RABBI ZE'EV GREENWALD

A SUMMARY OF LAWS
FOR JEWISH LIVING

FELDHEIM PUBLISHERS
JERUSALEM · NEW YORK

Originally published in 1983 in Hebrew as
Sha'arei Halachah: Kitzur Ha-Halachos Ha-Ma'asiyos

First published 2000
ISBN 1-58330-434-7

Copyright © 2000 by
Ze'ev Greenwald
POB 43015, Jerusalem
Tel: 02-6527417

distributed by:
FELDHEIM PUBLISHERS
POB 35002, Jerusalem, Israel 91350
200 Airport Executive Park, Nanuet, N.Y. 10954

www.feldheim.com

Printed in Israel

10 9 8 7 6 5 4 3 2 1

Letters of Appropriation from the
Original Hebrew Edition

הרב נסים קרליץ
רמת אהרן
רח' ר' מאיר 6, בני ברק

בס"ד ז' ניסן תשמ"ג

ראיתי את הספר היקר שערי הלכה מעשה ידי הרב המאה"ג מוה"ר זאב גרינולד
שליט"א אשר בו הביא בקיצור ההלכות המצויות על סדר היום. וניכרין הדברים רב העמל
שהושקע בדבר ללבן ולסדר הדברים בצורה ברורה ומובנת לכל.
והנני לחתום בברכה יזכה להמשיך בפעלו החשוב לקרב לבן של ישראל לאביהם
שבשמים ולזכות את הצבור בספרים חשובים ויקרים.

נסים קרליץ

הרב יהודא צדקה
ראש ישיבת פורת יוסף, ירושלים

גם אני החתום מטה מצטרף לדברי הגאון הנזכר לעיל, ומברכו שיזכה עוד בפעולות
כאלו להרביץ תורה בישראל לאורך ימים ושנות חיים וכל טוב סלה.

ברכת התורה

י. צדקה

הרב יצחק זילברשטיין
רב שכונת רמת אלחנן
בני ברק

בס"ד כ"ו אייר תשמ"ג

נעים לנו להעיד על ספרו של הרה"ג ר' זאב גרינולד שליט"א אשר בשם "שערי הלכה"
יכונה, כספר העשוי מעשה אומן ורב תועלת. כי השכיל ללקט וגם להסביר את עיקרי
יסודות ההלכה לבאים בשערי ההלכה בבחינת שימה בפיהם. והוא כשלחן ערוך עם כל
פרטי ההלכות שבו.
ספר זה היה למראה עיניו של אחד הגדולים בתורה, אשר עבר כמעט על כל הספר היקר
הזה ומצא אותו ערוך ומדוקדק. ובנוסף לכך אתמחי גברא כבקי ומדקדק ומבאר היטב
בסגנון בהיר מלא ברכת ה' ויראת ה' היא אוצרו והספר הוא צורך ותועלת השעה.
והנני לברך את הרב המחבר שעמל ויגע, שיפוצו מעינותיו חוצה להגדיל תורה
ולהאדירה.

יצחק זילברשטיין

Contents

Laws concerning both the *tallis* and *tefillin* 34, If one has no *tefillin* 35, Putting on *tefillin shel yad* (*Tefillin* for the arm) 35, Putting on *tefillin shel rosh* (*Tefillin* for the head) 35, Additional laws pertaining to wearing *tefillin* 36, The holiness of *tefillin* 38, Taking off the *tefillin* 38, The *kashrus* of *tefillin* 39, Inspecting the *tefillin* 40

Chapter Seven - Shacharis (The morning service)..................... 41

List of Tables

Introduction

In recent years we have witnessed an inspiring phenomenon. The thirst for the eternal values of Judaism is constantly increasing. The spirit of repentance encompasses many sectors of our people. Numerous people are returning to the Torah's path, striving to properly observe its *mitzvos*.

The same trend exists within the religious community, with people striving to reach spiritual heights through careful mitzvah observance and by refraining from that which the Torah forbids.

These people need a clear, easy-to-read compendium of Halachah. This volume must be easily understood by all those who leaf through it. Our goal when organizing the *halachos* presented in this volume was to compile such a compendium. We set out to present in clear, colloquial language the foundations of practical Halachah as it is observed daily, on Shabbos, and throughout the year.

This book serves as a gateway to Halachah. There is no substitute for studying the halachic texts written by the great Torah scholars throughout the generations. This book is nothing more than a brief compendium of the *halachos* discussed in depth in the above-mentioned texts. The reader must be aware that this book only contains the most common, frequently observed *halachos*.

Each person must strive, over time, to be able to study the volumes of halachic texts, and to be able to study all the details of Halachah in depth, from the original sources. By studying these texts, one is propelled towards a life filled with the love of Torah and careful observance of Halachah.

The *halachos* presented in the first four sections of this volume follow the halachic rulings of the *Mishnah Berurah*, which is the most comprehensive, relied-upon commentary to the *Orach Chayim* section of the *Shulchan Aruch*. We have also noted the halachic rulings followed by Sephardic Jewry when those rulings differ from those of the *Mishnah Berurah*. Therefore, this book is suitable for both Ashkenazic and Sephardic Jews.

One should consult a *rav* or an expert in Halachah any time a question arises regarding what Halachah requires in a specific situation. Although this book is written in a clear, easily understandable way, at times the *halachos* within are presented concisely. The reader should therefore pay close attention to the details of the *halachos* presented.

With God's help, the Hebrew edition of *Sha'arei Halachah* has been well received, by educational institutions as well as by individuals. We consulted with halachic authorities and leading educators while preparing the English edition of this book. Our goal was to prepare a book that would be suitable for students as well as for adults.

I would like to sincerely thank all those who were instrumental in preparing this edition of *Sha'arei Halachah*. I am especially grateful to my late dear friend, R. Avraham Saslow *z"l*, of Rechasim-K'far Chasidim, who tirelessly reviewed the English edition of *Sha'arei Halachah*. R. Saslow's comments were indispensable. R. Saslow was tragically killed in a traffic accident, together with his six-year-old son, Refael.

We pray to God that no halachic errors should result from use of this book. It is our sincere hope that this volume assists all those individuals and families who are striving to come closer to their Creator.

Part One: The Daily Routine

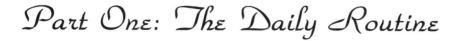

A Jew's day is replete with *mitzvos*, from the prayer of *Modeh Ani* upon arising in the morning, to the prayer of *Shema* before retiring at night. These
mitzvos are discussed in the following chapters, according to their order during the day.

By observing the *mitzvos* and abstaining from the prohibitions of the Torah,
we are obeying God's will and fulfilling our Divinely ordained task and purpose in life. Every Jew should strive for higher spiritual achievements by
studying the Torah and observing its *mitzvos*. Our daily *mitzvos* and prayers
deepen our faith and instill in us the awareness that we stand before God. The
verse, "I have set the Lord before me always" (*Tehillim* 16:5), expresses the
highest spiritual level to which one should aspire, wherein one feels that
God is always with him, and constantly watching over him.

The *Shulchan Aruch* elaborates:

> "I have set the Lord before me always" is a fundamental concept of the Torah,
> and is among the virtues of the righteous ones who walk before God. When a
> man is alone, he sits, moves and behaves differently than he would sit, move
> and behave if he would be before a great king. How much more so will his
> conduct be different when he realizes that he is before the mighty King,
> the Holy One, blessed be He, Whose glory fills the world, Who is looking
> down upon him and watching him. " 'Can anyone conceal himself in secret
> places, so that I not see him?' says the Lord" (*Yirmeyahu* 23:24). If a man ac-
> quires this attitude, he will be filled with fear of God, and piety, and he will be
> humble before God at all times. (*Orach Chayim* 1:1)

The awareness that we are always under God's supervision is an incentive to
self-improvement.

3

Chapter One

Arising

1. Rabbi Yosef Karo, the author of the *Shulchan Aruch*, opens the section of *Orach Chayim* with the words: "One should be strong like a lion to arise in the morning to serve his Creator."[1] From the moment he arises in the morning, a Jew is at his Creator's service, ready to faithfully observe all His *mitzvos*. *Mitzvos* impose a Divine order upon our lives, lifting us above the materialism of day to day life to a level full of spiritual content and meaning.

Through observing *mitzvos* upon arising in the morning, man announces his entry into God's service for that day: he washes his hands just as a *Kohen* (priest) would do before serving in the Temple; he dresses modestly, because he knows God's glory fills the entire world; and he covers his head out of reverence for the *Shechinah* (Divine Presence).

2. One should make every effort to arise early enough to recite *Shacharis* (the morning prayer) with a congregation, in the synagogue.[2]

Reciting *Modeh Ani*

3. When we sleep, we entrust God with our soul. God, in His kindness, restores our soul to us in the morning, leaving us feeling rested and refreshed. Therefore, when a Jew wakes up, he thanks his Creator by reciting *Modeh Ani*: "I thank You, living and eternal King, that You have returned my soul to me with compassion; Your trustworthiness is great." One should pause slightly between reciting the words *b'chemlah* ("with compassion") and *rabbah* ("great").[3]

Netilas yadayim shel Shacharis
(Washing the hands upon arising)

4. We wash our hands with water as soon as possible after awakening. Children should also observe *netilas yadayim* upon arising.[3*]

5.   Therefore, one should try to arrange having the water close to where he sleeps, so that he will not have to walk more than four *amos* before being able to wash his hands.[4]

One should not touch bodily orifices, such as his mouth, eyes, nose or ears before performing *netilas yadayim*. Similarly, one should not touch any food before performing *netilas yadayim*.[5]

Reasons for *netilas yadayim shel Shacharis*

6.   Several reasons for this *netilas yadayim* are cited in halachic literature.

In the Temple, the *Kohanim* would sanctify their hands by washing them before beginning the sacrificial service. When we arise in the morning it is as if we were created anew, and are about to begin serving our Creator. Therefore, we wash our hands and recite the blessing *al netilas yadayim* at the start of the day, before we begin performing *mitzvos*.

Another reason for this *netilas yadayim*, is that while sleeping, one's hands most likely touched the parts of the body that are normally covered, rendering them unclean. Since in such a case one is required to wash his hands before praying, our sages ordained that we wash our hands upon arising.[6] Because of these reasons, we recite a blessing on having washed our hands before reciting *Shacharis*.

A spiritual impurity rests on a person after he has slept. We remove it by pouring water three times on each hand.[7]

How to perform the morning *netilas yadayim*

7.   One should take a utensil filled with water in his right hand and pass it to his left hand in order to wash the right hand first.[8] One should wash each hand three times in this order: right, left, right, left, right, left. (Some people wash each hand four times.)[9] It is preferable to wash the hand up to the wrist.

8.   It is preferable to use an uncracked utensil for *netilas yadayim*. At least a *revi'is* of water must be used.[10] (For the exact measure of a *revi'is*, see the Table of Measures at the end of Chapter 15.)

9. The water used for *netilas yadayim* may not be used for any other purpose, nor may it be walked upon. Therefore, it should be spilled out in a place where people do not normally walk.[11]

Additional *halachos*

10. If one has a limited amount of water, he may wash his fingers until the knuckles three times.[12]

11. If no water is available, one should clean his hands (the palm, back of his hand and all sides of the fingers) by rubbing them on anything that cleans, i.e. a garment, earth, etc. In this case, the blessing recited is *al nekiyus yadayim*, instead of *al netilas yadayim*. Even though his hands were not washed, one may now recite blessings and study Torah.[13] Later, when water is available, he should wash his hands three times.

12. When one rises after having taken a nap during the day, he should wash his hands three times without reciting a blessing.[14] (See Chapter 3, Section 10 regarding what procedure to follow regarding the blessing of *al netilas yadayim* and the other blessings if one was awake all night.)

13. It is commendable to rinse one's mouth every morning, so one will pronounce God's Name, in the prayers and blessings, with a clean mouth. On fast days, one should not rinse his mouth.[15] (For more details, see Chapter 25, Section 3.)

Other occasions when the hands must be washed

14. There are other times during the course of the day when one must wash his hands.[16] Some of these times are:

＊ Upon leaving a bathroom, even without having relieved oneself or having bathed.

＊ After a haircut, shaving or cutting one's nails.

＊ After visiting a cemetery or attending a funeral. (It is customary not to enter a house after leaving the cemetery or attending a funeral without first washing the hands.)

In each of the above cases, the hands must be washed immediately.

One should also wash his hands after scratching his scalp, or touching shoes, feet, and parts of the body that are required to be covered.

Covering one's head

15.   Every man should wear a *yarmulke* or hat throughout the day as a sign of respect for the *Shechinah*.[17] The Talmud teaches (*Shabbos* 156b) that covering one's head imbues man with the fear of God and humility, and helps him improve his *middos* (character traits). It is virtuous to have one's head covered while sleeping.

Getting dressed

16.   The prophet Michah called out to Israel, "Walk modestly with your God" (*Michah* 6:8). All aspects of a Jew's behavior should be unobtrusive. *Tzeniyus*, unobtrusive behavior and dress, and *bushah*, a sense of shame at impropriety, are exalted virtues which draw a person close to the Torah. *Tzeniyus* requires that a Jew not bare his body unnecessarily, even when undressing. A person who rationalizes, "Who will see me?" ignores the fact that the Almighty's glory fills the entire world, and that He sees everything.[18]

17.   The right side of a garment should be put on first, since the Torah ascribes more importance to the right side than to the left.[19]

However, when tying a knot, the left side precedes the right, because *tefillin* are bound to the left arm.

Therefore, shoes should be put on in the following manner: First, the right shoe should be put on, then the left shoe, then the left shoelaces are tied, then the right shoelaces are tied.[20] When taking off shoes, one should begin with the left shoe,[21] since removing the left shoe first demonstrates the importance of the right side.

Similarly, when washing oneself, the right side should precede the left. When bathing the whole body, a person should first wash his head, since it is the most important part of his body.[22]

The mitzvah not to adopt the practices of the gentiles

18.   We are forbidden to imitate the dress or behavior of other peoples. This is derived from the verses: "you shall not follow the practices of the gentile..." (*Vayikra* 20:23), and "...do not follow their practices" (ibid. 18:3).

God bestowed an exalted spiritual mission upon the Jewish people. Not only are we to draw close to the Almighty by observing His 613 *mitzvos*, we must also be a guiding light and a spiritual inspiration to all other nations. Because of our spiritual merit and calling, we must not let ourselves be lured to the gentiles' practices.

19. The refinement we seek for our character is promoted through modest, inconspicuous clothing and praiseworthy behavior. Therefore, our mode of dress should be without overtones of conceit or immodesty. This also applies to the way we wear our hair, our manner of speech, and general conduct.

A Jew should conduct himself, and all his affairs, in a way that demonstrates that he is a member of God's people who faithfully strives to fulfill his Creator's will. (Details concerning these laws appear in the *Shulchan Aruch, Yoreh De'ah* 178).

Chapter Two

Introduction to Prayer

1. Belief in the Creator, and the desire to connect oneself with the One Who is the source of life, health and happiness, is inherent to all humanity. In some people, this feeling predominates and directs them throughout their lives. In others, this feeling is latent, surfacing only in times of crisis, when they cry out to God for help.

The text of the prayers is fixed

2. Although prayer comes naturally to every human being, it needs a framework and a specific text. Man needs modes of expression that will encompass all his heart's desires, both his obvious needs as well as his hidden ones. One needs a framework within which to pray for his family, his people, and for the whole world; a framework within which he can stand before the King of the universe and express his most private thoughts.

The text of the prayers was fixed by the Men of the Great Assembly. They concealed within the prayers kabbalistic secrets and mysteries of the *Ma'aseh Merkavah* (extremely profound kabbalistic concepts which are cryptically described in the first chapter of *Yechezkel*). No human being alive today is capable of composing a text as perfect and profound as the one we have possessed for generations, of which only a few of its infinite mysteries are comprehensible to master kabbalists.

The text of the prayers, established by the sages according to rules transmitted by the Almighty at Sinai, constitute the service of the heart. When we pray in the prescribed form, we fulfill the obligation to pray daily. At the same time, we also have the chance to express our thoughts and innermost feelings to God.

Personal prayers

3.   A personal prayer in which a person expresses his feelings and wishes
           in his own words is also valuable. A person may pour out his soul be-
fore his Creator and ask for anything he desires in a personal prayer. These
extra prayers are desirable at all times, even at times not set aside for prayer.
These prayers may also be incorporated in the fixed text of the *Shemoneh
Esreh*, either in the paragraph of *Shema koleinu* ("Hear our voice"), or in the
last section which begins *Elokai netzor* ("My God, guard my tongue"), as is
explained in Chapter 7, Section 35.

4.   Prayer is like a "ladder set upon the earth whose top reaches the hea-
           vens" (*Bereshis* 28:12). Prayer is close to man's heart and with it man can
reach high spiritual levels. Every prayer has value and every prayer reaches
heaven. It is the most intimate expression of a person's feelings, and the
more pure and intimate it is, the more it is accepted in heaven. Nevertheless, every prayer is important. Even if a person finds it difficult to concentrate on his prayers, God still listens to him.

The source of the halachic requirement of prayer

5.   The verse "and to serve Him with all your heart" (*Devarim* 11:13) refers
           to the mitzvah of prayer. The *Sifri* (ad loc.) explains: " 'to serve Him'
refers to prayer."

The Rambam explains that the obligation to pray is an explicit commandment
from the Torah:

> It is a positive mitzvah to pray every day, as it says, "You shall serve the
> Lord, your God." This service refers to prayer, as it says "and to serve
> Him with all your heart." What is "service of the heart?" This is prayer. A
> person fulfills this commandment by beseeching and praying to God every
> day. First, he should praise the Holy One, blessed be He; then he should pe-
> tition and entreat Him for his personal needs; finally, he should give thanks
> and express gratitude to God for all the goodness He bestowed upon him.
> (*Hilchos Tefillah* 1:1,2)

Other sources for this mitzvah may be found in the Ramban's glosses on the
Rambam's *Sefer Ha-Mitzvos* (*Asseh* 5) and in *Sefer Ha-Chinnuch* (*Ekev*, mitzvah
433).

Times of prayer

6.   The three Patriarchs fixed the times of prayer:

Avraham instituted *Shacharis* in the morning, Yitzchak instituted *Minchah* in the afternoon, and Ya'akov instituted *Ma'ariv* (*Arvis*) in the evening.

"We will offer the words of our lips instead of calves" (*Hoshea* 14:3). The prayers that we recite are a substitute for the sacrifices offered in the Temple:

> *Shacharis*, the morning prayer, corresponds to the *tamid*-sacrifice offered in the morning;

> *Minchah*, the afternoon prayer, corresponds to the *tamid*-sacrifice offered in the afternoon;

> *Ma'ariv*, the evening prayer, corresponds to the burning of the sacrifices' parts at night.

> *Musaf* is recited after *Shacharis* on Shabbos, *Yom Tov* (festivals), and *Rosh Chodesh* (the first day of the Hebrew month), corresponding to the *Musaf* (additional) sacrifice offered on those days.

Our prayers include a petition for the speedy restoration of the Temple, so that we may once again serve God with the sacrificial service. The Temple service will elevate our entire nation to great spiritual heights and closeness to God.

Chapter Three

Birchos Ha-Shachar
(The morning blessings)

1. Every morning we recite a number of blessings thanking God for His constant kindness to us. These blessings are called *Birchos Ha-Shachar* (the Morning Blessings).

These blessings, instituted by the sages, instill in us the realization that all we possess comes from God. Reciting *Birchos Ha-Shachar* intently impresses upon us that life, clothes, vision and all of man's other capacities and possessions are gifts from Heaven.

When contemplating life, a person realizes how much he should thank his Creator for the abundance of good that he was given. *Birchos Ha-Shachar* express this gratitude towards God.

2. The sages ordained blessings to be recited before partaking of various pleasures available in the world. "A person is forbidden to derive enjoyment from this world without first reciting a blessing. Whoever derives enjoyment without reciting a blessing is like one who misappropriates a sacred object" (*Berachos* 35a). Since everything in the world belongs to God, taking anything for personal use without reciting a blessing is like misappropriating a holy object. However, once a person recites the blessing he is permitted to derive benefit from the object.[1]

The text of *Birchos Ha-Shachar*

The text of *Birchos Ha-Shachar* appears in the *Siddur* before *Shacharis*. It will be helpful to study the following laws of prayer with an open *Siddur*.

3. *Birchos Ha-Shachar* begin with the blessing *al netilas yadayim* ("Who has commanded us to wash our hands"). This is followed by the blessing of *asher yatzar* ("Who has formed man with wisdom"), in which we thank God for creating our body, and *Elokai neshamah* ("My God, the soul You have

13

given me"), in which we thank God for creating the soul.[2] When reciting *Elokai neshamah*, one should pause between the first word, *Elokai* ("My God"), and the rest of the blessing.[3]

4.   After that, the blessings from *asher nasan la-sechvi* ("Who gives the heart [or 'rooster'] understanding") until *ha-gomel chasadim* ("Who bestows great kindness") are recited.[4]

5.   One should not respond Amen after hearing the blessing *ha-ma'avir sheinah* ("Who removes sleep"), since the section following it is considered part of the blessing.

One must not recite a blessing, or any phrase containing words of Torah, or God's names, if one's hands are not clean (i.e. if they have touched the body, shoes, etc.), as is explained in Chapter 4, Sections 11-12.[5]

Birchos Ha-Torah (The blessings on the Torah)

6.   Every morning we recite *Birchos Ha-Torah* with *Birchos Ha-Shachar*.

Torah study is the basis of all mitzvah observance. Through study, one gains knowledge of his Creator, and learns how to observe His *mitzvos*. This is why the obligation to study Torah spans the life of a Jew, as God told Yehoshua, "You shall study it day and night" (*Yehoshua* 1:8). The reward for Torah study is exceedingly great; our sages tell us that, "The study of Torah equals all other [*mitzvos*]" (*Mishnah Pe'ah* 1:1).

7.   The *Birchos Ha-Torah* express the great importance of Torah study. These blessings must be recited intently, with a feeling of joy, as we are thanking God for choosing us as His chosen people from among the other nations, and for giving us His Torah.[6]

We may not study Torah (this includes all holy subjects) before reciting these blessings. A person who wishes to study early in the morning before reciting *Shacharis*, should recite *Birchos Ha-Torah* before he begins to study.[7]

8.   *Birchos Ha-Torah* is made up of three parts. First we thank God for commanding us to study His Torah (*la-asok b'divrei Torah*). Then we pray that we find our Torah study pleasant, and that we and our offspring merit to study Torah for its own sake (*v'ha-arev na*). Finally, we thank God for choosing us from among all the nations, and giving us His Torah (*asher bachar banu*).

The *Mishnah Berurah* advises parents to continually pray to God that their children become Torah students, and righteous men with good character traits. They should have this in mind when they recite the prayer *Ahavah rabbah* ("You have loved us with great love") before *Shema*, and in *Birchos Ha-Torah*, when reciting the passage *v'nihiyeh anachnu v'tze'etza'einu* ("may we and our offspring"), as well as in *u'Va l'Tzion go'el* ("And a redeemer shall come to Zion"), when they recite the words *l'ma'an lo nigah larik v'lo neiled la-behalah* ("so that we do not struggle in vain nor produce in futility"). Thus, parents should pray that their children succeed in Torah study and spiritual endeavors.[8]

9.   Immediately after reciting *Birchos Ha-Torah* we observe the mitzvah of Torah study by reciting *Birkas Kohanim* (the *Kohanim's* Blessing; *Bemidbar* 6:24-26) as well as a section from the mishnah. These appear in the *Siddur* after *Birchos Ha-Torah*.[9]

The procedure to follow if one remained awake all night

10.   There are different halachic opinions concerning how a person who did not sleep deeply[10] on his bed all night should recite the blessings of *al netilas yadayim*, *Elokai neshamah*, *ha-ma'avir sheinah*, and *Birchos Ha-Torah*.

The *Mishnah Berurah* sets down the following procedure:

* Before *Shacharis*, the person should relieve himself, wash up, and then perform *netilas yadayim* and recite the blessings *al netilas yadayim* and *asher yatzar*.[11] If he does not need to relieve himself, he should listen to someone who slept during the night recite these blessings, and reply Amen to them. Both the one reciting the blessings and the listener should intend for the listener to fulfill his obligation to recite the blessings by listening. The listener should reply Amen.

* The person should not recite the blessings of *Elokai neshamah* and *ha-ma'avir sheinah*, but should listen to someone else recite them. Both the one reciting the blessings and the listener should intend for the listener to fulfill his obligation to recite the blessings by listening. The listener should reply Amen.[12]

* The person should listen to someone else recite *Birchos Ha-Torah*, and both should intend for the listener to fulfill his obligation to recite the blessings by listening. The listener should reply Amen. He should then recite the

verses mentioned in Section 9 above, in order to observe the mitzvah of studying Torah following *Birchos Ha-Torah.*[13]

If a person slept during the day (he slept a *sheinas keva*, i.e. the way one normally sleeps at night), and then stayed awake the following night, he may recite *Birchos Ha-Torah* in the morning.

＊ A person who wore his *tzitzis* throughout the night, whether or not he was asleep, should not recite the blessing for *tzitzis* in the morning. Rather, he should wrap himself in a *tallis gadol*, and recite the blessing for *tzitzis* over it, intending to include his *tallis katan* in this blessing.[14]

The other *Birchos Ha-Shachar* are recited even by a person who stayed awake all night.

If one did not recite *Birchos Ha-Shachar* before *Shacharis*

11.   If one did not recite *Birchos Ha-Shachar* before *Shacharis*, he may recite them after *Shacharis*. The exceptions to this rule are the blessings *al netilas yadayim*,[15] *Elokai neshamah*, and *Birchos Ha-Torah*. There are doubts regarding whether or not these *berachos* are recited then.[16] Therefore, one should always recite these blessings before *Shacharis*.

Reciting *asher yatzar* ("Who has formed man") during the day

12.   Every time one relieves himself, he should wash his hands with water and recite the blessing *asher yatzar*. He should not recite the blessing of *al netilas yadayim* after washing his hands.[17] When using the bathroom, a person should not bare his body more than necessary.[18]

13.   One should wash his hands outside the bathroom. If it is not possible to wash his hands outside, he should wash his hands in the bathroom and dry them outside.[19]

One should wash his hands after leaving a bathroom, even if he did not make use of it.[20]

14.   When reciting the blessing of *asher yatzar* we give thanks to God Who created man's body with marvelous wisdom, and Who keeps a person's organs functioning throughout his life. If one of a person's organs did not function correctly, he would not be able to continue living. Only through the grace of God, "Who heals all flesh and acts wondrously," are we able to exist at all. The text of this blessing appears in the *Siddur* among the *Birchos Ha-Shachar*.

Chapter Four

Preparations for Prayer, Minyan, and the Synagogue

1.   When praying, one is standing in the presence of God, the King of kings. A person must prepare himself for this encounter, as the prophet says, "Prepare yourself for your God, Israel" (*Amos* 4:12). Standing before God calls for preparation and contemplation. A person who is preparing to pray should feel as if he were going to meet a king or an important minister.

2.   Preparing oneself for prayer includes dressing with the proper decorum. One should wear the type of clothing that people wear when they go to meet a prominent person. One who usually wears a hat when going out should wear one when praying.[1] Even when one prays at home, his attire should be appropriate.

These preparations prepare a person to stand before the King of the universe, and impress upon him the significance of prayer.

It is commendable to give *tzedakah* (charity) before praying. This is derived from the verse, "As for me, I will behold Your face in *tzedek* (righteousness)" (*Tehillim* 17:15). The Ari *z"l* used to give *tzedakah* while standing, when he reached the words *v'attah moshel ba-kol* ("And You preside over all"), in the paragraph of *Va-yevarech David* in *Pesukei D'zimrah*.[2]

3.   Mothers who find it difficult to recite all the prayers because they are caring for their children should ask a *rav* how to proceed.

The prohibition to become occupied with extraneous matters before praying

4.   Once it is time for *Shacharis*, one should not visit a friend and greet him before having prayed. If one meets a friend in the street, though, he may greet him. Although it is permissible to greet him with "Shalom," it is

customary to say "good morning" or something similar. This helps one re-member not to deviate to other matters before praying.[3]

Similarly, one should not engage in his profession, perform any form of work, or travel until he has prayed. In situations of great urgency, for instance, if one will miss his means of transportation, and no other means is available, the person may travel first and pray later.[4]

One should not begin to study Torah once it is time to recite *Shacharis*. How-ever, if one regularly prays with a *minyan*, he is permitted to study before prayer, since it is unlikely that he will exceed the permitted time for prayer without praying. One may also study Torah if he asks a friend who is not studying to remind him to pray.[5] One who studies Torah before *Shacharis* must recite *Birchos Ha-Torah* before beginning to study. For more details, see Chapter 3, Section 7.

5.   One should not eat or drink before praying. However, one may drink water, coffee or tea (without milk or sugar), if this will enable him to concentrate better on his prayers. One may eat or drink before praying if his health requires it.[6]

Preparing oneself for prayers, a location suitable for praying

6.   Both the status of one's body and the place where one recites his prayers and blessings must be in keeping with the sanctity of prayer.[7] This is derived from the first verse of *Tehillim* 103, "My soul, bless God! and all that is within me, His holy Name!" Therefore, if one needs to relieve himself, he should do so before he begins praying. Afterwards, he should make sure that his body is clean and fit to stand before God.[8]

When one recites blessings or studies Torah, the upper part of the body should be separated from the lower part by a belt or a garment that is fitted at the waist. The reason for this is so that "the heart should not see the body's nakedness."[9]

7.   Our sages taught that whenever God is amongst us (e.g. when we are praying or busy with Torah study), our surroundings must be holy (*Berachos* 25). Our sages derived this from the verse, "For the Lord your God goes in the midst of your camp... and your camp should be holy" (*Devarim* 23:14). Care should be taken that no unpleasant odors or body

wastes, such as dirty diapers, are detectable from the place where one is pray-ing. Similar care must be taken with regard to Torah study. One may not speak or even think about Torah subjects, or pray, in a bathroom. Standing in front of a bathroom with its door open is like standing in the bathroom itself. If one has reason to question the appropriateness of his surroundings, he must check the place before he is allowed to pray.

If one is ill, confined in a hospital, or in a situation where it is not possible to observe the laws of a clean body and proper surroundings, a *rav* should be consulted concerning what procedure to follow.

8.   A man may not pray facing an improperly dressed woman. Similarly, a man may not pray facing a married woman whose hair is uncovered.[10]

9.   Although a man should never listen to a woman singing, he should be particularly careful when he is praying or studying Torah. If one is in a place where a woman is singing, and he cannot leave the place, or ask her to stop, he may study Torah and pray in that place. However, he should make every effort to concentrate on the holy matters he is occupied with, and not pay attention to the singing.[11]

Netilas yadayim before prayer

10.   One should always wash his hands before praying (i.e. before *Shacharis*, *Minchah*, and *Ma'ariv*).[12] The blessing *al netilas yadayim* is not recited after washing one's hands before praying. The only exception is when recit-ing *al netilas yadayim* during *Birchos Ha-Shachar* (see Chapter 3, Section 3).[13]

The hands must be kept clean

11.   One should not pray or recite a blessing while his hands are unclean, i.e. after touching his shoes or a part of the body which must be covered, and after scratching his scalp.[14] Parts of the body that must be covered in-clude the torso, the arms above the elbow, the legs, and the feet.[15]

12.   One must wash his hands after touching one of these places.[16] If one's hands became unclean while reciting the *Shemoneh Esreh*, when he can-not leave his place, he should clean his hands by rubbing them on a garment or on the wall. The palm, the back of the hand to the wrist, and all sides of the fingers should be washed or rubbed.[17]

Praying with a congregation

13. A person should make every effort to pray with a congregation in a synagogue.[18] God accepts our prayers when we pray alone, but communal prayer is more readily accepted and is of greater value. Our sages comment on the verse, "As for me, my prayer is to You, O God, at a time of favor" (*Tehillim* 69:14): "When is it a time of favor? When a congregation prays" (*Berachos* 7a).

14. There is another benefit to praying with a congregation. *Kaddish, Kedushah, Birkas Kohanim,* Torah readings, etc. may only be recited if a congregation is present. These prayers are omitted when one prays by himself.

A *minyan*

15. A *minyan* is a group of ten or more Jewish men, thirteen years of age or older, who pray together. All ten men, including the *sheliach tzibur* (the man who leads the prayers), must pray in one place. If some of the men are in one room, and the rest are in another room, they are not counted as one group, even if there is an opening between the two rooms. There are certain situations where men in two separate rooms can be combined to form a *minyan.* For example, in situations of great urgency, if some of the men in each room can see each other, they can be counted as one *minyan.*[19]

When a *minyan* reaches *Kaddish* or *Kedushah,* anyone hearing them, even if he is in another room or is a distance away, may join them in answering Amen, *Yehei Shemeh rabbah,* etc. The reason why people who are not part of the *minyan* are permitted to join in answering is because the *Shechinah* is present where there is a *minyan.* Once it is present, "even an iron wall cannot separate between Israel and their Father in heaven" (*Pesachim* 85b).

16. One should make every effort to come to the synagogue on time so he can recite the entire service with a *minyan.*[20] The most important prayer to recite with a *minyan* is the *Shemoneh Esreh.* If a person came late, he should try to catch up so he will be able to begin the *Shemoneh Esreh* with everyone else.[21] (For additional details see Chapter 7, Sections 10-14.)

17. One who is unable to join a *minyan* in the synagogue, and cannot gather ten men to pray with him at home, should try to pray at the same time as the *minyan* in the synagogue, since that time is considered a "time of favor."[22]

When a boy and girl become bar mitzvah or bas mitzvah

18. A boy becomes obligated in *mitzvos* and is counted in a *minyan*, after thirteen complete years have passed since his birth, according to the Jewish calendar. Here are some examples of this *halachah*.[23]

If a boy was born on the first day of Nissan, even if he was born at the end of the day, he becomes bar mitzvah (i.e. obligated to observe *mitzvos*) at the beginning of the night of the first of Nissan, thirteen years later.

19. If a boy was born on the twentieth of Adar in a regular year (which has only one month of Adar), and the year he becomes thirteen is a leap year, his bar mitzvah is on the twentieth day of the second month of Adar.

If a boy was born in the first month of Adar during a leap year, and the year he becomes thirteen is also a leap year, his bar mitzvah is in the first month of Adar.

If a boy was born in Adar, during a leap year, and the year he becomes thirteen is a regular year, he becomes bar mitzvah in Adar, whether he was born in the first or second Adar.

The same rules apply to a girl, the only difference being that she becomes bas mitzvah when twelve full years have passed since her birth (one year earlier than a boy).

These calculations are done exclusively according to the Jewish calendar. When doubts exist about the Jewish date of birth, they must be clarified so the boy or girl will know on which day they become obligated to observe *mitzvos* as adults.

The synagogue

20. A synagogue is a place designated for prayer. Prayers recited there are of greater value than prayers recited in other places. Therefore, one should do his utmost to pray in a synagogue, with a congregation.

Even if one cannot find a *minyan* and has to pray alone, he should nevertheless pray in a synagogue. This is because it is a holy place, and prayers recited there are more acceptable to God.[24]

21. A person should pray in a set place in a specific synagogue. He should not change places unless there is a good reason for it. We know that

Avraham had a set place for prayer from the verse, "And Avraham woke up early in the morning to (go to) the place where he had stood before the Lord" (*Bereshis* 19:27). When one prays at home, he should pray in a place where he will not be disturbed by family members.[25]

22.   It is a mitzvah to hurry when going to synagogue, as well as when going to perform any other mitzvah. This is derived from the verses, "...let us hasten to get awareness of God..." (*Hoshea* 6:3), and "I will run along the way of Your commandments" (*Tehillim* 119:32). However, when a person leaves the synagogue, he should go slowly, unless he is on his way to study Torah or perform another mitzvah. One should not rush about in synagogue.[26]

The sanctity of the synagogue

23.   The holiness of a synagogue is very great, akin to the holiness of the Temple. This is derived from the verse, "...and I have given to them a small sanctuary" (*Yechezkel* 11:16). Our sages explained, "These refer to the synagogues and study halls" (*Megillah* 29a). The verse, "...and you shall revere My sanctuary" (*Vayikra* 19:30) cautions us to stand in awe of these places wherein God abides.

24.   One's conduct in synagogue should be in keeping with its sanctity. A person should not behave frivolously, or engage in idle talk. Of course, one should shun prohibited speech, such as slander, gossip, and quarreling. Besides these types of speech being grave sins in themselves, committing these sins in a holy place multiplies a person's guilt immensely, because he is brazenly insulting the *Shechinah*. A synagogue should only be used for studying Torah and reciting prayers.[27]

25.   Parents should make sure that their children do not make a commotion or disturb the service. Parents should teach their children to sit next to them and behave properly in synagogue, and to answer Amen, *Yehei Shemeh rabbah*, etc. Children who are too young to understand the sanctity of the synagogue, or who are unable to behave properly, should not be brought to synagogue, since they disturb the adults during the service, and they get used to desecrating the holiness of the place.[28]

26.   One is prohibited to enter a synagogue in order to escape the heat, cold, or rain.

If one has to speak with a friend who is in synagogue, he should enter the synagogue, recite a verse from the Torah or a passage from any of the religious writings, and then speak with his friend. If he does not know how to recite any verse, he should at least sit down a moment, because just sitting in a synagogue is a mitzvah.[29]

One may not walk through a synagogue as a shortcut (i.e. one may not walk through a synagogue because it is quicker than walking around it).

It is a mitzvah for one who entered a synagogue to pray or study Torah to leave through another door, thereby showing that he cherishes the place.[30]

27.   It is forbidden to eat, drink, or sleep in a *Bais Knesset* and *Bais Midrash*.

The only exception to this rule is a Torah scholar who studies in a *Bais Midrash* regularly. This person may eat and sleep there, since leaving to eat or sleep causes him to lose precious study time.[31]

Holy books and religious articles

28.   Holy books and religious articles must also be accorded due respect. The following are some of the laws:

* One should not sit on a chair or a bench on which holy books are lying.

* All holy books, including those which are worn out or torn, as well as sheets of paper on which Torah thoughts were written, may not be thrown out. They must be put in a *genizah* (a special burial place). Many synagogues have a special box or place where these books and papers are set aside until they are taken for burial.

* Holy books must not be placed face down. If one sees a book that is face down, he should turn it to its right side.

* A *Chumash* (one of the five books of the Torah) may be placed on top of a volume of *Nevi'im* or *Kesuvim* (Scriptures), and *Nevi'im* and *Kesuvim* may be placed one on top of the other. *Nevi'im* and *Kesuvim* may not be placed on top of *Chumashim*. Other holy books must not be placed on top of any of these books.

* Papers which have no religious significance should not be inserted in holy books, unless they facilitate studying the holy book.

* A person who was studying from a holy book should not leave the book open when he leaves, even if he expects to return shortly.[32]

Chapter Five

The Mitzvah of Tzitzis

1. "...They shall make for themselves *tzitzis* ("fringes") on the corners of their garments..." (*Bemidbar* 15:38). It is a mitzvah to put *tzitzis* on garments which have four square corners.[1]

The importance of the mitzvah of *tzitzis*

2. "...These shall be your *tzitzis*, and when you see them, you shall remember all of God's commandments, so as to keep them" (*Bemidbar* 15:39). *Tzitzis* have the unique ability to remind us of God's commandments, and to motivate us to fulfill them. The number of its threads, windings, and knots all hint to God's Name and the 613 *mitzvos*. The numerical value of the word *tzitzis* is 600; when added to the eight threads and five knots, the sum is 613.[2]

3. Wearing *tzitzis* regularly instills us with an awareness of our love of Torah and *mitzvos*. Fulfilling the *mitzvos* creates a pure heart within us, and forms the framework for a sanctified life replete with eternal values and closeness to God. This is mentioned clearly in the continuation of the section which discusses *tzitzis* in the Torah: "...You will thus remember and keep all My commandments and be holy to your God" (*Bemidbar* 15:40).

It is explained in the *Mishnah Berurah* that if a person received a gift from a king which was inscribed with the king's signature, he would surely take great pride in it, and show it to everybody. *Tzitzis* hints to the Name of the King of kings; how much more so should every Jew take pride in this mitzvah![3]

4. The mitzvah of *tzitzis* can be fulfilled all day long by wearing a *tallis katan* (a four-cornered garment with fringes on each corner which is part of a man's daily garb). The Rambam writes:

> A person should be meticulous when observing the commandment of *tzitzis*, for the Torah ascribed special value to it, and ascribed the fulfillment of all the *mitzvos* to it. This is derived from the verse, "and you shall see it and remember all of God's commandments." (*Hilchos Tzitzis* 3:12)

25

The *Shulchan Aruch* (at the end of *Hilchos Tzitzis*) states: "The punishment for one who ignores the mitzvah of *tzitzis* is great... while one who is careful in its fulfillment will merit to behold the *Shechinah.*"[4]

5.   It is a mitzvah to make a beautiful *tallis katan* and *tzitzis*. This is derived from the verse, "This is my God and I shall beautify Him" (*Shemos* 15:2). Our sages explained that we "beautify" God by performing His *mitzvos* in a beautiful manner.[5]

Tallis katan

6.   Men must wear a *tallis katan* with *tzitzis* attached to it throughout the day. (This garment is commonly referred to as *tzitzis*.) Men should put on a *tallis katan* immediately after washing their hands in the morning, so as not to walk four *amos* without wearing *tzitzis*.[6]

7.   One should be careful that his *tallis katan* is not too small. If the *tallis katan* does not meet the halachically required measurements, one has not fulfilled the mitzvah.

There are several opinions regarding the minimum width of the shoulders of the *tallis katan*. According to the Chazon Ish, each shoulder should be at least as wide as the neck-hole.

According to the Chazon Ish, the minimum width of the *tallis katan* is an *amah*. The Chazon Ish ruled that an *amah* is 58 cm (22.7 in), while Rav Chaim Na'eh ruled that an *amah* is 49 cm (18.9 in).[7] The *tallis katan* should be at least three-quarters of an *amah* long in front and in back. It is preferable for the *tallis katan* to be a complete *amah* in front and in back. If each shoulder is wider than the neck-hole, they may be included as part of the length of the *tallis katan*. Otherwise, the length of the front and back sections of the *tallis katan* are measured from under the neck-hole.

It is advisable for a new *tallis katan* to be a little larger than the measurements given, as it may shrink when washed.

8.   One who does not wear a *tallis gadol* (a prayer shawl, commonly referred to as a *tallis*) while reciting *Shacharis*, recites the blessing *al mitzvas tzitzis* ("concerning the commandment of *tzitzis*")[8] before putting on his *tallis katan* in the morning. One must remember, however, that the blessing may only be recited if the *tallis katan* is the required size.

A person who wore his *tzitzis* throughout the night does not recite the blessing *al mitzvas tzitzis* over it in the morning. Instead, the person should wrap himself in a *tallis gadol*, and recite the blessing for *tzitzis* over it, intending to include his *tallis katan* in this blessing.

9. Before reciting the blessing on the *tallis gadol* or *tallis katan*, one should examine the strings of the *tzitzis* to make sure they are not torn. The part of the strings which pass through the holes in the corners of the garment should also be examined.[9] The strings should be separated from each other, so that they do not become entangled.[10]

Tallis gadol

10. Before *Shacharis*, one wraps himself in a *tallis gadol* and wears it throughout the service. Before wrapping himself, a person stands[11] and holds the *tallis* in his hands, and recites the blessing *l'his'ataif ba-tzitzis* ("to wrap oneself in *tzitzis*").[12] After reciting the blessing, one wraps himself in the *tallis*, making sure to cover his head and body with it, and flings the four *tzitzis* to his left side. One remains in this position for the amount of time it takes to walk four *amos*. Afterwards, one pushes the *tallis* back from his head until the *tefillin* can be seen, and he arranges the *tallis* so that two corners are in the front and two are in the back.[13]

Some communities have their own custom regarding how to wrap oneself in a *tallis*. Each person should follow his community's custom.

11. While wrapping himself in a *tallis gadol* or *tallis katan*, one should remember that he is doing this to fulfill the mitzvah of *tzitzis*. One should also have in mind that God commanded him to wear *tzitzis* for the purpose of remembering and fulfilling His *mitzvos*.[14]

It is customary for those who wear a *tallis gadol* during *Shacharis* to include their *tallis katan* in its blessing. In this case, no blessing is recited when putting on the *tallis katan* in the morning.[15]

The *tallis gadol* should cover the body while one is reciting *Shacharis*. It should not be worn around the neck like a shawl. One should be careful not to let the *tzitzis* drag on the floor, as this shows disrespect for the mitzvah, and may cause the strings to tear.[16]

Additional laws

12.   If one took off his *tallis gadol* for a short time, for example, to go to the bathroom, he does not recite another blessing when he puts it back on.[17] If, however, the *tallis* unintentionally fell off his body (even if he still held it in his hand), he must recite the blessing a second time when he wraps himself in it again, even if he replaces it immediately.[18] Some Sephardic Jews do not repeat the blessing in this case.

13.   The mitzvah of *tzitzis* is a positive commandment which applies to garments that are worn during the daytime. Women are exempt from such *mitzvos*, and are not obligated to observe the mitzvah of *tzitzis*.[19]

Instructions on how to prepare *tzitzis*

14.   A. Insert four *tzitzis* strings through one of the four holes in the corners of the garment. Eight strings now hang from the corner of the garment.[20] One of the four strings should be longer than the others. This string is called the *shamash*. Before inserting the strings into the hole of the garment, one should explicitly state that he is about to fulfill the mitzvah of *tzitzis*.[21] This is because the *tzitzis* must be hung, knotted and wound for the express purpose of the mitzvah.

15.   There are various customs regarding the number of times the strings are wound. The following method is the one described by the *Shulchan Aruch* and the *Mishnah Berurah*:

B. Take the four strings hanging from one side of the hole in one hand, and the four strings hanging from the other side with the other hand and tie two knots with them.

C. Take the *shamash* and wind it around the seven other strings seven times. Once again, make two knots with the two groups of four strings.

D. Now wind the *shamash* around the other strings eight times, make two knots as before, wind the *shamash* around the other strings eleven times, make another two knots, wind the *shamash* around thirteen times, and make two more knots.

E. When finished, the *tzitzis* will have five double knots with four spaces in between them where the *shamash* is wound around the other threads seven, eight, eleven and thirteen times. This process is repeated for each corner of the garment.

Another method designates winding the *shamash* around ten, five, six, and five times, which is the numerical value of each of the letters of the sacred four-letter Name of God.[22]

16.   The *tzitzis* look better if the windings appear equal in length, so one should try to make the first two windings slightly more spread apart and the last two windings closer together.[23]

17.   The length of the *tzitzis* from the knot closest to the garment to the end of the *tzitzis* should be at least twelve *agudalim*. According to the Chazon Ish the minimum length is 30 cm (11.8 in) (or at least 29 cm [11.4 in]). According to Rav Chaim Na'eh, the minimum length is 24.5 cm (9.65 in). The *tzitzis* look best when the knots and windings measure approximately one-third of the length of the *tzitzis* (i.e. four *agudalim*) and the hanging strings measure two-thirds of the length (i.e. eight *agudalim*). If the strings are longer than twelve *agudalim*, the knots and the windings should be spread apart so that they still measure one-third of the entire length.[24]

When making *tzitzis* for the first time, it is advisable to get practical instruction from an experienced person, due to the details involved.

The garment of a *tallis*

18.   The *Shulchan Aruch* maintains that according to the Torah woolen garments require *tzitzis*, while garments which are made from materials such as cotton only require *tzitzis* due to a rabbinical decree. Those who follow this opinion are particular that both their *tallis katan* and *tallis gadol* be made of wool, so that they are fulfilling a mitzvah from the Torah, rather than a rabbinic decree. The Rema (Rav Moshe Isserlis) maintains that the Torah requires *tzitzis* on four-cornered garments regardless of what material the garment is made of.[25]

19.   Woolen *tzitzis* are suitable for all garments regardless of what material they are made from. (The exception to this rule is linen garments, to which special laws apply.)

Tzitzis made of a material other than wool may only be used for a garment made of the same kind of material, i.e. cotton *tzitzis* can only be used on a cotton garment, etc.[26]

The mitzvah of *tzitzis* does not only apply to a *tallis katan* or *tallis gadol*. Any garment requires *tzitzis* if it has four corners, opens at the sides or the back, and is open for more than half of its length (e.g. a poncho). If one does not want to put *tzitzis* on these garments, he should round off one of the corners. It is not enough to fold the corner and sew it down so it appears round; the corner must be cut to exempt the garment from the requirement of *tzitzis*.[27]

20. According to the Chazon Ish, the distance between the hole for the *tzitzis* and the edge of the garment (not the diagonal from the corner) should be 4-7 cm (1.6-2.75 in), and preferably between 4.5 and 6 cm (1.8-2.3 in). According to Rav Chaim Na'eh, the distance should be 3.5-6 cm (1.4-2.3 in), and preferably 4-5 cm (1.6-2 in).[28]

If the *tzitzis* were initially inserted in the hole at the required distance from the edge, and later the hole tore, causing the distance to become smaller, the *tzitzis* may still be used. It is advisable to reinforce the stitching around the hole and the edge of the entire garment.[29]

The fringes of the *tzitzis*

21. The fringes of the *tzitzis* should be specially spun and interwoven for the purpose of being used as *tzitzis*. This is derived from the verse, "You shall make for yourself bound tassels" (*Devarim* 22:12), which our sages interpret as meaning, "'You shall make for yourself' — for the sake of fulfilling your obligation (to wear *tzitzis*)."[30] Therefore, one should be careful to buy *tzitzis* which bear reliable certification that they were spun and interwoven as required by Halachah.

22. If part of a string becomes fully unraveled, that part is considered as if it tore off. Therefore, if the thread's twining is loose, some people knot the end of the string to prevent it from unraveling.[31]

23. If only one of the eight threads is torn below the knots, the *tzitzis* may still be used. If the string is torn above the knots (i.e. the part of the string which is in the hole of the garment), it may no longer be used.[32]

If two or more strings tear, several factors must be considered, and a *rav* should be consulted regarding whether the garment may still be used.

24. As long as the *tzitzis* are attached to the garment, they may not be used for any purpose (e.g. tying objects with them), since this is disrespectful of the mitzvah. Similarly, strings that were torn off or removed from a *tallis katan* should not be treated disrespectfully. Some people go beyond the letter of the law and bury the strings like they bury holy books.[33]

The prescribed time for the mitzvah of *tzitzis*

25. The timetable below indicates the earliest time when one may recite the blessing on *tzitzis*. The blessing may not be recited before that time.

The table is arranged according to the solar calendar, as these times depend on the solar year.

The times listed are according to the *Shulchan Aruch's* opinion (18:3), that one may recite the blessing on a *tallis* when there is enough daylight to allow one to recognize an acquaintance from a distance of four *amos*, and when one is able to distinguish between sky-blue and white. This is also the earliest time when *tefillin* may be put on, as is explained in Chapter 6, Section 9.

The times are cited at ten-day intervals. One can estimate the times for the days in between.

The times are listed according to standard time.

Timetable for the Mitzvah of *Tzitzis*

DATE		JERUSALEM	NEW-YORK	LONDON	DATE		JERUSALEM	NEW-YORK	LONDON
Jan.	1	5.47	6.20	6.51	July	10	3.45	3.26	2.13
Jan.	11	5.48	6.20	6.49	July	20	3.52	3.36	2.32
Jan.	21	5.47	6.17	6.42	July	30	4.00	3.47	2.53
Jan.	31	5.43	6.10	6.31	Aug.	9	4.08	3.59	3.14
Feb.	10	5.37	6.01	6.17	Aug.	19	4.15	4.11	3.35
Feb.	20	5.28	5.49	5.59	Aug.	29	4.23	4.22	3.55
Mar.	2	5.18	5.35	5.39	Sep.	8	4.30	4.33	4.14
Mar.	12	5.06	5.19	5.17	Sep.	18	4.36	4.44	4.32
Mar.	22	4.53	5.02	4.53	Sep.	28	4.43	4.54	4.49
Apr.	1	4.40	4.45	4.29	Oct.	8	4.49	5.05	5.06
Apr.	11	4.27	4.28	4.04	Oct.	18	4.56	5.15	5.23
Apr.	21	4.14	4.11	3.39	Oct.	28	5.03	5.25	5.39
May	1	4.02	3.55	3.14	Nov.	7	5.10	5.36	5.55
May	11	3.52	3.41	2.50	Nov.	17	5.18	5.47	6.10
May	21	3.45	3.29	2.29	Nov.	27	5.26	5.57	6.24
May	31	3.39	3.21	2.11	Dec.	7	5.34	6.06	6.36
June	10	3.37	3.16	1.58	Dec.	17	5.40	6.13	6.45
June	20	3.37	3.16	1.54	Dec.	27	5.45	6.18	6.50
June	30	3.40	3.19	2.00					

Chapter Six

Tefillin
(Phylacteries)

1. The verse, "And you shall bind them as a sign upon your arm, and let them be as an emblem in the center of your head" (*Devarim* 6:8) refers to the mitzvah of wearing *tefillin*. *Tefillin* are put on every day (except for Shabbos and *Yom Tov*, as is explained below).

The preciousness of *tefillin*

2. The Rambam writes:

    The holiness of the *tefillin* is very great. As long as one wears *tefillin* on his head and on his arm, he will be humble and God-fearing, and will not be drawn to mockery, idle talk or evil thoughts. Instead, he will direct his thoughts to words of truth and righteousness.

    Therefore, a person should strive to wear them all day, as the mitzvah requires. It was said of Rav, the disciple of *Rabbeinu Ha-kadosh* (Rabbi Yehudah Hanassi) that throughout his life he was never seen walking four *amos* without discussing Torah, and wearing *tzitzis* and *tefillin*.

    Although it is a mitzvah to wear *tefillin* throughout the day, it is a greater mitzvah to do so when praying. Our sages said, "If one says the *Shema* without wearing *tefillin*, it is as if he is giving false testimony concerning himself." One who does not put on *tefillin* transgresses eight positive commandments, since in four different passages the Torah commands us to put on *tefillin shel rosh* (*tefillin* worn on the forehead) and *tefillin shel yad* (*tefillin* worn on the arm). One who regularly puts on *tefillin* will live long, as it says: "God is upon them and they shall live" (*Yeshayahu* 38:16). (*Hilchos Tefillin* 4:25-26)

3. "And it shall be as a sign to you upon your arm and a reminder in the center of your forehead so that God's Torah will be on your tongue. For it was with a show of strength that God brought you out of Egypt" (*Shemos* 13:9). The mitzvah of *tefillin* is a sign and a reminder for us. When we wear *tefillin* we impress upon our heart the essentials of our belief that

are written in its passages, as well as the memory of the Exodus from Egypt. Remembering the Exodus is essential because it was then that we became God's people, who received the Torah and are obligated to keep its *mitzvos*.

What are *tefillin*?

4. The two *tefillin* boxes and their straps are made from the hide of a kosher animal.[1] The *tefillin* boxes are filled with parchments which are also made from the hide of a kosher animal. Four passages from the Torah are handwritten on the parchments by a *sofer stam*, an authorized scribe. *Stam* is an acronym for *Sifrei Torah*, *Tefillin*, and *Mezuzos*.

The four passages inside the *tefillin* are *Kadesh Li* (*Shemos* 13:1-10); *V'hayah ki yevi'acha* (ibid. 13:11-16); *Shema Yisrael* (*Devarim* 6:4-9); and *V'hayah im shamo'a* (*Devarim* 11:13-21). Each of these passages discusses the mitzvah of *tefillin* and essentials of the Jewish faith.[2]

These four passages are inserted in the *tefillin shel yad* (that are worn on the arm) and in the *tefillin shel rosh* (that are worn on the head). In the former they are written on one piece of parchment, and in the latter, on four separate pieces.[3]

5. The *tefillin* and their straps are painted black with a specially prepared paint. The *tefillin* must be painted especially for the sake of the mitzvah.[4] If the color faded or was rubbed off, the *tefillin* must be repainted with the special paint. Before painting the *tefillin*, one should say, *L'shem kedushas tefillin*, "For the sake of the holiness of *tefillin*." The *tefillin* may be painted by a woman, but not by a child.

The *tefillin* boxes must be exactly square. One must ask a *rav* if the *tefillin* have to be repaired if any of the corners have become uneven.[5] Only an expert *tefillin*-maker can repair *tefillin*.

6. According to the Chazon Ish, the *tefillin* straps must be 11 mm (.433 in) wide. According to Rav Chaim Na'eh, the *tefillin* straps must be 10 mm (.394 in) wide. One must be careful that the straps are not torn or crimped at the place where they are tightened around the arm, lest their width decrease and they become invalid.[6]

On which days *tefillin* are worn

7.   *Tefillin* are worn every day, except for Shabbos and *Yom Tov* (as is explained in Section 8 below). This is a very important mitzvah and forgoing it for even one day is a great sin.[7]

8.   It is prohibited to wear *tefillin* on Shabbos and *Yom Tov*.[8] This includes the second day of *Yom Tov* observed by those living outside of Israel. *Tefillin* are worn on Chanukah and Purim.

The custom in Israel as well as in some communities in the Diaspora, is that *tefillin* are not worn on *Chol Ha-mo'ed* (the Intermediate days of Pesach and Succos). There are additional details concerning this *halachah* which are not mentioned here.[9]

The mitzvah of *tefillin* is a positive commandment which is bound by time. Therefore, women are exempt from this mitzvah.[10]

The prescribed time for putting on *tefillin*

9.   It is forbidden to sleep while wearing *tefillin*. Therefore, one may not put on *tefillin* at night, since he might fall asleep while wearing them.[11]

The earliest time to put on *tefillin* is when one can recognize an acquaintance from a distance of four *amos*. This time is the same as the earliest time one may recite a blessing on *tzitzis*. For more information regarding the exact time that one may put on *tefillin*, see the timetable in Chapter 5, Section 25.

Laws concerning both the *tallis* and *tefillin*

10.   *Tefillin* are put on before *Shacharis*, after wrapping oneself in a *tallis*, and are worn until the end of *Shacharis*.

11.   The *tallis* and *tefillin* should be placed in their bags in such a way that when one is taking them out, he reaches the *tallis* first. If one reached the *tefillin* first, he must put them on before the *tallis*. This is because of the principle that one should not pass by a mitzvah that comes his way.[12] Sephardic Jews always put on the *tallis* first even if they inadvertentiy reached the *tefillin* first.

There is great significance to entering the synagogue wearing a *tallis* and crowned with *tefillin*. Therefore many people put on their *tallis* and *tefillin* before entering the synagogue.[13]

If one has no *tefillin*

12.   A person who has no *tefillin* to put on should not recite *Shacharis* until he can borrow a pair from someone. This is because reciting the *Shema* without wearing *tefillin* is like giving false testimony concerning oneself (i.e. one recites the verse, "and you shall bind them on your arm," but does not have *tefillin* bound to his arm). If one may miss the proper time for reciting *Shema* while waiting for *tefillin* to become available he may recite *Shacharis*, including the *Shema*, without wearing *tefillin*, and fulfill his obligation to put on *tefillin* later.[14] (See Chapter 7, Section 26 for the latest time to recite *Shema*.)

13.   Putting on *tefillin* is a mitzvah independent of other *mitzvos*. If one recited *Shacharis* without wearing *tefillin*, he must put on *tefillin* some time during the day (but not at night). In this case, he recites the blessings for the *tefillin* and reads the *Shema*, a passage from the Torah or a chapter of *Tehillim*.[15]

Putting on *tefillin shel yad* (*Tefillin* for the arm)

14.   The *tefillin shel yad* is put on before the *tefillin shel rosh* (the *tefillin* for the head). The *tefillin shel yad* is placed on the lower half of the left biceps (referred to as the *kibbores* by our sages), closer to the elbow than to the armpit. According to the Gra (Rabbi Eliyahu of Vilna),the *tefillin shel yad* may be placed on any part of the biceps, including the part on the upper half of the upper arm.[16]

The *tefillin shel yad* should be turned slightly towards the body. When one lays his arm flat against the side of his body, the *tefillin shel yad* should be inclined towards his heart, so as to fulfill the verse, "And these words... shall be on your heart."[17]

15.   Before one tightens the strap that holds the *tefillin shel yad* to his arm, he recites the blessing *l'hani'ach tefillin* ("to put on *tefillin*"). Then he tightens the strap and winds it around his forearm (between the elbow and the wrist) seven times.[18]

Putting on *tefillin shel rosh* (*Tefillin* for the head)

16.   After putting on the *tefillin shel yad*, one places the *tefillin shel rosh* on his head, and tightens its strap around the head.[19] Before tightening it, many Ashkenazic Jews recite a separate blessing, *al mitzvas tefillin* ("Who has commanded us concerning the mitzvah of *tefillin*"). After tightening it, they say *Baruch Shem kevod malchuso l'olam va-ed*.

Sephardic Jews do not recite the blessing when putting on the *tefillin shel rosh*[19*] unless they inadvertently spoke between putting on the *tefillin shel yad* and the *tefillin shel rosh*. Some Ashkenazic Jews observe this practice as well.[20]

17. The *tefillin shel rosh* is placed above the hairline, exactly in the center of the head, corresponding to the spot which is exactly in between the eyes. One should be very careful that the entire *tefillin shel rosh* lies above the hairline and not on the forehead.[21] The knot of the *tefillin shel rosh* should also lie at the center within the hairline (and not below it), preferably at the bottom tip of the skull slightly above the nape of the neck.

18. One should make sure that the strap around the head fits his head. If the strap's length is not precise, the *tefillin shel rosh* will not lie properly on the head, and the *tefillin* or the knot might move from its proper place.[22]

19. After putting on the *tefillin shel rosh*, one finishes winding the strap of the *tefillin shel yad* by winding it around the middle finger three times (once on the middle bone and twice on the lower bone). The rest of the strap is wound around the palm. One then recites the verse: *v'eirastich li...* which is printed in *Siddurim*.[23]

20. According to the Rema and the *Mishnah Berurah*, both *tefillin shel yad* and *tefillin shel rosh* are put on while standing. Sephardim sit while putting on the *tefillin shel yad* and stand while putting on the *tefillin shel rosh*.[24]

21. It is prohibited to speak between putting on *tefillin shel yad* and *tefillin shel rosh*. If one hears *Kaddish* or *Kedushah* being recited while putting on his *tefillin*, he should listen and think the response instead of reciting it. It is preferable not to pause in silence between putting on the *tefillin shel yad* and the *tefillin shel rosh*.[25]

Additional laws pertaining to wearing *tefillin*

22. It is proper that the *tefillin shel rosh* appear prominently on one's head. This is derived from the verse, "And all the nations of the world will realize that God's Name is associated with you" (*Devarim* 28:10). However, those who follow the custom of the Ari *z"l* cover their *tefillin shel rosh* with their *tallis*. It is preferable for the *tefillin shel yad* to be covered.[26]

23. The side of the straps that is painted black must always face outward. This applies to the part of the straps that surround the head and the first part of the strap that is wound and tightened on the biceps, but not to the other parts. It is preferable that the black side of the other parts of the straps faces outwards too, because of *noi mitzvah* (beautifying the mitzvah).[27]

24. Nothing should be between one's body and the *tefillin*. This applies to the boxes of the *tefillin*, the first part of the strap that encircles the head, and the first part of the strap that is wound around the biceps.

If one has a thin bandage on his head or arm, and the *tefillin* boxes lie on the skin, and only the straps are on the bandage, the *tefillin* may be worn and the blessing may be recited.

If the bandage covers the entire biceps, the *tefillin shel yad* should be worn over the bandage without reciting a blessing. Similarly, if the bandage covers the front center of the head, the *tefillin shel rosh* are worn over the bandage without reciting a blessing. In these cases the *tefillin* should be covered.[28]

One may not wear the *tefillin shel yad* on his other arm, even if the arm he usually wears it on has a bandage on it.

25. One should be careful that the knot which forms the letter *yud* in the strap should not be detached from the box of the *tefillin shel yad*. Some people are careful that this knot does not become detached from the *tefillin* box, even when the *tefillin* are not being worn.[29]

26. One who performs all his actions with the left hand ties his *tefillin shel yad* to his right arm.[30] A person who is ambidextrous, or who writes with one hand and does his other actions with the other hand, should consult a *rav* to determine to which arm he should tie his *tefillin*.[31]

27. One who took off his *tefillin* to go to the bathroom must repeat the blessing when he puts them on again.[32] Sephardic Jews do not recite the blessing in this case.

28. One should place the *tefillin* in their bag in a way that he always reaches for the *tefillin shel yad* first. This way he will avoid passing over the *tefillin shel rosh* when reaching for the *tefillin shel yad*. If one inadvertently reached for the *tefillin shel rosh* first, he still puts on the *tefillin shel yad* first, according to the order specified in the Torah, "Bind them as a sign on your arm and as *tefillin* between your eyes."[33]

The holiness of tefillin

29.   When one is wearing tefillin, he should behave in a manner befitting their holiness. He may not engage in light or frivolous talk. It is best if one fixes his thoughts on the tefillin he is wearing so that his mind does not stray to improper thoughts. However, when one concentrates on prayer or Torah study, he need not focus his attention on the tefillin.[34] If one is wearing tefillin when it is not a time of prayer, he should touch them every so often, so he remembers he is wearing them. He should first touch the tefillin shel yad, and then the tefillin shel rosh.[35] Touching the tefillin helps the person focus his attention on them.

30.   It is prohibited to sleep or expel intestinal gas while wearing tefillin.[36] If one feels he will be unable to prevent this from happening, he must take off the tefillin.[37]

A person suffering from an intestinal illness is exempt from putting on tefillin if he cannot prevent himself from expelling intestinal gas. If he can control himself long enough to recite the Shema, he should put on his tefillin between Ahavah rabbah and Shema, recite the blessings for the tefillin, recite Shema, and then remove the tefillin.[38]

31.   Tefillin should be treated as the sacred objects that they are. A person may not sit on a chair or a bench if tefillin are lying there. One must be extremely careful that tefillin do not fall to the ground. It is customary to fast if the tefillin fell from one's hands when it wasn't in its box. If one is too weak to fast, he should give tzedakah (charity) instead.

32.   Tefillin are kept in a special bag, which is considered a tashmish kedushah (an accessory to a holy object, which has sanctity of its own). The bag may not be used for any other purpose. When the bag becomes worn out or torn, it requires burial, like holy books.[39]

If the boxes of one's tefillin cover them from all sides so that they do not come in contact with the bag, the bag is not considered a tashmish kedushah.

Taking off the tefillin

33.   It is a custom of chachamim (the wise) to kiss their tefillin before putting them on and after removing them.[40]

The usual custom is not to remove the *tefillin* until after the *Kedushah* in the prayer *u'Va l'Tzion go'el* ("A redeemer shall come to Zion"). The Ari z"l only removed his *tefillin* after reciting *Al ken nekaveh* in *Aleinu L'shabe'ach*. It is good to remove one's *tefillin* after the *Kaddish Yasom* following *Aleinu L'shabe'ach* has been recited.[41]

The *tallis* and *tefillin* may not be folded while *Kaddish* is being recited, because one has to concentrate on the words of the *Kaddish*, and nothing else may be done during that time.[42]

34. When removing the *tefillin*, the straps which are wound around the hand and middle finger are unwound first. Then the *tefillin shel rosh* is removed. Some men do this with their left hand to show their reluctance at removing the *tefillin*; this demonstrates their reverence for the *tefillin*.[43] The straps of the *tefillin shel rosh* are folded, and it is put into the bag. The *tefillin shel yad* is then taken off, its strap is folded, and it is also put into the bag. As was mentioned above, one should place the *tefillin* in their bag in a way that the *tefillin shel yad* is always taken out first.[44]

35. The Rema and the *Mishnah Berurah* maintain that one must stand while removing their *tefillin*. Sephardic Jews have the custom to remove the *tefillin shel rosh* while standing, and the *tefillin shel yad* while sitting.[45] The *tallis* is taken off after the *tefillin* are removed.

The *kashrus* of *tefillin*

36. There are many *halachos* concerning the *kashrus* of *tefillin*. Hundreds of details must be stringently observed when processing the hide for the boxes and straps, shaping the boxes, writing the Scriptural passages, etc. Once the *tefillin* are completed, it is no longer possible to verify if many of these details were done according to Halachah. (For example, the animal hides must be prepared explicitly for the sake of the mitzvah of *tefillin*, the Scriptural passages must be written in their proper sequence, the straps must be painted explicitly for the sake of the mitzvah of *tefillin*, etc.) Great expertise and uncompromising *yir'as shamayim* (fear of God) are essential if a *tefillin*-maker is to make *tefillin* according to Halachah.

A person who puts on *tefillin* which are not kosher not only fails to observe this great mitzvah, but he also recites the blessings before putting on the *tefillin* in vain. Therefore, not only must one be careful to buy his *tefillin* from a reliable and God-fearing person who can attest to their *kashrus*, but he should also have them checked by a Torah scholar to verify if the *tefillin* are ritually fit.

Inspecting the *tefillin*

37.   *Tefillin* that were verified to be kosher do not have to be inspected again if they are used daily, and the outside appears complete. There is no reason to assume that the letters on the parchment have become damaged or erased. Although the Halachah does not require that a person check his *tefillin*, it is proper to inspect the *tefillin* over the course of time since they can be damaged by sweat or other factors.

Tefillin that are only used occasionally must be inspected twice in seven years.

Tefillin that fell into water, were left in a damp place, were subjected to high temperatures, or were damaged in any way must be inspected immediately. In these cases, it is likely that the script was damaged or that the *tefillin* were rendered invalid in some other way.[46]

Chapter Seven

Shacharis
(The morning service)

1. Before reciting *Shacharis*, men put on a *tallis* and *tefillin*. The text for *Shacharis* is printed in the Siddur.

The greatness of prayer

2. At the start of the day, man raises his face heavenward, to give thanks to his Father for all the goodness He has bestowed upon him, and to express his entreaties and heart's desires. Prayer recited with *kavanah* (concentration on every word) instills a person with the awareness that all events in this world are under the full control of God, the Creator of all.

In *The Kuzari*, Rabbi Yehudah Halevy explains the greatness of a prayer that springs from the depths of one's heart, the exalted level achieved by one whose prayer is this pure, and the influence prayer has on a person's entire day. These are his words:

> A pious man does not pray by rote. He does not enunciate words thoughtlessly and inattentively like a parrot. Rather, he says every word with the thought and intention befitting it. His heart and tongue are at one with each other, for he will not express with his tongue what his mind does not truly think.
>
> The time he sets aside for prayer is the most important time of the day. The other hours are auxiliary, and only lead up to it. In effect, the fruition of his day and night are the three periods of prayer.
>
> Prayer is as vital for the soul as material food is for the body, for the soul's sustenance is prayer. The positive effect of one prayer accompanies him until the next prayer, just as one meal fortifies the body until the next. As time passes since the last time he prayed, his soul begins to feel darkness and melancholy because of its encounters with the materialistic world. During prayer, the soul becomes purified from these contacts and prepares itself for the stretch of time until the next prayer. (*The Kuzari* 3:5)

The parts of *Shacharis*

3.   *Shacharis* includes the following parts:

* *Birchos Ha-Shachar* — The Morning Blessings (discussed in Chapter 3).

* *Parashiyos Ha-Korbanos* — The Passages of the Sacrifices.

* *Pesukei D'zimrah* — The Section of Praises.

* *Kerias Shema* — The Recitation of the *Shema* and its blessings.

* *Shemoneh Esreh* (*Amidah*) — The Prayer of Eighteen Blessings (and the leader's repetition of it when a *minyan* is present).

* *Tachanun* — Supplications.

* *Kerias Ha-Torah* — Torah Readings (read on Monday, Thursday, *Rosh Chodesh*, etc.).

* The prayers at the end of the service.

Parashiyos Ha-Korbanos — the passages of the sacrifices

4.   It is commendable to read the passages which discuss the *Akedah* (the binding of Yitzchak; *Bereshis* 22:1-19), the sacrifices, and the other sections appearing after *Birchos Ha-Shachar* in the *Siddur*.[1]

The *Mishnah Berurah* explains that the passage discussing the *Akedah* is recited daily to remind us of our forefathers' merits, and to help us subdue our evil inclinations, as Yitzchak did when he was prepared to allow himself to be sacrificed to God.[2]

Our sages teach that since the Temple has been destroyed, and we can no longer offer sacrifices, one who recites the passages which discuss the sacrifices will be credited as if he actually offered them. "Whoever occupies himself with the section about the *olah* (burnt-offering) is regarded as having offered an *olah*."

It is a mitzvah to study the passages which discuss the sacrifices and their halachic details, so that one fully understands what he is reciting.[3]

Pesukei D'zimrah
(The section of praises)

5.   We preface our petitions to God with *Pesukei D'zimrah*. *Pesukei D'zimrah* is an anthology of chapters and verses from *Tehillim* and other holy books, whose content is the praise and glorification of God.

6.   *Pesukei D'zimrah* is preceded by the blessing of *Baruch She-Amar* ("Blessed is He Who said"), and is followed by the blessing of *Yishtabach*.

There are eighty-seven words in *Baruch She-Amar*. This is hinted to in the verse, "His opening words were *paz* (finest gold)" (*Shir Ha-Shirim* 5:11). Since the numerical value of the Hebrew word *paz* is eighty-seven, this phrase may be understood as a hint that at the beginning of the service there is a blessing with eighty-seven words.

Baruch She-Amar is recited while standing. One holds the two front *tzitzis* of his *tallis* in his right hand while reciting this prayer, and kisses them at the end of the blessing.[4]

7.   One must not talk from the beginning of *Baruch She-Amar* until after reciting the *Shemoneh Esreh*.[5] The table provided in Section 29 below indicates when one may interrupt his prayers to respond Amen or to *Kedushah*, etc.

Pesukei D'zimrah must be recited calmly, without haste, and without skipping any words. A person should not swallow his words. One should articulate the words as carefully as he would count coins. He should concentrate on each word's meaning.[6]

8.   *Mizmor l'sodah* is omitted on Shabbos, Yom Tov, *erev* Pesach, the intermediate days of Pesach, and *erev* Yom Kippur.[7] Sephardic Jews only omit *Mizmor l'sodah* on Shabbos and Yom Tov.

When reciting the verse, *pose'ach es yadecha* ("You open Your hand and satisfy the desire of every living thing") during *Ashrei*, one should concentrate on the fact that God watches over and provides for all His creations. If one recited this verse without *kavanah*, he must repeat it; according to the *Mishnah Berurah* he should repeat from this verse until the end of *Ashrei*.[8]

It is customary to stand while reciting the following passages of *Pesukei D'zimrah*: *Baruch She-Amar*, from *Va-yevarech David* ("And David blessed") until *Attah Hu Hashem Ha-Elokim* ("You are the Almighty God"), and *Yishtabach* ("Your name shall be praised").[9] Sephardic Jews do not stand when reciting *Yishtabach*.

9.   When praying with a *minyan*, half-*Kaddish* is recited after *Yishtabach*. The *halachos* concerning *Kaddish* are discussed in Sections 105-108 below.

After *Kaddish*, the leader says *Barechu es Hashem Ha-Mevorach* ("Bless the blessed God"), and the congregation responds, *Baruch Hashem Ha-Mevorach l'olam va-ed* ("Blessed is the blessed God forever and ever"). The leader then repeats the congregation's response.[10] This is followed by *Kerias Shema* and its blessings.

The procedure for one who came late to services

10.   One should come to synagogue on time, so as to be able to recite all of *Pesukei D'zimrah* with a *minyan*.[11]

Shemoneh Esreh is the most important prayer to recite with a *minyan*. Therefore, our sages permitted a latecomer to skip some passages of *Pesukei D'zimrah* to enable him to recite *Shemoneh Esreh* with the congregation. However, nothing may be omitted from *Kerias Shema* and its blessings.

11.   One who came to synagogue late should put on his *tallis* and *tefillin* and recite their blessings. Then, he should recite the blessings *al netilas yadayim*, *Elokai neshamah* ("My God, the soul You have given me") and *Birchos Ha-Torah*. These blessings must always precede the rest of *Shacharis*. (For more information regarding *Birchos Ha-Shachar*, see Chapter 3, Section 11.)

If one does not have enough time to recite the remaining *Birchos Ha-Shachar*, he may recite them after he has finished praying. If he is very pressed for time, he should just recite *Baruch She-Amar*, *Ashrei* and *Yishtabach*, and then continue with the blessings of *Kerias Shema*.

12.   Depending on how much more time a person has, the other prayers should be added with certain ones taking precedence over others. Here they are listed according to precedence:

A. The third and fifth of the *Hallelukahs* in the *Pesukei D'zimrah* (*Hallelu es Hashem min ha-shamayim*, and *Hallelu kel b'kadesho*).

B. The other three *Hallelukahs*.

C. *Va-yevarech David* until the words *l'shem tif'artecha* ("for the sake of Your glory").

D. The first part of *Hodu la-Hashem* ("Praise God; call in His Name") until *V'Hu rachum* ("And He is merciful"), and then skip until the *V'Hu rachum* before *Ashrei*.

13.   One who arrived at the synagogue when the congregation was reciting *Yotzer or* ("He creates light"), should recite *Baruch She-Amar, Ashrei* and *Yishtabach,* and *Kerias Shema* with all its blessings, and try to begin *Shemoneh Esreh* together with the congregation. (See Section 11 above, concerning *Birchos Ha-Shachar.*) According to the *Shulchan Aruch,* if the person will not be able to begin *Shemoneh Esreh* together with the congregation, he should begin *Yotzer or* with the congregation. After the service he should recite *Pesukei D'zimrah,* omitting *Baruch She-Amar* and *Yishtabach.* The *Mishnah Berurah*[12] cites the *Mishkenos Ya'akov's* halachic opinion, that it is better for a person to recite his prayers in the proper order without a *minyan,* rather than to skip *Baruch She-Amar* and *Yishtabach.*

14.   If one came late on Shabbos or *Yom Tov,* he should recite *Baruch She-Amar, Ashrei, Nishmas,* and *Yishtabach.* If possible, the passages from the daily *Pesukei D'zimrah* should be added. (These chapters of *Tehillim* take precedence over those added on Shabbos because they are recited more frequently.) If more time is available, one should add the special chapters of *Tehillim* for Shabbos in the following order: *La-menatze'ach, L'David b'shanoso,* and *Tefillah l'Moshe.*[13] These passages are printed in the *Siddur* with the Shabbos prayers.

Our sages permitted us to skip parts of *Pesukei D'zimrah* to enable us to recite *Shemoneh Esreh* with the congregation, but only on the condition that *Kerias Shema* and its blessings are recited meticulously, according to Halachah. If a person rushing to catch up to the congregation for *Shemoneh Esreh* will recite *Kerias Shema* without the requisite *kavanah,* it is better for him not to recite *Shemoneh Esreh* with the congregation. In this case the person should recite the prayers in their proper order, without skipping any of them.[14]

Kerias Shema
(Shema and its blessings)

15. *Kerias Shema* and its blessings are recited after *Pesukei D'zimrah* (and *Kaddish* and *Barechu* when praying with a *minyan*). Two blessings precede the *Shema*. The first blessing ends with the words *yotzer ha-me'oros* ("Who has formed the luminaries") and the second blessing ends with the words *ha-bocher b'ammo Yisrael b'ahavah* ("Who has chosen His people Israel with love").

Shema is recited after these two blessings. The mitzvah to recite *Shema* twice a day, in the morning and in the evening, is derived from the *Shema* itself, from the words, "when you lie down and when you arise" (*Berachos* 2a).

The importance of *Kerias Shema*

16. *Kerias Shema* is comprised of three passages: *Shema Yisrael* (*Devarim* 6:4-9), *V'hayah im shamo'a* (*Devarim* 11:13-21), and *Parashas tzitzis* (*Bemidbar* 15:37-41). These passages contain three fundamentals of our faith: belief in God, the acceptance of His sovereignty over us, and our commitment to observe His *mitzvos*.

Jews in every generation have proclaimed their faith and devotion to God, His Torah and *mitzvos* by reciting the verse *Shema Yisrael Hashem Elokeinu Hashem Echad* ("Hear O Israel, the Lord is our God, the Lord is one").

17. The *Shema* should be recited with awe and reverence, and with total concentration. Halachic authorities write that when one recites *Shema*, he should intend to accept the heavenly yoke by being prepared to give up his life for the sanctification of God's name. This is derived from the words "with all your soul," i.e. even if He takes your soul.[15]

The *Tur* cites Rav Amram Gaon as saying that one should read *Kerias Shema* just as he would read a new decree from a king to his subjects. People would certainly read the new decree while trembling with fear and reverence; how much more so should a person tremble when reading the *Shema*, which is a decree from the King of kings!

A person must not hasten through the *Shema*. Rather, one should recite it slowly and calmly, trying to understand every detail that God commands.[16]

Reciting the *Shema* meticulously

18.   *Kerias Shema* should be recited with great precision. Every syllable and sound must be enunciated correctly so that, for example, the letter *zayin* (the sound "z") is distinguishable from the letter *sin* (the sound "s"). One syllable must not be combined with another. One should pause between two words where the first word ends with the same letter with which the second word begins (i.e. *bechol - levavecha, eisev - b'sadecha, va-avadetem - meheirah, eschem - me-eretz, ha-kanaf - pesil*). All rules of pronunciation should be followed, e.g. when a letter should be emphasized (*dagesh*) and when not (*rafui*).[17]

The words of *Kerias Shema* should be recited aloud so that one can hear what he is saying.[18]

What to have in mind when reciting *Kerias Shema*

19.   A person must have in mind that he is reciting *Shema* for the purpose of fulfilling a mitzvah. He must understand and concentrate on the meaning of the words. This especially applies to the first verse of *Shema*. If the first verse is not recited with *kavanah*, the person has not fulfilled his obligation.[19]

The following explanations of the words of the first verse of *Shema* will help one recite it with the proper *kavanah*:

Shema Yisrael (Hear, O Israel) — Believe, Israel (that)

Hashem (God) — He Who is Lord over all, and Who was, is, and will ever be

Elokeinu (is our Almighty God) — Who is powerful and omnipotent

Hashem — He is Lord over all, and He was, is, and will ever be

Echad (One) — the One and Only, and the sole Ruler of the universe.[19*]

It is customary to recite the first verse of *Kerias Shema* in a loud voice, while covering one's eyes with the right hand.[20] This is to enhance one's concentration. The sentence following it (*Baruch Shem kevod*) is recited in a whisper.[21] This verse must also be recited with special concentration.[21*]

20.   The three passages of the *Shema* contain 245 words. To attain the number 248 — which corresponds to the number of limbs in a person's body — the leader repeats the last words of *Kerias Shema, Hashem Elokeichem emes*. If one is not praying with a *minyan*, he says *Kel melech ne'eman* ("God, trustworthy king") before the *Shema*, instead of repeating the last three words.[22] Sephardic Jews do not say *Kel melech ne'eman* because they repeat *Hashem Elokeichem emes* when praying alone.

How to conduct oneself when reciting *Kerias Shema*

21. When reciting the first passage of *Shema*, it is prohibited to gesture to others with one's hands or eyes, even if it is for the sake of a mitzvah. During the rest of *Shema*, gesturing is permitted if it is for the sake of a mitzvah.[23]

22. During *Kerias Shema*, it is a mitzvah to hold the *tzitzis* (fringes) against one's heart. (This is derived from the verse, "And these words... shall be upon your heart.") One holds the *tzitzis* betwen the fourth and fifth fingers of his left hand. When one reaches the third passage of the *Shema*, which discusses the mitzvah of *tzitzis*, he holds the *tzitzis* in both hands, and looks at them. Some men have the custom to look at the *tzitzis* when reciting the words *u're'isem osso* ("so that you may look upon them").

One should continue holding his *tzitzis* until he reaches the words *ne'emanim v'nechemadim la-ad* ("trustworthy and pleasant forever"), in the passage beginning *Emes v'yatziv*. One kisses his *tzitzis* before letting go of them.[24]

When reciting the *u'keshartam l'os al yadecha* (bind them as a sign upon your arm), one should touch his *tefillin shel yad*. When reciting the words *v'hayu l'totafos bein einecha* (and let them be *tefillin* between your eyes), one should touch his *tefillin shel rosh*. When reciting the words *u're'isem osso*, which refers to the *tzitzis*, one should touch his front two *tzitzis*.[24*]

23. One may stand or sit when reciting *Shema* in the morning, but if one was sitting, he may not stand up for *Shema*.[25]

If one has already recited *Shema*, when he hears a congregation reciting it he should join in reciting the first verse (*Shema Yisrael*), so it does not appear as if he does not wish to accept the Almighty's sovereignty with everyone else.[26]

The earliest time for reciting *Shema*

24. According to Halachah, one may recite *Shema* in the morning beginning from the time when one can recognize an acquaintance from a distance of four *amos*. This is the same time that one may recite the blessing on *tzitzis*.[27]

(For more information regarding the earliest time for reciting *Shema*, see the timetable in Chapter 5, Section 25.)

The best time to recite *Shema* is at *vasikin*, i.e. just before sunrise, so one can begin *Shemoneh Esreh* exactly at sunrise.[28]

25. If one has to pray very early, e.g. he is going on a trip, and will not be able to recite *Shema* later, he may recite *Shema* immediately after dawn (*alos ha-shachar*). The time of daybreak is listed in many halachic timetables. Since the earliest time for putting on *tefillin* is somewhat later, one who is traveling very early should not put on *tefillin* until the correct time.[29] (For more information, see Chapter 6, Section 9.)

The latest time for reciting *Shema*

26. The daylight hours are divided into twelve equal parts, called *sha'os zemanios*. *Shema* may be recited during the first three *sha'os zemanios* (a fourth of the daylight hours). The number of minutes in each *sha'ah zemanis* varies according to the season. In the winter, each *sha'ah zemanis* has less than sixty minutes, and in the summer each *sha'ah zemanis* has more than sixty minutes.

One must rise early in the morning, so as to recite *Shacharis* before it is too late to recite *Shema*. One should note that the time for reciting *Shema* ends earlier in the summer, since dawn is earlier in the summer.[30]

According to the *Magen Avraham*, the day is measured from dawn (*alos ha-shachar*) to when the stars appear (*tzeis ha-kochavim*), while according to the Gra (the Vilna Gaon), it is measured from sunrise (*netz ha-chamah*) to sunset (*shekiah*). According to the Gra, the latest time for reciting *Shema* is a little later than the latest time according to the *Magen Avraham*.

The table on p. 50 lists the latest time for reciting *Shema* each morning. The times are listed at ten-day intervals. One can estimate the times for the days in between. The times are listed according to standard time.

The Latest Time for Reciting *Kerias Shema*

DATE		JERUSALEM		NEW-YORK		LONDON	
		MAGEN AVRAHAM	THE GRAH	MAGEN AVRAHAM	THE GRAH	MAGEN AVRAHAM	THE GRAH
Jan.	1	8.32	9.11	8.55	9.39	9.09	10.05
Jan.	11	8.35	9.14	8.57	9.41	9.11	10.06
Jan.	21	8.36	9.14	8.58	9.41	9.10	10.03
Jan.	31	8.35	9.13	8.56	9.38	9.06	9.58
Feb.	10	8.33	9.10	8.52	9.33	8.59	9.50
Feb.	20	8.28	9.05	8.45	9.26	8.50	9.40
Mar.	2	8.22	8.59	8.38	9.18	8.39	9.29
Mar.	12	8.15	8.51	8.29	9.09	8.27	9.17
Mar.	22	8.07	8.44	8.19	9.00	8.13	9.04
Apr.	1	7.59	8.36	8.08	8.50	7.59	8.51
Apr.	11	7.51	8.28	7.57	8.40	7.43	8.38
Apr.	21	7.43	8.21	7.47	8.31	7.28	8.26
May	1	7.36	8.15	7.38	8.24	7.12	8.15
May	11	7.30	8.10	7.29	8.17	6.55	8.06
May	21	7.25	8.07	7.22	8.13	6.38	7.59
May	31	7.23	8.06	7.17	8.10	6.16	7.54
June	10	7.22	8.06	7.15	8.09	6.00	7.52
June	20	7.23	8.07	7.15	8.10	6.02	7.52
June	30	7.25	8.10	7 18	8.13	6.04	7.55
July	10	7.29	8.13	7.23	8.17	6.04	8.00
July	20	7.33	8.16	7.29	8.21	6.39	8.06
July	30	7.38	8.19	7.36	8.26	6.58	8.13
Aug.	9	7.42	8.22	7.43	8.30	7.13	8.20
Aug.	19	7.45	8.24	7.49	8.34	7.26	8.27
Aug.	29	7.48	8.26	7.54	8.37	7.37	8.34
Sept.	8	7.50	8.28	7.58	8.41	7.47	8.40
Sept.	18	7.52	8.29	8.02	8.44	7.55	8.47
Sept.	28	7.54	8.30	8.06	8.47	8.03	8.53
Oct.	8	7.56	8 32	8.10	8.51	8.10	9.00
Oct.	18	7.58	8.34	8.14	8.55	8.17	9.07
Oct.	28	8.00	8.37	8.18	9.00	8.24	9.15
Nov.	7	8.04	8.41	8.23	9.05	8.32	9.24
Nov.	17	8.08	8.46	8.29	9.12	8.40	9.33
Nov.	27	8.14	8.52	8.36	9.19	8.48	9.43
Dec.	7	8.19	8.58	8.42	9.26	8.56	9.52
Dec.	17	8.25	9.04	8.48	9.32	9.03	9.59
Dec.	27	8.30	9.09	8.53	9.37	9.08	10.04

27.   If one did not recite *Shema* and its blessings within the first three *sha'os zemanios* of the day, he recites them within the fourth *sha'ah zemanis*. In this case, however, he has not fulfilled the mitzvah of reciting the morning *Shema*.

If the fourth *sha'ah zemanis* passed, it is nonetheless proper to recite *Kerias Shema* anytime throughout the day, so to accept God's sovereignty. In this case, one should not recite the accompanying blessings. In any case, a person is required to recite *parashas tzitzis* so as to recall the Exodus from Egypt (this is an independent mitzvah which can be performed throughout the day).[31]

28.   One blessing is recited after *Kerias Shema*. This blessing ends with the words *Ga'al Yisrael* ("Who redeemed Israel"). It is customary to stand up in preparation for reciting *Shemoneh Esreh* when the leader begins to recite the words *Tehillos l'Kel Elyon*, "Praises to the Supreme God."[32]

One should begin reciting *Shemoneh Esreh* immediately after concluding the blessing of *Ga'al Yisrael*. This is in accordance with the rule that the *Shemoneh Esreh* should be adjoined to the blessing of Redemption.[33]

When One May Interrupt His Prayers
(To respond to Baruch Hu U'varuch Shemo, Amen, Kedushah, Barechu and Modim)

29.   These *halachos* have been arranged in the table on p.52 so as to facilitate locating the *halachah* regarding interruptions at various points in the service. The notes below the table include halachic references, as well as additional details. The table illustrates the *Mishnah Berurah's* ruling regarding these *halachos*.

Shemoneh Esreh (The eighteen blessings)

30.   The *Shemoneh Esreh*, also referred to as *Tefillas Ha-Amidah* ("Standing Prayer") or as *Tefillah* ("Prayer"), is recited three times every day: as part of *Shacharis*, *Minchah* and *Ma'ariv*.

Responding during Prayers to Amen, etc.

Where one is in the service / The response	Pesukei D'zimrah (from Baruch She-Amar until after Yishtabach)[1]	Kerias Shema and its Blessings (between sections)[2]	Kerias Shema and its Blessings (in the middle of a section)
Baruch Hu u'varuch Shemo	Prohibited[3]	Prohibited	Prohibited
Amen (to all blessings except those specified below)	Permitted[4]	Permitted[6]	Prohibited
Amen (to Ha-Kel Ha-Kadosh and Shome'a tefillah in Shemoneh Esreh; Amen before Yehei Shemeh Rabbah and after da'amiran b'alma v'imru during kaddish; and responding Baruch Hashem ha-mevorach to Barechu)	Permitted[5]	Permitted	Permitted[7]
Kedushah	Permitted[5]	One may only recite the verses Kadosh, and Baruch kevod	One may only recite the verses Kadosh, and Baruch kevod
Modim d'rabbanan	Permitted[5]	Bow and recite the three words Modim anachnu lach	Bow and recite the three words Modim anachnu lach

1. Before reciting Baruch She-Amar it is permitted to recite all responses including Baruch Hu u'varuch Shemo. One should conclude all short blessings without any interruptions after mentioning God's Name. (M.B. 54 [3]; see also Chayei Adam 5:13 regarding interrupting a lengthy berachah.)   2. "Between sections" means: between Yotzer ha-me'oros and Ahavah rabbah; between ha-bocher b'ammo Yisrael b'ahavah and Shema; between u'vi-she'arecha and V'hayah im shamo'a, between ki-mei ha-shamayim al ha-aretz and Va-yomer Hashem el Moshe. For more details see S.A. 66. The halachos regarding interruptions during Kerias Shema during Ma'ariv are the same as those regarding interruptions during Shacharis. Between the Kaddish following Yishtabach and Barechu is considered "between sections," while immediately after Barechu is considered "in the middle of a section" (M.B. 54 [13]). One may never interrupt in middle of the first verse of Shema and in middle of the verse Baruch Shem kevod and between the verses of Shema and Baruch Shem kevod, between Hashem Elokeichem and emes at the end of the third section of Shema, and between Ga'al Yisrael and the Shemoneh Esreh. One should not even pause between Ga'al Yisrael and the Shemoneh Esreh.   3. M.B. 51 (8).   4. One may respond Amen during Pesukei D'zimrah even if he is in the middle of a verse, as long as he is not in the middle of a phrase. (Ibid. See also Be'ur Halachah there beginning with the word tzarich).   5. It is permitted to interrupt to recite all these responses, even if one is in the middle of a phrase. (Ibid. See also Ha-Kel Ha-Kadosh or Shome'a tefillah he should try to finish the verse he is reciting before responding. If this is not possible, the person should respond Amen, and then recite the verse from the beginning. It   6. M.B. 59 (18). See also M.B. 66 (23).   7. If one is in the middle of a section when it is time to answer Amen to Ha-Kel Ha-Kadosh and Shome'a tefillah if they are in the middle of a section of Shema. is customary among Sephardic Jews not to respond Amen to Ha-Kel Ha-Kadosh and Shome'a tefillah if they are in the middle of a section of Shema.

When one is praying one should feel that he is pouring out his heart to God. This is derived from the verse, "Pour out your heart like water before God" (*Eichah* 2:19). It is written in *Mesillas Yesharim* (Chapter 19):

> A person must be mindful when engaged in prayer or performing a mitzvah that he is praying or performing the deed before the King of kings. This is what the sage exhorted us about, "When you pray, know before Whom you are standing" (*Berachos* 28b).
>
> ...With a minimum of reflection, a person can establish the reality in his heart that he is fully communicating with God, saying his supplications and placing his requests while God listens.

31. Before reciting the *Shemoneh Esreh*, a person should contemplate His Creator's exaltedness and his own insignificance. These thoughts will help him concentrate properly on this prayer.[34]

It is commendable to study the meanings and *kavanos* of the various prayers. Books have been written for this purpose, and there are *Siddurim* available with a commentary printed on the same page as the prayers. In view of the special importance of the *Shemoneh Esreh*, its structure and laws are discussed below in detail.

The text of the *Shemoneh Esreh*

32. The text of the *Shemoneh Esreh* was instituted at the beginning of the Second Temple period by the Men of the Great Assembly. According to *Maseches Megillah* 17b, the Men of the Great Assembly included Ezra the Scribe, and the last prophets, Chaggai, Zecharyah and Malachi. The Men of the Great Assembly instituted the eighteen blessings that comprise this prayer. After the destruction of the Second Temple, the Sanhedrin moved to Yavne, and a nineteenth blessing was added, the blessing of *V'lamalshinim*. Thus, although the prayer retained its name *"Shemoneh Esreh"* ("Eighteen Blessings"), it is actually comprised of nineteen blessings.

In Chapter 2, Section 5, we cited the Rambam's opinion that prayer is a mitzvah mandated by the Torah. The Men of the Great Assembly composed a set text for prayer.

Parts of the *Shemoneh Esreh*

33. Immediately preceding the *Shemoneh Esreh* one recites the verse, "O Lord, open my lips, and my mouth shall recite Your praise" (*Tehillim* 51:17). We begin by asking God to assist us in praying to Him.

The *Shemoneh Esreh* is divided into three sections:

A. Praises — the first three blessings

B. Petitions — the thirteen middle blessings

C. Thanksgiving — the last three blessings

Praises — Before submitting our petitions, we commence with God's glory and praises. Our sages said, "One should always cite God's praises before petitioning Him" (*Berachos* 32a). The three blessings in this category are *Avos* (ending with the words *Magen Avraham*), *Gevuros* (ending with the words *mechayeh ha-meisim*), and *Kedushah* (ending with the words *Ha-Kel Ha-Kadosh*).

Petitions — In the thirteen middle blessings we petition God for all our needs. These prayers are stated in the plural form, because we are praying for the entire Jewish people. We request that every Jew be assisted in his spiritual endeavors (in the blessing *Chonen ha-da'as*), in his Torah study, and in repenting to God for his sins; and that he be redeemed from his sufferings, and enjoy good health and a livelihood. We also pray for the community's general needs. For example, we pray for the return of the exiles, that Torah law be restored (in the blessing *Hashivah shofteinu*), that the Temple be rebuilt in Jerusalem, that the *Mashiach* should come (in the blessing *Es tzemach David*), etc. The last of these thirteen blessings is *Shema koleinu*, in which we ask God that our prayers be acceptable to Him.

Thanksgiving — The last three blessings are *Retzei*, *Modim*, and *Sim shalom*. In these blessings we thank God for listening to our prayers and for His eternal kindness towards us. We also make a few general requests for God's goodwill towards the Jewish people, the reinstitution of the Temple service, that our prayers be received with love and favor, and that God bestow peace, goodness and blessings upon His people.

The *Tur Orach Chayim* explains that these general petitions are inserted in this section because the fact that the entire nation is in constant need of His benevolence is in itself part of God's praise.

The paragraph *Elokai netzor*, which is recited at the end of the *Shemoneh Esreh*,

was composed by the sages of the Talmud (*Berachos* 11a). Among the requests we make in this paragraph, we ask God to improve our *middos* (character traits), and to open our hearts to Torah.

34.   On Shabbos and *Yom Tov* the *Shemoneh Esreh* only contains seven bles-
          sings: the first three and the last three blessings that are recited on
weekdays; and one middle blessing whose subject is the theme of the day,
along with requests pertaining to it. The laws concerning Shabbos and
Yom Tov prayers are discussed in the chapters that deal with Shabbos and
Yom Tov.

Private petitions

35.   One may insert private prayers and petitions in the following places: in
          the blessing of *Shema koleinu* before the words *ki attah shome'a* ("For
You hear"), and at the end of *Elokai netzor*, before the sentence *yiheyu l'ratzon
imrei fi* ("May the words of my mouth be"). One uses his own words here,
praying for whatever he wishes; he is free to pour out his soul before
God, expressing his most intimate feelings.[35]

Personal prayers may be inserted in other blessings, if one has fulfilled certain
halachic stipulations.[36]

One's Conduct When Reciting the Shemoneh Esreh

Kavanah

36.   When reciting the *Shemoneh Esreh*, one must keep in mind that he is
          standing and praying before the King of the universe. One should be
sure to concentrate well on the meaning of the words that he is reciting.

The *Shulchan Aruch* tells us:

> One who prays must concentrate on the meaning of the words that he recites,
> imagining that the *Shechinah* is in front of him. He should free himself of all
> distractions so he is able to concentrate solely on his prayer. He should con-
> sider that if he were speaking with a human king, he would carefully prepare
> his words and make sure that he didn't stumble. How much more so should he
> be prepared before the King of kings Who searches out everyone's thoughts.

> The *chasidim* of the past would seek solitude in which to concentrate intensely
> on their prayers until their intellect overcame and spiritualized their corporeal
> bodies. They achieved a level close to prophecy.

If a profane thought enters one's mind while he is praying, he should keep silent until it passes. He should reflect on matters which humble the heart and which direct him towards God. Before praying he should contemplate the exaltedness of God, and man's insignificance, and should remove from his mind all thoughts of worldly pleasures.[37]

37.   One is obligated to concentrate well on the meaning of the words of the first blessing of the *Shemoneh Esreh* (the blessing of *Avos*). In this blessing one begins listing God's praises, and it is not proper to think about other matters at this time.

If one realizes that he recited the first blessing without proper *kavanah* before mentioning God's name in the blessing *Magen Avraham*, he should return to the words *Elokei Avraham* ("the God of Avraham"), and repeat the blessing from there.

Some halachic authorities maintain that the blessing of *Modim* should be recited with special *kavanah*, similar to that of the first blessing.[38]

38.   While reciting *Shemoneh Esreh*, one should not let his eyes wander. One should pray with his eyes closed, or from within a *Siddur*.[39]

It is prohibited to pray in front of a mirror, because it gives the impression that one is praying and bowing towards his own reflection. Similarly, one should not pray in front of pictures or drawings, since he may gaze at them and then his attention will be diverted from his prayers.[40]

One may not gesture or motion to others while reciting the *Shemoneh Esreh*. The only exception is if a child is crying and disturbing the prayer. In this case one may gesture to the child to stop crying.[41]

39.   When one is reciting *Shemoneh Esreh*, *Pesukei D'zimrah*, or *Shema* and the accompanying blessings, one should not hold anything in his hands other than a *Siddur*. All other objects are likely to divert a person's attention from his prayers.[42]

Answering Amen, *Kaddish*, *Kedushah* and *Barechu* during *Shemoneh Esreh*

40.   One who is in the middle of the *Shemoneh Esreh* may not interrupt his prayer, to answer Amen, *Kaddish*, *Kedushah* or *Barechu*. Rather, he should stop and listen to what the leader is reciting without joining in.[43]

41. In communities which allow saying *Elokai netzor* at the end of the *Shemoneh Esreh* before reciting the verse *yiheyu l'ratzon*, after saying *Hamevoriech es amo Yisroel Bashalom* and in *Elokai netzor*, it is permitted to make the same interruptions as are allowed between the sections of *Kerias Shema* (see the table in Section 29 above). If possible, one should recite the verse *yiheyu l'ratzon imrei fi* ("May it be Your Will that the words of my mouth") before making the interruption.

Since Sephardic Jews always recite the verse *yiheyu l'ratzon imrei fi* before *Elokai netzor*, they may interrupt for *Kaddish*, *Kedushah*, etc., anywhere during the paragraph of *Elokai netzor*. However, according to this custom, one may not interrupt for *Kaddish*, etc., after *Hamevoriech es amo Yisroel Bashalom* before reciting *yiheyu l'ratzon*.

If one finished reciting *Shemoneh Esreh*, but cannot take three steps backwards because someone is reciting *Shemoneh Esreh* behind him, (see Section 52 below), he may answer any Amen, and may even respond *Baruch Hu u'varuch Shemo*.[44]

Verbalizing the prayers

42. The words of the prayers should be verbalized, and not merely thought in one's mind.[45]

There is immeasurable significance to a prayer that is verbalized. Speech is the feature which distinguishes man from all other creatures. Moreover, reciting the words emphasizes the content of the prayer, and facilitates *kavanah*. However, one should maintain his voice at a whisper, so that it remains inaudible to those around him. This is derived from the way Chanah (the mother of the prophet Shmuel) prayed: "Only her lips moved, but her voice was not heard" (*Shmuel I* 1:13).[46]

Facing towards Jerusalem

43. Wherever one is in the world, he should face the Land of Israel when reciting *Shemoneh Esreh*. One who is praying in Israel should face towards Jerusalem, and one who is praying in Jerusalem should face towards the site of the Temple.

When praying, a person should imagine that he is standing in the Temple in Jerusalem, at the site of the *Kodesh Ha-Kodashim* (the Holy of Holies), just as

King Shlomo prayed, "and they shall pray to God by way of the city which You have chosen and the house that I have built for Your Name" (*Melachim I* 8:45).[47]

A place for prayer

44.   As mentioned above (Chapter 4, Section 21), one should have a permanent place to pray, which should be changed as little as possible. It is best to have a place right near the eastern wall.[48]

One should pray in an enclosed place, and not in an open field. If one is traveling, he may pray in an open area, although it is better to pray in a more private place, such as among trees.[49]

Modes of prayer

45.   It is written in the *Shulchan Aruch* that our prayers replace the sacrifices which were offered in the Temple. Consequently, there are a number of customs which we observe while praying which resemble laws that pertained to the sacrifices. Some of them are:

* One should not allow his mind to wander while he is praying. This is similar to sacrifices which were made unfit due to extraneous thoughts.

* The *Shemoneh Esreh* must be recited while standing. This is similar to sacrifices, which were offered while the owner was standing.

* One should have a set place where he prays. It is preferable for this place to be near a wall. This is similar to the sacrifices, which were offered in specific places, where there was nothing between them and the wall.[50]

The three steps before one begins reciting *Shemoneh Esreh*

46.   One takes three steps forward before beginning to recite *Shemoneh Esreh*. This is to show that one is approaching God in reverence. It is customary to take three steps backwards before taking the three steps forward.[51]

Standing during the *Shemoneh Esreh*

47.   The *Shemoneh Esreh* is recited while standing. One should not lean against a table, pillar, etc.[52] According to the *Shulchan Aruch*, one should stand with his feet together so that, "it appears as if his feet were one foot, similar to the angels, about whom it says, 'and their feet are like a straight foot' (i.e. appearing like one foot)."[53]

Bowing during the *Shemoneh Esreh*

48. One bows down four times while reciting the *Shemoneh Esreh*: at the beginning and end of the first blessing (*Avos*), and at the beginning and end of the blessing of *Modim*. Bowing down is an expression of our submission to and reverence for God. One must not bow at the beginning or end of the other blessings in the *Shemoneh Esreh*.[54]

Bowing down is done in the following manner: When one says *Baruch* he bends the knees, while saying *Attah*, he bows his head and body. Before saying *Hashem*, one straightens up slowly, first lifting his head, and then his body.[55]

At the beginning of *Modim*, one bows his head and body, and remains in this position until he reaches the word Hashem. One straightens up slowly before saying the word Hashem. At the end of *Modim*, one bows in the same manner as for the blessing of *Avos*.[56]

Concluding the *Shemoneh Esreh*

49. At the conclusion of the *Shemoneh Esreh*, after reciting the verse *yiheyu l'ratzon imrei fi* at the end of *Elokai netzor*, one bows and takes three steps backwards, thereby taking leave of God's presence. One takes the first step with his left foot to convey his reluctance at parting from God. The steps backward should be the size of the person's foot, and the last step should be taken with the left foot, bringing it alongside the right foot.

Then, while still bowing, one turns to his left side and recites the verse, *Oseh shalom bi-meromav* ("He makes peace in the heavens"); then one turns to his right and continues *Hu ya'aseh shalom aleinu* ("He shall make peace for us"); finally, one bows forward and concludes *v'al kol Yisrael v'imru amen* ("and for all of Israel, and let us say Amen").

The passage *yehi ratzon milfanecha* ("May it be Your will"), in which we pray for the reinstitution of the sacrificial service in the Temple, is then recited. Since prayers are in place of the Temple service, we end our prayers by asking that the Temple be restored, and that we merit to serve God in the Temple.[57]

50. One should remain in the place where the three steps ended until the leader reaches *Kedushah*. However, if the place is confining or uncomfortable, one may return to his place when the leader begins the Repetition of the *Shemoneh Esreh*. When praying privately, one should remain in his place the amount of time he would wait if he were praying with a congregation. The minimum amount of time one should wait is the amount of time it takes to walk four *amos*.[58]

Because these *halachos* involve so many details, it is advisable to learn how to practically fulfill them from an expert in these *halachos*.

The prohibition of sitting near or passing in front of a person reciting the *Shemoneh Esreh*

51. It is prohibited to sit within four *amos*, in any direction, of a person reciting *Shemoneh Esreh*. If one is praying, or involved in a matter pertaining to prayer, he may sit within four *amos* of someone who is reciting *Shemoneh Esreh*. Some halachic authorities also allow a person who is verbally studying Torah (instead of just thinking Torah thoughts) to sit within four *amos* of one who is reciting *Shemoneh Esreh*. Nevertheless it is proper to follow the more stringent opinion unless it causes inconvenience. There is an opinion that one may not sit directly in front of a person reciting *Shemoneh Esreh* for as far as his line of vision extends, even when one is involved in Torah study and prayer. It is proper to follow this opinion.[59]

52. It is prohibited to walk within four *amos* in front of a person reciting *Shemoneh Esreh*, because it may divert his attention.[60]

A person who finished reciting *Shemoneh Esreh* may not take three steps backwards if he will enter within four *amos* of someone who is still reciting *Shemoneh Esreh* behind him. He must wait until the other person finishes reciting *Shemoneh Esreh*.[61]

Additions and changes in the *Shemoneh Esreh*

53. On special days, and during certain periods of the year, a few passages are changed or added in the *Shemoneh Esreh*. These passages are printed in the *Siddur*. They are:

* The words *Mashiv ha-ruach u'morid ha-gashem* ("He blows the wind and sends down rain") are recited in the blessing of *Mechayeh ha-meisim* dur-

ing the winter. This passage is recited from *Musaf* on Shemini Atzeres (the twenty-second of Tishrei) until *Shacharis* on the first day of Pesach (the fifteenth of Nissan). During the summer, the words *Morid ha-tal* ("He sends down dew") are recited instead of *Mashiv ha-ruach u'morid ha-gashem.*[62] *Morid ha-tal* is recited from the first day of Pesach until Shemini Atzeres. Some communities outside of Israel do not recite *Morid ha-tal* during the summer (these communities recite *Mechalkel chayim* immediately after the words *rav l'hoshia* during the summer). For more details, see Chapter 29, Sections 67-68, and Chapter 33, Section 19. Section 56 below has a table that illustrates how to proceed if one erred regarding *Mashiv ha-ruach u'morid ha-gashem* or *Morid ha-tal.*

* *Attah chonantanu.* This paragraph is added in the blessing of *Attah chonen* during *Ma'ariv* following Shabbos and *Yom Tov.*[63] For more details regarding *Attah chonantanu,* see Chapter 19, Section 3.

* *The Petition for Rain.* The blessing of *Bareich aleinu,* differs depending on if it is summer or winter. In the winter *v'sein tal u'matar li-verachah* (give dew and rain for a blessing) is recited, while in the summer we only recite the words *v'sein berachah* (give blessing).

Sephardic Jews have a different version of this blessing for each season. The winter version is, "Bless on our behalf, Hashem, our God, this year and all the varieties of its produce for the best." The summer version is, "Bless us Hashem, our God, in all our endeavors, and bless our year with favorable dew."

The winter version is recited in Israel from *Ma'ariv* on the seventh of Cheshvan until after *Minchah* on *erev Pesach,* the fourteenth of Nissan. The summer version is recited from *Ma'ariv* on the first night of *Chol Ha-mo'ed Pesach,* until after *Minchah* on the sixth of Cheshvan.[64] Additional laws, as well as the *halachos* concerning one who did not recite the proper version, are listed below in Section 57.

Outside of Israel, the winter version is recited from *Ma'ariv* on either the fourth or the fifth of December, whichever is sixty days after the autumnal equinox (*Tekufas Tishrei*). Since this date is based on the solar cycle, it always occurs on one of the same two days in December. (One should check a Jewish calendar every year to find out the correct day.)

Nachem is added in *Minchah* on Tish'ah b'Av in the blessing of *Boneh Yerushalayim.* For more details see Chapter 35, Section 31.

* *Aneinu* is added on fast days in the blessing of *Shema koleinu*. For more details, see Chapter 25, Section 8.

* *Ya'aleh V'yavo* is added on *Rosh Chodesh* and *Chol Ha-mo'ed* in the blessing of *Retzei*, in *Shacharis*, *Minchah* and *Ma'ariv*. See Chapter 23, Section 5 for the *halachos* pertaining to reciting *Ya'aleh V'yavo* on *Rosh Chodesh*, and Chapter 29, Section 54 for the *halachos* pertaining to reciting *Ya'aleh V'yavo* on *Chol Ha-mo'ed*.[65]

* *Al Ha-Nissim* is added on Chanukah and Purim in the blessing of *Modim*. For more details, see Chapter 30, Section 5 and Chapter 31, Section 16.[66]

* There are several changes and additions to the *Shemoneh Esreh* during the Ten Days of Repentance. For detailed list of these additions, see Chapter 26, Sections 5 and 6.[67]

54.   Before one begins his prayers, he should note any changes or additions to that day's prayers. The prayers for special days like *Rosh Chodesh* and the *Yamim Tovim* should be reviewed beforehand, so one is acquainted with what he must say. Otherwise, he should recite the holiday service from within a *Siddur*. *Piyutim* (hymns which are added on *Yom Tov*) and other prayers whose meaning is obscure should be reviewed beforehand, even if they will be recited from a *Siddur* or *Machzor* (holiday prayer book).[68]

55.   The following tables explain how to proceed if one forgets *Mashiv ha-ruach* and *v'sein tal u'matar*.

56. Mistakes with "Mashiv Ha-ruach" and "Morid Ha-tal"[1]

When one realized his error	If one forgot to recite morid ha-gashem during the winter[2]	If one recited morid ha-gashem during the summer[3]
Before mentioning God's name at the end of Mechayeh ha-meisim	Finish the phrase,[4] recite mashiv ha-ruach u'morid ha-gashem and then continue reciting the Shemoneh Esreh where he left off. After reciting v'ne'eman Attah but before mentioning God's Name at the end of Mechayeh ha-meisim, Recite mashiv ha-ruach u'morid ha-gashem and begin reciting v'ne'eman Attah[5]	Return to the beginning of the blessing Attah gibor, and recite the Shemoneh Esreh from there[6]
After mentioning God's Name but before completing the blessing Mechayeh ha-meisim	Say lamedeini chukecha[7] and go back to mashiv ha-ruach u'morid ha-gashem.[8] If one recited morid ha-tal instead of mashiv ha-ruach u'morid ha-gashem,[9] he countinues with Mechayeh ha-meisim and does not recite mashiv ha-ruach	Say lamedeini chukecha[7] and go back to the beginning of the blessing Attah gibor[10]
After completing Mechayeh ha-meisim but before saying Attah kadosh	Recite mashiv ha-ruach u'morid ha-gashem and continue with Attah kadosh.[11] If one recited morid ha-tal instead of mashiv ha-ruach u'morid ha-gashem, he does not recite Mashiv ha-ruach	Repeat the Shemoneh Esreh[6]
After beginning Attah kadosh (even after completing the Shemoneh Esreh)	Repeat the Shemoneh Esreh.[12] If one recited morid ha-tal instead of mashiv ha-ruach u'morid ha-gashem, he does not repeat the Shemoneh Esreh	Repeat the Shemoneh Esreh[6]

1. According to the M.B. (114 [10]), if one forgot to recite the two words mashiv ha-ruach during the winter, or recited them by mistake during the summer, he does not have to repeat anything. If one recited the words morid ha-gashem during the summer he must repeat the blessing, or the entire Shemoneh Esreh. What one has to repeat depends upon where he realizes his error (S.A. 114:4). If one is not sure if he recited the Shemoneh Esreh with the correct change the rule is as follows: Within the first thirty days of implementing the change one assumes he recited the Shemoneh Esreh without the appropriate change. After the first thirty days, one assumes he recited the Shemoneh Esreh with the appropriate change (S.A. 114:8). One who is sure he intended to recite the Shemoneh Esreh with the appropriate change, but some time after praying cannot remember if he actually recited the Shemoneh Esreh correctly does not have to repeat the Shemoneh Esreh. However, if one is in doubt immediately after praying, he must repeat the Shemoneh Esreh (M.B. 114 [38]). 2. S.A. 114:5-6. 3. If one did not recite Morid ha-tal during the summer, he does not repeat anything. (There are communities in the Diaspora that do not recite morid ha-tal at all.) 4. M.B. 114 (29). See also Be'ur Halachah there, starting from the words Ba-makom she-nizkar. 5. M.B. 114:4. 6. S.A. 114:4. 7. This is Tehillim 119:12 Baruch Attah Hashem lamedeini chukecha. By completing the sentence Baruch Attah Hashem with the final words of the verse (lamedeini chukecha) one recites a verse from Tehillim rather than mention God's Name in vain (see M.B. 114 [32]). 8. Ibid. 9. S.A. 114:5. One living in Israel or any other community where morid ha-tal is recited during the summer, may assume he recited morid ha-tal. 10. M.B. 114 (20). 11. In this case it is preferable to recite mashiv ha-ruach u'morid ha-gashem immediately after reciting Mechayeh ha-meisim (i.e. without pausing the time of toch kedei dibbur (M.B.114 [31]). 12. S.A. 114:5. See also note 8, above.

57. Mistakes Regarding V'sein Tal U'matar Li-verachah

Where one realized his error	If one did not recite[1] v'sein tal u'matar li-verachah in the winter[2]	If one recited[1] v'sein tal u'matar li-verachah in the summer[3]
Before mentioning God's Name at the end of the blessing mevarech ha-shanim	Return to the words v'sein tal u'matar li-verachah	Return to the words Bareich aleinu, and recite the Shemoneh Esreh from there[9]
After mentioning God's Name but before reciting the words mevarech ha-shanim	Continue until the words ki Attah shome'a in Shema koleinu. Recite v'sein tal u'matar li-verachah there[4]	Say lamedeini chukecha,[5] and return to the words Bareich aleinu[9]
After reciting the words mevarech ha-shanim but before reaching the words ki Attah shome'a in Shema koleinu	Continue until the words ki Attah shome'a in Shema koleinu. Recite v'sein tal u'matar li-verachah there[4]	Return to the words Bareich aleinu, and recite the Shemoneh Esreh from there[9]
If one remembered after mentioning God's name preceding the words Shome'a tefillah	Say lamedeini chukecha, recite v'sein tal u'matar li-verachah, and continue from ki Attah shome'a[6]	Return to the words Bareich aleinu, and recite the Shemoneh Esreh from there[9]
After finishing Shema koleinu, but before beginning Retzei	Recite v'sein tal u'matar li-verachah, and continue with Retzei[7]	Return to the words Bareich aleinu, and recite the Shemoneh Esreh from there[9]
After begining Retzei	Return to the words Bareich aleinu[8]	Return to the words Bareich aleinu, and recite the Shemoneh Esreh from there[9]
After reciting the words yiheyu l'ratzon imrei fi, at the end of the passage Elokai netzor, even without having taken the three steps backwards[10]	Repeat the entire Shemoneh Esreh	Repeat the entire Shemoneh Esreh

1. If one is not sure if he recited the Shemoneh Esreh with the correct change (i.e. v'sein tal u'matar li-verachah during the winter, or omitting it during the summer), the rule is as follows. Within the first thirty days of implementing the change one assumes he recited the Shemoneh Esreh without the appropriate change After the first thirty days, one assumes he recited the Shemoneh Esreh with the appropriate change (S.A. 114:8). One who is sure he intended to recite the Shemoneh Esreh with the appropriate change, but some time after praying cannot remember if he actually recited the Shemoneh Esreh correctly does not have to repeat the Shemoneh Esreh. However, if one is in doubt immediately after praying, he must repeat the Shemoneh Esreh. (M.B. 114 [38]). 2. S.A. 117:4-5. 3. S.A. 117:3. If one is in an area of the world that needs rain in the summer, see 117:2. 4. See M.B 117 (15). 5 This is Tehillim 119:12 Baruch Attah Hashem lamedeini chukecha. By completing the sentence Baruch Attah Hashem with the final words of the verse (lamedeini chukecha) one recites a verse from Tehillim rather than mention God's Name in vain (see M.B. 422 [5]). 6. M.B. 117 (19). 7. S A. 117:5. 8. Ibid 9. M.B 117 (14). See also the Be'ur Halachah in 114:4 beginning with the word v'im. 10. M.B. 117 (18).

The earliest time to recite *Shacharis*

58. The principal time for reciting *Shemoneh Esreh* begins at sunrise and lasts four *sha'os zemanios* (one-third of the daylight hours).[69]

The best time to recite the *Shemoneh Esreh* is exactly at sunrise. This is derived from the verse, "They shall fear You with the sun" (*Tehillim* 72:5). Prayers recited at this time are called *Tefillas vasikin* (the prayer of the pious).[70]

59. If one must to recite *Shacharis* before sunrise, he should consult a *rav* regarding when to recite *Shemoneh Esreh* (as well as when to put on *tefillin* and recite *Shema*).[71] This situation may arise if one has to travel early in the morning, and will not be able to pray while traveling.

60. The following timetable lists the times of sunrise for the entire year. The times are cited at ten-day intervals. One can estimate the times for the days in between.

The times are listed according to standard time, not Daylight Savings Time.

Timetable of Sunrise

DATE	JERUSALEM	NEW-YORK	LONDON	DATE	JERUSALEM	NEW-YORK	LONDON
Jan. 1	6.39	7.19	8.07	July 10	4.41	4.33	3.54
Jan. 11	6.40	7.19	8.03	July 20	4.47	4.41	4.06
Jan. 21	6.38	7.14	7.54	July 30	4.53	4.50	4.20
Jan. 31	6.33	7.07	7.41	Aug. 9	5.00	4.59	4.35
Feb. 10	6.26	6.56	7.25	Aug. 19	5.06	5.09	4.51
Feb. 20	6.17	6.43	7.06	Aug. 29	5.12	5.19	5.07
Mar. 2	6.06	6.29	6.45	Sep. 8	5.18	5.29	5.23
Mar. 12	5.54	6.13	6.22	Sep. 18	5.25	5.38	5.39
Mar. 22	5.41	5.56	6.00	Sep. 28	5.31	5.48	5.55
Apr. 1	5.28	5.40	5.37	Oct. 8	5.37	5.58	6.12
Apr. 11	5.16	5.24	5.14	Oct. 18	5.44	6.09	6.29
Apr. 21	5.04	5.08	4.53	Oct. 28	5.52	6.20	6.46
May 1	4.54	4.55	4.33	Nov. 7	6.00	6.32	7.04
May 11	4.45	4.43	4.15	Nov. 17	6.09	6.44	7.22
May 21	4.39	4.34	4.00	Nov. 27	6.17	6.55	7.38
May 31	4.35	4.27	3.50	Dec. 7	6.26	7.05	7.51
June 10	4.33	4.24	3.43	Dec. 17	6.33	7.13	8.01
June 20	4.34	4.24	3.42	Dec. 27	6.38	7.18	8.06
June 30	4.37	4.27	3.46				

The latest time to recite *Shemoneh Esreh*

61.   One may recite *Shemoneh Esreh* for *Shacharis* until the end of the fourth *sha'ah zemanis*, i.e. for a third of the daylight hours.[72] Since dawn and sunrise are earlier in the summer, the time when one can recite *Shemoneh Esreh* is earlier in the summer than in the winter.

There are two opinions regarding how to calculate the latest time for reciting *Shemoneh Esreh*. According to the *Magen Avraham*, daytime is from dawn until the stars come out, while according to the Gra daytime is from sunrise until sunset. (For more details, see Section 26 in this chapter.) Both times are usually listed on daily halachic timetables.

The Leader's Repetition of the Shemoneh Esreh

62.   When there is a *minyan*, the leader repeats the *Shemoneh Esreh* aloud after he has finished reciting his own *Shemoneh Esreh*.[73] The leader takes three steps backwards, and waits the amount of time it would take to walk four *amos* before returning to his place. Then he returns to his place and recites the verse, *Hashem sefasai tiftach u'fi yagid tehilasecha* ("God, open my lips and my mouth will speak your praises") and recites the *Shemoneh Esreh* again, this time aloud.[74]

63.   The congregation should pay attention to the Leader's Repetition and should concentrate on the blessings being recited. If there are not at least nine men paying attention to the Repetition of the *Shemoneh Esreh*, the leader's blessings may be considered "blessings made in vain." Therefore, everyone should make an effort to follow the Leader's Repetition.[75]

It is prohibited to talk during the Repetition of the *Shemoneh Esreh*.

64.   During every blessing, when the leader recites *Baruch Attah Hashem*, the congregation responds *Baruch Hu u'varuch Shemo* ("Blessed is He, and blessed is His Name"). Similarly, when the leader finishes reciting each blessing, the congregation responds Amen. The *halachos* regarding *Baruch Hu u'varuch Shemo* and Amen, as well as the *kavanah* one should have when answering Amen, are cited in Chapter 10, Sections 9-11

The leader should pause when the congregation responds *Baruch Hu u'varuch Shemo* so the congregation can hear which blessing he is finishing. The leader must not begin the next blessing until a majority of the congregation finished answering Amen for the previous blessing.[76]

65.   Fathers should teach their children to listen to the Leader's Repetition and answer Amen. As soon as a child can answer Amen, he gains a portion in the world to come.[77]

During the Leader's Repetition, the congregation joins in reciting *Kedushah* and *Modim d'Rabbanan*. In Israel, the *Kohanim* bless the congregation during the Leader's Repetition.

Kedushah

66.   After the leader finishes the blessing of *Mechayeh ha-meisim*, the congregation joins him in reciting *Kedushah*. The text for *Kedushah* is printed in the *Siddur*.[78]

When reciting *Kedushah*, one should reflect on his readiness to sanctify God's Name. One should intend to fulfill the verse from the Torah, "I will be sanctified in the midst of Israel" (*Vayikra* 22:32). When we recite *Kedushah* with the proper *kavanah*, God endows us with His holiness.[79] According to the *Tur*, reciting *Kedushah* properly gives God great joy.

67.   When one recites *Kedushah*, he stands with his feet together, similar to the way one stands when reciting the *Shemoneh Esreh* itself.[80] One's eyes should be raised towards heaven when reciting *Kedushah*. One should sway his body, and raise his heels and body upwards, while reciting *Kadosh Kadosh Kadosh*, *Baruch* and *Yimloch*.[81]

If one already recited *Kedushah* when he hears another congregation reciting it, he should recite it again with the second congregation.

Modim d'Rabbanan

68.   When the leader reaches *Modim*, the congregation bows with him and recites the *Modim d'Rabbanan* which is printed in the *Siddur*. This passage begins with the words, *Modim anachnu lach she-Attah Hu Hashem Elokeinu, Veilokei avoseinu, Elokei kol bassar* ("We are thankful to You, that You Hashem are our God, and God of our fathers, God of all flesh").[82]

While the congregation recites *Modim d'Rabbanan*, the leader continues to recite *Modim* aloud.[83]

Birkas Kohanim
(The Kohanim's blessing)

69.   It is a mitzvah for *Kohanim* to bless their fellow Jews. This mitzvah is derived from the verse, "So shall you bless the children of Israel" (*Bemidbar* 6:23).

The *Sefer Ha-Chinnuch* writes:

> Among the reasons for this mitzvah is that God, in His goodness, wants to bless His people through his servants [the *Kohanim*]. Since they are constantly present in His Temple, and their every thought is cleaving to His service and their souls are bound with fear of Him all day long, their merit will confer blessing upon them [the Jewish people]. Thus, all the deeds of His people will be blessed, and God's grace will be upon them. (Mitzvah 378)

Every *Kohen* in the synagogue must lift his hands and bless the congregation.[84]

Birkas Kohanim is only recited if there is a *minyan* present. The *Kohanim* are counted in the *minyan*.[85]

Men who are not *Kohanim* are forbidden to recite *Birkas Kohanim*.[86]

Prior to **Birkas Kohanim**

70.   A *Kohen* who cannot bless the congregation due to weakness, etc. must leave the synagogue before the leader calls out "*Kohanim!*" The *Kohen* should leave before the leader begins *Retzei*. It is customary for the *Kohen* not to re-enter the synagogue until after *Birkas Kohanim* is completed.[87]

71.   Before the *Kohanim* approach the *Aron Ha-Kodesh* (the Holy Ark), their hands are washed by a *Levi* (Levite). The *Levi* pours water on the *Kohen's* hands, up to the wrist. This commemorates the practice of washing one's hands before performing the sacrificial service in the Temple.[88] Among Sephardic Jews the *Levi* washes his own hands before washing the *Kohen's* hands.

72.   When the leader begins *Retzei*, all the *Kohanim* present begin to approach the *Aron Ha-Kodesh*. A *Kohen* who did not begin to approach the *Aron Ha-Kodesh* before the leader finished reciting *Retzei* is not allowed to participate in *Birkas Kohanim*, and must leave the synagogue while *Birkas Kohanim* is being recited.[89]

73. After the *Kohanim* recite *Modim d'Rabbanan* with the congregation, they recite the following passage: *Yehi ratzon milfanecha Hashem Elokeinu she-tehei berachah zo she-tzivanu l'varech es amcha Yisrael berachah sheleimah v'lo yehei bah micheshol v'avon me-attah v'ad olam* ("May it be Your Will, Hashem our God, that this blessing which You commanded us to bless Your people, Israel, be a perfect blessing, without flaw or sin from now and forever"). The *Kohanim* recite this prayer slowly, ending when the leader completes the blessing *ha-tov shimcha u'lecha na'eh l'hodos*, so that when the congregation responds Amen, they are responding to both blessings. The *Kohanim* also respond Amen to the leader's blessing.[90]

The order of *Birkas Kohanim*

74. The *Kohanim* must concentrate when they bless the congregation. They should not look at the congregation. Their eyes should be downcast, as is generally done while praying, and their heads should be covered with their *talleisim*. The congregation should concentrate on the words of the blessing, and they should face the *Kohanim*, although they should not look at the *Kohanim*'s faces or hands.[91]

75. The *Kohanim* raise their hands to shoulder height, with the right hand a little higher than the left. They stretch out their hands with the palms facing downwards, and spread their fingers so that five intervals are formed by the fingers of both hands (i.e. a space between the two pairs of fingers, a space between the index finger and the thumbs, and one space between the two thumbs).[92]

At first the *Kohanim* stand facing the *Aron Ha-Kodesh*. If there are at least two *Kohanim* present, one of the congregants calls out "*Kohanim!*" after the leader finishes reciting *Modim*. In some congregations, the leader calls out "*Kohanim!*" Some of these congregations have the custom that the leader recites the passage *Elokeinu*, and when he reaches the word "*Kohanim*" in the passage, he calls it out loud.

Then the *Kohanim* begin to recite the blessing *asher kideshanu b'kedushaso shel Aharon*. At this point they turn around towards their right and face the congregation, and continue *v'tzivanu l'varech es ammo Yisrael b'ahavah.* The congregation responds Amen to this blessing. The leader does not respond Amen to this blessing.[93]

The leader recites the words of *Birkas Kohanim* aloud, word by word, and the *Kohanim* repeat each word after him. When the *Kohanim* finish each sentence, the congregation responds Amen.[94]

76. The person who calls out the word "*Kohanim*" must wait until most of the congregation has answered Amen to the blessing of *Modim.* The *Kohanim* may not begin reciting *Birkas Kohanim* until they hear "*Kohanim*" being called out. During *Birkas Kohanim*, neither the *Kohanim* nor the leader may call out the next word until the other one has finished his turn, and, where required, until most of the congregation has replied Amen.[95]

When the *Kohanim* recite the words of the blessing which end with the suffix *cha* ("you"), and the last word *shalom*, they turn to their sides. The reason for this is to include the congregants standing at their sides.[96]

Additional laws

77. Only people standing in front of or on the sides of the *Kohanim* receive the *Kohanim's* blessing (i.e. those standing in back of the *Kohanim* do not receive the blessing). Therefore, congregants who sit at "*mizrach*," the eastern wall of the synagogue, which is usually behind the *Kohanim*, should leave their places and stand where they will be facing the *Kohanim* during *Birkas Kohanim*.[97] Everyone in the congregation should face the *Kohanim*. The people who are directly or indirectly in front of the *Kohanim* should face east, while those on the *Kohanim's* sides should turn to face the *Kohanim*.

78. *Birkas Kohanim* must be recited aloud, in Hebrew, while the *Kohanim* are standing with outstretched hands. All these details are derived from the Torah. A *Kohen* who is unable to observe all of these details may not recite the blessing, and must leave the synagogue before the leader recites *Retzei*.[98]

After *Birkas Kohanim* has been recited

79. After *Birkas Kohanim*, the leader begins reciting the blessing of *Sim shalom.* The *Kohanim* turn around (towards their right) to face the *Aron Ha-Kodesh* and recite the following passage: *Ribon ha-olamim assinu ma she-gazarta aleinu asseh Attah ma she-hivtachetanu hashkifah mi-me'on kode-*

shecha min ha-shamayim u'varech es amecha es Yisrael ("Master of all worlds, we have done what You commanded us; now do what You have promised us: Look down from Your holy dwelling place in Heaven and bless Your people, Israel"). The *Kohanim* recite this prayer slowly, ending when the leader finishes reciting *Sim shalom*, so when the congregation answers Amen, it applies to both prayers. If the *Kohanim* finish before the leader, they add the following: *Adir ba-marom shochen bi-gevurah Attah shalom v'shimecha shalom yehi ratzon she-tasim aleinu shalom* ("The Mighty One in Heaven, Who dwells in strength, You are peace and Your name is peace. May it be Your will to establish peace upon us").[99]

The *Kohanim* may not turn towards the *Aron Ha-Kodesh* before the leader begins reciting *Sim shalom*. Once facing the *Aron Ha-Kodesh* the *Kohanim* lower their hands. The *Kohanim* remain in front until the leader finishes reciting *Sim shalom*, and most of the congregation has answered Amen.[100]

When there are no *Kohanim* present

80.   When there are no *Kohanim* in the synagogue, the leader recites a short prayer (which is printed in the *Siddur*) after *Modim*. This prayer begins *Elokeinu v'Elokei avoseinu*, and includes the text of *Birkas Kohanim*. The congregation answers *Ken yehi ratzon* after each of the three verses, instead of Amen.[101]

Which prayers include *Birkas Kohanim*

81.   *Birkas Kohanim* is recited during *Shacharis* every day, as well as during *Musaf* on Shabbos, *Rosh Chodesh* and *Yom Tov*. See the respective chapters regarding whether *Birkas Kohanim* is recited during *Minchah* on fast days, and during *Ne'ilah* on Yom Kippur.

In some communities outside of Israel, the *Kohanim* only recite *Birkas Kohanim* during *Musaf* on *Yom Tov*. This is because people are infused with joy at this time. In this case, the leader recites *Elokeinu v'Elokei avoseinu* during the daily and Shabbos *Shacharis*, as well as during the Shabbos and *Rosh Chodesh Musaf*, instead of *Birkas Kohanim*.[102]

The laws of *Birkas Kohanim* cited above are abridged. Certain details were not included, such as which *Kohanim* may not recite the blessing, and how to proceed if the leader is a *Kohen*. Every *Kohen* should be proficient in these *halachos*, as they are his special domain.

Tachanun

82.   *Tachanun* is recited after *Shemoneh Esreh* (and when a *minyan* is present, after its repetition by the leader). The prayer is comprised of supplications to God to forgive and redeem us for His sake.

83.   The section beginning *Rachum v'chanun* is recited while one falls down on his face (this is called *nefilas apayim*). Today, this is not done in a literal sense. It is customary to sit, bow one's head to the side, and cover one's face. One covers his face with a cloth, e.g. his sleeve.[103] During *Shacharis* a right-handed man lowers his face to the right side and covers it with his right arm because his *tefillin* are on his left arm. During *Minchah*, or if one does not have *tefillin* on his left arm, he lowers his head to the left side and covers his face with his left arm.[104]

Sephardic Jews do not recite the passage *Rachum v'chanun*. Instead, they sit down and recite the psalm *L'David, eilecha Hashem*, without *nefilas apayim*.

84.   *Nefilas apayim* is done while one is sitting. One may only stand while doing *nefilas apayim* in a situation where he cannot sit down, e.g. when another person is still reciting *Shemoneh Esreh* behind him.[105]

After *nefilas apayim*, one remains seated until after reciting the words *va'anachnu lo neida*. The rest of the prayer, from the words *ma na'aseh*, is recited while standing.[106]

Nefilas apayim is only done in a place where there is a *sefer Torah*. If there is no *sefer Torah*, *tachanun* is recited without *nefilas apayim*. The *Mishnah Berurah* cites various opinions regarding whether or not *nefilas apayim* should be done in places where there is no *sefer Torah*, but there are holy books.[107] The custom observed in Jerusalem is to do *nefilas apayim* in places where there is no *sefer Torah*, but where there are holy books.

85.   One's recitation of *tachanun* will not be as acceptable in heaven if one discusses other matters at length between *Shemoneh Esreh* and *tachanun*. However, one may interrupt for a holy matter, such as answering Amen,

Yehei Shemeh rabbah, etc. Halachically one is even permitted to interrupt for a short conversation with a friend.[108]

Some people recite *Viduy* and the Thirteen Divine Attributes before *tachanun*. *Viduy* is the standard sinner's admission of his guilt. The text (which is printed in the *Siddur*) includes a list of transgressions according to the order of the Hebrew alphabet; i.e. *"Ashamnu, Bagadnu, Gazalnu"* etc.

Reciting *Tachanun* on Monday and Thursday

86. Monday and Thursday are considered days of grace. After the Israelites made the Golden Calf, Moshe ascended Mount Sinai, and returned forty days later, bringing the news that God forgave them. Moshe ascended Mount Sinai on a Thursday, and returned on a Monday. Therefore, more supplications are recited on Mondays and Thursdays. These supplications are recited while standing, and are read slowly with great concentration.[109]

Half-*Kaddish* is recited after *tachanun*. On Monday and Thursday half-*Kaddish* is followed by *Kel erech apayim*. This prayer is omitted on days when *La-menatze'ach* (before *u'Va l'Tzion*) is not recited (for more details, see Section 101, below). On the Monday, Thursday and Monday following the Shabbos after *Rosh Chodesh Cheshvan* and *Rosh Chodesh Iyar*, special *selichos* (penitential prayers) and *Avinu Malkeinu* are recited. These are called *Selichos BaHaB* (*"selichos* for the second, fifth, and second day"). These *selichos* are printed in some *Siddurim*. Sephardic Jews do not recite these *selichos*.

Days when *Tachanun* is omitted

87. *Tachanun* is not recited on Shabbos, *Yom Tov* and *Rosh Chodesh*. *Tachanun* is also omitted on the following days (which are listed according to their order in the year):

* *Erev Rosh Hashana* (although *tachanun* is included in the *selichos* which precede *Shacharis* on *erev Rosh Hashana*).

* From *erev Yom Kippur* (the ninth of Tishrei) until after *Isru Chag* of Succos. Many people do not recite *tachanun* until after *Rosh Chodesh Cheshvan*.

* All eight days of Chanukah.

* Tu bi-Shevat.

* Purim and Shushan Purim (the fourteenth and fifteenth of Adar). During a leap year, *tachanun* is omitted on the fourteenth and fifteenth of both Adars.

* The entire month of Nissan.

* Many people do not recite *tachanun* on Pesach Sheini (the fourteenth of Iyar).

* Lag ba-Omer (the eighteenth of Iyar).

* From *Rosh Chodesh Sivan* until after *Isru Chag* of Shavuos.

* Many people do not recite *tachanun* on the six days following Shavuos.

* Tish'ah b'Av (the ninth of Av).

* The fifteenth of Av.[110]

88.   *Tachanun* is not recited in a mourner's house during the seven days of mourning. *Tachanun* is not recited if a *chasan* (a bridegroom) who is celebrating the seven days of rejoicing after his wedding is present. (If the bride and groom had been married previously, e.g. if they are a widow and widower, *tachanun* is only omitted for the first three days following their wedding.) Similarly, *tachanun* is not recited if a *bris milah* (circumcision) will take place in the synagogue that day, or if the *mohel* (the one performing the circumcision), the *sandek* (the one honored to hold the child during the ceremony) or the father of the child is present.[111] This applies even if the *bris milah* will be held elsewhere. See Chapter 8, Section 3 for further details.

Torah Readings
on Monday and Thursday

The edicts of Moshe and Ezra the Scribe

89.   Moshe decreed that the Torah be read on Monday and Thursday (in addition to the readings on Shabbos and *Yom Tov*), so that the Jewish people should not have three days go by without reading from the Torah. Ezra the Scribe decreed that three people be called to the Torah on these days, and that no less than ten verses be read on each day.

On Monday and Thursday the first part of the weekly Torah portion (*parashas ha-shavua*) which will be read on the upcoming Shabbos is recited.[112] The portion that is read and the breaks in the text where each of the three people is called up to the Torah are printed in some *Siddurim*. The Torah is only read if a *minyan* is present.

Taking out the Torah

90.   The leader and the congregation recite several verses and prayers while the Torah is taken out of the *Aron Ha-Kodesh* (the Holy Ark). These verses and prayers are printed in the *Siddur*.[113] The congregation stands while the *sefer Torah* (Torah scroll) is taken out of the *Aron Ha-Kodesh* and is carried through the synagogue, until it is laid down on the reading table (the *bimah*).

The one who carries the *sefer Torah* should hold it in his right arm.[114] He walks to his right around the *bimah* until he is standing in front of it.[115] It is a mitzvah for the congregants to honor the Torah by accompanying the *sefer Torah* to the *bimah*.

The *aliyos* to the Torah

91.   Three men receive successive *aliyos* (i.e. are called up to recite a blessing on the *sefer Torah*). A *Kohen* receives the first *aliyah*, a *Levi* receives the second *aliyah*, and a *Yisrael* receives the third *aliyah*. The Torah states, "You shall sanctify him" (*Vayikra* 21:8), referring to a *Kohen*. We learn that a *Kohen* is given precedence in all matters of sanctity from this verse. For example, the *Kohen* is the lead speaker, leads *Birkas Ha-mazon*, etc. We learn that a *Levi* is given precedence after a *Kohen* from the verse, "and He gave it [the Torah] to the *Kohanim*, the sons of *Levi*" (*Devarim* 31:9).[116]

There are many details regarding *aliyos* which also apply to the Torah readings on Shabbos and *Yom Tov*. Some of the more common laws are:

* Two brothers or a father and son do not receive two consecutive *aliyos*.

* If there is no *Kohen* in the synagogue, the first *aliyah* is given to a *Levi* or *Yisrael*. In this situation a *Levi* may not receive the second *aliyah*; only a *Yisrael* may.

* If there is a *Kohen* in the synagogue, but no *Levi* is present, the *Kohen* receives both the first and second *aliyos*. A *Yisrael* receives the third and subsequent *aliyos*.

* If there is neither a *Kohen* nor a *Levi* in the synagogue, *Yisraelim* receive all the *aliyos*.

92. The person receiving the *aliyah* should take the shortest path to the *bimah* to show how dear the Torah is to him, and to prevent the congregation from waiting unnecessarily. If the paths to the *bimah* are of equal length, the person approaches from the right.[117] The person receiving the *aliyah* then opens the scroll and looks at the beginning verse of his *aliyah*, over which he recites his blessing. (This is so he knows for which verses he is reciting his blessing.)[118] He then grasps the wooden handles of the Torah (the *atzei chayim*) with both hands.[119] He is forbidden to touch the Torah's parchment with his hand, but may do so with a cloth, garment, etc.[120]

93. The person then closes his eyes[121] and proclaims in a loud voice, so that the entire congregation can hear, *Barechu es Hashem ha-mevorach* ("Bless Hashem, the Blessed One"). The congregation responds, *Baruch Hashem ha-mevorach l'olam va-ed* ("Blessed is Hashem, the Blessed One, for all eternity").[122] He repeats the congregation's response, and then recites the blessing, *asher bachar banu mi-kol ha-amim v'nasan lanu es Toraso* ("Who chose us from all the nations and gave us His Torah").[123]

Kerias ha-Torah (The reading of the Torah)

94. After the congregation answers Amen to the blessing on the Torah, the *ba'al korei* (official reader) reads from the *sefer Torah*. The person who received the *aliyah* reads the Torah quietly, together with the *ba'al korei*, while holding the *atzei chayim*.[124] Both the *ba'al korei* and the person receiving the *aliyah* must stand during the Torah reading, without leaning on anything (e.g. a wall or the table).[125] It is customary that at least three people (the *ba'al korei*, the person receiving the *aliyah*, and one other person) stand at the *bimah* while the Torah is read.[126]

95. The *ba'al korei* must be proficient in the *halachos* concerning the Torah readings. He must also know that day's Torah portion well, along with its proper cantillation (the *te'amim*), so that he reads it properly.

The congregation must listen to the Torah reading. It is prohibited to talk from the time the *sefer Torah* is opened to be read until the reading is finished.[127] It is commendable to stand while the Torah is being read, just as the Israelites stood while receiving the Torah at Mount Sinai. In fact, one should feel as if he is receiving the Torah during the Torah reading. However, one who finds it difficult to stand, may sit down.[128] When *Barechu* and *Baruch Hashem ha-mevorach* are recited before the reading, everyone must stand due to the sanctity of these verses.[129] However, it is customary among Sephardic Jews to sit while the Torah is read and the blessings are recited.

96. It is prohibited to leave the synagogue from the time the *sefer Torah* is opened to be read until the reading is finished. When the Torah is not being read, such as between one *aliyah* and the next, one may leave for an urgent reason. This only applies if one has already heard the Torah reading for that day, or if he is planning to return immediately. At least ten men must remain in the synagogue when someone leaves.[130]

After reading the Torah

97. It is customary for the person who received the *aliyah* to kiss the Torah after it is read.[131] He then rolls the scroll closed and recites the blessing *asher nasan lanu Toras emes v'chayei olam nata b'socheinu* ("Who has given us a Torah of truth and has planted eternal life in our midst") aloud.[132] The *Shulchan Aruch* explains that the words "a Torah of truth" refer to the Written Torah, and the words "planted eternal life in our midst" refer to the Oral Law. Some communities recite a slightly different version of this blessing, *asher nasan lanu Toraso, Toras emes* ("that He gave us His Torah, a Torah of truth").

98. It is customary for the person who received the *aliyah* to remain at the *bimah* until the next person's Torah reading is finished (this custom is not observed in all communities). Then he leaves the *bimah* from the opposite side from which he came, returning to his place by way of a longer route. He returns to his place slowly, so as not to give the impression that the Torah reading was a burden to him.[133]

After the Torah reading for the day is completed, half-*Kaddish* is recited. The only time half-*Kaddish* does not follow the Torah reading is during *Minchah* on Shabbos and on fast days.

Lifting the *sefer Torah*

99. After half-*Kaddish* has been recited, the *sefer Torah* is lifted up high. The one who lifts the Torah opens it three columns wide and then, holding it by its handles, turns it to the right, left, front, and back, so that the entire congregation can see its script. It is a mitzvah for all those present to look at the Torah's script, to bow towards it and recite the passage *V'zos ha-Torah,* "And this is the Torah" (the complete passage is printed in the *Siddur*).[134] It is written in kabbalistic books that one merits a great spiritual light if he discerns the letters of the *sefer Torah* enough to be able to read them while the Torah is raised.[135]

In Sephardic and several other congregations, the *sefer Torah* is raised, and its script shown to the congregation before the Torah is read.[136]

The scroll is raised and rolled closed in such a way that a seam connecting two lengths of parchment is in the middle. This is done so that if — God forbid — the Torah scroll tears, only the seam will be torn and the parchment will remain intact.[137]

If it is necessary to touch the parchment while closing the scroll, it should only be done with a *tallis* or garment. The parchment should not be touched directly.[138]

Returning the Torah to the *Aron Ha-Kodesh*

100. After the *sefer Torah* has been rolled closed the leader recites *Yehi ratzon* (the complete passage is printed in the *Siddur*). This passage is omitted on days when *tachanun* is omitted. Sephardic communities do not recite this passage.

When the *sefer Torah* is brought back to the *Aron Ha-Kodesh*, it is carried on the opposite side from which it was brought to the *bimah*. While the Torah is being brought to the *Aron Ha-Kodesh*, the congregation stands and recites certain verses which are printed in the *Siddur*. The men who raised and closed the *Sefer Torah* accompany it (by walking behind it) to the *Aron Ha-Kodesh*, and wait there until the *sefer Torah* is placed inside.[139] It is a mitzvah for those whom the *sefer Torah* passes to accompany it on its way to the *Aron Ha-Kodesh*. It is even a mitzvah for those outside the synagogue to enter and look on while the Torah is being taken out or put back, because of the principle that, "A king is glorified when a multitude joins to honor him" (*Mishlei* 14:28).

The Final Passages
of the Service

101. The service continues with *Ashrei* (*Tehillim* 145). When reciting the verse, "You open Your hand and satisfy the desire of every living thing," one should reflect on the fact that God watches over and provides for all His creatures. *Ashrei* is followed by *La-menatze'ach* (*Tehillim* 20). *La-menatze'ach* is omitted on Shabbos, *Yom Tov*, *Rosh Chodesh*, *erev Yom Kippur*, Chanukah, Purim (the fourteenth and fifteenth of both Adars), *erev Pesach*, and Tish'ah b'Av. In some communities *La-menatze'ach* is also omitted on *erev Succos*, *erev Shavuos*, and on the days following a *Yom Tov* (*Isru Chag*). Sephardic Jews do not recite *La-menatze'ach* on days when *tachanun* is omitted.

102. *U'Va l'Tzion* is then recited. This section includes the verses *Kadosh, Kadosh, Kadosh Hashem Tzeva'os melo chol ha-aretz kevodo*, and *Baruch kevod Hashem mi-mekomo*, as well as an Aramaic translation of these verses. These verses are known as *Kedushah d'Sidra*. According to the Talmud, *Kedushah d'Sidra* is an especially important prayer. Therefore, one must concentrate intently while reciting it. One should not leave the synagogue before reciting *Kedushah d'Sidra* with the congregation, unless an emergency arises.[140]

Since it is preferable to recite *Kedushah d'Sidra* with the congregation, if one has not yet recited *Ashrei* or *La-menatze'ach*, and the congregation has already begun reciting the verse *v'Attah kadosh* (which immediately precedes *Kedushah d'Sidra*), one should join them, and then recite the verses he skipped. When reciting *Kedushah d'Sidra* with a congregation, the Aramaic translation should be recited quietly.[141]

The end of the service

103. The hymn of the day (*Shir shel Yom*) is then recited. This is the psalm which the *Levi'im* sang in the Temple when the daily sacrifice was offered. There is a special hymn for each day of the week.[142] Some people recite additional psalms before the *Shir shel Yom*. These psalms are printed in the *Siddur*.

Shir shel Yom is followed by *Ein k'Elokeinu* and *Pitum Ha-Ketores*. One should try to read *Pitum Ha-Ketores* carefully from the *Siddur*, so as not to skip any of the ingredients of the incense which are mentioned in it.[143]

Aleinu L'shabe'ach ("It is our duty to praise")

104. *Aleinu L'shabe'ach* is recited at the end of the service. Yehoshua Bin Nun composed this prayer of praise after he entered the Holy Land. In *Aleinu L'shabe'ach* we express superlative praises of God Who chose Israel from among all the peoples, and pray for God's rule to be acknowledged by all the nations. This prayer is considered to be highly valued Above. Therefore, it should be recited with great *kavanah*. One should bow when reciting the words *va-anachnu kor'im u'mishtachavim* ("and we bend and bow").[144]

A number of communities (particularly those who recite *Nussach Ashkenaz*) recite *Aleinu L'shabe'ach* before the *Shir shel Yom*.

Kaddish

105. *Kaddish* is recited at certain set places in the service, for example after *Pesukei D'zimrah*, *u'Va l'Tzion*, and *Aleinu L'shabe'ach*. *Kaddish* is also recited during *Minchah* and *Ma'ariv*.

Kaddish is a prayer in Aramaic, in which we sanctify God's Name, and pray that His Name and dominion be speedily recognized and praised by all mankind.

106. *Kaddish* is only recited with a *minyan* (See Chapter 4, Sections 15-17, regarding the laws pertaining to a *minyan*).[145]

All those present should concentrate when *Kaddish* is recited, and should answer Amen and *Yehei Shemeh rabbah* aloud, where required. Our sages tell us that one who responds to *Kaddish* with full concentration is greatly rewarded.

Talking when *Kaddish* is recited is a grave sin. Therefore, one should be extremely careful not to talk during *Kaddish*. One should hasten to a place where *Kaddish* is being recited so as to hear it, and to be able to join in answering Amen.[146]

There are several kinds of *Kaddish*: half-*Kaddish*, *Kaddish Tiskabel* and *Kaddish d'Rabbanan*. Each one has a different ending. Each one is printed in the *Siddur* in the appropriate place.

107. One should stand from the beginning of *Kaddish* until after *Yehei Shemeh rabbah*, or after the Amen following *d'amiran b'alma*. Eglon, king of

Moab, rose from his throne when Ehud, the judge, told him, "I have a message from God to you" (*Shoftim* 3:20). Thus, we learn from Eglon to stand up when hearing "a holy matter" (*davar she-b'kedushah*) such as *Kaddish*.[147]

There is one halachic opinion that the congregation only has to stand when *Kaddish* is recited if they were standing anyway, such as for the *Kaddish* following *Hallel*. According to this opinion, one does not have to stand for the other *Kaddishim*. Sephardic Jews follow this opinion. However, Sephardic Jews do stand for the *Kaddish* which precedes *Ma'ariv* on Friday night. Sephardic Jews have different customs regarding whether or not to stand during *Kaddish Tiskabel*.

108.   *Kaddish Yasom* (the Mourner's *Kaddish*) is recited by a son (or another man) in memory of a deceased person. The details of the *halachos* concerning *Kaddish Yasom*, such as who recites this *Kaddish* if there are several mourners in the synagogue, are cited in *Be'ur Halachah*, at the beginning of Chapter 132.

It is possible to honor one's parents even after their death, and to accrue immense merits for them in the eternal world, where their souls repose. The Midrash states that a son who recites *Kaddish* for his deceased parent earns great merit on his parent's behalf in the Heavenly Court. The son earns further spiritual merits for his parents by receiving the *maftir aliyah* and by leading the congregation in prayer, especially for *Ma'ariv* after Shabbos.

The *Zohar* at the end of *Parashas Bechukosai* states that a son fulfills the mitzvah of honoring his parents, even after their death, by being an upright individual and by conducting his life according to the Torah. His *mitzvos* and good deeds have the power to elevate his parents' souls in the World Above.

Making Up a Missed Shemoneh Esreh

Who is required to make up a missed Shemoneh Esreh

109.   If one forgot to recite *Shacharis*, *Minchah* or *Ma'ariv*, he should make it up by reciting the *Shemoneh Esreh* from the next service twice. For example, if one did not recite *Ma'ariv*, he recites *Ashrei* following the Leader's

Repetition of the *Shacharis Shemoneh Esreh* and *tachanun*, and then immediately recites another *Shemoneh Esreh* to make up for the *Ma'ariv* that was
missed. The same rule applies for one who did not recite *Shacharis*: when
one makes it up during *Minchah*, he first recites *Ashrei*, and then recites a
second *Shemoneh Esreh*. There are two opinions as to whether *Ashrei* is recited when making up a missed *Minchah* after *Ma'ariv*. According to the opinion that *Ashrei* is not recited, the person should pause for the amount of time
it takes to walk four *amos* and then recite the second *Shemoneh Esreh*.[148]

One who intentionally skipped one of the services may not make up that
service.[148*]

If when reciting *Shemoneh Esreh* one erred in such a way that he is required to
recite it again, but he only realized his mistake after the prescribed time for
that service had passed, the person must make it up by reciting an additional
Shemoneh Esreh during the next service. For example, one who recited *v'sein
tal u'matar* during the *Shemoneh Esreh* for *Shacharis* during the summer, and
only realized his mistake after the time for *Shacharis* had passed, then must
make up the *Shemoneh Esreh* when he recites *Minchah*.

How one makes up a missed *Shemoneh Esreh*

110.   When a person recites two *Shemoneh Esreh*s to make up for one that
           was missed, the first *Shemoneh Esreh* is recited as part of the service
he is currently reciting, and the second *Shemoneh Esreh* is the one he is making up.[149] The *Shemoneh Esreh*s should follow one another, separated only
with *Ashrei* or the short pause, as noted above. However, a person should
listen to the Leader's Repetition of *Shemoneh Esreh* before he begins reciting
the second *Shemoneh Esreh*, since the Repetition is considered part of the first
Shemoneh Esreh. The person should also recite *tachanun* when applicable after
the first *Shemoneh Esreh*.[150]

111.   The second *Shemoneh Esreh* is always the same as the first *Shemoneh
           Esreh*. For example, if one missed *Minchah* on *erev Shabbos*, he recites
the *Shemoneh Esreh* for *Ma'ariv* on Shabbos twice, even though the second
Shemoneh Esreh is in place of a weekday service.[151]

Additional laws

112. A missed *Shemoneh Esreh* may only be made up during the next service.

Shacharis may be made up during *Minchah*, and *Minchah* may be made up during *Ma'ariv*. *Shacharis* is made up during *Minchah* even if *Musaf* was recited in between.[152] If one missed *Musaf* (i.e. he did not recite it during the daytime) he cannot make it up.[153]

If the leader of the congregation has to make up a service, he absolves himself when he recites the Repetition of the *Shemoneh Esreh*. He should have in mind that his Repetition is in place of the missed *Shemoneh Esreh*.[154]

Torah Study after Prayer

113. Torah study is a mitzvah of paramount importance. It is essential for proper mitzvah observance. The Mishnah in *Pe'ah* (Chapter 1) states that Torah study is, "equal to all the other [*mitzvos*]." This mitzvah is discussed in detail in Chapter 38, Sections 8-10.

The Talmud relates (*Shabbos* 31) that when one comes to the next world, he is immediately asked, "Did you set aside time for Torah [study]?" Besides utilizing all his free time for Torah study, one is obligated to set aside time to study Torah, both during the day and at night. One must insure that these fixed times are not missed in order to fulfill other obligations.[155]

114. The Talmud further states that a person who goes straight from the synagogue to the *Beis Midrash* (study hall) to study Torah, will merit to behold the *Shechinah*. This is derived from the verse, "They will go from strength to strength, they will appear before God in Zion" (*Tehillim* 84:8).

Therefore it is good to study Torah immediately after *Shacharis*. An important advantage of a regular study time after *Shacharis* is that it prevents a person from becoming involved in his affairs and missing the Torah study he planned for later in the day.[156]

One who cannot study Torah regularly after praying, should study at least one verse from the Torah or one *halachah* before leaving the synagogue.[157]

Chapter Eight

Minchah
(The afternoon prayer)

The significance of *Minchah*

1.   The *Tur Orach Chayim* (Chapter 232) explains that *Minchah* is considered very precious by God:

> One should be sure to recite this prayer when its time arrives, as Rabbi Chelbo said in the name of Rabbi Huna: One should be scrupulous about reciting *Minchah*, for we find that the prophet Eliyahu was only answered when he recited *Minchah*, as it says, "And it was at the time of the *Minchah* sacrifice, Eliyahu stepped forward and prayed..." (*Melachim I* 18:36).

> *Minchah* is considered more precious than *Shacharis* and *Ma'ariv*. *Shacharis* is recited in the morning, as soon as one arises from his sleep, and before he becomes occupied with his work. Similarly, *Ma'ariv* is recited after one comes home from his work and his time is free from his occupations. *Minchah*, however, is recited in the middle of the day, when one is still busy with his affairs. A person must keep it uppermost in his mind, and stop whatever he is doing in order to recite *Minchah*. One who recites *Minchah* is greatly rewarded.

2.   A person should perform *netilas yadayim* before reciting *Minchah*, even if his hands are clean. No blessing is recited for this *netilas yadayim*.[1] If water is not available, one should rub his hands on anything that cleans, like a garment, cloth, etc. If one's hands are not clean, e.g. if he has touched a part of his body that is normally covered, he should perform *netilas yadayim* even if it means going to another place because there is no water where he is.[2]

The different parts of *Minchah*

3.   The *halachos* pertaining to *Shemoneh Esreh* are explained in detail in Chapter 7. Therefore, the *halachos* of *Minchah* listed below only provide a general outline. The text for *Minchah* is printed in the *Siddur*.

The parts of *Minchah* (which are recited in the following order) are:

* Some people observe the custom to recite the passages which discuss the *tamid*-sacrifice and the incense offering (*Pitum Ha-Ketores*) before reciting *Minchah*. These passages are printed in some *Siddurim*.

The *tamid*-sacrifice and the incense offering were offered twice daily in the Temple, once in the morning and once in the afternoon. Therefore, the passages which discuss these offerings are recited twice daily.[3] If it is late, and one is afraid that he might miss the prescribed time for reciting *Minchah*, he should skip these passages.[4]

* *Ashrei* (*Tehillim* 145).

When reciting the verse *pose'ach es yadecha* ("You open Your hand and satisfy the desires of every living thing"), one should concentrate on the fact that God watches over and provides for all of His creations.[5] When a congregation is reciting *Minchah*, *Ashrei* should not be started before there is a *minyan* present, so that the *Kaddish* following it may be recited.[6]

* The *Shemoneh Esreh*.

* The Repetition of the *Shemoneh Esreh* (when a *minyan* is present).

Birkas Kohanim is not recited during *Minchah*, unless it is a fast-day, in which case special *halachos* apply. For more details, see Chapter 25, Section 8.

* *Tachanun*.

The *halachos* pertaining to *tachanun* and *nefilas apayim* are discussed in Chapter 7, Sections 82-88. During *Minchah*, *nefilas apayim* is done with the left arm. As mentioned above, Sephardic Jews recite *tachanun* sitting down, without doing *nefilas apayim*.[7]

Nefilas apayim is not done at night. Therefore, if *Minchah* lasts until nightfall, *tachanun* is recited without *nefilas apayim*. (It is customary to do *nefilas apayim* until *tzeis ha-kochavim*.)[8]

On days when *tachanun* is omitted during *Shacharis* it is also omitted during *Minchah*. For a complete list of these days see Chapter 7, Section 87.[9] *Tachanun* is omitted during *Minchah* on the day preceding a day when *tachanun* is omitted during *Shacharis*. Exceptions to this rule are the twenty-eighth of Elul (the day before *erev Rosh Hashana*), the eighth of Tishrei (the day before *erev Yom Kippur*) and the thirteenth of Iyar (the day before erev Pesach Sheini). Tachanun is recited during Minchah preceding these days in spite of the fact that tachanun is omitted on these days.

Those present at a bris milah (circumcision) do not recite tachanun if they recite Minchah in the house where the child is, and it is before or during the festive meal made in honor of the occasion. If the meal is over and they have already recited Birkas Ha-mazon, they recite tachanun during Minchah. The father of the child, the sandek (the one who holds the child during the circumcision) and the mohel (the one who performs the circumcision) do not recite tachanun at all on the day of the child's bris.[10] It is customary among Sephardic Jews for the entire congregation to omit tachanun if the father of the child, the sandek or the mohel are present.

When a minyan is present, Kaddish Tiskabel is recited after tachanun. On days when tachanun is not recited, Kaddish Tiskabel is recited after the Repetition of the Shemoneh Esreh. Sephardic Jews recite La-menatze'ach bi-neginos (Tehillim 67) after Kaddish Tiskabel.

> * Aleinu L'shabe'ach concludes Minchah.

The prescribed time for reciting Minchah

4. Minchah corresponds to the tamid-sacrifice which was offered in the Temple during the afternoon. The prescribed time for offering this sacrifice began half an hour after midday (six-and-a-half sha'os zemanios after daybreak). However, except for erev Pesach, the sacrifice was offered after nine-and-a-half sha'os zemanios had passed. This was to enable other sacrifices to be offered before it. Consequently, the main time for reciting Minchah begins nine-and-a-half sha'os zemanios after the beginning of the day (i.e. two-and-a-half sha'os zemanios before nightfall). This period of time is called Minchah Ketanah.

The period of time from six-and-a-half sha'os zemanios until nine-and-a-half sha'os zemanios is called Minchah Gedolah. Some halachic authorities are lenient and maintain that one may recite Minchah during this period of time. All halachic authorities maintain that a person should recite Minchah Gedolah with a minyan if he is about to set out on a journey, or if for some reason he will not be able to find a minyan for Minchah Ketanah.[11] The times for Minchah Gedolah and Minchah Ketanah are listed on daily halachic calendars.

5. There are two opinions regarding the latest time *Minchah* may be re-
       cited. According to Rabbi Yehuda, the latest time to recite *Minchah*
is *Pelag Ha-Minchah*, which is one-and-a-quarter *sha'os zemanios* before sunset. According to the other *Tanna'im*, one may recite *Minchah* until sunset.
The earliest time to recite *Ma'ariv* is when the time for *Minchah* has
passed. According to Rabbi Yehuda, the earliest time one may recite
Ma'ariv is *Pelag Ha-Minchah*. According to the other *Tanna'im*, the earliest
time to recite *Ma'ariv* is at nightfall. One should note that even according
to Rabbi Yehuda, *Kerias Shema* for *Ma'ariv* must be recited after *tzeis ha-
kochavim*, i.e. when three small stars can be seen in the sky. One may follow
either of the two opinions, provided that he follows that opinion consistently.
In pressing circumstances one may follow the other opinion, provided he
does not recite *Minchah* after *Pelag Ha-Minchah* and *Ma'ariv* before nightfall
on the same day. The reason for this is that one may not recite both services
during the same time period.[12]

One who follows the opinion of the *Tanna'im*, and recites *Minchah* until sunset, should finish the entire service before sunset. If he cannot find a *minyan*
that finishes *Minchah* before sunset, he should recite *Minchah* by himself at
the proper time.

(One should consult a *rav* regarding how to proceed if he must recite
Minchah after sunset.)

6. The table on p. 88 indicates the time of sunset for the entire year, in
       ten-day intervals. The time for a date in between can be approximated
from the times before and after it. The times listed in this table are according
to standard time, and not Daylight Savings Time.

One may not sit down to a meal before *Minchah*

7. One may not sit down to eat a meal before he has recited *Minchah*, in
       accordance with the following rules:

One may not eat a meal (even a small meal), if it is almost the time of *Minchah Ketanah* (i.e. half a *sha'ah zemanis* before the beginning of the time period
of *Minchah Ketanah*). This is so one will not miss reciting *Minchah* at the
proper time, due to the meal becoming drawn out. However, one may
snack on up to a *k'beitzah* of bread (see the Table of Measures at the end
of Chapter 15 for the exact measure of a *k'beitzah*). One may also have as

much fruit and non-alcoholic beverages as he wants, even during the time of *Minchah Ketanah*.

A festive meal such as is served on the occasion of a *bris milah, pidyon ha-ben,* or a wedding may not be started at midday (i.e. six *sha'os zemanios* after the beginning of the day). The participants must wait until the time of *Minchah Gedolah* and recite *Minchah* before sitting down for the meal.[13]

One may not go to a barber or a bathhouse when the time of *Minchah Ketanah* is approaching. One should wait until after he has recited *Minchah*.

Timetable of Sunset

DATE		JERUSALEM	NEW-YORK	LONDON	DATE		JERUSALEM	NEW-YORK	LONDON
Jan.	1	16.46	16.38	16.01	July	10	18.47	19.28	20.17
Jan.	11	16.54	16.48	16.14	July	20	18.44	19.22	20.07
Jan.	21	17.03	16.59	16.30	July	30	18.37	19.13	19.53
Jan.	31	17.02	17.11	16.47	Aug.	9	18.29	19.02	19.36
Feb.	10	17.21	17.24	17.05	Aug.	19	18.19	18.48	19.16
Feb.	20	17.30	17.36	17.24	Aug.	29	18.07	18.33	18.55
Mar.	2	17.37	17.47	17.42	Sep.	8	17.55	18.17	18.32
Mar.	12	17.45	17.58	17.59	Sep.	18	17.42	18.00	18.09
Mar.	22	17.52	18.09	18.16	Sep.	28	17.29	17.43	17.46
Apr.	1	17.58	18.20	18.33	Oct.	8	17.16	17.27	17.23
Apr.	11	18.05	18.30	18.50	Oct.	18	17.04	17.11	17.02
Apr.	21	18.12	18.40	19.07	Oct.	28	16.54	16.57	16.41
May	1	18.19	18.51	19.23	Nov.	7	16.45	16.46	16.23
May	11	18.26	19.01	19.39	Nov.	17	16.39	16.36	16.09
May	21	18.33	19.11	19.54	Nov.	27	16.36	16.30	15.58
May	31	18.39	19.19	20.07	Dec.	7	16.35	16.28	15.52
June	10	18.44	19.26	20.16	Dec.	17	16.38	16.29	15.51
June	20	18.47	19.29	20.22	Dec.	27	16.43	16.35	15.56
June	30	18.49	19.30	20.22					

Chapter Nine

Ma'ariv
(The evening prayer)

1. *Ma'ariv* is recited in the evening. Since many of the laws and explanations pertaining to *Ma'ariv* were explained in detail in Chapter 7, the laws of *Ma'ariv* below are listed in brief.

If water is available, one should perform *netilas yadayim* before praying, even if his hands are clean. No blessing is recited for this *netilas yadayim*.

If one washed his hands for *Minchah* and was careful that they did not become unclean (i.e. he made sure not to touch any part of his body that is normally covered, etc.), he does not have to wash his hands again before reciting *Ma'ariv*. For further details, see Chapter 8, Section 2.[1]

The different parts of *Ma'ariv*

2. **The opening verses:** On weekdays, *Ma'ariv* begins with the passage *v'Hu Rachum y'chaper avon* ("And He is merciful, forgiving of sins").[2]

The *Midrash Tanchuma* relates that as long as the Temple stood in Jerusalem, no one passed the night in the city with a sin on his record. The morning *tamid*-sacrifice atoned for sins committed the previous night, and the afternoon *tamid*-sacrifice atoned for sins committed during the day. Therefore, our sages ordained that we pray that our sins be forgiven as part of *Ma'ariv*.

Some congregations recite *Shir ha-ma'alos hineh barechu* (*Tehillim* 134) during *Ma'ariv*. This psalm is printed in some *Siddurim*.

Barechu: On weekdays, Shabbos and *Yom Tov*, when *Ma'ariv* is recited with a *minyan*, the leader proclaims *Barechu es Hashem ha-mevorach*, and the congregation responds *Baruch Hashem ha-mevorach l'olam va-ed*.

3. After *Barechu* is recited, one may not talk until he has finished reciting *Shemoneh Esreh*.[3] For details regarding when one may interrupt his

89

prayers to respond Amen, *Yehei Shemeh rabbah* and *Barechu*, refer to the table in Chapter 7, Section 29. The *halachos* regarding when one may interrupt between sections and in the middle of sections of the *Shema* and its blessings are the same for *Ma'ariv* as they are for *Shacharis*.[4]

4.   *Kerias Shema* and its blessings: Two blessings are recited before *Kerias Shema* for *Ma'ariv*. The first blessing ends with the words *ha-ma'ariv aravim* ("Who brings on evening") and the second blessing ends with the words *ohev ammo Yisrael* ("Who loves His people Israel").

5.   One fulfills a mitzvah from the Torah when he recites the *Shema* during *Ma'ariv*. This is derived from the verse "and you shall speak [these words]... when you lie down and when you arise" (*Devarim* 6:7).

All three passages of *Shema* are recited during *Ma'ariv*: *Shema Yisrael* (*Devarim* 6:4-9), *V'hayah im shamo'a* (*Devarim* 11:13-21) and *Parashas tzitzis* (*Bemiubar* 15:37-41). *Kerias Shema* should be recited very carefully. Every syllable and sound must be pronounced correctly. One should concentrate particularly well when reciting the first sentence. If a person does not recite the first sentence with the proper *kavanah*, he has not fulfilled his obligation to recite *Shema*. For more details concerning the laws of *Kerias Shema*, as well as an explanation of the verse *Shema Yisrael*, see Chapter 7, Sections 18-19.

One may recite *Shema* for *Ma'ariv* while standing or sitting, but if one was standing, he may not sit down to recite *Shema*.[5]

6.   Two blessings follow *Kerias Shema*: The first blessing ends with the words *Ga'al Yisrael* ("Who redeemed Israel"), and the second blessing ends with the words *shomer ammo Yisrael la'ad* ("Who guards His people Israel forever").

Some communities outside of Israel add a section after the second blessing which is comprised of various verses (*Baruch Hashem l'olam amen v'amen,* etc.) and the blessing *Yir'u eneinu*. This section is printed in some *Siddurim*.[6]

When reciting *Ma'ariv* with a *minyan*, half-*Kaddish* is recited before the *Shemoneh Esreh*.

7.   The *Shemoneh Esreh*: This prayer is discussed at length in Chapter 7. There is no Leader's Repetition of the *Shemoneh Esreh* during *Ma'ariv*. Similarly, *tachanun* is not recited.

8.   *Aleinu L'shabe'ach*: This prayer concludes *Ma'ariv*. Some communities recite *Shir la-ma'alos* (*Tehillim* 121) before *Aleinu*.

The time to recite *Kerias Shema* for *Ma'ariv*

9.   The best time to recite *Shema* for *Ma'ariv* is at *tzeis ha-kochavim*, when three small stars can be seen in the sky after sunset. (Large stars can be seen before *tzeis ha-kochavim*.)[7]

10.   *Shema* may be recited until *chatzos*, which is the midpoint between sunset and sunrise. One who erred and recited *Ma'ariv* after *chatzos*, but before dawn, has nonetheless fulfilled the mitzvah.[8] The times when *tzeis ha-kochavim*, *chatzos*, and dawn occur throughout the year are printed in halachic timetables.

11.   One may not sit down to a meal or take a nap from half an hour before *tzeis ha-kochavim* until after he has recited *Shema*. This is because the meal or nap may take longer than planned, causing the person to miss reciting *Shema* within the prescribed time. However, a person may snack on fruit or less than a *k'beitzah* of bread (see the Table of Measures at the end of Chapter 15 for the exact measure of a *k'beitzah*).

If one arranged for someone to remind him to recite *Ma'ariv*, he may eat a complete meal. However, one may not nap before reciting *Ma'ariv*, even if he only intends to sleep for a short while.[9]

See Chapter 8, Section 5 regarding when *Shemoneh Esreh* for *Ma'ariv* may be recited.

12.   It is a mitzvah to set a time to study Torah at night. One who does this is widely praised by our sages. The Talmud states, "Whoever studies Torah at night is looked upon graciously by God during the day, as it says, 'God will command His kindness in the day, and in the night His song is with me' (*Tehillim* 42:9)." Therefore, a person should make every effort to study Torah at night. One should be especially careful not to miss the fixed times he has set aside for Torah study. A person who missed his regular study time in the morning or who fell behind in his daily study, should make up the missed time at night.[10]

Kerias Shema al Ha-Mittah

13. Before going to sleep, one recites the blessing *Ha-mapil chevlei sheinah* ("Who makes the bonds of sleep fall"), and at least the first paragraph of *Shema*.[11] It is best to recite all three paragraphs of *Kerias Shema*, because they contain 248 words, which correspond to the 248 limbs of a person's body.[12] Various petitions and passages are also recited, in which we beseech God to guard us while we sleep. The complete text is printed in *Siddurim*.

14. *Shema* and *Ha-mapil* are recited right before one goes to sleep. This is because one should not talk or do anything else after reciting these prayers. If one has only recited *Shema*, he may speak if necessary, and he may drink if he is thirsty. In this case one should repeat the first passage of *Shema*. However, once one has recited *Ha-mapil* he must go to sleep immediately.[13]

If one is afraid that he will fall asleep while reciting *Shema*, he should recite *Ha-mapil* first. Otherwise, *Shema* is recited first so that *Ha-mapil* is recited right before falling asleep.[14]

It is best to recite *Kerias Shema al ha-mittah* while sitting or standing (before lying down).[15]

It is prohibited for a man to sleep on his back or his stomach. Therefore, men should accustom themselves to sleep on their side.[16]

15. Our holy books advise a person to think about the things he did during the day, before going to sleep. If a person realizes that he committed a sin, he should confess it, and resolve not to repeat it. Sins that are commonly transgressed, such as *lashon ha-ra* (derogatory talk) and *bittul Torah* (neglect of Torah study) should be scrutinized.

It is also proper for a person to forgive anyone who wronged or insulted him during the day. (There is a declaration to this effect may be found in the *Siddur* before *Kerias Shema al ha-mittah*.) The Talmud states that one who forgives those who wronged him is rewarded with long life.[17]

* * *

Review of Part One

Part One of this book discusses the *halachos* pertaining to prayer. One should continually try to deepen his understanding of the meanings of the prayers he recites, since prayer is called the "service of the heart."

One who prays from the depths of his heart, concentrating his thoughts and feelings upon the profound contents of the prayers, will actually feel that he is standing before God. *Tehillim* 84:6 states, "Praiseworthy is the man for whom You are his strength, in whose heart tracks are lain." Over the years, prayer lays tracks in a person's heart that bring him closer to God.

Each service is different. Almost every service is recited in a different frame of mind. Sometimes we recite our prayers inspired by the exaltedness of man and the Creation, other times we approach God overwhelmed by our insignificance before God's unapproachable greatness. A moving prayer can arouse thoughts of repentance. It can imbue a person with yearnings to bring the divine into his own life.

The many prayers and intimate feelings that a person has expressed before God throughout the years eventually crystallize and penetrate his heart. He begins to sense that he is in the presence of the Omnipotent Creator, Whose *Shechinah* is eternally watching over him. At this point one has reached the exalted perception implicit in the verse "I have set the Lord before me always" (*Tehillim* 16:5).

Part Two: Blessings

—⟨⟩—

The chapters in this section deal with the laws pertaining to the blessings recited before eating, upon enjoying certain things, before performing *mitzvos*, or upon special occasions.

The purpose of these blessings is to praise God for creating these various pleasures, and for commanding us to perform His *mitzvos*.

Expressing gratitude to our Creator

A blessing is one of the ways we verbalize our recognition that the whole world, and all that is ours in it, are gifts from heaven. It is our way of saying thank you. Furthermore, one who recites a blessing with the proper *kavanah* (concentration) deepens his awareness of God's kindness and goodness, which He showers upon all His creations.

"Who in His goodness continually renews Creation each day" (*Siddur*). A juicy peach, the scent of freshly mown grass, the pale expectant aura of the approaching morning, the *shofar* blast piercing the tense atmosphere of Rosh Hashana, the birth of a child — all these are gifts from God. It is incumbent upon us to acknowledge His goodness and kindness towards us.

Blessings help one acknowledge the wonders of Creation, elevating him from a life of daily routine to a life of depth and meaning. When we praise God "that all things came into being by His word" (*she-ha-kol niheyah bi-devaro*), as well as when we recite any other blessing, we are acknowledging that whatever our eyes behold and whatever pleasures we enjoy are gifts from God.

Chapter Ten

General Halachos
Pertaining to Blessings

The types of blessings

1.   The various blessings can be divided into three categories:

* *Birchos Ha-nehenin* — "Blessings recited before enjoying an object." These blessings are recited before partaking of food and drink, and before smelling a fragrance.

* *Birchos Ha-mitzvos* — "Blessings recited before performing *mitzvos*." These blessings are recited before performing certain *mitzvos*, such as taking the *lulav* on Succos, putting on *tefillin*, lighting Shabbos candles, etc.

* *Birchos Ha-shevach* — "Blessings of Praise." When we recite these blessings we thank God for His kindness to us and we praise Him for His greatness. This category includes the following blessings: *She-hecheyanu* (recited, among other times, before eating a new fruit), *she-kocho u'gevuraso malei olam* (recited when hearing thunder), *Birkas Ha-gomel* (recited after escaping from danger). The more common of these blessings are cited in Chapter 15.

2.   Every blessing begins by mentioning God's Name (*Baruch Attah Ha-shem Elokeinu*, "Blessed are You, God our Lord"), and His sovereignty over the universe (*Melech ha-olam*, "King of the universe"). Our sages state that, "A blessing which does not include God's Name and His sovereignty is not considered a blessing."

The specific reason for reciting the blessing is mentioned in the second half of the blessing. For example, *asher kideshanu b'mitzvosav v'tzivanu al netilas yadayim* ("Who has sanctified us by His commandments and commanded us regarding washing the hands") or *ha-motzi lechem min ha-aretz* ("Who has caused bread to come forth from the earth").

97

(When transliterating blessings and prayers, the words *Hashem Elokeinu* and *Elokai* are used instead of God's actual Name. This is due to the great holiness of God's Name. However, when a person recites a blessing, he must pronounce God's Holy Names in the correct manner.)

In the following chapters the laws and the wording of various blessings are discussed. One must be familiar with them so that he is able to recite each blessing when necessary.

Reciting a blessing with *kavanah*

3.   One should pay attention to the meaning of the words when reciting a blessing. This applies to all blessings. Rabbi Yehudah He-Chasid (who lived at the time of the *Rishonim*) writes:

> When one recites a blessing after washing his hands, before eating a fruit or performing a mitzvah — [blessings which are recited] routinely by every person — he must intend to praise God Who dealt kindly with him by allowing him to enjoy the fruit or the bread, and by giving him the opportunity to perform the mitzvah. He must not thoughtlessly go through the motions of pronouncing words. For such behavior, God's anger burns and, through Yeshayahu the prophet, He rebuked the Jews: "The people draw near, honoring Me with their mouth and lips, but their heart is distant from Me. Their fear of Me is merely an action performed by rote" (*Yeshayahu* 29:13). (*Sefer Chasidim*)

4.   When one begins to recite a blessing, and particularly when he is reciting God's Name, he should be aware of which blessing he is about to recite. He should not be doing anything else while reciting the blessing, lest it appear that the blessing is unimportant and perfunctory to him.[1]

It is best to recite a blessing out loud, since this fosters concentration.[2]

One should not have anything in his mouth when reciting a blessing. This is derived from the verse, "Let my mouth be filled with Your praise" (*Tehillim* 71:8). This means that God's blessing alone should fill one's mouth.[3]

The prohibition of mentioning God's Name or reciting a blessing needlessly

5.   It is prohibited to mention God's Name needlessly.[4] The Torah states, "You shall fear Hashem your God and serve Him, and swear in His

Name" (*Devarim* 6:13). The mitzvah of fearing God includes the prohibition of needlessly mentioning His Name in any language.

6. It is also prohibited to recite a *berachah l'vatalah*, a blessing which one is not required to recite. Similarly, one may not recite a *berachah she-einah tzerichah*, a blessing which could have easily been avoided.[5]

An example of a *berachah l'vatalah* is a blessing recited before eating a food during a meal which includes bread. The blessing is unnecessary, since the blessing of *ha-motzi* recited at the beginning of the meal generally exempts one from reciting additional blessings during the meal. (See Chapter 11, Section 12 for details.) An example of a *berachah she-einah tzerichah* is when one recites a blessing before eating a food, and then immediately recites *ha-motzi*, and eats a meal that includes this food. Instead, a person should wait and eat the food during the meal so as to avoid having to recite the extra blessing.[6]

One who recited a *berachah l'vatalah* should immediately recite *Baruch Shem kevod malchuso l'olam va-ed*, "Blessed be the Name of His glorious kingdom forever."[7]

7. There is a verse in *Tehillim* (119:12), *Baruch Attah Hashem lamedeini chukecha*, "Blessed are You, Hashem, teach me Your statutes." If a person recited the first three words of a blessing (*Baruch Attah Hashem*), and then remembers that he does not have to recite a blessing, he should immediately finish with the words of this verse (*lamedeini chukecha*). In this way, he will not recite God's Name needlessly, but will recite a verse instead.

Studying the *halachos* pertaining to reciting blessings (i.e. when to recite a blessing, and when not; which blessing is suitable for which situation, etc.) will greatly assist a person in avoiding the transgression of needlessly mentioning God's Name.

When there is a doubt if one recited a blessing

8. When one is in doubt as to whether or not he recited a blessing, he does not recite it again.[8] The only exceptions to this rule are: 1) *Birkas Ha-mazon* (Grace After Meals), 2) *Birchos Ha-Torah* (the blessings on the Torah), 3) the blessing *Me'ein Shalosh* (the blessing recited after eating any of the seven species for which the Land of Israel is praised in the Torah). If one is unsure whether he recited *Birkas Ha-mazon* after eating a slice of bread when he had a filling meal, he must recite it again.[9] If one is unsure whether he recited *Birkas Ha-Torah* in the morning, or the blessing *Me'ein Shalosh* (after being sated), he should ask a halachic authority how to proceed.[10]

Baruch Hu U'varuch Shemo and Amen

9.   When one hears God's Name being recited at the beginning of a blessing, one responds with *Baruch Hu u'varuch Shemo* ("Blessed is He and blessed is His Name").[11] At the end of the blessing, one should immediately respond Amen.[12]

One does not answer Amen to his own blessing.[13]

When responding Amen, one should know which blessing he is responding to. He should clearly articulate the word Amen, being careful not to swallow the "A" or the "n".[14] One who is not careful with these rules is likely to end up responding with an *Amen chatufah* (a "snatched" Amen). *Amen chatufah* is when the "A" is pronounced like a short "e" or when the person began to answer Amen before the other person finished reciting the blessing. One should also be careful not to answer an *Amen yesomah* (an "orphaned" Amen). *Amen yesomah* is when the person does not respond Amen immediately after the end of the blessing, or when the person does not know which blessing he is responding to.

The meaning of Amen

10.   Amen means "Truth". The person who responds Amen is verifying the words of the blessing he just heard. For example, responding Amen to the blessing *she-ha-kol niheyah bi-devaro* (all things came into being through God's word) is stating that, "It is true that 'by God's word all things came into being'."[15]

When one answers Amen after a blessing which is a supplication, e.g. the middle blessings of the *Shemoneh Esreh*, it has a further connotation of praying that the request will be fulfilled in the future. For example, "It is true, and may it be His will, that these things will occur."

Amen responded during *Kaddish* only refers to the future: "May it be His will that these things occur, and that His Name be glorified and exalted soon."

Answering Amen in the middle of one's prayers

11. There are many prayers which may not be interrupted by speaking, e.g. during *Shacharis*, one may not interrupt from *Baruch She-Amar* until after the *Shemoneh Esreh*. During these prayers, one is not allowed to recite *Baruch Hu u'varuch Shemo* when hearing another person recite a blessing.[16]

Regarding answering Amen while praying, there are places where one may answer Amen, and places where one may not. The table in Chapter Seven, Section 29 indicates when one may interrupt to answer Amen during the various prayers. One may not interrupt the *Shemoneh Esreh* until one reaches the last paragraph of *Elokai netzor*.

When one hears another person recite a blessing, with the intent of being exempted from that blessing (for example, *Kiddush* or *Havdalah*), he must not interrupt the blessing to respond *Baruch Hu u'varuch Shemo*, or to respond Amen to someone else's blessing.

When one recites a blessing he may not interrupt his blessing to respond Amen or *Baruch Hu u'varuch Shemo*.[17] If one only recited the words *Baruch Attah* but did not mention Hashem (God's name), one may answer Amen to another's blessing. He then recites his blessing from the beginning.[18]

The blessings recited during the course of a meal are discussed in the following chapters (e.g. *al netilas yadayim*, *ha-motzi*, and *Birkas Ha-mazon*). This is followed by a discussion of the *Birchos Ha-nehenin* (the blessings recited before enjoying something), and the blessings recited after eating various foods. The most common Blessings of Praise are discussed in Chapter 15.

Chapter Eleven

Netilas Yadayim and Ha-Motzi

1.   One must perform *netilas yadayim* before eating bread.[1] Challahs, rolls,
      pitas, bagels and matzah are halachically considered bread. Therefore,
one must perform *netilas yadayim* before eating them.

Sephardic Jews recite the blessing *borei minei mezonos* instead of *ha-motzi* before eating sweet breads, and they recite the blessing *Me'ein Shalosh* as the
berachah acharonah (the blessing after eating). However, if they eat a meal
with sweet bread, the *halachah* is different. For more details regarding this
case, see Chapter 13, Section 11.

Sephardic Jews also recite *borei minei mezonos* before eating matzah (unless it is
eaten with a meal). On Pesach, however, Sephardim perform *netilas yadayim*
and recite *ha-motzi* before eating matzah.

Eating a small amount of bread

2.   When one eats more than a *k'zayis*, but less than a *k'beitzah* of bread (see
      the Table of Measures at the end of Chapter 15), one should perform
netilas yadayim without reciting the blessing *al netilas yadayim*. Even when
eating less than a *k'zayis* of bread, it is proper to perform *netilas yadayim* as
well. One does not recite the blessing *al netilas yadayim* in this case either.[2]
Like other *Birchos Ha-nehenin*, the blessing of *ha-motzi* is recited no matter
how little bread one is planning to eat.

How to perform *netilas yadayim* before a meal

3.   *Netilas yadayim* must be done with a whole, unbroken vessel. The vessel
      may not have any holes, and its upper rim must be straight, and with-
out defects. The vessel must hold at least a *revi'is* of water. (According to the
Chazon Ish, a *revi'is* is 150 cc (5.07 fl oz). According to Rav Chaim Na'eh, a
revi'is is 86 cc (2.9 fl oz).)[3]

4.   Before performing *netilas yadayim*, one must be sure that his hands are clean, and that nothing is sticking to them. Nothing may come between the water and one's hands.[4] Therefore, rings should be removed before *netilas yadayim*. A ring which is never removed does not have to be removed before *netilas yadayim*.[5]

5.   The water must be poured on the entire hand up to the wrist.[6] It is proper to wash the right hand before the left hand.[7] A *revi'is* of water should be poured onto each hand. (Various *halachos* must be observed if less than a *revi'is* of water is used.)[8]

If one has enough water, it is preferable to pour a *revi'is* of water on each hand twice.[9]

One should be careful not to let the hand that was already washed touch the hand that was not yet washed.[10]

6.   One recites the blessing *al netilas yadayim* ("Who has commanded us regarding the washing of the hands") before drying his hands.[11] Drying one's hands is part of the mitzvah of *netilas yadayim*.[12]

Additional laws

7.   One who has a bandage on the palm of his hand which cannot be removed because it will be painful, should wash the part of the hand which is not covered. At least a *revi'is* of water should be poured over the hand in one motion. If the bandage falls off during the meal, the person must perform *netilas yadayim* by pouring water over his whole hand.

If one cannot wash his hand at all because he is ill or has a wound, he should cover his hand with a napkin, glove, etc. during the meal.[13]

8.   Water which lost its transparency because an object or liquid fell into it may not be used for *netilas yadayim*. However, water which is dusty or sandy (even if the water is not clear) may be used for *netilas yadayim*.

Water which had been used previously, e.g. to wash dishes or vegetables, or to cool drinks, may not be used for *netilas yadayim*.[14]

9.   According to some halachic opinions, one who used the bathroom before performing *netilas yadayim* for a meal should wash his hands twice. The first time he should wash his hands in a manner different than that required for *netilas yadayim* before a meal, and recite the blessing *asher yatzar*.

Then he should perform *netilas yadayim* as is required for the meal, and recite the blessing *al netilas yadayim*.[15] However, according to the Chazon Ish one in this situation is only required to perform *netilas yadayim* once. The person should wash his hands as required for *netilas yadayim* before a meal. Then he recites *al netilas yadayim*, followed by *asher yatzar*. Most people follow the Chazon Ish's ruling in this matter.

Ha-motzi (The blessing for bread)

10.   One should not talk or become busy with anything else from the time one performs *netilas yadayim* until after he has swallowed a piece of bread.[16] One should recite *ha-motzi* and have a bite of the bread as soon after he has dried his hands as possible. It is best to avoid pausing, even without speaking, between *netilas yadayim* and reciting *ha-motzi*.[17]

One should hold the bread in his hands while reciting the blessing *ha-motzi lechem min ha-aretz* ("Who causes bread to come forth from the earth"). One should hold the bread with all ten fingers when reciting the blessing.[18]

Ha-motzi is recited no matter how little bread one is planning to eat.

It is a mitzvah to have salt on the table where one is eating.[19]

11.   It is preferable to recite a blessing on a large or complete food. Therefore, one should not slice the loaf of bread before reciting *ha-motzi*.[20] To shorten the time between reciting the blessing and eating the bread, one should make a small cut in the loaf, recite *ha-motzi*, and then finish slicing the piece of bread. On Shabbos and *Yom Tov* one should not cut into the loaf before reciting *ha-motzi* (for more details, see Chapter 17, Section 18).

Food eaten with bread

12.   The blessing of *ha-motzi*, which is recited at the beginning of the meal, generally exempts a person from reciting additional blessings on other food or drinks during the meal.[21]

However, if one drinks wine during the meal, he must recite the blessing *borei peri ha-gafen*. This is because wine is considered an especially important beverage. Blessings are also recited for foods which are eaten during the meal, but which are halachically not considered a part of the meal, such as desserts.[22]

A food is considered a part of the meal if it is usually eaten with bread or if it is eaten to satisfy one's hunger. Examples of foods which are considered part of a meal are meat, fish, eggs, vegetables, cheese, pickled foods, and cereals. It is best to clarify the status of individual foods with an expert in Halachah.

Halachos which apply to a meal

13.   During a meal one should not touch any parts of his body that are covered. Similarly, one should not scratch his scalp during a meal. One who did either of these things, or who relieved himself, or who did not concentrate on keeping his hands clean, must perform netilas yadayim again.[23]

We do not talk while eating, lest the food enter the windpipe instead of the esophagus. However, it is a mitzvah to discuss Torah thoughts between courses, when one is not eating.[24]

The Shulchan Aruch (Sections 170, 171, 180) discusses what is considered proper behavior during meals. It mentions, for instance, that food should be treated respectfully, and that one should have good table manners.

14.   One should not leave his place or go out of his house while in the middle of a meal. This applies even if the person intends to return and finish his meal. There are many details pertaining to this halachah, e.g. when one may leave his place, and how one should proceed if he did leave. The Halachah is different for one who ate a meal with bread as opposed to one who only ate pastries or fruit.

If a number of people are eating a meal together, and some of the people left their places, as long as one person remained at his place the others do not have to repeat any blessings when they return and resume their meal. Since someone remained at the table, it is not considered as if the others interrupted their meal.[25]

Chapter Twelve

Birkas Ha-Mazon
(Grace after meals)

1. "When you have eaten and are satisfied, you shall bless Hashem your God" (*Devarim* 8:10). *Birkas Ha-mazon* is recited after eating bread.[1]

One is only required to recite *Birkas Ha-mazon* if he ate a *k'zayis* or more of bread.[2] A *k'zayis* of bread must be eaten within a unit of time called *toch kedei achilas pras*. The exact measures of a *k'zayis* and *toch kedei achilas pras* are listed in the Table of Measures at the end of Chapter 15.

2. One should sit when reciting *Birkas Ha-mazon*, as this helps one concentrate. One should not recline impertinently in his chair. Rather, one should sit reverently, and concentrate on the blessings he is reciting.[3] *Birkas Ha-mazon* must be recited where the meal was eaten.[4]

3. A person who forgot to recite *Birkas Ha-mazon* immediately after his meal, may recite it as long as he still feels sated. Once the person is hungry again, he may no longer recite *Birkas Ha-mazon*. If one only ate a small amount, he may only recite *Birkas Ha-mazon* within 72 minutes after finishing the meal. In this case it is preferable to eat a *k'zayis* of bread (without reciting *ha-motzi*, provided that the person did not specifically decide to end his meal) before reciting *Birkas Ha-mazon*.[5]

4. When *Birkas Ha-mazon* is recited after a meal, no *berachos acharonos* are required for the various foods that were eaten during the meal. This rule even applies to foods that require a separate blessing during the meal (e.g. wine and desserts).[6]

Mayim acharonim (Washing the hands after a meal)

5. One is required to wash his hands at the end of the meal[7] (even if his hands are clean[8]), before reciting *Birkas Ha-mazon*. This *netilah* is called *mayim acharonim*. The water is poured on the fingers up to the second joint. If

there is enough water, it is preferable to pour water up to the knuckles.[9] The water is poured over the fingers into a vessel, which should be removed from the table before *Birkas Ha-mazon* is recited. One should not eat or drink between washing *mayim acharonim* and reciting *Birkas Ha-mazon*.

Some people rely on the opinion that today *mayim·acharonim* is not required.[10]

On weekdays it is customary to remove or cover any knives on the table before beginning *Birkas Ha-mazon*.

Zimmun (*Birkas Ha-mazon* recited in a group)

6.   Three or more men over the age of thirteen who ate a meal together that included bread are obligated to recite *Birkas Ha-mazon* as a group.[11] This is called *zimmun*. One of the men recites a passage, inviting the others to join him in reciting *Birkas Ha-mazon*. The others recite another passage in response. If ten or more men ate together, they add the word *Elokeinu* when reciting the passage.[12] The text of *zimmun* is printed in the *Siddur* before *Birkas Ha-mazon*, as well as in small printed copies of *Birkas Ha-mazon*. The leader recites the first *berachah* of *Birkas Ha-mazon* out loud, and the others recite the *berachah* quietly word by word. They end the *berachah* before the leader does, and answer Amen to his *berachah*. It is proper that the rest of *Birkas Ha-mazon* be recited in the same manner. Among Sephardic Jews, everyone ends the *berachah* in unison.

The text of *Birkas Ha-mazon*

7.   *Birkas Ha-mazon* is comprised of four blessings:

Birkas Ha-Zan: In this blessing we thank God for His kindness in giving us food.

Birkas Ha-Aretz: This blessing begins with the words *Nodeh lecha Hashem*. In this blessing we express general gratitude for having been given the Land of Israel as our heritage, as well as thank God for taking us out of Egypt, making a covenant with us, and giving us the Torah. On Chanukah and Purim *Al ha-nissim* is added in this blessing.[13] (In Section 9, below, there is a table which indicates how to proceed if one forgot to recite any of the additions to *Birkas Ha-mazon*.)

Birkas Boneh Yerushalayim: This blessing begins with the words *rachem na Hashem*. This blessing includes a prayer requesting God's compassion on His people, on Jerusalem, and on His Temple, as well as a request for the Temple to be rebuilt speedily in our days. On Shabbos, *Retzei* is included in this blessing. On *Yom Tov* and *Rosh Chodesh*, *Ya'aleh V'yavo* is included in this blessing.[14]

Birkas Ha-Tov V'Ha-Metiv: This blessing begins with the words *Ha-Kel avinu*. In this blessing, we thank God for the great kindness He has done for us in the past, and request that He continue to grant us His kindness in the future. These four blessings are followed by additional supplications.

Birkas Ha-mazon when newlyweds are present and at the meal following a circumcision

8.   At a meal where a *chasan* (bridegroom) and a *kallah* (bride) are present, and at least ten men over the age of thirteen are present, seven blessings (*sheva berachos*) are recited after *Birkas Ha-mazon*. The *halachos* that apply to these blessings, such as how many days after the wedding they are recited, and the requirement that someone who has not been to the couple's previous *sheva berachos* be among the ten men, are listed in the *Shulchan Aruch, Even Ha-ezer*, Section 62.

Special supplications are added at the end of *Birkas Ha-mazon* following the festive meal that follows a circumcision (*bris milah*). These additions are printed in the *Siddur*.

Kos shel berachah: Birkas Ha-mazon recited over a cup of wine

When *Birkas Ha-mazon* is recited with a *zimmun*, it is considered praiseworthy to recite *Birkas Ha-mazon* over a cup of wine. This cup of wine is called the *kos shel berachah*. The one who leads the *zimmun* holds the cup while reciting *Birkas Ha-mazon*. After concluding *Birkas Ha-mazon*, the one who led the *zimmun* recites the blessing for wine (*borei peri ha-gafen*) and drinks from the *kos shel berachah*.[15] If the host led the *zimmun*, he then passes a bit of wine to his wife, as well as to the other men who took part in the *zimmun*. (Further details are cited in halachic sources.)[16]

9.   The charts below reflect the *Mishnah Berurah's* rulings regarding how one should proceed if he forgot to add *Retzei, Ya'aleh V'yavo*, or *Al ha-nissim* in *Birkas Ha-mazon*.

Forgetting *Retzei V'hachalitzenu* during *Birkas Ha-mazon*[1]

When one realized his error	During the evening and first daytime Shabbos meals	During any meal other than the first two meals·(seudah shelishis)[2]
Before mentioning God's Name at the end of the blessing *U've-neh Yerushalayim*	Recite *Retzei* and then recite *U'veneh Yerushalayim*[3]	Recite *Retzei* and then recite *U'veneh Yerushalayim*[3]
After mentioning God's Name at the end of the blessing, but before reciting the word *boneh*	Say *lamedeini chukecha*,[4] recite *Retzei*,[5] and then repeat *U'veneh Yerushalayim*	Say *lamedeini chukecha*,[4] recite *Retzei*,[6] and then repeat *U'veneh Yerushalayim*
After finishing the blessing[7]	Recite the blessing *Baruch Attah Hashem Elokeinu melech ha-olam she-nasan Shabbasos li-menuchah l'ammo Yisrael bi-ahavah l'os v'li'veris. Baruch Attah Hashem mekadesh ha-Shabbos*, and continue with the next blessing[8]	If it is not yet night, recite the blessing *Baruch Attah Hashem Elokeinu melech ha-olam she-nasan Shabbasos li-menuchah l'ammo Yisrael bi-ahavah l'os v'li'veris. Baruch Attah Hashem mekadesh ha-Shabbos*, and continue with the next blessing[9]
After beginning the next blessing	Repeat *Birkas Ha-mazon* from the beginning[10]	Do not repeat *Birkas Ha-mazon*[11]

1. *M.B.* 188 (16) and *M.B.* 422 (10).   2. *S.A.* 188:8.   3. *M.B.* 188 (22).   4. This is *Tehillim* 119:12 *Baruch Attah Hashem lamedeini chukecha*. By completing the sentence *Baruch Attah Hashem* with the final words of the verse (*lamedeini chukecha*) one recites a verse from *Tehillim* rather than mention God's Name in vain (see *M.B.* 422 [5]).   5. *M.B.* 188 (22), and *Sha'ar Ha-Tzion* there,(18).   6. *M.B.* 188 (31).   7. According to the *Chayei Adam*, one who only recited the first few words of the blessing *Ha-tov v'ha-meitiv* (i.e. the words *Baruch Attah Hashem Elokeinu melech ha-olam*) when he realized he omitted the passage *Retzei* should conclude *She-nasan Shabbasos li-menuchah...* . The *Be'ur Halachah* cites the halachic opinion that one who began reciting *Ha-tov v'ha-meitiv*, and realized he omitted the passage *Retzei* should repeat *Birkas Ha-mazon*. *M.B.* 188 (23), and *Be'ur Halachah* there.   8. *S.A.* 188:6.   9. *M.B.* 188 (31). One who omitted *Retzei* during *Birkas Ha-mazon* following the third Shabbos meal, and who is reciting *Birkas Ha-mazon* after nightfall, does not recite the blessing *She-nasan Shabbasos li-menuchah*. In this situation one may recite the blessing without mentioning God's Name, in the following manner: *Baruch she-nasan Shabbasos li-menuchah l'ammo Yisrael b'ahavah l'os u'li-veris* (*Shoneh Halachos* 188:14).   10. *S.A.* 188:6.   11. *M.B.* 188 (31).

Forgetting[1] Ya'aleh V'yavo during Birkas Ha-mazon

WHEN	YOM TOV	ROSH CHODESH	CHOL HA-MO'ED
When one realized his error	During the first two meals	During any meal other than the first two meals[2]	During any meal[3]	During any meal
Before mentioning God's Name at the end of the blessing Boneh Yerushalayim	Return to Ya'aleh V'yavo,[4] and recite Birkas Ha-mazon from there	Return to Ya'aleh V'yavo,[4] and recite Birkas Ha-mazon from there	Return to Ya'aleh V'yavo,[4] and recite Birkas Ha-mazon from there	Return to Ya'aleh V'yavo,[4] and recite Birkas Ha-mazon from there
After mentioning God's Name at the end of the blessing, but before reciting the word boneh	Say Lamedeini chukecha,[5] return to Ya'aleh V'yavo[6] and recite Birkas Ha-mazon from there	Say Lamedeini chukecha,[5] return to Ya'aleh V'yavo[6] and recite Birkas Ha-mazon from there	Say Lamedeini chukecha,[5] return to Ya'aleh V'yavo[6] and recite Birkas Ha-mazon from there	Say Lamedeini chukecha,[5] return to Ya'aleh V'yavo[6] and recite Birkas Ha-mazon from there
After completing the blessing	Recite the blessing below and recite the rest of Birkas Ha-mazon[7]	If it is not yet night, recite the blessing below, and recite the rest of Birkas Ha-mazon[8]	If it is not yet night, recite the blessing below, and recite the rest of Birkas Ha-mazon[9]	Recite the blessing below, and recite the rest of Birkas Ha-mazon[10]
After beginning the next blessing[15]	Repeat Birkas Ha-mazon from the beginning[11] (See note 16 regarding how to proceed on Rosh Hashana)	Continue reciting Birkas Ha-mazon without repeating any sections[12]	Continue reciting Birkas Ha-mazon without repeating any sections[13]	Continue reciting Birkas Ha-mazon without repeating any sections[14]

Compensatory Blessings

Shabbos	Rosh Chodesh	Rosh Hashana	Yom Tov	Chol Ha-mo'ed
Recite the blessing Baruch Attah Hashem Elokeinu melech ha-olam she-nasan Shabbasos li-menuchah l'ammo Yisrael bi-ahavah l'os v'li'veris. Baruch Attah Hashem mekadesh ha-Shabbos (Who gave Shabbos for contentment to His people Israel with love, for a sign and a covenant, Blessed are You God Who sanctifies the Shabbos.)	She-nasan rashei cha-dashim l'ammo Yisrael l'zikaron (Who gave new moons to His nation Israel for a remembrance.)	She-nasan yamim tovim l'ammo Yisrael es Yom ha-Zikaron ha-zeh. Baruch Attah Hashem me-kadesh Yisrael v'Yom Ha-zikaron (Who gave festivals to His nation Israel this day of remembrance, Blessed are You God Who sanctifies Israel and the day of remembrance).	Asher nasan Yamim Tovim l'ammo Yisrael l'sasson u'l'simchah es Yom (choose the appropriate day) **Pesach:** chag ha-matzos; **Shavuos:** chag ha-Shavuos; **Succos:** chag ha-Succos; **Shemini Atzeres / Simchas Torah:** Shemini chag ha-Atzeres; ha-zeh. Baruch Attah Hashem meka-desh Yisrael v'ha-zemanim (Who gave festivals to His nation Israel for happiness and joy, this day of (insert the appropriate day). Blessed are You God Who sanctifies Israel and the seasons.)	She-nasan mo'adim l'ammo Yisrael l'sas-son u'l'simchah (Who set aside times for His nation Israel for happi-ness and joy).

One who has to recite these blessings on Yom Tov or Rosh Chodesh that is on Shabbos, recites a combined version that mentions Shabbos and the other special day. See S.A. 188:6, M.B. 188 (20), S.A. 188:7, and M.B. 188 (30). The text for these blessings is printed in some Siddurim.

1. One who is certain that he intended to recite Ya'aleh V'yavo, but some time after reciting Birkas Ha-mazon cannot remember whether or not he actually recited the passage does not have to repeat Ya'aleh V'yavo. However, one who is not sure if he recited Ya'aleh V'yavo immediately after reciting Birkas Ha-mazon must recite Birkas Ha-mazon again. M.B. 188 (16).   2. M.B. 188 (26) and 298 (5).   3. S.A. 188:7. See also Be'ur Halachah starting with the words bein ba-laylah   4. M.B. 188 (22).   5. This is Tehillim 119:12 Baruch Attah Hashem lamedeini chukecha. By completing the sentence Baruch Attah Hashem with the final words of the verse (lamedeini chukecha) one recites a verse from Tehillim rather than mention God's Name in vain. M.B. 422 (5).   6. M.B. 188 (22), and Sha'ar Ha-Tzion (18).   7. S.A. 188:6.   8. If one forgets to recite Ya'aleh V'yavo on Yom Tov during any meal other than the first two meals, and it is already night, the blessing below is not recited. One may recite an abbreviated version of the blessing without mentioning God's Name (Baruch Attah asher nasan yamim tovim l'ammo Yisrael l'sasson u'l'simchah es yom chag [fill in the name of the Yom Tov] ha-zeh. Baruch mekadesh Yisrael v'ha-zemanim). M.B. 188 (31). See also Shoneh Halachos 188:14.   9. S.A. 188:7, and M.B. 188 (25).   10. S.A. 188:7 and M.B. 188 (27).   11. S.A. 188:6.   12. M.B. 188 (31).   13. S.A. 188:7.   14. Ibid. M.B. 188 (31). See also Shoneh Halachos 188:14.   15. According to the Chayei Adam, one who remembers that he did not recite Ya'aleh V'yavo after reciting the words Baruch Attah Hashem Elokeinu Melech ha-olam at the beginning of the next blessing should conclude with the appropriate blessing. M.B. 188 (23). There are halachic authorities who disagree with this opinion. According to these halachic authorities, one who realizes that he did not recite Ya'aleh V'yavo after beginning the next blessing should repeat Birkas Ha-Mazon from the beginning (Be'ur Halachah 188, from the words ad she-hitchil).

Forgetting *Al ha-nissim* during *Birkas Ha-mazon*[1]

When one realized his error	How to proceed
Before mentioning God's Name at the end of the *V'al ha-kol*	Recite *Al ha-nissim*,[1] and then repeat *V'al ha-kol*
Anytime after mentioning God's Name at the end of *V'al ha-kol*	Recite *Birkas Ha-mazon* until the special *Ha-rachamans* for Shabbos and *Yom Tov*, and then recite: *Ha-rachman ya'aseh lanu nissim v'nifla'os k'shem she-asisah la-avoseinu ba-yamim ha-hem ba-zeman ha-zeh,*[2] and then continue... On Chanukah: *Bi-mei Mattisyahu...* On Purim: *Bi-mei Mordechai v'Esther...*

1. *S.A.* 682:1 (Chanukah), 693:2 (Purim).   2. Ibid. When reciting this *Ha-rachaman* on *Rosh Chodesh* on Chanukah, one first recites the special *Ha-rachaman* for *Rosh Chodesh*, and then this *Ha-rachaman* (*M.B.* 682 [5]).

Chapter Thirteen

Birchos Ha-Nehenin
(Blessings recited before enjoying a food or fragrance)

1. "The earth and all that is in it is God's" (*Tehillim* 24:1). Everything that exists in the world belongs to God. Man is permitted to enjoy God's world, but first he must recite a blessing. Reciting a blessing is akin to asking God's permission to benefit from His creations.

Our sages teach that, "One may not benefit from this world without first reciting a blessing. One who does so is like one who misappropriates a holy object" (*Berachos* 35a). One is only permitted to benefit from and enjoy the various things that exist in this world after reciting a blessing. The blessings included in this category are *Birchos Ha-nehenin*.

When one recites a blessing, he is expressing his gratitude to God, Who has given him of His goodness. One is also praising God for creating the object from which he is deriving pleasure.

Blessings instill in us the realization that everything belongs to God, and that all we possess is due to His kindness. One who recites his blessings with *kavanah* gains a deepened faith in God and a stronger awareness of Divine Providence.

Laws pertaining to *Birchos Ha-nehenin*

2. One must recite a blessing before eating or drinking, no matter how small the quantity of food.[1] One should hold the food or drink in his right hand while reciting the blessing; one who is left-handed holds the food or drink in his left hand.[1*]

One should not pause between reciting the blessing and eating the food over which the blessing was recited. If one paused but did not speak, he does not have to repeat the blessing as long as his attention was not diverted from eating the food. If, however, the person spoke about something other than the food he is about to eat, he must repeat the blessing.[2]

3.   There are different blessings for different types of food. The more common *Birchos Ha-nehenin* are listed below.

* *Borei minei mezonos* ("Who creates various kinds of nourishment")[3] is recited before eating foods made from the five species of grain (except bread), like cake, noodles, wafers, cookies, etc. The five species of grain are: wheat, barley, spelt, oats, and rye.

Borei minei mezonos is also recited before eating rice. (It should be noted that the blessing recited after eating rice is *Borei Nefashos*, and not the blessing *Me'ein Shalosh* that usually follows *mezonos*. For more details regarding the blessing *Me'ein Shalosh*, see Chapter 14, Sections 2-4.)

* *Borei peri ha-gafen* ("Who creates the fruit of the vine") is recited before drinking wine. Due to its importance, wine was assigned a special blessing.[4]

* *Borei peri ha-etz* ("Who creates the fruit of the tree") is recited before eating fruits that grow on trees.[5]

* *Borei peri ha-adamah* ("Who creates the fruit of the earth") is recited before eating vegetables and fruits that grow from the ground, such as melon, watermelon, and strawberries. This blessing is also recited before eating bananas.

* *She-ha-kol niheyah bi-devaro* ("by Whose word all things came into being") is recited before eating or drinking food that does not grow from the earth, such as cheese, eggs, fish, meat and drinks (including fruit and vegetable juices).[6]

Blessings recited before smelling fragrances

4.   Before smelling a pleasant fragrance, one must recite one of the following blessings:

* Before smelling fragrant grasses or their flowers, one recites *borei isvei vesamim* ("Who has created fragrant grasses").

* Before smelling fragrant woody plants such as bushes, trees, or their flowers, one recites *borei atzei vesamim* ("Who has created fragrant trees").

* Before smelling fragrant edible fruits, one recites *ha-nosein re'ach tov la-peros* ("Who has given a pleasant smell to fruits").[7]

* Before smelling a fragrance which is not included in any of the categories listed above, one recites *borei minei vesamim* ("Who has created various kinds of fragrances").[8]

If one erred and recited *borei minei vesamim* before smelling a fragrance that required a different blessing, he has fulfilled his obligation and does not have to recite the correct blessing.[9]

Priority in blessings

5.   When one intends on eating several foods of the same blessing, there is an order as to which food to make the blessing on. The basic rules are listed below.

Any of the fruits for which the Land of Israel is praised in the Torah has priority over all other fruits. When one is about to eat several of these fruits, he recites the blessings for the fruits in the following order: olives, dates, grapes, figs, and pomegranates.

One recites a blessing over a whole food, rather than over a food that is cut up (even if he likes the cut food better and even if it is larger).

One recites a blessing over the larger food, rather than over the smaller one.

One recites a blessing over the food he usually prefers, rather than over the food he likes less. If one usually enjoys both equally, he recites a blessing over the food he prefers now.

If one is going to eat foods that require different blessings, he should recite the blessings in this order (even if the other food is of the seven fruits of Israel and is usually preferred): *ha-motzi, borei minei mezonos, borei peri ha-gafen, borei peri ha-etz* or *borei peri ha-adamah, she-ha-kol niheyah bi-devaro.*

When one is going to eat foods that require *borei peri ha-etz* and *borei peri ha-adamah*, one recites a blessing over the food he usually prefers if he prefers it now too. If one usually enjoys both equally and one is of the seven fruits of Israel, he recites a blessing over it. If one usually enjoys both equally and both or neither are of the seven fruits of Israel, *borei peri ha-etz* is said first.

These *halachos* are listed in more detail in *Shulchan Aruch, Orach Chayim*, Section 211.[10]

Errors when reciting blessings

6.   If one has recited the incorrect blessing for a food, he may or may not
      have to recite the correct blessing, depending on which blessing he re-
cited. The following are examples of common errors:

   * If one recited *borei peri ha-adamah* before eating a fruit that grows on a
tree, he does not recite the blessing *borei peri ha-etz*, because trees grow from
the ground.

   * If one recited *borei peri ha-etz* before eating vegetables, he must recite
the blessing *borei peri ha-adamah*.[11]

   * If one recited *she-ha-kol* on any type of food, including wine and
bread, he does not have to recite the correct blessing.[12]

When one is required to recite a
blessing before taking medicine

7.   The following *halachos* apply when taking medicine, or when eating or
      drinking a food solely for medicinal purposes:

   * One recites a blessing before ingesting food or medicine that has a
pleasant taste. If one swallowed a *k'zayis* of food or a *revi'is* of something
to drink, he should also recite a *berachah acharonah*.

   * One does not recite a blessing before ingesting food or medicine that
has an unpleasant taste. This rule only applies if the person does not eat the
unpleasant tasting food because he is hungry.

   * One does not recite a blessing before drinking water to help swallow
medicine or food which became stuck in his throat (i.e. he is not drinking to
quench his thirst). However, one must recite a blessing before drinking other
beverages for these same reasons, since he enjoys their taste.[13]

Tasting food

8.   There are two opinions regarding whether one is required to recite a
      blessing before tasting and swallowing a bit of food (e.g. to see if
the food is fully cooked). In order to avoid this *safek* (doubt) in *halachah*,
one who is tasting food should intend to enjoy the food. This way he is required to recite a blessing before tasting the food. One who tastes a bit of
food without swallowing it (i.e. he spits out the food) also avoids the *safek*,
as one is not required to recite a blessing for food that he does not swallow.[14]

Food that became wet

9.   One should wash his hands without reciting *al netilas yadayim* before
       eating wet food (e.g. fruit which was rinsed in water and not dried,
or a pastry that was dipped in a glass of tea).[15]

This *halachah* applies to food which is usually eaten without cutlery, even if
the person is eating it with cutlery. One does not have to wash his hands
before eating wet food that is usually eaten with cutlery, such as cooked
dishes.

Two foods where one is subordinate to the other

10.   When a person eats two kinds of food, and one food is only eaten be-
       cause of the other one, the person only recites a blessing for the main
food. This blessing exempts one from reciting the blessing over the other
food.

The definitions of a "main" food and a "subordinate" food depend on several
factors. The practical details of this *halachah* must be verified with a person
who is proficient in these *halachos*.[16]

Basing a meal on baked goods

11.   If one is planning to eat baked goods (cakes, pastries, etc.) in a quantity
       considered sufficient for a complete meal, the baked goods acquire the
same status as bread. Therefore, one must perform *netilas yadayim* and recite
the blessing *al netilas yadayim*, and recite *ha-motzi* (instead of reciting *borei
minei mezonos*) before eating the baked goods. Similarly, one must recite *Birkas Ha-mazon* (instead of reciting *Me'ein Shalosh*) after eating.

The exact amount of baked goods that is considered sufficient for a meal is
not clear. According to the Chazon Ish up to 200 cc (6.8 fl oz, approximately
the volume of a teacup), is clearly not considered a meal. According to Rav
Chaim Na'eh up to 168 cc (5.7 fl oz) is clearly not considered a meal. It is
praiseworthy to eat more than this amount of baked goods only during a
meal with bread, or when eating enough to definitely require reciting *ha-
motzi* and *Birkas Ha-mazon*.

According to the *Mishnah Berurah*, *ha-motzi* and *Birkas Ha-mazon* are recited if
the quantity of baked goods eaten equals the quantity of bread usually eaten

with a meal. If the entire meal consists of baked goods, then the quantity eaten must equal the amount of bread that would be eaten at a meal where bread is the only food being eaten. If other foods are eaten together with the baked goods, then the quantity eaten must equal the amount of bread that would be eaten during a meal that consists of bread as well as other foods. (It is advisable to discuss this rule with a halachic authority.)[17]

Food whose shape and texture were changed

12. *She-ha-kol* is recited before eating fruits or vegetables which were completely pureed or mashed so that their natural shape and texture became completely indistinguishable. The regular blessing is recited if the fruits or vegetables were not completely mashed (i.e. *borei peri ha-etz* for fruits, and *borei peri ha-adamah* for vegetables).

Food that is usually eaten mashed or pureed (e.g. spices eaten with sugar) requires the regular blessing.[18] This *halachah* has many detailed practical applications. Therefore, each person is advised to study the *halachah* in depth.

Chapter Fourteen

Berachos Acharonos
(Blessings recited after eating)

1. One must recite a *berachah acharonah*[1] after eating a *k'zayis* or more of food, or drinking a *revi'is* or more of liquid. When one recites this blessing he thanks and praises God for the good things he just enjoyed. A *berachah acharonah* is only recited if a *k'zayis* of food was eaten within a period of *toch kedei achilas pras*. For more information regarding the exact measure of a *k'zayis*, *revi'is*, and *toch kedei achilas pras*, refer to the Table of Measures at the end of Chapter 15.

There are two opinions regarding whether one must recite a *berachah acharonah* after eating a complete unit of food such as a grape or pomegranate seed if the total amount of food eaten is less than a *k'zayis*. To avoid this, one is advised not to eat less than a *k'zayis* of such a food, unless one eats it during a meal, or with other fruits which, together, amount to more than a *k'zayis*. The fruit is not considered whole if a small part is missing, or if the seed is removed.[3]

Besides *Birkas Ha-mazon*, which is recited after eating bread, there are two other *berachos acharonos* which are recited after eating food: *Me'ein Shalosh* and *Borei Nefashos*.

Me'ein Shalosh

2. *Me'ein Shalosh* is recited after eating food made from the five species of grain (wheat, barley, rye, oats and spelt), such as cakes, noodles, wafers, etc. (Buckwheat is not one of the five grains and its *berachah acharonah* is *Borei Nefashos*.) *Me'ein Shalosh* is also recited after drinking wine and grape juice, and after eating one of the fruits for which the Land of Israel is praised in the Torah (grapes, figs, pomegranates, olives, and dates).[4] This blessing is

119

called *"Me'ein Shalosh"* ("a summary of three") because it contains the first three blessings of *Birkas Ha-mazon* in an abridged form.

The text of the blessing

3. The beginning and the end of the blessing vary according to the food after which it is recited:

    * After eating food made from the five types of grain (for example, cake, cookies, wafers, pasta, etc.), one recites the passage *al ha-michyah v'al ha-kalekalah*.[5]

    * After drinking wine or grape juice, one recites the passage *al ha-gefen v'al peri ha-gefen*.[6]

    * After eating fruits for which the Land of Israel is praised, one recites the passage *al ha-etz v'al peri ha-etz*.[7]

The full text of *Me'ein Shalosh* is printed in the *Siddur*, as well as in small pamphlets containing *Birkas Ha-mazon*.

If one ate several of these foods together, e.g. cakes and grapes, or wine and cake, one recites *Me'ein Shalosh* once, with both passages. This combined version is usually printed in the *Siddur* as well.[8]

On Shabbos, *Yom Tov*, and *Rosh Chodesh*, a sentence referring to the holiness of the day is included when reciting *Me'ein Shalosh*. This sentence is printed in the *Siddur*. If one forgot to include the extra sentence, he does not have to repeat the blessing.[9]

Reciting the *berachah acharonah* in the place where one ate

4. According to the Gra, one who eats food made from the five grains must recite the *berachah acharonah* where the food was eaten. It is proper to follow a stricter opinion of some halachic authorities, who hold that *Me'ein Shalosh* must always be recited where one ate. One should not leave the area until he has recited the *berachah acharonah*. If one did leave, he should return to the place where he ate to recite the *berachah acharonah*. If one left unintentionally before reciting the *berachah acharonah*, in case of necessity he may recite the blessing without going back.[10] According to some halachic authorities, *Me'ein Shalosh* should always be recited sitting

down. According to the Gra, however, one is only required to sit when reciting *Me'ein Shalosh* after eating food made from one of the five grains.[11]

Borei Nefashos

5.   *Borei Nefashos* ("Who makes many living things and provides for their needs, for all that you have created. Blessed are You, the provider of life in the worlds") is recited after eating foods and drinks for which neither *Birkas Ha-mazon* nor *Me'ein Shalosh* is the *berachah acharonah*.[12]

One must recite this blessing after eating at least a *k'zayis* of food or drinking a *revi'is* of a beverage, as specified in Section 1 of this chapter.

It is preferable not to leave the place where one ate before reciting *Borei Nefashos*.[13]

6.   When reciting *Borei Nefashos*, we thank God for creating mankind, as well as "their needs," i.e. the sustenance which is vital for man's existence, like bread and water. When we thank God "for all that You have created," we are referring to the countless additional things which benefit man although they are not essential for his existence.

Additional laws

7.   A person who erred and recited *Borei Nefashos* instead of *Me'ein Shalosh*, or vice versa,[14] has not fulfilled his obligation. However, if one ate a fruit for which the Land of Israel is praised, as well as other kinds of fruits (e.g. grapes and apples), one only recites *Me'ein Shalosh* (the passage beginning *al ha-etz v'al peri ha-etz*).[15]

In certain situations, the *berachos* one recites when drinking wine exempts him from reciting *berachos* over the other beverages he will drink.[16] This applies to the blessing recited before drinking wine as well as to the *berachah acharonah*.

8.   One who did not recite the *berachah acharonah* after eating a meal may recite it as long as he is still sated. Once one feels hungry, he may no longer recite the *berachah acharonah*.

If one only ate a small amount of food, he may only recite the *berachah acharonah* within 72 minutes after having eaten.[17]

Chapter Fifteen

Other Blessings

1. Some blessings are recited at various events, and on certain occasions. These blessings are called *Birchos Ha-shevach*, Blessings of Praise.

Various blessings are recited upon seeing certain natural phenomena such as lightning, a rainbow, majestic mountains, etc. Other blessings are recited upon hearing things, such as thunder, good news, a bad message, etc. Each situation has its special blessing.

The *halachos* regarding these blessings are cited in the *Shulchan Aruch, Orach Chayim*, Chapters 218-230. These blessings are often listed in the *Siddur*. The following are the most common of these blessings.

She-hecheyanu

2. *She-hecheyanu v'kiyemanu v'higi'anu la-zeman ha-zeh* ("Who has kept us alive and sustained us and enabled us to reach this time").

This blessing is recited when one eats a seasonal fruit from the new crop for the first time.[1] *She-hecheyanu* is recited in addition to the regular blessing for the fruit (*borei peri ha-etz*).[2] It is preferable to recite *She-hecheyanu* before the regular blessing, but if *She-hecheyanu* is recited after the regular blessing, it is not considered an interruption.

She-hecheyanu is also recited for foods requiring *borei peri ha-adamah*, such as melon, watermelon and strawberries, since these foods are only available during the new season. One does not recite *She-hecheyanu* for fruits that are available throughout the year, because it is not obvious when their season begins.[3]

3. *She-hecheyanu* is also recited when one buys an important article of clothing (or when one makes any other major purchase).[4] If the garment requires alterations, the blessing is recited after all the alterations have been completed, and one is wearing it for the first time.[5]

She-hecheyanu is recited before performing a mitzvah which occurs infrequently, like sitting in a *succah*, eating matzah, etc. The blessing is recited before the mitzvah is performed for the first time during the holiday. *She-hecheyanu* is also included in the *Kiddush* recited on the first night of all *Yamim Tovim*.

Ha-gomel

4.   The text of the blessing of *Ha-gomel* is: *ha-gomel l'chayavim tovos she-gemalani kol tov* ("Who does good to the undeserving and Who has rendered every kindness to me"). This blessing is recited after recovering from a grave illness, safely crossing an ocean or desert, or after being released from prison.

A person who has recovered from a serious illness must ask someone who is proficient in Halachah if he is required to recite *Ha-gomel*. This is because *Ha-gomel* is only recited after recovering from certain diseases. Similarly, one who has been released from prison must determine if he is required to recite the blessing.

A person who crossed a sea or a desert must recite *Ha-gomel*, even if he was not in any obvious danger.[6]

A person who survived other life-threatening situations (e.g. a serious car accident, or the collapse of a building) also recites *Ha-gomel*. One should consult with an expert in Halachah regarding whether a given situation is halachically considered "life threatening."[7]

5.   *Ha-gomel* must be recited when ten men are present. When the blessing is concluded, the listeners respond *Mi she-gemalecha tov Hu yigemalecha kol tov selah* ("May He Who rendered you every kindness continue to deal kindly with you forever"). It is customary to recite *Ha-gomel* after *Kerias ha-Torah*, since ten men are always present then.[8]

Blessings recited for thunder, lightning, and a rainbow

6.   One recites the blessing *oseh ma'aseh bereshis* ("Who does the act of Creation")[9] immediately after seeing a flash of lightning.

One recites the blessing *she-kocho u'gevuraso malei olam* ("Whose strength and might fill the world") immediately after hearing a clap of thunder.[10]

One must recite the blessings within the time period of *toch kedei dibbur* (i.e. the amount of time required to say three words[11]) after seeing the lightning or hearing the thunder.[12] If one saw the lightning and heard the thunder simultaneously, he only recites *oseh ma'aseh bereshis*.[13]

These blessings may only be recited once a day. The only exception to this rule is if the storm clouds dispersed and the sky cleared, and then a new storm arose. In this case, one recites the blessings for thunder and lightning twice in one day.[14]

7.   When one sees a rainbow he recites the blessing *zocher ha-bris v'ne'eman bi-veriso v'kayam b'ma'amaro* ("Who remembers the covenant, and is faithful to His covenant and keeps His word").[15] Halachic sources mention that one should not look at the rainbow for too long.

Blessings recited when one sees a tree in bloom

8.   One who sees fruit trees blossoming during the month of Nissan[17] recites the blessing: *she-lo chisar ba-olamo klum* ("Who ensured that nothing is lacking in His world, and Who created in the world beautiful creations and beautiful trees so as to delight man").[16] Some people recite *she-lo chisar ba-olamo davar*, instead of *she-lo chisar ba-olamo klum*.

Sephardic Jews recite various prayers when they recite this blessing. This blessing is recited only once a year, during the month of Nissan.

Tefillas Ha-Derech (The traveler's prayer)

9.   *Tefillas Ha-Derech* is recited when traveling.[18]

The text of this prayer includes a request for God's protection from any dangers or misfortunes during the trip, as well as a request to arrive safely at the destination. This prayer is customarily followed by various verses whose theme is God's protection and His salvation from troubles. *Tefillas Ha-Derech*, as well as the additional verses, are printed in the *Siddur*.

If possible, one should stop his vehicle (or stop walking) when reciting *Tefillas Ha-Derech*.[19]

10.   *Tefillas Ha-Derech* is only recited when one's route includes a stretch of unpopulated land one *parsah* long.[20] A *parsah* is 8000 *amos*. According

to the Chazon Ish, one *parsah* is about 4610 meters (5041.5 yards). According to Rav Chaim Na'eh, one *parsah* is about 3820 meters (4177.6 yards).

11.   *Tefillas Ha-Derech* should be recited within the first *parsah* after leaving the environs of the city or populated area. If one did not recite *Tefillas Ha-Derech* within the first *parsah* after leaving the populated area, he may recite it anywhere along the way. One who remembers that he did not recite *Tefillas Ha-Derech* when he is within one *parsah* of his destination should recite *Tefillas Ha-Derech* without the closing blessing, *shome'a tefillah.*[21]

12.   *Tefillas Ha-Derech* is only recited once a day. This rule even applies to a person who rested for several hours during his trip. If the trip spans a few days, one should recite *Tefillas Ha-Derech* each day.[22]

If a person traveled through the night he recites *Tefillas Ha-Derech* in the morning, but omits the concluding blessing.[23] This rule applies to someone who rested for a short time during the night.

A person who planned to spend the night at a certain place, and then changed his mind and decided to continue his trip, must recite *Tefillas Ha-Derech* even if he already recited it that day.

A table of measurements can be found on p. 126.

Table of Measurements

This table is cited at various points in the text, where the measurements defined here are listed. This table lists three views. With regard to *mitzvos* of the Torah we usually follow a stringent opinion, whereas with regard to rabbinically ordained *mitzvos* we follow a lenient opinion. Sometimes the larger measure is the more stringent opinion, while at other times the smaller measure is the more stringent. The views sometimes give two measurements as a conversion of single Torah measure. One should receive direction regarding when to apply each measurement. One should also receive direction from an expert in these *halachos* as to which opinion one should use in a given situation (e.g. how much one must eat to be able to recite a *berachah acharonah*, etc.)[1]

	According to the Chazon Ish	According to Rav Chaim Na'eh	According to Rav Moshe Feinstein
LENGTH			
Agudal, width of a thumb	.95 inch (2.4 cm)	.8 inch (2 cm)	.9 inch (2.24 cm)
Tefach, width of a fist	3.8 inches (9.6 cm)	3.2 inches (8 cm)	3.5 inches (9 cm)
Amah, cubit (the length of an arm from the elbow to the tips of the fingers)	22.7 inches (57.6 cm)	18.9 inches (48 cm)	21.3 inches (54 cm)
VOLUME			
K'zayis, size of an olive one-half egg[2] one-third egg[2]	1.7 oz (50 cc) 1.2 oz (33 cc)	.9-1 oz (27-30.2 cc) .58-.65 fl oz (17.3-19.3 cc)[4]	1.1-1.5 oz (32.5-44.3 ml) .7-1 oz (20.7-29.6 ml)
L'chumrah,[3]	as small as an average olive, 3 cc		
K'beitzah,[5] size of an egg	1.7-3.38 oz. (50-100 cc)[6]	1.95 fl oz (57.6 ml)	1.9-2.95 fl oz (52-87.1 ml)
LIQUID CAPACITY			
Revi'is, one-quarter of a *lug*	5.07 oz (150 cc)	2.9 oz (86 cc)	3.3-4.4 oz (97.6-130.7 ml)
TIME			
Kedei Achilas Pras,[7]	2-9 minutes	4-9 minutes	3-9 minutes

1. *K'zayis, k'beitzah,* and *revi'is* are cubic measures. We have converted these measures into their cubic equivalents because different articles have different densities.   2. One opinion holds a *k'zayis* to be a half egg, another holds it to be a third of an egg.   3. According to the Chazon Ish, although a *k'zayis* is the size of an actual olive, one must conduct himself according to an opinion that the measure is far greater as well, hence the two measures.   4. Rav Na'eh brings an opinion that 14.4 cc of food is considered a *safek k'zayis.*   5. A *k'beitzah* is the measure of an egg with its shell.   6. The smaller measure is based in todays' average size egg, the larger measure assumes eggs in early times were twice the size of today's.   7. The time required to eat 3-4 *k'beitzim* of bread. One should observe the shorter amount of time for *kedei achilas pras* when dealing with the maximum time period for eating. One who must eat on Yom Kippur should observe the longer amount of time for *kedei achilas pras.*

Metric conversions: Length, One inch = 2.54 centimeters. **Volume,** One fluid ounce (USA) or 1.8 cubic inches = 29.57 milliliters or cubic centimeters.

Part Three: Shabbos

⟨⟨⟩⟩

"The Holy One said to Moshe, 'I have a precious gift in My treasure house called Shabbos, and I wish to give it to Israel'" (*Shabbos* 10b).

God blessed Shabbos and declared it to be holy. This is derived from the verse, "And God blessed the seventh day and declared it to be holy, for it was on this day that He ceased from all the work that He had been creating (so that it would continue) to function" (*Bereshis* 2:3).

By observing Shabbos, we demonstrate our faith in God, Who created heaven and earth. Just as God created the world in six days and rested on the seventh, we rest from our work on the seventh day. This is derived from the verse, "The Israelites shall thus keep the Shabbos, making it a day of rest for all generations, as an eternal covenant. It is a sign between Me and the Israelites forever that God made heaven and earth in six days, and on the seventh day He ceased working and rested" (*Shemos* 31:16-17).

Shabbos also commemorates the Exodus from Egypt. This is derived from the verse, "And you shall remember that you were a slave in the land of Egypt, and the Almighty, your God took you out from there with a strong hand and a show of power. Therefore, the Almighty, your God commands you to keep the Sabbath day" (*Devarim* 5:15). At the Exodus from Egypt, we ceased being a nation of slaves, and became a nation of free men, the people of God.

The Exodus from Egypt is one of the firm foundations of our faith in God. By observing the Shabbos, we express the freedom we attained at the Exodus, as well as our faith and devotion to God Who took us out from slavery to freedom, and gave us His Torah.

Rest and holiness

Shabbos is not merely an opportunity for physical rest; it is an exalted and sublime day that we utilize for spiritual inspiration. We state in the Shabbos

127

Minchah service, "You have given a day of rest and holiness to Your people. Avraham rejoices, Yitzchak sings joyously, and Ya'akov and his sons rest thereon. A rest of love and free will, a rest of truth and faithfulness, a rest of peace and tranquility, and of serenity and security, a perfect rest with which You are pleased. Your children will realize and know that their rest comes from You, and through their rest, they sanctify Your Name."

Shabbos has the power to release us from weekday concerns. This enables us to rise above the mundane atmosphere of the six weekdays, and feel the spirituality of the seventh day — a taste of, "the cessation of work and the rest of the eternal world" (*Birkas Ha-mazon* recited on Shabbos). For one who truly observes Shabbos, the spirituality and special mood of the Shabbos prayers and meals extends to the other days of the week. Thus, Shabbos becomes a source of inspiration and holiness to the days that precede and follow it.

Shabbos has its own *mitzvos* and prayers. The *mitzvos*, prayers and festive meals are discussed in the following chapters. This discussion is followed by an explanation of the laws concerning activities which are prohibited on Shabbos.

Chapter Sixteen

Preparing for Shabbos and Lighting Candles

General preparations

1. On Friday one prepares for Shabbos. The preparations for Shabbos are similar to those that are done for an important guest.[1]

"And you shall call Shabbos a delight, and show honor to the day made holy by God" (*Yeshayahu* 58:13). The mitzvah to honor the Shabbos applies to everyone. Even when one's family and servants can make all the necessary preparations for Shabbos, one should nevertheless personally prepare at least one thing for Shabbos.[2]

2. It is a special mitzvah to buy things for Shabbos early on Friday morning. This mitzvah is derived from the Torah's account of the manna that fell for the Israelites in the Sinai desert. The Torah relates that a double portion of manna fell on Friday for that day and for Shabbos. "On Friday, [the Israelites] shall prepare that which they will bring in" (*Shemos* 16:5). We know the manna fell early in the morning, from the verse, "They gathered it [the manna] early in the morning" (*Shemos* 16:21). The manna was also prepared on Friday morning for Shabbos.

Nevertheless, foods which require lengthy preparation should be bought on Thursday. In the winter, when the days are short, it is preferable to shop on Thursday.[3]

Our Sages relate that God determines a person's income for the entire year on Rosh Hashana. The two exceptions are the expenses incurred to honor Shabbos and *Yom Tov*, and the expenses incurred to teach his children Torah. In these specific areas, if one increases his expenditures, he is fully compensated.

129

Therefore, a person can freely purchase delicacies and special food items for Shabbos without worrying that he is diminishing his disposable income.

Tasty dishes should be prepared for all the Shabbos meals. It is a mitzvah to taste the dishes while they are being prepared to ensure that they are appetizing. (See Chapter 13, Section 8, regarding reciting a blessing when tasting food.) Everyone should have meat, wine, and other foods for their Shabbos meals, according to their means.[4]

It is desirable to have fish at each of the three Shabbos meals, unless one dislikes fish. (Shabbos is meant to be enjoyed, not to be cumbersome.)

It is customary for women to bake challahs (special braided bread) on Friday. This is done to honor Shabbos by making especially festive foods, and to give women the opportunity to fulfill the mitzvah of "separating *challah*." The *halachos* of separating *challah* are discussed in Chapter 37, Sections 21-25.

3.   The house should be cleaned and put in order in honor of Shabbos.
     Tablecloths should be put on the tables in the dining room, and the table should be set in honor of Shabbos. It is fitting to cover all the tables in the house with tablecloths. The tables should remain covered throughout Shabbos.[5]

Some people put two tablecloths on the table, so the table will not be exposed if the top tablecloth is removed to shake off the crumbs.

The Shabbos table should be set before Shabbos begins so that everything is ready for the meal when the family members return from the synagogue on Friday night.[6]

Our holy books advise that one should spend time repenting for his misdeeds, and improving his ways on *erev Shabbos*. This is so he can enter Shabbos clean from sin.[7]

Bathing, haircuts, nail-cutting

4.   One should bathe with hot water on Friday, in honor of Shabbos. If one is unable to bathe, he should at least wash his face, hands, and feet with hot water.

Some men have the custom to immerse themselves in a *mikveh* in honor of Shabbos.

If a person needs a haircut, it is a mitzvah to have it done in honor of Shabbos.[8]

5.   One should cut his fingernails on Friday. Some details pertaining to nail cutting are as follows. Some people do not cut their finger- and toenails on the same day. These people cut their toenails on Thursday and their fingernails on Friday. Some people do not cut their hair or nails on *Rosh Chodesh*. The Gemara states that one who burns his nails is pious; one who buries them is righteous; and one who throws them to where people walk is wicked. Therefore, one should not leave his nail clippings around. If his nail clippings fell to the floor the person should sweep them up. It is preferable not to cut one's nails in order. Rather, the left hand's nails should be cut in this order (the thumb is A): D-B-E-C-A. Similarly, the right hand's nails should be cut in this order: B-D-A-C-E.[9]

6.   The prophet *Yeshayahu* says about Shabbos, "You shall honor it, and not conduct your regular affairs on it" (*Yeshayahu* 58:13). Regarding the words "honor it," our sages comment, "Your Shabbos clothing should not be like your weekday clothing."

A person should wear nicer clothes on Shabbos. If possible, a man should have a special *tallis* for Shabbos.[10] One should change into his Shabbos clothing before Shabbos begins.

Clothes that are needed for Shabbos should be washed on Thursday, so there will be sufficient time on Friday for the other Shabbos preparations.[10*]

Halachos pertaining to meals, work, and travel on Friday

7.   One way we honor Shabbos is by not eating a large meal on Friday afternoon, so we will have an appetite for the Shabbos night meal.

There are many *halachos* regarding the meals eaten on Friday. The following are a few of the details relating to these *halachos*:

   * One should not eat the kind of festive meal on Friday that one does not usually eat during the week. For example, one should not have a party with friends or a *siyum* celebration upon the completion of a Talmudic tractate.

   * A meal celebrating a mitzvah which must be done on a specific day, such as a *bris milah*, or a *pidyon ha-ben* (the redemption of a firstborn son), is eaten on Friday. However, it is a mitzvah to have the meal before noon.

* A normal meal may be eaten on Friday, but it is a mitzvah to avoid eating a meal during the last quarter of the day.

During the short winter days, it is a mitzvah to refrain from eating a meal even before the last quarter of the day, so that one will have an appetite for the Shabbos night meal.

* It is permitted to have a snack throughout the day.[11]

8.   One should not set Friday afternoon aside for doing substantial work. This rule applies from the earliest time for reciting *Minchah*. One may rely on the halachic opinion that this prohibition only begins from the time of *Minchah Ketanah* (i.e. two-and-a-half *sha'os zemanios* before sunset).

However, casual work, like letter-writing, etc., is permitted throughout the day. Work that is required for Shabbos, like mending a Shabbos dress, cooking, baking, cleaning, etc., may be done anytime on Friday.[12]

One may travel on Friday if he is expected at his destination, and people have prepared his Shabbos meals. This rule even applies to traveling to distant locations. However, it is essential not to start one's trip too late in the day. One must make sure not to arrive after Shabbos begins. One must leave enough time so that if he is delayed unexpectedly, he will not transgress Shabbos. If one must prepare for Shabbos upon his arrival at his destination, he should plan to arrive early enough to take care of the necessary preparations before Shabbos.

To help avoid transgressing *melachos* on Shabbos, it is advisable to prepare various things before Shabbos, as is discussed in Chapter 21.

The Mitzvah of Lighting Shabbos Candles

9.   One lights candles before Shabbos begins. The candlelight creates an atmosphere of peace and tranquility in the home. It is also one of the ways in which we honor Shabbos, and demonstrate its importance.

10.   The primary mitzvah is to light candles in the room where the Shabbos meal will be served. One recites the appropriate blessing after lighting the candles. There must also be sufficient light in the other rooms of the house that will be used.[13]

The mitzvah of lighting the Shabbos candles is principally the woman's. Every member of the household fulfills his mitzvah to light Shabbos candles when the woman lights her Shabbos candles. It is commendable for her husband to place the candles in the candlesticks and prepare them for lighting.

When there is no woman in the house, the man lights the Shabbos candles.[14]

11. From the moment a woman lights the candles, she must observe the sanctity of Shabbos, and refrain from doing things which are forbidden on Shabbos. (The activities which are prohibited on Shabbos are discussed in Chapter 20.)

A woman who normally recites *Minchah* must do so before she lights the candles, because once she has accepted the sanctity of Shabbos, she may no longer recite weekday prayers.[15]

Lighting Shabbos candles

12. After lighting the Shabbos candles, one recites the blessing *asher kideshanu b'mitzvosav v'tzivanu l'hadlik ner shel Shabbos* ("Who sanctified us with His *mitzvos* and commanded us to light the Shabbos candles").[16] The woman covers her face with her hands while reciting the blessing, so as not to derive benefit from the light until after she has recited the blessing.[17]

Some Sephardic women have the custom to recite the blessing before lighting the candles.

A man who lights Shabbos candles has not accepted the sanctity of Shabbos upon himself. Some halachic authorities maintain that he should recite the blessing first, and then light the candles.

13. There are two verses in the Torah regarding Shabbos: "Remember the Shabbos day to sanctify it" (*Shemos* 20:8), and "Observe the Shabbos day to sanctify it" (*Devarim* 5:12). God said both verses at the Revelation on Mount Sinai. Many women light two candles, which correspond to the words "remember" and "observe," that are mentioned in these two verses.[18] Other women light more than two candles. Many women have the custom to light one candle for each member of their immediate family (one for themselves, one for their husband, and one for each of their children).

14.   One must make sure that the candle's wick (or the wick of the oil lamps, if one is using oil) was well lit, so that the flame will burn brightly when the match is removed.

One may not open a window or door if the draft will blow out the candles.[19]

One may not taste anything, including water, from the beginning of Shabbos until after *Kiddush*.[20] Children till bar or bas mitzvah may eat before *Kiddush*.

Some people who light the candles on the table where the Shabbos meals will be eaten place a challah on the table before lighting the candles. This prevents the table from being *muktzeh* (an item forbidden to be moved on Shabbos; for more details, see Chapter 20, Section 97).[21]

Where a guest should light candles

15.   A person who is sleeping at home, but is eating the Friday night meal in another place, should light Shabbos candles at home.

A guest who was given his own room to sleep in should light the candles in that room, even if he is not eating in that room, and even if his wife is lighting candles at home.[22]

One who lights the candles in a room where he will not be eating the Shabbos meal must use large candles which will burn long enough for him to benefit from the light when he returns to that room.[23]

A guest who does not have his own room to sleep in should join in his host's Shabbos candles by giving his host a token sum to cover his portion in the candles. Alternatively, the host may give the guest a portion of the candles as a gift.[24]

If the guest's wife is lighting candles at home, and he does not have his own room to sleep in, he does not have to share in his host's Shabbos candles.

16.   If a number of women are lighting candles in one room, each one lights her own candles and recites the blessing.

Some Sephardic Jews have the custom that each woman lights her own candles, but only one woman recites the blessing, exempting all the others. She must intend to exempt them, and they must answer Amen and intend to be exempted by her blessing.[25]

If a number of men are sharing a room, and their host is not sleeping with them, only one man is required to light Shabbos candles. The others partake by giving a token sum for their share of the candles. The one who lights the candles must intend to exempt all the others with his blessing, and they must intend to be exempted from their obligation when he lights his Shabbos candles.[26] See Section 15, above, regarding how to proceed if the host is sleeping in the same room as his guests.

"A mitzvah is a candle and Torah is light" (*Mishlei* 6:23)

17. The Talmud (*Shabbos* 23b) states that in the merit of lighting Shabbos candles, parents are blessed with sons who will be Torah scholars. This is derived from the verse *ner mitzvah v'Torah or*, "a mitzvah is a candle and Torah is light" (*Mishlei* 6:23), i.e. through the mitzvah performed with candles, one merits the light of Torah.

Therefore, many women recite a prayer after lighting the Shabbos candles requesting that their sons become Torah scholars, that their children follow in the way of Torah, and that they be given Divine assistance in all their endeavors.

For many women, these moments are a special time when they feel spiritually uplifted and close to God.

The prescribed time to light Shabbos candles

18. Shabbos officially begins at sunset. However, one is required to "add to the holy from the ordinary," i.e. to refrain from doing work some time before sunset. This refraining from doing work is called *tosefes Shabbos*, and it must be observed even if one has not yet accepted Shabbos upon himself.

If one did not light candles on time, and sunset is imminent, one may no longer light the candles since this is a form of work that may not be done on Shabbos.

Shabbos candles should be lit at a certain determined time before sunset.

The weekly time for candle-lighting in various cities can be found on Jewish calendars. The candle-lighting times are calculated on the basis of a set amount of minutes before sunset. This amount of time can be between eighteen and forty minutes, depending on local custom.

One may light the candles and accept the sanctity of Shabbos upon himself from as early as *Pelag Ha-Minchah* (one-and-a-quarter *sha'os zemanios*) before sunset. (See Chapter 7, Section 26, for the definition of a *sha'ah zemanis*.)

19.   Below is a table listing the time for lighting candles in selected cities. The times are listed according to standard time, not Daylight Savings Time.

Candle Lighting Times

DATE		JERUSALEM	TEL-AVIV	HAIFA	DATE		JERUSALEM	TEL-AVIV	HAIFA
Jan.	**1**	16.11	16.25	16.14	**July**	**1**	18.13	18.29	18.22
Jan.	**10**	16.18	16.32	16.22	**July**	**10**	18.12	18.28	18.21
Jan.	**20**	16.27	16.41	16.31	**July**	**20**	18.08	18.24	18.17
Feb.	**1**	16.38	16.52	16.42	**Aug.**	**1**	18.01	18.16	18.09
Feb.	**10**	16.46	17.00	16.50	**Aug.**	**10**	17.53	18.08	18.01
Feb.	**20**	16.54	17.09	16.59	**Aug.**	**20**	17.43	17.58	17.50
Mar.	**1**	17.01	17.16	17.07	**Sep.**	**1**	17.28	17.43	17.35
Mar.	**10**	17.08	17.23	17.14	**Sep.**	**10**	17.17	17.32	17.23
Mar.	**20**	17.15	17.30	17.21	**Sep.**	**20**	17.04	17.19	17.10
Apr.	**1**	17.23	17.38	17.30	**Oct.**	**1**	16.49	17.04	16.55
Apr.	**10**	17.29	17.44	17.36	**Oct.**	**10**	16.38	16.53	16.43
Apr.	**20**	17.36	17.51	17.43	**Oct.**	**20**	16.27	16.41	16.32
May	**1**	17.43	17.59	17.51	**Nov.**	**1**	16.15	16.29	16.19
May	**10**	17.50	18.05	17.58	**Nov.**	**10**	16.08	16.22	16.12
May	**20**	17.57	18.12	18.05	**Nov.**	**20**	16.02	16.17	16.06
June	**1**	18.04	18.19	18.12	**Dec.**	**1**	16.00	16.14	16.03
June	**10**	18.09	18.24	18.17	**Dec.**	**10**	16.00	16.14	16.04
June	**20**	18.12	18.27	18.21	**Dec.**	**20**	16.03	16.18	16.07

Chapter Seventeen

Friday Night

Kabbalas Shabbos (Welcoming Shabbos)

1.　The Shabbos evening service begins with the recitation of *Kabbalas Shabbos*. *Kabbalas Shabbos* is comprised of a selection from *Tehillim*, the poem *Lechah Dodi* (composed by the sixteenth-century kabbalist, Rabbi Shlomo HaLevy Alkabetz, in Safed), and other prayers.

When it is close to sunset, the congregants welcome the Shabbos by reciting *Mizmor shir l'yom ha-Shabbos*, as well as other chapters of *Tehillim* that comprise *Kabbalas Shabbos*. *Kabbalas Shabbos* should be recited on time, and the congregation should not wait for congregants who have not yet arrived.

It is proper to arrive at the synagogue on time, and recite *Kabbalas Shabbos* with the congregation. *Minchah* must be recited at its proper time, before *Kabbalas Shabbos*.

2.　After reciting the concluding words of *Lechah Dodi* (*bo'i kallah*), or after beginning the psalm *Mizmor shir l'yom ha-Shabbos*, work that is prohibited on Shabbos may no longer be done. This rule applies even if the sun has not yet set.[1] This cessation of work before Shabbos begins is called *tosefes Shabbos*, as is mentioned in Chapter 16, Section 18, above.

One may not perform work some time before sunset, whether or not one recited *Kabbalas Shabbos*. Women accept Shabbos upon themselves when they light Shabbos candles.

If the majority of a congregation has already accepted the Shabbos, other members who usually join in the service must also begin to observe Shabbos, even if they are not in the synagogue at that time. They may not perform any work prohibited on Shabbos, even if the sun has not yet set.[2]

Shabbos *Ma'ariv*

3.   *Ma'ariv* for Shabbos is recited after *Kabbalas Shabbos*. *Ma'ariv* includes *Kerias Shema* and its blessings, and the *Amidah*. (See Chapter 9 regarding the *halachos* pertaining to *Ma'ariv*.)

4.   The paragraph of *Hashkivenu* does not end with the words *shomer ammo Yisrael la'ad* as on weekdays. Instead it ends with the words *Ha-pores succas shalom*, etc. ("Who spreads His shelter of peace"). If one recited the weekday ending (*shomer ammo Yisrael la'ad*) and realized his mistake within the time of *toch kedei dibbur*, he may correct himself and recite the proper ending for Shabbos. If the person realized his error later, he need not repeat the blessing.[3] *Toch kedei dibbur* is the amount of time it takes to say the sentence *shalom aleicha rabbi u'mori*.[4]

5.   All the *Amidah* prayers which are recited on Shabbos (*Ma'ariv*, *Shacharis*, *Musaf*, and *Minchah*) contain seven blessings. The first three blessings and the last three blessings are the same as those recited during the week. The middle blessing focuses on the theme of Shabbos, and contains requests pertaining to this holy day. This blessing differs for each of the Shabbos services. The exact text for these blessings is printed in the *Siddur*.

6.   If after reciting the first three blessings of the *Amidah* during *Shacharis*, *Minchah* or *Ma'ariv*, one erred and continued reciting the weekday *Shemoneh Esreh* (i.e. he recited *Attah chonen*), he should conclude the blessing he was reciting when he realized his mistake, and then continue with the fourth blessing of the Shabbos *Amidah*. He does not repeat the first three blessings of the *Amidah*.[5] Regarding an error during *Musaf*, see Chapter 18, Section 14.

7.   After the *Amidah* of *Ma'ariv*, the passage of *Va-yechulu* (*Bereshis* 2:1-3) is recited aloud, while standing. It is best to recite it together with the congregation, or at least together with another person.[6]

The leader then recites the blessing *Me'ein Sheva*, which is a shortened version of the *Amidah*. *Me'ein Sheva* is also known as *Magen Avos* ("Shield of our Fathers"). One should not talk while *Va-yechulu* and *Me'ein Sheva* are being recited.[7] *Me'ein Sheva* is only recited by a *minyan* that always prays in the same place.[8] (In Jerusalem, it is customary to recite *Magen Avos* even if the *minyan* does not meet regularly.)

Rabbi Yosei said in the name of Rabbi Yehudah: "Two angels, one good and one bad, accompany a Jew home from the synagogue on Friday night. When they enter his home and find the candles lit, the table set, and the house in order, the good angel exclaims, 'May the next Shabbos be the same!' and the bad angel is forced to answer, 'Amen!' But if this is not the situation, the bad angel exclaims, 'May the next Shabbos be the same!' and the good angel is forced to answer, 'Amen!'" (*Shabbos* 119b). Therefore, the Shabbos table should be set before the family members return from the synagogue on Friday night, and everything should be ready when they return.

Before *Kiddush*

8.   Upon returning home from *Ma'ariv*, the song *Shalom Aleichem* is sung to the accompanying angels, and the passage *Eshes Chayil* ("Woman of Valor," *Mishlei* 31) is customarily recited or sung. *Eshes Chayil* is a hymn composed by *Shlomo Ha-Melech*, which praises the virtues of the Jewish woman, who is accomplished and successful in carrying out all her tasks, for the sake of God and His Torah. Additional prayers are printed in the *Siddur*.

It is customary for parents to bless their sons with the words *Yesimcha Elokim k'Efrayim v'chi-Menashe* ("May God make you like Efrayim and Menashe"), and their daughters with the words *Yesimeich Elokim k'Sarah, Rivkah, Rachel, v'Leah* ("May God make you like Sarah, Rivkah, Rachel, and Leah"). The three verses that comprise *Birkas Kohanim* are then recited: "May God bless and protect you. May God shine His countenance upon you. May God lift His countenance towards you and grant you peace" (*Bemidbar* 6:24-26).

Kiddush

9.   *Kiddush* is then recited over a cup of wine or grape juice.[9] The text for *Kiddush* is printed in the *Siddur*. As mentioned above, one should not taste anything from the time he accepts Shabbos until after *Kiddush*.

The Rambam writes in *Hilchos Shabbos* (Chapter 29:1,6):

> It is a positive mitzvah from the Torah to make the day of Shabbos holy with words. This is derived from the verse in the Torah, "Remember the Shabbos day to sanctify it" (*Shemos* 20:8), which means: Remember it with a commemorative (mention) of praise and *Kiddush* (sanctification), etc. According to the words of the *Sofrim* (this means) to make *Kiddush* over wine.

10.   Women are obligated to observe the mitzvah of *Kiddush*, as well as all the other laws of Shabbos.[10]

Halachos pertaining to *Kiddush*

11.   The cup used for *Kiddush* should hold at least a *revi'is*. According to the Chazon Ish, a *revi'is* is 150 cc (5.07 oz). According to Rav Chaim Na'eh, a *revi'is* is 86 cc (2.9 oz). The cup must be full when *Kiddush* is recited.[11]

The cup used for *Kiddush* must be whole, without any cracks.

Before *Kiddush*, the cup should be thoroughly rinsed with water, both inside and out. If someone took a drink from the cup of wine (or directly from the wine bottle) before *Kiddush*, the wine is considered *pagum* (unfit for ritual use), and may not be used for *Kiddush*. One may remedy this situation by adding a little wine, or another liquid (that is not considered *pagum*) to the wine.[12]

The one who is reciting *Kiddush* should pick up the cup with both of his hands. (This is a way of demonstrating one's love of the mitzvah.) One should hold the cup in his right hand when he starts reciting *Kiddush*. According to *Kabbalah*, the base of the cup should rest on the palm of the person's hand, with his fingers facing upwards around the cup. The cup should be lifted at least a *tefach* above the table (see the Table of Measures at the end of Chapter 15).

God's Name is hinted at with the initial letters of the first four words of *Kiddush*: *Yom Ha-shishi Va-yechulu Ha-shamayim* and so it is customary to stand when saying these words. There are various customs concerning whether to sit or stand while reciting the rest of *Kiddush*. The text for *Kiddush* is printed in the *Siddur*.

If wine is left over in the cup after *Kiddush*, and one would like to pour the wine back in the bottle to be used another time, it is customary to add unused wine to the cup before pouring it back into the bottle. This is done so the wine in the bottle does not become *pagum*.

Fulfilling one's obligation during *Kiddush*

12.   When a number of people are having their Shabbos meal together, it is customary for the host or one of the other participants to recite *Kiddush* aloud and exempt the others. This is done because, "A king is more glorified when a multitude joins to honor him" (*Mishlei* 14:28). That is to say, God is more revered when many people jointly participate in one *berachah*, than if each person present recited his own *berachah*. The one reciting *Kiddush*

must intend to exempt all those present, and those present must listen to every word of the *Kiddush*, intending to be exempted. They should respond Amen at the end of each blessing. Those being exempted do not reply *Baruch Hu u'varuch Shemo* while listening to the blessing.

13. The one who recited *Kiddush* drinks a *melo logmav* (a *melo logmav* is equal to the greater part of a *revi'is*). He should drink this amount of wine without pausing. If, in the middle of drinking, he pauses for longer than *kedei achilas pras* he has not fulfilled this requirement.[13] (For the exact time of *kedei achilas pras*, see the Table of Measures at the end of Chapter 15.) It is important that there be no interruption (e.g. talking) between hearing *Kiddush* and drinking the wine.

If the one who recited *Kiddush* did not taste the wine, and one of the listeners drank the required amount in his place, all the listeners have fulfilled their obligation. It is preferable for all those present to taste the wine too.

If no one drank an entire *melo logmav* of wine, but all the participants together consumed a *melo logmav* within the time of *kedei achilas pras*, all those who heard *Kiddush* have fulfilled the mitzvah.[14]

Additional laws

14. If there is no wine available, the Friday night *Kiddush* is recited over bread. In this case, *netilas yadayim* is performed before *Kiddush*, and *ha-motzi* is recited during *Kiddush* instead of *borei peri ha-gafen*. This is the only change made during *Kiddush*. The one who recites *Kiddush* should place his hands on the bread until he has finished reciting *Kiddush*.[15]

15. *Borei peri ha-gafen* recited during *Kiddush* exempts one from having to recite *borei peri ha-gafen* before wine one intended on drinking during the meal. Similarly, *Birkas Ha-mazon* recited at the end of the meal exempts one from having to recite a separate *berachah acharonah* for the wine he drank during *Kiddush* or during the meal.[16]

16. The table should be covered with a tablecloth, and a cloth should be spread over the challahs. The challahs should remain covered until after *Kiddush*. Some keep the challas covered till after *ha-motzi*.

One reason why the two challahs are covered on the top and the bottom, is to commemorate the manna which the Israelites ate in the desert, which was protected by an upper and lower layer of dew.[17]

The Halachos Pertaining to the Shabbos Meal

Netilas yadayim and *ha-motzi*

17.   "*Kiddush* must be recited where the meal will be held." One must begin the meal immediately after *Kiddush*, in the place where *Kiddush* was recited.[18] (The *halachos* of *netilas yadayim*, the blessings recited during a meal, and the *halachos* of *Birkas Ha-mazon* are cited in Chapters 11-12.)

One washes his hands, recites the blessing *al netilas yadayim*, dries his hands, and recites *ha-motzi* over *lechem mishneh* (two whole loaves of bread). Two loaves of any type of bread (buns, challahs, pitas, etc.) may be used as long as they are whole. *Lechem mishneh* commemorates the double portion of manna which fell on Friday, sufficing for both Friday and Shabbos.[19]

Cutting the challah

18.   One holds both challahs in his hand while reciting *ha-motzi*. He should lift the challahs when mentioning God's Name. Many people have the custom to place one challah on top of the other while reciting the blessing. On Friday evening, the lower challah should be placed slightly closer to the person reciting the blessing than the one on top. One cuts the lower loaf after concluding the blessing.[20] See Chapter 18, Section 18 for the details regarding how to cut the challah during the Shabbos day meal.

One should not cut the *lechem mishneh* before he has recited *ha-motzi*. It is customary for the person reciting *ha-motzi* to mark the loaf with the knife at the place where he will cut it after reciting the blessing.[21]

One may not speak from the time he washes his hands until he swallows some of the bread, as mentioned above in Chapter 11, Section 10.

Exempting others

19. When a group is eating a Shabbos meal together, one person may recite *ha-motzi* aloud and exempt the others. The person reciting *ha-motzi* must intend to exempt the other members of the group, and they must intend to be exempted with this blessing.[22] They should respond Amen to the blessing. As was mentioned above, many people have the custom for one person to exempt the others because of the principle, "A king is more glorified when a multitude joins to honor him" (*Mishlei* 14:28).

The one who cuts the bread should give each of those present a piece at least the size of a *k'zayis*.

All of those present must wait to taste the challah until the one who recited the blessing tastes it. The only exception to this rule is if each person has his own *lechem mishneh*.[23]

The Shabbos meal

20. It is a mitzvah to honor Shabbos by serving fish, meat, wine, and other food and drinks that a person enjoys. This is derived from the verse, "call the Shabbos a delight" (*Yeshayahu* 58:13).[24]

It is preferable to eat at least a bit more than a *k'beitzah* of challah during the Shabbos meal.

21. The section of *Retzei* is added in *Birkas Ha-mazon* (the complete passage is printed in the *Siddur*). The table in Chapter 12, Section 9 indicates how one should proceed if he forgot to recite *Retzei*.[25]

22. When *Birkas Ha-mazon* is recited with a *zimmun* (i.e. when three or more men over the age of thirteen recite *Birkas Ha-mazon* as a group), it is praiseworthy to recite it with a cup of wine (*kos shel berachah*). The one who leads the *zimmun* holds the cup of wine until he finishes reciting *Birkas Ha-mazon*. Then he recites *borei peri ha-gafen*, and drinks the wine. See Chapter 12, Section 8, for more details regarding the *kos shel berachah*.

The Shabbos meals make a major contribution towards molding the family, strengthening its spiritual ties, and imbuing the children with exalted values. The family sings *zemiros* (Shabbos hymns, which are generally printed in the *Siddur*, as well as in special booklets) and other Jewish songs. They discuss ideas from the weekly Torah portion, and other topics that pertain to Torah study, Halachah, and Jewish ethical teachings. Shabbos meals are a potential source of spiritual light for the whole week.

Shabbos *zemiros*

23. The Ari *z"l* and other kabbalists and Torah luminaries composed the Shabbos *zemiros*. These hymns express the sublime holiness of Shabbos, and praise the Almighty for granting His nation such a holy day. They also express the yearnings of the Jewish soul for its Father in Heaven, and for the Shabbos day. For instance, the hymn written by Rabbi Avraham ibn Ezra, *Tzam'ah Nafshi*, has as its refrain:

> My soul thirsts for the Almighty, for the living God
>
> My heart and my flesh exult in the living God.

These songs also emphasize faith in God, Who created the world in six days and ceased creating on the seventh. For example, *Menuchah v'Simchah* (written by an unknown composer) begins:

> Rest and rejoicing, the Jews have light
>
> A day of rest, a day of pleasures
>
> Those who guard [the Shabbos] and keep it thereby testify
>
> That in six days all was created and established.

Shabbos rest is intimately connected to the Final Redemption. "The day when work ceased and one rests is akin to the world to come" *(me'ein olam ha-ba)*. The Shabbos hymns also express our yearnings for the eternal repose of the Messianic Era:

> With *mishneh lechem*, and a beautiful *Kiddush*
>
> Many tasty delights and a magnanimous spirit
>
> Those who delight in the Shabbos will merit much good
>
> In the world to come when the Redeemer arrives. (*Menuchah v'Simchah*)

Chapter Eighteen

Shabbos Day

Shacharis for Shabbos

1. *Shacharis* recited on Shabbos differs from that recited during the week in that it includes additional prayers. Various passages from *Tehillim* are added to *Pesukei D'zimrah*. *Nishmas Kol Chai* is recited before *Yishtabach*. When reciting *Nishmas Kol Chai*, we thank and praise God for His great kindness with us and the entire universe.

See Chapter 7, Sections 10-14, regarding how one should proceed if he arrived at synagogue when the congregation was in the middle of reciting *Pesukei D'zimrah*.

Various passages are added to the first blessing preceding *Kerias Shema* (*yotzer or*). These passages discuss Shabbos.

The Shabbos *Amidah* also differs from the weekday *Amidah*, as is discussed in Chapter 17, Section 5. The *halachah* regarding one who erred while reciting the *Amidah* on Shabbos is discussed in Chapter 17, Section 6.

The Torah reading

2. The weekly Torah portion is read from a *sefer Torah* after *Shacharis*.[1]
    The Torah is divided into sections (*parashiyos*) and one section is read every week. This section is called the *parashas ha-shavua*.[2] The reading of the entire Torah is completed every year on Simchas Torah. The *halachos* regarding reading the Torah are discussed at length in Chapter 7, Sections 89-100.

3. The Torah is only read if a *minyan* is present.[3] When the Torah is taken out of the *Aron Ha-Kodesh*, the leader and the congregation recite several verses and prayers which are printed in the *Siddur*.

145

4.   The *parashas ha-shavua* is divided into seven sections. A different man
received an *aliyah* before each section is read. A *Kohen* receives the first
aliyah, and a *Levi* receives the second *aliyah*.[5] *Yisraelim* receive the other
aliyos. The man who received the *aliyah*[4] recites the blessings before and
after his section is read. (For details regarding how this is done, see Chapter
7, Sections 93-97.)[6]

The Torah scroll is rolled closed before the man who recieved the *aliyah* recites the after-blessing and remains closed between *aliyos*. When a longer interruption occurs, for example when *Kaddish* or a *Mi she-berach* is recited, the
scroll is also covered.[7] Sephardic Jews cover the scroll with a cloth between
aliyos, and close the scroll when there is a longer interruption.

The different priorities concerning who receives an *aliyah* are discussed in
Be'ur Halachah, Chapter 136. Among those who have precedence is a man
on the day of his wedding, a man on the Shabbos before his wedding, and
a boy who just became bar mitzvah.

5.   Half-*Kaddish* is recited after the Torah portion is read.[8] Following half-
Kaddish, the last verses of the portion (called the *maftir*) are read again.
A *Kohen* or *Levi* may receive the *maftir aliyah*.

On a special Shabbos, such as *Shabbos Rosh Chodesh*, two scrolls are taken out
of the *Aron Ha-Kodesh*. The *parashas ha-shavua* is read from the first scroll, and
a passage which discusses the special sacrifices which were offered in the
Temple is read from the second scroll. This special passage is the *maftir*.

6.   After reading the *maftir*, the *sefer Torah* is lifted up high so that the
entire congregation can see its script. The scroll is then rolled closed
and covered with its mantle.

In Sephardic and several other communities, the *sefer Torah* is raised and its
script shown to the congregation before the Torah is read.[9]

The *haftarah* (Reading from the prophets)

7.   After the *sefer Torah* is lifted, the *haftarah* is read.[10] The *haftarah* is a
section from the Prophets, whose content is in some way connected
to the *parashas ha-shavua*. On a special Shabbos, when two scrolls are read
from, the *haftarah* pertains to the week's special event (i.e. *Rosh Chodesh*, or
the upcoming holiday). (The *haftarah* is usually printed in the *Chumash*,

after the *parashas ha-shavua*.)[11] The man who receives the *maftir aliyah* recites the blessings before and after the *haftarah*. (These blessings are printed in the *Siddur* and *Chumash*.) Those who receive *aliyos* should recite their blessings aloud, so the congregation can hear them, and respond Amen after each one.[12]

8. The congregants should listen attentively when the Torah and *haftarah* are read aloud. They may not speak when the Torah and *haftarah* are being read, or when the blessings for them are recited.

The obligation to read the Torah twice and the *Targum* once

9. Men must study the *parashas ha-shavua* every week, before hearing it read in the synagogue. One fulfills this obligation by reading the text of the *parashah* twice, and the *Targum* once.[13] (The *Targum* is the Aramaic translation and explanation of the Torah authored by Unkelus, a contemporary of the *Tanna'im*.) Most *Chumashim* have the *Targum* printed alongside the text of the Torah. Some people read each verse of the Torah twice, followed by the *Targum* for that verse. Others read each subsection (i.e. the Torah is divided into subsections with the letter *phey* or *samech* inbetween them) twice, and then study the *Targum*.[14] This course of study is referred to as *shenayim mikra v'echad Targum*, "reading the Torah twice, and the *Targum* once." It is also referred to by its Hebrew acronym, *SHeMOT*.

10. One may substitute the *Targum* with Rashi's commentary. Verses for which Rashi has no commentary should be read three times. One who is God-fearing studies both the *Targum* and Rashi.[15]

One who does not understand Rashi's commentary may substitute a commentary which explains the *parashah* according to Rashi's commentary, and is based on the Talmud. This commentary may be studied in any language one understands.

11. There are two very good ways to fulfill one's obligation to study the Torah twice and the *Targum* once. Either one can study the entire *parashas ha-shavua* and the accompanying *Targum* on Friday, or one can study a section of what he is obligated to study each day of the week, and complete the entire portion on Friday. If one was unable to complete the course of study before Shabbos, he should complete it before the Shabbos day meal.

If he delayed past that time, he should complete it before *Minchah*, or at least no later than the following Tuesday. If one missed this, he should nevertheless complete his reading of all the weekly portions by Simchas Torah.[16] One can begin studying *parashas ha-shavua* and *Targum* for the following week after reciting *Minchah* on Shabbos, which is when the first section of the next weekly portion is read.[17]

Musaf

12. After *Shacharis* and the Torah reading, *Ashrei* and some additional prayers are recited, followed by the *Amidah* for *Musaf*.[18] This prayer corresponds to the *Musaf* sacrifice which was offered in the Temple on Shabbos. The *Musaf Amidah* includes verses describing the *Musaf* sacrifice, as well as a request for God to restore the Temple service, and that we once again merit offering the sacrifices.

13. The prescribed time for reciting *Musaf* is after *Shacharis*. It should not be delayed later than the seventh *sha'ah zemanis*, i.e. one *sha'ah zemanis* after midday. (The exact time of midday is usually indicated on the halachic timetables published annually.) If one did not recite *Musaf* on time, he may recite it until sunset.[19]

14. If, after reciting the first three blessings in the *Musaf Amidah*, one erred and continued reciting the weekday *Shemoneh Esreh* (i.e. the passage of *Attah chonen*), he should immediately stop where he is and begin the middle blessing of *Musaf* (i.e. *Tikanta Shabbos*).[20]

The *Musaf Amidah* and its repetition by the leader are followed by *Ein k'Elokeinu*, *Pitum Ha-Ketores*, *Aleinu L'shabe'ach*, and some other prayers. All these prayers are printed in the *Siddur*.

The Shabbos day *Kiddush*

15. *Kiddush* is recited over a cup of wine (or grape juice) before the Shabbos morning meal. The main part of the Shabbos morning *Kiddush* is the blessing recited over the wine, *borei peri ha-gafen*. Some people precede *Kiddush* with various verses which discuss the holiness of Shabbos. One should not begin *Kiddush* with the words *al ken berach Hashem* etc. because they are in the middle of a verse. Rather, one must recite the verse from the beginning (*Ki sheshes yamim*).[21] The verses that comprise the Shabbos morning *Kiddush* are printed in the *Siddur*, following the Shabbos morning service.

If a number of people are eating the Shabbos meal together, the host or one of the participants can exempt the others with his recital of *Kiddush*. (For more details regarding how this is done, see Chapter 17, Sections 12-13, where *Kiddush* for Friday night is discussed.)

16. If no wine or grape juice is available for the morning *Kiddush*, the blessing can be recited over *chamar medinah* — a popular, respectable beverage. One who recites *Kiddush* over this type of beverage, recites the blessing *she-ha-kol niheyah bi-devaro* instead of *borei peri ha-gafen*. One only recites *Kiddush* over bread in the morning if he cannot obtain wine or *chamar medinah*. Beer is considered a *chamar medinah*. Some people recite *Kiddush* over brandy and similar beverages. One should check with a halachic authority as to which beverages are considered *chamar medinah* in his locale.[22]

17. One may not eat or drink anything before *Kiddush*. However, one may drink a beverage that is permitted before praying, before reciting *Shacharis*. (For more details, see Chapter 4, Sections 3-5.) The obligation to recite *Kiddush* in the morning only applies after reciting *Shacharis*.[23] This is because one is forbidden to eat a meal until he has recited *Shacharis*, and *Kiddush* is always connected to the following meal. One who is permitted to eat before praying, e.g. because of medical reasons, is obligated by the mitzvah of *Kiddush* before praying. Someone in this situation must recite *Kiddush* over wine or grape juice if he wants to eat.

According to the *Mishnah Berurah* (Chapter 269:1), children under bar mitzvah or bas mitzvah may eat before *Kiddush*.

The Shabbos morning meal

18. The table should be set on Shabbos morning so it is ready for the meal when the family returns from the synagogue. This is one of the ways in which we honor Shabbos.

The *halachos* pertaining to the Shabbos morning meal are the same as those pertaining to the evening meal (see Chapter 17, above). One must begin the meal immediately after *Kiddush*, in the place where *Kiddush* was recited. *Ha-motzi* is recited over *lechem mishneh* (during the day the upper loaf is sliced instead of the lower one), and *Retzei* is recited in *Birkas Ha-mazon*. Chapter

12, Section 9 has a table illustrating how to proceed if one forgot to recite *Retzei* during *Birkas Ha-mazon*.

19.   One can fulfill his obligation to eat a meal where *Kiddush* was recited by eating a *k'zayis* of baked goods following *Kiddush*.[24] However, since one is required to have three proper meals on Shabbos (i.e. to eat three meals with bread), he must still recite *ha-motzi* over *lechem mishneh* and eat a Shabbos day meal, in addition to the third meal (*Se'udah Shelishis*), which is eaten later.

One hundred blessings each day

20.   A person should try to recite at least one hundred blessings every day.

The blessings recited during prayers are included among the one hundred blessings.[25] Since the Shabbos *Amidah* only has seven blessings (instead of the nineteen blessings in the weekday *Amidah*), one must recite many extra blessings on Shabbos to reach the number one hundred. Therefore, a person should partake of fruits and pastries, smell spices, etc., so as to recite one hundred blessings on Shabbos.[26] However, when reciting a blessing before eating these foods, one should be careful not to recite a *berachah she-einah tzerichah*. (For details regarding a *berachah she-einah tzerichah*, see Chapter 10, Sections 6-7.)

Torah study on Shabbos

21.   The *Tur Orach Chayim* (290) cites the following Midrash:

> The Torah complained to the Holy One, blessed be He: "Master of the world! When (the people of) Israel will enter their Land, this one will hasten to his vineyard, and that one to his field — what will be with me?" The Almighty answered: "I have a partner for you, called Shabbos. On Shabbos they will set aside their work and will occupy themselves with Torah study."

After the Shabbos morning meal, one should set aside time for Torah study (this is referred to as *kov'im midrash*). Liberated from our weekday chores, there is time to devote to the pleasure of Torah study. Every man is obligated to study Torah on Shabbos but those who are busy with their livelihood during the week will especially welcome the opportunity to study Torah on Shabbos. It is advisable for these people to study the practical applications of the *halachos* so they will be able to properly observe the *mitzvos* and avoid transgressions.[27]

Minchah recited on Shabbos

22. *Minchah* begins with *Ashrei* and *u'Va l'Tzion*. (Some people recite *Pitum
     Ha-Ketores*, as well as other passages, which are printed in some
Siddurim.) This is followed by *Kerias Ha-Torah*. Before the *sefer Torah* is
taken out of the *Aron Ha-Kodesh*, various verses are recited including the
verse *va-ani tefillasi*, "But, as for me, I turn to You in prayer, God, at a
time of good will. O God, in Your great kindness, answer me with the
truth of Your salvation" (*Tehillim* 69:14).[28]

23. The Torah reading for *Minchah* consists of the first section of the next
     week's *parashas ha-shavua*. Three men — a *Kohen*, a *Levi*, and a *Yisrael*
— receive *aliyos*. The *halachos* relating to the Torah reading, raising the Torah
scroll, and rolling it up, are discussed in detail in Chapter 7, Sections 89-100.

24. The *Amidah* is recited, followed by the Leader's Repetition. After this,
     three verses beginning with the words *Tzidekasecha* are recited (the com-
plete text is printed in the *Siddur*). These verses are omitted on dates on which
tachanun would have been omitted had it been a weekday.[29] (These dates are
listed in Chapter 7, Section 87, as well as in Chapter 8, Section 3.)

Minchah ends with *Aleinu*. Additional details regarding *Minchah* are listed in
Chapter 8.

25. On Shabbos during the winter, some people recite the passage *Barchi
     nafshi*, and the fifteen chapters of *Tehillim* which begin with the
words *Shir Ha-Ma'alos*. These passages are printed in the *Siddur* following
Minchah for Shabbos. During the summer, beginning from the Shabbos
after Pesach, many people have the custom to study one chapter of *Pirkei
Avos* each Shabbos. *Avos* is a tractate of the Mishnah which contains ethical
instructions and moral teachings of our sages. Jewish calendars often list
which chapter of *Avos* is being studied each Shabbos.

Se'udah Shelishis (The third Shabbos meal)

26. It is a mitzvah to eat three meals on Shabbos. The prescribed time for
     the third meal is in the afternoon, from the time of *Minchah Gedolah* (i.e.
half a *sha'ah zemanis* after midday) onwards.[30] *Kiddush* is not recited before
this meal.[31] One must begin the meal before sunset, but it may continue
into the night.

After reciting *ha-motzi* over *lechem mishneh,* the upper loaf is sliced as was done during the morning meal. If one eats more than three meals on Shabbos, he must recite *ha-motzi* over *lechem mishneh* each time.[32]

One should plan to eat the Shabbos morning meal early enough so that he will have an appetite for *Se'udah Shelishis* later on. If one is very full, and finds it difficult to eat bread for the third meal, he may eat baked goods instead.[33]

27.   *Retzei* is added in *Birkas Ha-mazon.*[34] (The table on p. 109 indicates how to proceed if one forgot to add *Retzei* in *Birkas Ha-mazon* after *Se'udah Shelishis.*) If one continues *Se'udah Shelishis* into the night, he still recites *Retzei* in *Birkas Ha-mazon.* However, if one recited *Ma'ariv* before he recited *Birkas Ha-mazon,* he does not add *Retzei* because the sanctity of Shabbos has ended for him.[35]

If *Rosh Chodesh* begins on Saturday night, it is preferable to refrain from eating bread during *Se'udah Shelishis* after it becomes dark. If one does so, he encounters the halachic problem of whether he should recite *Retzei* and/or *Ya'aleh V'yavo* in *Birkas Ha-mazon.*[36] If, however, he did not eat bread after it became dark, he only recites *Retzei* in *Birkas Ha-mazon.*

Chapter Nineteen
Motza'ei Shabbos
(Saturday evening when Shabbos ends)

1. Shabbos ends at *tzeis ha-kochavim* (when three small stars appear in the sky near each other). The exact time varies from place to place. Jewish calendars often include the time Shabbos ends in various cities. One may not resume work that is prohibited on Shabbos before the time listed for his particular locale, and before reciting *Baruch ha-mavdil bein kodesh l'chol*.

The timetable below lists the time of *tzeis ha-kochavim* in various cities The times are cited at ten-day intervals. One can calculate the times for the days in between. The times are listed according to standard time, not Daylight Savings Time.

Timetable of *Tzeis Ha-kochavim*

DATE		JERUSALEM	NEW-YORK	LONDON	DATE		JERUSALEM	NEW-YORK	LONDON
Jan.	1	17.26	17.24	17.00	July	10	19.29	20.17	21.28
Jan.	11	17.33	17.33	17.11	July	20	19.24	20.10	21.14
Jan.	21	17.41	17.43	17.25	July	30	19.17	20.00	20.56
Jan.	31	17.50	17.54	17.41	Aug.	9	19.08	19.47	20.34
Feb.	10	17.58	18.06	17.57	Aug.	19	18.57	19.32	20.12
Feb.	20	18.06	18.17	18.14	Aug.	29	18.44	19.15	19.48
Mar.	2	18.14	18.28	18.31	Sep.	8	18.31	18.58	19.23
Mar.	12	18.21	18.39	18.49	Sep.	18	18.18	18.41	18.59
Mar.	22	18.28	18.50	19.06	Sep.	28	18.05	18.24	18.35
Apr.	1	18.35	19.01	19.24	Oct.	8	17.52	18.07	18.13
Apr.	11	18.42	19.12	19.42	Oct.	18	17.40	17.52	17.52
Apr.	21	18.50	19.24	20.02	Oct.	28	17.31	17.39	17.33
May	1	18.58	19.35	20.22	Nov.	7	17.23	17.28	17.16
May	11	19.06	19.47	20.42	Nov.	17	17.17	17.20	17.03
May	21	19.13	19.58	21.01	Nov.	27	17.14	17.15	16.54
May	31	19.20	20.08	21.18	Dec.	7	17.14	17.13	16.50
June	10	19.26	20.16	21.30	Dec.	17	17.17	17.15	16.50
June	20	19.30	20.20	21.37	Dec.	27	17.22	17.20	16.55
June	30	19.31	20.21	21.36					

Ma'ariv on *Motza'ei Shabbos*

2.   One recites the weekday *Ma'ariv* after *tzeis ha-kochavim*. (For more details regarding the *halachos* pertaining to *Ma'ariv*, see Chapter 9.)[1]

3.   One adds the passage of *Attah chonantanu* ("You have favored us") to *Attah chonen*, the fourth blessing of the *Amidah*. In this passage, we declare the difference between the holy and the ordinary: "You have differentiated between the sacred and the ordinary, between light and darkness, between Israel and the nations, between the seventh day and the six days of work..."[2]

If one forgot to recite *Attah chonantanu*

4.   If one forgot to recite *Attah chonantanu*, but he remembered before mentioning the name of Hashem at the conclusion of *Attah chonen*, he should return to the beginning of the blessing, and recite *Attah chonantanu*. The person then continues reciting the *Amidah* from there. If one remembers that he did not recite *Attah chonantanu* after he already mentioned the name of Hashem at the conclusion of *Attah chonen*, he does not return to the beginning of the blessing.

The Repetition of the *Shemoneh Esreh* is not recited during *Ma'ariv*. After the *Amidah* for *Ma'ariv*, the leader recites half-*Kaddish*. This is followed by the passages *Vi-hi no'am*, *Yoshev be-seser elyon*, and *V'Attah Kadosh* (for the complete text, see the *Siddur*). The verse *Vi-hi no'am* is recited while standing.[3] Moshe blessed the Jews with this verse (*Tehillim* 90:17) when they had completed the Tabernacle. Since God's Presence rested upon the Jews through the Tabernacle, we follow this verse with other verses from *Tehillim*, which discuss God's resting His Presence on Israel.[4]

These sections are not recited when a holiday on which work is forbidden occurs during the following week. Sephardic Jews always recite these verses.

Kiddush Levanah (The blessing on the renewal of the moon)

5.   *Kiddush Levanah* is recited in the first half of the month,[7] during a night when the moon can be seen clearly. *Kiddush Levanah* is recited once a month, while one is standing under the open sky.[5] *Kiddush Levanah* is recited at some point after the third day of the moon's *molad*, when the moon passes between the earth and sun (*molad* tables are sometimes printed in Jewish calendars). Sephardic Jews recite *Kiddush Levanah* seven or more days after the *molad*.[6] One reason why special importance is attached to each new lunar cycle is that the Jewish calendar, and all the Festivals, are calculated according to the lunar month.

Kiddush Levanah is only recited during the first half of the month. The last day for reciting *Kiddush Levanah* is listed on some Jewish calendars.

6.   *Kiddush Levanah* is generally recited on *Motza'ei Shabbos* (Saturday night). However, if it was impossible to recite it on *Motza'ei Shabbos* (e.g. because clouds were covering the moon), it should be recited on the first night when the moon is visible.[8]

Various prayers are recited together with *Kiddush Levanah*. The full text is printed in the *Siddur*.

Havdalah

7.   The *Havdalah* ceremony separates the holy from the mundane; Shabbos from the other days of the week. *Havdalah* is recited over a cup of wine at the conclusion of Shabbos. The cup must contain at least a *revi'is* of wine. According to the Chazon Ish, a *revi'is* is 150 cc (5.07 oz), and according to Rav Chaim Na'eh, a *revi'is* is 86 cc (2.9 oz).

The *halachos* concerning the cup used for *Havdalah* are the same as those concerning the cup used for *Kiddush*. During *Havdalah*, the cup should be held the same way it is held during *Kiddush*. The cup is filled until it overflows, to symbolize abundant blessing.[9] One should be careful that no one drinks from the cup of wine before *Havdalah* is recited. If someone did drink from the cup, one may render the wine usable for *Havdalah* by adding a little more wine to the cup.[10]

The text of *Havdalah*

8.   The text for *Havdalah* is printed in *Siddurim*. It includes various verses followed by *borei peri ha-gafen*[11] and three other blessings.

After reciting *borei peri ha-gafen*, one recites *borei minei vesamim* over fragrant spices. After reciting this blessing, all those present smell the fragrance.

During *Havdalah*, one recites *borei minei vesamim*, no matter which kind of fragrance is smelled, although it is preferable to smell a fragrance which requires this specific blessing.[12] However, Sephardic Jews recite the specific blessing required for whatever fragrance they use, i.e. *borei atzei vesamim*, *borei isvei vesamim*, or *borei minei vesamim*. (The *halachos* regarding the blessings recited before smelling fragrances are discussed in detail in Chapter 13, Section 4.)

9.   After reciting *borei minei vesamim*, *borei me'orei ha-esh* is recited over a candle. One looks at his fingernails and the palms of his hands by the candle's light.[13] One may use a large candle with more than one wick. One may also use two candles which are held so their flames are touching.[14]

One holds the cup of wine in his left hand while reciting the blessings for the fragrance and the flame.

10.   After reciting *borei me'orei ha-esh*, one recites the blessing of *Havdalah*: *ha-mavdil bein kodesh l'chol*, "Who separates between the holy and the ordinary." This is the main blessing of *Havdalah*, after which one drinks the wine.

Ordinarily, the one who recites *Havdalah* drinks the entire cup of wine,[15] so that he can then recite the *berachah acharonah* of Me'ein Shalosh (*al ha-gefen v'al peri ha-gefen*). (For the details pertaining to this blessing, see Chapter 14, Sections 2-3.)

If no wine or grape juice is available, one may recite *Havdalah* over *chamar medinah* (for details regarding what is considered *chamar medinah*, see Chapter 18, Section 16). In this case, *she-ha-kol* and *borei nefashos* are recited instead of *borei peri ha-gafen* and Me'ein Shalosh.[16]

Exempting others with *Havdalah*

11.   If one recites *Havdalah* for a number of people, he must intend to exempt them with his blessings, and they must intend to fulfill their obligation by listening to his blessings. Those being exempted must answer Amen to all the blessings, and may not speak while the blessings are being

recited. All those present should watch the *Havdalah* cup and the flame, so their minds do not wander during the ceremony.

If there is a man to recite *Havdalah*, it is customary for women to fulfill their obligation by listening to the man recite it. Similarly, women do not customarily drink from the *Havdalah* wine. A man who has already fulfilled his obligation of *Havdalah* should not recite it for women unless he is also reciting it for other men or boys.[17] Therefore, if a man intends to recite *Havdalah* for his family he should intend not to fulfill his obligation when hearing *Havdalah* in the synagogue.

If no man is present to recite *Havdalah* for her, a woman must recite *Havdalah* herself and, of course drink the wine. However, she should not recite *borei me'orei ha-esh*.[18]

Eating or performing work on *Motza'ei Shabbos*

12.   It is prohibited to eat or drink anything besides water before reciting *Havdalah* on *Motza'ei Shabbos*.[19]

13.   Work which is prohibited on Shabbos may not be done before *Havdalah* is recited. Work may be done after saying *Attah chonantanu* in the *Amidah* of *Ma'ariv*. If one has to do work after the conclusion of Shabbos, but has not yet prayed or did not recite *Attah chonantanu* in the *Amidah* of *Ma'ariv*, he should say the words *Baruch ha-mavdil bein kodesh l'chol* ("Blessed is the One Who separates between the holy and the ordinary), and may then do the work. However, one may not eat or drink anything except water until after reciting *Havdalah*. Women who do not recite *Ma'ariv* on *Motza'ei Shabbos* and therefore do not recite *Attah chonantanu*, must recite *Baruch ha-mavdil bein kodesh l'chol* before doing any work after Shabbos.[20]

When a *Yom Tov* begins on *Motza'ei Shabbos*, *Havdalah* is recited during the *Yom Tov Kiddush*. In this case, the last blessing is different, and ends with the words *ha-mavdil bein kodesh l'kodesh*, "Blessed are You, Who separates between the holy and the holy" (i.e. Who separates between the holiness of Shabbos and the holiness of *Yom Tov*). This version is printed in the *Machzor*. In this situation, it is not customary to recite *borei minei vesamim*, although *borei me'orei ha-esh* is recited. The order that the blessings are recited at the combined *Kiddush/Havdalah* ceremony on *Motza'ei Shabbos* forms the acronym of YaKNeHaZ: Yayin (borei peri ha-gafen), Kiddush, Ner (borei me'orei ha-esh), Havdalah (ha-mavdil), Zeman (She-hecheyanu, which is recited on the first night of Yom Tov).

14. It is a nice custom to fold the *tallis* that one used on Shabbos on *Motza'ei Shabbos*. (One may not fold his *tallis* in the normal manner on Shabbos. This *halachah* is cited in detail in Chapter 20, Section 42.) The reason for this custom is to ensure that one begins the new week with something connected with a mitzvah.

Melaveh Malkah

15. One should set the table on *Motza'ei Shabbos*, and eat a meal called a *Melaveh Malkah* ("Escorting the Shabbos Queen"). With this meal we take leave of Shabbos, and honor it as it departs before a new week.[21] It is preferable for one to eat bread with this meal. However, if one is already sated, he may eat baked goods and the like instead.[22] Some people have the custom to light candles for the *Melaveh Malkah*, and to sing hymns composed especially for *Motza'ei Shabbos*.

It is preferable to eat the *Melaveh Malkah* soon after Shabbos ends. However, if a person has no appetite just then, he may have the meal later. It is proper not to do any work other than casual work before one has eaten his *Melaveh Malkah*. One should eat the meal before midnight.

Chapter Twenty

The Melachos
(The types of work prohibited on Shabbos)

Keep the day of Shabbos holy

1. Keep the Shabbos day holy, as the Almighty your God commanded you. Six days you may labor and do all your work, and the seventh day is Shabbos for the Almighty your God. You shall not do any work. (*Devarim* 5:12-14)

Many principles and fundamentals of the Jewish faith are included in the concept of Shabbos. Shabbos commemorates Creation and the Exodus from Egypt. It is also considered a "foretaste of the world to come," as the Shabbos hymn *Me'ein Olam Ha-ba* so beautifully describes it. The tranquility and sanctity of Shabbos is a Jew's opportunity to rise above the ordinary atmosphere of the six weekdays to reach new spiritual levels.

The special character of Shabbos emanates from observing its *mitzvos*, avoiding its prohibited activities, and conducting oneself in accordance with the sanctity of the day. By desecrating any of its prohibitions one divests himself of the exalted ideas and lofty spiritual concepts which characterize Shabbos.

Avos and *tolados*

2. The command to build the Tabernacle in the Sinai Desert (*Shemos* 31:1-11) was said together with the warning not to violate Shabbos. In *Parashas Vayakhel* (*Shemos* 35:1-3) the warning not to transgress Shabbos also appears together with the building of the Tabernacle. We derive two *halachos* from this: 1) it was prohibited to build the Tabernacle on Shabbos, and 2) any work done in connection with the Tabernacle may not be done on Shabbos.

3. Thirty-nine types of *melachos* ("labors") were done in connection with the construction of the Tabernacle. These thirty-nine *melachos* are the *avos melachah*, i.e. catagories of the types of work prohibited on Shabbos.

There are also other types of prohibited work, which are derived from these catagories. These are called *tolados*. They resemble the *avos melachah* in their purpose and in the manner in which they are executed. The *tolados* must be observed as strictly as the *avos melachah*.

It is important to note the following: There is a popular assumption that work is forbidden on Shabbos because it is difficult to do. This is absolutely not true. There are *melachos* which are forbidden on Shabbos which are easy to do. The Torah forbade doing things which are "works of creation." Exact rules were given at Mount Sinai. The details of the laws of Shabbos were set according to these rules.

The following sections discuss each of the thirty-nine *melachos*, along with examples of related *tolados*. The examples presented also include a number of prohibitions instituted by the sages because these acts resemble the thirty-nine *melachos*. Each *melachah* is explained, followed by its common applications and restrictions. The laws are categorized to facilitate learning.

One can enter the palace of Shabbos and feel the pleasure, tranquility, and holiness that pervade it. Prior preparation and familiarity with Halachah help one experience the pleasure of this special day.

The thirty-nine *melachos*

4.   The thirty-nine *melachos* are usually divided into the following groups:

Melachos 1-11 are connected to the preparation of food: (1) Plowing (2) Sowing (3) Reaping (4) Sheaf-making (5) Threshing (6) Winnowing (7) Selecting (8) Sifting (9) Grinding (10) Kneading (mixing) (11) Baking (cooking)

Melachos 12-24 are connected to the preparations required to produce clothing: (12) Shearing (13) Bleaching (laundering) (14) Combing raw material (15) Dyeing (16) Spinning (17) Preparing the loom for weaving (18) Arranging the warp on a weaving loom (19) Weaving (20) Separating into threads (21) Tying a knot (22) Untying a knot (23) Sewing (24) Tearing

Melachos 25-33 are connected to writing or the preparation of parchment: (25) Trapping (26) Slaughtering (27) Skinning (28) Tanning (29) Scraping (30) Engraving lines (31) Cutting to shape (32) Writing (33) Erasing

Melachos 34-35 are connected to building: (34) Building (35) Demolishing

Melachos 36-37 involve fire: (36) Kindling a fire (37) Extinguishing a fire

Melachah 38. The final hammer-blow (completing an object)

Melachah 39. Carrying from one domain to another

Explanation of the thirty-nine *melachos* and examples of activities included in them

5.   Before reading the following activities which are prohibited on Shabbos, it should be noted that these are only selected examples. There are many other forbidden activities which could not be included in the limited space of this compendium.

(1) The *melachah* of Plowing involves preparing the soil for sowing or planting. This includes removing anything that might interfere with plant growth.

Forbidden activities include: digging or making furrows in the ground (This includes furrows that are made by dragging a heavy object, like a bench on the ground); clearing stones, weeds, or stubble from a field; fertilizing or draining the soil; leveling the ground (filling in holes or leveling mounds); spreading earth on the ground; sweeping an outdoor earthen floor (such as a garden); and playing games (like marbles) on the ground which might lead one to level the ground to facilitate the game.

These forbidden activities and the ones that follow apply to the earth in flowerpots as well as to the ground. (Preparing the ground for construction purposes is forbidden. This is included in the *melachah* of Building (*melachah* 34).)

(2) The *melachah* of Sowing involves sowing, planting, or any other action which facilitates the growth of plants.

Forbidden activities include: throwing seeds on arable soil (this includes throwing down pits from fruit); planting; bending branches to plant them; grafting; pruning or cutting off branches from a plant attached to the ground; watering plants; putting flowers in water, changing the water in or adding water to a vase of flowers; weeding; thinning out plants; tarring trees; fertilizing; and covering plants in a nursery in order to stimulate growth.

(3) The *melachah* of Reaping involves uprooting a plant from its place of growth.

Forbidden activities include: harvesting grain; picking fruits or flowers; mowing the lawn; breaking or sawing branches off trees; and moving flowerpots that are on the ground. One may not remove honey from a beehive.

Our sages also prohibited actions which may cause one to break branches. For example, one may not climb a tree or make use of a tree in any way; ride or make use of an animal; travel in a wagon drawn by an animal (this is because one might tear off a branch in order to prod the animal).

(4) The *melachah* of Sheaf-making involves gathering scattered objects that grew from the ground, or combining scattered objects into one bunch.

Forbidden activities include: gathering fruit which fell from a tree; gathering twigs or straw; making a wreath of flowers; threading fruits on a string, and pressing fruits into one bunch (e.g. a fig roll).

(5) The *melachah* of Threshing involves removing something edible from its natural attached cover.

Forbidden activities include: threshing grain; removing peas and other legumes from their pods (if the pods are inedible); squeezing juice from fruits or vegetables; and milking animals. (One should consult with a person who is proficient in Halachah regarding a permissible way to milk animals on Shabbos.)

(6) The *melachah* of Winnowing involves dividing an object into its different components, or removing the waste material from food by fanning it or blowing at it.

(7) The *melachah* of Selecting involves separating unwanted matter from wanted matter, or sorting objects into different groups.

Forbidden activities include: sorting a pile of objects according to their various types; straining liquids containing unwanted matter; soaking fruits or vegetables in a container with water so that dirt and other waste materials will either float to the top or sink to the bottom; and separating unwanted matter from food. (The permitted way to select food from its unwanted matter is discussed in Sections 27-31, below.)

(8) The *melachah* of Sifting involves separating waste from food or separating objects into their different components by shaking them in a sieve, e.g. sifting flour.

(9) The *melachah* of Grinding involves crumbling or grinding an object into small particles.

Forbidden activities include: grinding grain into flour; grinding coffee, pepper, and other foods; filing metal; sanding wood; and cutting up vegetables or fruits into tiny pieces.

(10) The *melachah* of Kneading involves mixing and joining small solids together with a liquid (for example, mixing flour with water, or dirt or cement with water) to form a single unit.

Forbidden activities include: mixing a dough, or other mixtures of solids and liquids. Sometimes the initial act of pouring a liquid onto a solid — even without mixing them — is included in the prohibition of kneading.

(11) The *melachah* of Baking involves changing food, drinks or other materials through heat.

Forbidden activities include: baking, cooking, roasting, grilling, or frying; melting solid materials like wax or metals; and drying wood in an oven.

The *melachah* of Baking is discussed in greater detail in Sections 8-16, below.

(12) The *melachah* of Shearing involves removing any natural growth from a person's body or that of an animal.

Forbidden activities include: shearing or plucking wool, feathers, or hairs; cutting fingernails or toenails; tearing off bits of skin around the nails; removing hairs or calluses from the body, whether by cutting them off or through electrical or chemical means; and plucking hairs off a fur coat.

One may not comb his hair on Shabbos because hairs may be torn out. (The *halachos* regarding how to brush one's hair on Shabbos are discussed in detail in Section 63, below.)

(13) The *melachah* of Bleaching involves any action which cleans or improves the appearance of clothes or fabrics.

Forbidden activities include: soaking fabrics or clothes in water or other fluids; scrubbing clothes; shaking fluids out of garments or wringing out garments; ironing; cleaning stains; shaking or brushing off dust from clothes or hats whose appearance one is particular about; using a sponge; hanging up wet laundry; and squeezing the water from one's wet hair. One may not refold a *tallis* or clothes along their original folds (there are many details regarding this *halachah*).

(14) The *melachah* of Combing raw material involves separating a solid or entangled material into threads.

Forbidden activities include: combing raw wool and beating flax.

(15) The *melachah* of Dyeing involves changing or reinforcing the natural or artificial color of an object or fluid.

Forbidden activities include: painting objects; dyeing cloths with a solution; dissolving colors in water or other fluids; making chemical solutions which cause color reactions; developing film; applying makeup to one's face, eyes, or lips; and applying nail polish.

(16) The *melachah* of Spinning involves making threads from raw materials by pulling, stretching, twisting, or rolling.

Forbidden activities include: making threads or ropes; and twisting new threads or threads which became loose.

(17) The *melachah* of *Mesech* is an activity which prepares a loom for weaving. Some people define it as setting up the warp on a loom.

(18) The *melachah* of *Oseh batei nirim* is another activity that prepares the loom for weaving. It involves arranging the warp in such a way that the woof threads can be easily woven through them.

(19) The *melachah* of Weaving involves weaving the woof through the warp to form material.

These three *melachos* (*Mesech*, *Oseh batei nirim*, and Weaving) include the following activities: weaving material; knitting and crocheting; interweaving metal wires to make a wire fence; and weaving pliant twigs and straw into baskets.

(20) The *melachah* of Separating into threads involves separating a woven or braided material into threads.

Forbidden activities include: separating a cloth into its threads; removing a thread from a garment, cloth, or bandage; pulling out a thread from embroidery; unraveling; removing the basting thread from a garment; and untwining a thick thread.

(21-22) The *melachos* of Tying and Untying a knot include all kinds of permanent knots (these *melachos* are discussed in greater detail in Sections 53-54, below).

(23) The *melachah* of Sewing involves connecting two pieces of cloth or other material to each other.

Forbidden activities include: sewing; gluing together pieces of paper, cloth, leather, or any other material; tightening a loose thread in a garment; and stapling together papers or a booklet.

(24) The *melachah* of Tearing involves tearing paper, cloth, and other materials; and separating anything that is glued together.

(25) The *melachah* of Trapping involves catching animals or limiting their freedom of movement so that they can easily be caught.

Forbidden activities include: trapping animals (this includes insects) by hand or with an instrument; chasing animals into an enclosure where they can be caught easily; closing a window in a room to prevent a bird from escaping; closing a container which a fly entered; and setting up traps or snares to catch animals.

(26) The *melachah* of Slaughtering involves doing anything to shorten the life of a living creature.

Forbidden activities include: any form of killing, including removing fish from water; killing insects; causing bleeding; and making a wound or causing a bruise. It is also prohibited to press on a wound so that it will bleed.

(27) The *melachah* of Skinning involves skinning and flaying the hide of animals.

One is permitted to remove the skin from a piece of cooked chicken when he eats it. This is because skin from a cooked chicken is edible and is considered food. Feathers left on the chicken skin may not be removed.

(28) The *melachah* of Tanning involves tanning and processing leather and other materials.

Forbidden activities include: smearing oil on leather and shoes; processing materials in chemical solutions; pickling food; salting meat; and the like.

(29) The *melachah* of Scraping involves scraping and smoothing leather and other materials.

Forbidden activities include: smoothing and removing hairs from leather; smoothing creams or ointment on skin; using a bar of soap (for more details concerning soap, see Section 37, below); cleaning soiled shoes by vigorously scraping them with a scraper or a piece of metal; and smoothing materials with sandpaper.

(30) The *melachah* of Engraving lines involves marking lines or figures on various kinds of material.

Forbidden activities include: marking lines or other shapes on something using ink, paint, a sharp instrument, or a fingernail, in preparation for cutting or dividing that material.

(31) The *melachah* of Cutting to shape involves cutting, plucking, or tearing a material to a desired size or shape.

Forbidden activities include: cutting cloth, leather, paper, or other materials to size; sharpening pencils; and splitting a splinter from a piece of wood to use as a toothpick.

(32) The *melachah* of Writing involves writing letters, numbers, lines, or shapes which have some meaning.

Forbidden activities include: recording letters or shapes by writing, sketching, drawing, engraving, or embroidering; pouring into a mold which is in the shape of a letter; stamping with a rubber stamp; cutting out letters; and printing.

It is prohibited to write on any material on which writing is discernible, for example, paper, wood, ice, sand, a misty window, and liquids that spilled on a table.

Our sages prohibited a number of activities which might cause a person to write, for example, talking about business; purchasing items; measuring and weighing; reading business articles; reading a guest list; and playing games which ordinarily involve writing.

(33) The *melachah* of Erasing involves erasing or destroying a written form or character.

Forbidden activities include: any form of erasing, whether with an eraser or by chemical means; and scraping off or tearing up letters.

(34) The *melachah* of Building involves any action which aids in construction.

Forbidden activities include: digging a foundation; pouring cement; setting up a wall; installing doors and windows; leveling the ground or changing its surface in preparation for building; sweeping an unpaved floor; driving a nail into a wall; drilling a hole; reattaching a door or window that became detached; affixing a doorknob that fell off; setting up a tent; spreading a cover to form a roof; and erecting a partition. (For more details, see Sections 57-60, below.)

(35) The *melachah* of Demolishing involves demolishing or dismantling any structure described in the *melachah* of Building.

Forbidden activities include: demolishing buildings; removing nails, etc.

(36) The *melachah* of Kindling a fire involves lighting a fire, turning up a flame, and making a fire burn longer.

Forbidden activities include: any form of kindling a fire, whether with a match, a lighter, a magnifying glass, electricity, or by chemical means; lighting a new fire from an existing flame; stoking a fire; smoking; adding fuel to a fire, etc.

(37) The *melachah* of Extinguishing a fire involves putting out a fire, turning down a flame, or shortening the time that a fire will burn.

Forbidden activities include: extinguishing a fire by any means, for example with water, sand, foam, opening a door in front of it, blowing at it, stamping on it, covering it with a blanket, and removing the wood, gas, flammable liquids, etc. that serve as its fuel.

(38) The *melachah* of The final hammer-blow involves the final action which completes a job or finishes the production of an object.

Forbidden activities include: all actions customarily done by craftsmen when finishing a product, like cleaning and polishing the product; sharpening knives; removing the basting from a completed garment; banging on the anvil with a hammer to smooth it; completing the wiring of an electrical appliance; and connecting the handle to a tool.

(39) The *melachah* of Carrying from one domain to another involves any form of transporting an object from public domain to a private one, or vice versa, whether by carrying, throwing, handing an item to a person in a different domain, pulling, pushing, etc.

Moreover, one should not transport an object more than four *amos* in a public domain, even if the object did not come from a private domain. This prohibition does not include the clothes that one is wearing. (The basic *halachos* that apply to public and private domains are discussed in Sections 82-89, below.)

Actions Prohibited on Shabbos

6.   The following sections discuss common applications of the thirty-nine *melachos* in greater detail. Many *halachos* are not included. Therefore, one should not deduce that any action not mentioned below is permitted. If one is in doubt, he should refer to halachic books that specifically discuss the laws of Shabbos, or address one's questions to a *rav*.

Topics of Shabbos laws

The prohibitions of cooking on Shabbos
Kindling and Extinguishing a Fire/ Cooking on Shabbos

Food preparation on Shabbos
Squeezing Fruit for Juice/ Milking/ Grinding/ Snow and Ice on Shabbos/ Mixing (Kneading)/ Pickling/ Separating *Terumos* and *Ma'asros*/ Opening Cans and Packages

The prohibition of selecting
The Permitted and Prohibited Ways To Select

Housework
Using Soaps and Pastes/ Washing Dishes and Cutlery/ Cleaning the Table/ The Prohibition to Prepare for the Weekdays on Shabbos/ Sweeping and Washing Floors/ Laundering Clothes

Using appliances and building
Using Electricity/ Building and Spreading out a Cover

Miscellaneous work
Writing and Erasing/ Pasting/ Sewing, Cutting, and Tearing/ Tying and Untying a Knot/ Weighing and Measuring

Personal grooming
Washing/ Hair Care/ Nail-Cutting and Cosmetics/ Laws Pertaining to Medical Care/ Baby Care

Caring for plants and animals
Using Trees/ Working in the Field and Garden/ Tending Flowers/ Trapping/ Using Animals

Uvdin d'chol — weekday affairs
"Going on One's Way"/ "Pursuing One's Business"/ "Speaking Common Talk"/ Giving Instructions to a Non-Jew

The laws of Eruvin
The Different Types of Shabbos Domains/ The Laws of Eruvin/ The Prohibition of Techumin

The laws of Muktzeh
The Types of Muktzeh/ The Laws Pertaining to Moving Muktzeh

The prohibition of kindling and extinguishing a fire

7.   It is prohibited to kindle or extinguish a fire on Shabbos. It is also prohibited to make a flame larger or smaller on Shabbos. This prohibition applies to all kinds of fires and includes all kinds of fuel, regardless of how they are ignited. This prohibition includes extinguishing a flame on a stove after the pot has been removed.

Smoking is prohibited on Shabbos.

The prohibition of cooking on Shabbos

8.   It is prohibited to cook food on a fire or on any other source of heat. Food that was cooked before Shabbos may not be reheated directly on an electric hotplate, steamer, etc. This rule applies to solids and liquids. One may not put food on the fire on Shabbos for a short period of time, even if there is no chance the food will become cooked in that period of time.

The prohibition of cooking includes baking, roasting, grilling, and frying. It also includes melting solids, like wax or metal, and drying wood by means of heat or fire.

9.   It is prohibited to add food, liquids, or spices to a pot which is on a fire or other heat source.[1] Similarly, one may not stir food in a pot while it is on the fire.[2]

There are many complicated details regarding the prohibition of cooking on Shabbos. For instance, the *halachah* is different if the food is liquid or solid, and if the food is completely or only partially cooked. A few of the most common cases are cited in the following sections.

Placing one pot on top of another one

10.   Although it is prohibited to put food directly on a fire, one may put a cold solid food (without any soup or gravy) or a food that contains liquid that has not yet cooled off, that was completely cooked before Shabbos on top of a pot which had been standing on the fire since Shabbos began. Any food that contains a liquid (such as soup or gravy), may be put on top of a pot on a fire, electric hotplate, etc., if it will not reach a temperature of *yad soledes* (hot enough to cause the hand to recoil), even after being left there for a long time.[3]

A "first vessel" and a "second vessel"

11.   A "first vessel" is a pot which was heated up on a fire, electric hotplate, etc. It is prohibited to cook in a first vessel (i.e. by putting food, liquids, or spices into it). A pot is considered a first vessel after it is removed from the fire, if it is still *yad soledes*.[4] It is also prohibited to pour the contents of a first vessel onto food or liquids, because, halachically, this is considered cooking.[5] However, dry food which does not contain soup or gravy, and that was fully cooked before Shabbos, may be warmed up in a first vessel that was removed from the stove.[6]

12.   A "second vessel" is a container into which hot food from a first vessel was poured. It retains this status as long as the food remains as hot as *yad soledes*.[7] Some foods are easily cooked. Examples of such foods are eggs and tea leaves. Such foods may not be added to a second vessel on Shabbos. The *Mishnah Berurah* writes that since we are not sure which other foods are considered easily cooked, one should not place any uncooked food in a second vessel. The *Mishnah Berurah*, in his commentary *Sha'arei Tzion* (318:5, note 42:68), mentions that the two exceptions to this rule are water and oil.

Therefore, it is customary not to put food which is not cooked (e.g. bread, matzah) into a second vessel which contains food as hot as *yad soledes*. A person should be careful not to pour food or liquid from a first vessel onto food which is not cooked.[8] (There are additional details pertaining to this *halachah*. One should consult with someone who is proficient in Halachah regarding these details.)

One should not add spices, etc. to solid food (e.g. potatoes, pieces of meat, etc.) which are in a second vessel, and which are as hot as *yad soledes*. This is because some halachic authorities consider all hot solid food as if it were in a first vessel.[9]

Preparing tea and coffee on Shabbos

13. The correct way to make tea on Shabbos is described by the *Mishnah Berurah*[10] as follows: A strong tea essence should be prepared before Shabbos by cooking the tea leaves or teabag. When preparing the tea on Shabbos, first one should be pour the hot water into the cup, and then add the tea essence (and sugar). One should not pour the hot water on the tea essence from a first vessel (the teakettle or percolator) if the tea essence is cold. However, if the tea essence was kept warm, it is preferable to first pour the tea essence into the cup, and then add the hot water. This is to avoid doing an action similar to Dyeing.[11] According to the *Beis Yosef*, one may only pour the tea essence into the cup first if the essence is at a temperature of *yad soledes*. Many Sephardic Jews follow this ruling.

Since preparing coffee may involve cooking, many people only use instant coffee on Shabbos. To prepare instant coffee on Shabbos, first pour the hot water into a cup (this becomes the second vessel). Then add the instant coffee to the water. Preparing hot cocoa may also involve cooking. It is advisable to receive practical guidance in these matters.

Foods that were not fully cooked before Shabbos

14. It is recommended to make sure that all the food for Shabbos is fully cooked before Shabbos begins. If food that was not completely cooked was placed on a flame (or other heat source) before Shabbos, a number of laws must be observed that would not apply otherwise. For instance, one may not stir food in a pot if all the food in the pot is not fully cooked. Similarly, food may not be taken out of the pot if all the food is not completely cooked. This rule applies as long as the food is hot, including after the pot was removed from the flame or hotplate.[12] Another rule that applies in this case is that if the pot was uncovered, it may not be covered again.[13] Finally, if a pot was removed from its source of heat, it may not be returned.[14]

If food that is not completely cooked is in an oven, and someone opened the oven door, one may not close the oven door again.[15]

Hachzarah (Returning a pot to the stove)

15.   If one removes a pot of food from a source of heat on Shabbos, one may replace the pot if the following conditions are met:

A. One had intended to return the pot when he removed it.

B. The person was holding the pot the entire time it was off the fire. (According to the *Beis Yosef*, one may return the pot to the source of heat as long as it was not put down on the ground. Sephardic Jews follow this opinion.)

C. The food was fully cooked when it was removed from the flame.

D. The food is still hot when it is returned to the fire. According to the Rema, the pot may be returned to the source of heat as long as the food has not completely cooled off. The *Beis Yosef* maintains that the food must be as hot as *yad soledes*.[16] Sephardic Jews follow the *Beis Yosef's* opinion.

E. The fire must be "raked and covered." Many halachic authorities maintain that covering the flame with a sheet of metal or asbestos fulfills this condition. According to this opinion, one may replace food that was removed from the flame[17] if the flame is covered, and if all the conditions listed above are fulfilled. However, the Chazon Ish maintains that covering a flame does not fulfill the requirement of "raking and covering."[18]

A pot of food which was taken out of an oven (or removed from a fire) may not be returned to the oven, even if all the conditions mentioned above were fulfilled (see *Mishnah Berurah* 253:67).

Moreover, today most ovens are regulated by a thermostat. Opening or closing the oven door is likely to activate the thermostat — an act which is clearly forbidden on Shabbos. Therefore, one must determine how the oven works before using it on Shabbos. This is to avoid any Shabbos transgression.

Hatmanah
(Wrapping food before Shabbos so it retains its heat)

16. One may not wrap containers of hot food on *erev Shabbos* in a way that will increase the heat, and leave them that way for Shabbos. The *Shulchan Aruch* adds that pots which will be placed on the stove or other heat source for Shabbos may not be completely wrapped in blankets or cloths before Shabbos.

One may not completely wrap or surround a container of hot food to preserve its heat on Shabbos. This even applies if the wrapping does not add heat, or if the pot is wrapped when it is removed from the source of heat.[19] According to the *Beis Yosef*, it is also forbidden to partially wrap a container of food in order to preserve its heat.

Similarly, one may not heat up a jar or bottle of baby food on Shabbos by placing the jar into a container of hot water, when the hot water completely covers it. This even applies when the food in the bottle will not reach the temperature of *yad soledes*.[20]

Food Preparation on Shabbos
Squeezing Fruit, Grinding, Mixing (Kneading), etc.

The prohibition of squeezing

17. It is prohibited to extract juice from fruits or vegetables on Shabbos. This prohibition applies both when preparing and eating the food. In many cases, it is forbidden to drink juice that dripped from a fruit on Shabbos. One may cut up grapefruits and eat the pieces with a spoon even though some juice was unintentionally squeezed out. The juice that come out unintentionally may be drunk. However, one may not intend to squeeze out the juice.[21]

18. One may squeeze fruits and vegetables by hand (but not with a utensil made specifically for extracting juice) onto a solid food, if the juice is

immediately absorbed by the food, and aids in its preparation. The juice may not be squeezed into a liquid (e.g. squeezing lemon juice into tea). There is a halachic opinion that one may not squeeze olives or grapes at all (i.e. they may not even be squeezed over solid food). One who adheres to this stringent view will be blessed.[22]

19.   One may squeeze the juice from pickled vegetables if he intends to improve the vegetables (and he intends to dispose of the juice). The pickles should be squeezed shortly before they are eaten.[23]

20.   The *melachah* of squeezing fruit is included in the *melachah* of Threshing. This *melachah* includes threshing grain and removing peas from their pods, if the pods are inedible. The *melachah* of Threshing also includes milking animals. One who must milk animals on Shabbos should consult a *rav* regarding how to milk animals manually and with a milking machine on Shabbos. These *halachos* and their practical applications are very detailed.

Grinding

21.   Grinding food is prohibited on Shabbos. Crumbling, mashing, and pureeing food are included in the *melachah* of Grinding. This prohibition also applies to non-edible substances. For example, soil may not be crumbled, and wood may not be sawed to make sawdust.[24]

22.   Chopping or cutting vegetables or fruits into very small pieces is considered grinding. Therefore, one should cut these foods into somewhat large pieces, so as to avoid any possibility of transgressing this prohibition.[25]

Foods that don't grow from the ground (e.g. eggs, meat and cooked fish) may be ground on Shabbos with a spoon or fork, but not with a chopping or grinding utensil.

23.   One may not chop ice or crush snow on Shabbos to make it melt. However, one may put ice cubes in water or other drinks.[26] One may break ice on Shabbos to be able to use the water under it.[27]

Mixing and kneading

24.   Mixing and kneading are prohibited on Shabbos.[28] This *melachah* includes joining solid particles with a liquid, so that one substance is formed. It is prohibited to knead water with flour (or any other type of

dough), water with dust or cement, and honey or oil with various foods. (See *melachah* 10, Kneading, above.)[29]

Solids that will combine into a mixture without kneading or mixing may not be poured one into the other. (An example is honey and soft cheese.)

One may not make a hard or soft mixture on Shabbos. A soft mixture is defined as a liquid mixture which can be poured from one utensil to another. Sometimes, if one changes the way a mixture is formed, it is permitted to form a soft mixture on Shabbos. The change must entail the order in which the materials are mixed together, and the way the materials are mixed together (e.g. the materials might be mixed with a finger instead of a spoon, or by shaking the container). Since these *halachos* are very detailed, one should consult with a person who is proficient in Halachah.

Pickling food

25. On Shabbos it is prohibited to place vegetables in vinegar or brine to pickle them.[30]

One may not add salt to vegetables which are customarily pickled. Some of the vegetables included in this category are onions, radishes, and cucumbers. However, one may add salt to vegetables if he immediately adds oil or salad dressing to them too. One may also pour salt on each individual piece of vegetable just before eating it.[31]

Separating *terumos* and *ma'asros* (tithes) on Shabbos

26. It is prohibited to separate tithes (*terumos* and *ma'asros*) from fruits, vegetables, and other foods on Shabbos, unless one has made a special stipulation before Shabbos began. Similarly, one may not fulfill the mitzvah of separating *challah* from dough on Shabbos.

If one has *tevel* (fruits or vegetables which have not had tithes separated from them) in his home before Shabbos, and he has no time to separate *terumos* and *ma'asros* from it, he can recite the text for separating *terumos* and *ma'asros* in the future tense before Shabbos. This is explained in greater detail in Chapter 37, Section 19.

When one separates the *terumos* and *ma'asros* on Shabbos, he should recite the text again. One must be careful not to move the portion he separated (the little more than one one-hundredth which is *terumah*), since it becomes *muktzeh* after it is separated. This arrangement only applies to food which was in one's possession before Shabbos.

The Prohibition of Selecting

What is the *melachah* of selecting?

27.   It is prohibited to select and remove the unwanted part of a mixture from the part that one wants. Listed below are various things which are included in the prohibition of selecting.[32]

A. One may not separate unwanted material from food. Bones, seeds, and other inedible parts of food are considered its unwanted material.

B. If there is a mixture of two types of things, one may not separate the objects that he does not want from those that he wants. The prohibition even applies if the unwanted objects are fit for eating or some other use, but one does not want them at that particular moment.

C. One may not sort objects or foods into their respective groups; for example, one may not sort silverware into separate piles of spoons and forks. Nor may one sort different types of fruits, clothes, or toys into separate piles.

The permitted method of selecting
an object from a mixture

28.   One may only select food or other objects from a mixture when all three of the following conditions are present:

A. The object one wants must be removed from the other objects, and not the other way around. It is forbidden to take away the objects one does not want from the objects one wants. For example, it is prohibited to remove the bones from meat or fish, when one is eating these foods. Rather, one must separate the food from the unwanted matter, and leave the unwanted matter on the plate. Similarly, one may not remove the seeds from fruit that one is eating. The same principle applies to non-food items. One may not take a garment that is not needed at that moment from a pile of clothes.

B. The selecting must be done by hand and not with a tool for separating, like a sieve. A spoon or fork used in the normal way is not considered a special tool for separating.

C. The selecting may be done if the item is needed for immediate use, i.e. food may be separated if it will be eaten right away, and clothes may be selected if they will be worn right away. Items may not be selected if they are to be used later in the day.

Thus, one may only select items from a mixture if all three conditions are fulfilled.

1) The wanted object is separated from the unwanted objects.

2) The separation is done by hand.

3) The object is needed for immediate use.

Additional laws

29. One may not pour water on food mixed with unwanted matter for the purpose of causing the unwanted matter to float or sink, so it will be easier to remove.[33] Some halachic authorities consider washing fruit a form of selecting (i.e. one is using the water to select the fruit from the dirt). Therefore, it is advisable to rinse fruits that have dirt on them for Shabbos before Shabbos.

If a fly or any other unwanted object falls into a food or drink, it should not be removed alone. Rather, the unwanted object should be removed with a little of the food or drink, and thrown away.[34]

30. One may not filter or strain unwanted matter from liquids with a sieve or a piece of cloth.[35] One may slowly pour liquids from a utensil, even if he intends to leave the unwanted matter in the utensil. One must be careful to stop pouring as soon as the flow stops, and there are only drops coming out. When only drops are coming out, it is considered separating unwanted matter from the wanted matter, which is forbidden.[36]

31. One may not peel or shell fruits, vegetables, nuts, etc. for later use. They may only be peeled and shelled for immediate use.[37] It is preferable to avoid using a vegetable peeler, since there are different opinions concerning its use.

The *melachah* of Selecting arises frequently on Shabbos — while eating, washing dishes, and arranging clothes, toys, and books. It is essential to study these complex *halachos* in detail.

Opening cans, bottles and other food wrappers

32.   There are many things one must be careful of when opening bags, cans, or food wrappers on Shabbos.

Bags and cans should be opened in such a way that they do not become receptacles. One may not make a hole in a can or box in order to pour out its contents.[38] When opening a bag of food on Shabbos, one should tear the bag so it can no longer be used as a receptacle. (One should be careful not to tear any letters when tearing the bag.)

Many halachic experts forbid unscrewing screw-on bottle caps for the first time on Shabbos if the lower ring will be separated from the bottle cap, because one is creating a reusable cap.

Packages that are knotted closed may not be untied. (The *halachos* of Tying and Untying a knot are explained in Sections 53-55, below.)

33.   Wrappers and lids of boxes which bear written symbols, drawings, or letters must not be torn or opened if the writing will be torn in the process. Similarly, letters or pictures that are raised or depressed into lids or packages may not be crushed or defaced. Sometimes eggshells, salamis, orange peels, etc., are imprinted with letters or numbers. One must be careful not to cut these symbols when removing the peels and wrappers.[39]

It is best to open cans, food wrappers, and bottles before Shabbos, since opening them on Shabbos might entail a halachic transgression.

Washing dishes

34.   One must be careful not to do any wringing or squeezing while washing dishes on Shabbos.[40] Cloths and sponges[41] may not be used for cleaning purposes. Steel wool may not be used either. One may not use a bar of soap or a cleaning paste on Shabbos (this *halachah* is discussed at length in Section 37). It is advisable to seek practical guidance regarding how to wash dishes on Shabbos.

Cleaning the table and the tablecloth

35. If liquid is spilled on the table, one should wipe up the spill with a cloth about whose cleanliness one is not particular (e.g., a rag). This is to make sure the person will not wring out the cloth in an attempt to clean it. One should be careful not to wring the towel when drying dishes.

If water is spilled on a cloth tablecloth, one should not press down on it hard when wiping up the spill. This is to avoid inadvertently squeezing water from the tablecloth. If colored liquids, like juice or wine, are spilled on a cloth tablecloth, one should avoid spreading the liquid to other parts of the tablecloth when wiping it dry. This is to avoid performing the *melachah* of dyeing.[42]

The prohibition to prepare on Shabbos for weekdays

36. One may not prepare something on Shabbos for use on another day.
One may not even do something permitted on Shabbos, if it is not needed for Shabbos.[43] Therefore, dishes that will not be used anymore on Shabbos may not be washed on Shabbos (even in the permitted way). For example, one may not wash the dishes after *Se'udah Shelishis* (the third meal eaten on Shabbos), since they will not be used again on Shabbos. Glasses and cups which are continually in use may be washed throughout the day, unless one is certain that they will not be needed any more during Shabbos.

The prohibition of preparing on Shabbos for the weekdays is often encountered when one is straightening up the house or kitchen, and when putting garments, books, and other objects away.

Use of soaps, pastes and ointments

37. Bars of soap and soap pastes may not be used on Shabbos. Using these types of soaps involves the *melachah* of Scraping.[44] Thin liquid soap may be used on Shabbos. Washing up on Shabbos is discussed in greater detail in Section 64.

It is prohibited to use any kind of paste on Shabbos. This includes toothpaste, shoe polish,[45] cleaning paste, and hand cream.

It is prohibited to use soft materials, like wax or grease, to fill in holes.[46]

A *rav* should be consulted regarding how to apply ointments for medicinal purposes, since they must be applied differently on Shabbos than on weekdays.

Washing and ironing clothes, hanging laundry and polishing shoes

38. Washing and ironing clothes is prohibited on Shabbos. One may not wet a garment.[47] This includes soaking dirty diapers in water.

39. It is prohibited to remove a stain from a garment. If a damp piece of dirt or mud is stuck to a garment, one may remove it with his fingernail, as long as this will not clean the garment completely, i.e. there will still be a stain where the dirt was. One may not rub the material clean. If the mud is dry, it may not be removed.[48]

40. One may not shake dust off of clothes about whose appearance one is particular. One should put his Shabbos clothes and hat in a place where they will not fall and get dirty. This is so he will not accidentally forget this prohibition, and clean off these articles.[49]

41. It is prohibited to wring or shake off water from a garment or a cloth.[50] Wet laundry may not be hung up to dry on Shabbos. Clothes which became wet on Shabbos may not be hung up to dry, even in a place where no one will see them.[51]

Laundry which was wet at the beginning of Shabbos may not be moved, even after it has dried. Laundry is considered wet if it wets one's hand enough to dampen another item.[52]

42. One may only fold a *tallis* or other articles of clothing if a number of halachic conditions are fulfilled. Some halachic authorities permit folding things as long as one does not fold the item along the original folds.[53]

43. It is forbidden to give clothes any kind of scent on Shabbos.[54] Therefore, clothes should not be dabbed with perfume on Shabbos.

44. Shoes may not be brushed on Shabbos. This applies whether or not polish is used.[55]

Using appliances

45.   One may not turn a light fixture on or off, or dim or increase its light on Shabbos. Similarly, one may not turn on, regulate, or shut off electrical appliances. This prohibition includes battery-operated appliances. Motor vehicles, telephones, and all instruments and appliances which run on gas, petroleum, oil, etc., are included in this prohibition. Similarly, one may not activate or shut off a boiler or central heating system.

Since a vast number of electrical appliances and electronic gadgets are used daily, one must be careful not to accidentally activate them on Shabbos. For example, one must be careful not to pass through an automatic door which is activated when a person enters. Many electrical appliances, like ovens, are regulated by thermostats. Not only must one avoid directly using these appliances, one must be careful to avoid any act which may activate or shut off these appliances.

It is prohibited to wind up or set any kind of watch or clock.[56] Pressing the buttons on a battery-operated digital or analog electronic clock or watch is prohibited.

46.   One may not produce sounds by means of musical instruments, rattles, whistles, bells, etc.[57] One should not clap his hands on Shabbos, unless he claps in an unusual way. For example, one might hit the back of one hand on the palm of the other.[58] Some people do clap in the normal way.

Writing, erasing, and gluing

47.   It is prohibited to write on Shabbos.[59] This prohibition includes drawing,[60] painting,[61] sketching, stamping, and engraving.[62] Writing is forbidden on any material, including sand, dust, the vapor on windows, or liquids that have spilled on a table.[63]

48.   Erasing any kind of writing is prohibited on Shabbos.[64] (For more details, see *melachos* 32 and 33, Writing and Erasing, above.)

One may not break or cut, whether by hand or with a utensil, the letters and words on cakes or other foods. (Some halachic authorities also forbid cutting pictures on food.) According to the *Mishnah Berurah*, one may cut letters which are made from the same substance as the rest of the food, and which are either raised or pressed into the food.[65] The Chazon Ish prohibits this.

If wax, grease, or a similar substance dripped on written letters, one may not remove it on Shabbos.[66]

49.   It is prohibited to paste,[66*] sculpt or mold with clay, play-dough, or any other material.[67]

One may not take photographs, or develop the film on Shabbos.

Sewing, cutting, and tearing

50.   It is prohibited to sew, tighten a loose thread in a garment (e.g. if a button is about to fall off), or open a seam on Shabbos.[68] One may not cut material or paper on Shabbos. Tearing toilet paper is included in this prohibition.[69] Concerning opening packages and bags, see Sections 32-33 above, and *melachos* 19, 20, 23, 24, and 31 (Weaving, Separating into threads, Sewing, Tearing, and Cutting to shape).

51.   Papers or other materials which were intentionally glued together may not be separated on Shabbos.[70] The Torah prohibits separating the edges of pages of books, journals, and newspapers that were not cut before Shabbos.[71]

52.   A string or thread inserted in a collar or sleeve may not be pulled tight if it is inserted in the cloth itself, since this resembles sewing. This kind of tie is commonly found in knitted garments, baby clothes, and baby hats. One is permitted to tighten the string if the holes through which it is inserted are wide, and have a border sewn around them.[72]

Tying and untying a knot or a bow

53.   One may not make a knot on Shabbos or to tighten a knot which became loose.[73] (For example, men must be careful not to tighten the knots on their *tallis katan*.) One may only make a bow over a single knot (like when tying shoes) if he intends to open it on the same day that it was made.

54.   Any knot that may not be tied on Shabbos may not be untied on Shabbos.[74] If the bow of a shoelace became knotted, one may untie the knot to remove the shoe.[75]

55.   If a ribbon or string was pulled out of a shoe or a garment on Shabbos, it may be reinserted if the following conditions are met:

A. It was in the shoe or garment before Shabbos.

B. It is easy to insert (i.e. the holes into which it is inserted are wide).

C. The end of the string is not usually knotted or sewn after it has been inserted.

One may not insert a string or ribbon into a garment or shoe which never had a string or ribbon in it.[76]

Weighing and measuring

56.   Measuring is not permitted on Shabbos. If, on Shabbos, one uses a utensil which has measures marked on it, he should not fill the utensil to the exact measure. Rather, one should fill the utensil a little bit more or a little bit less than the exact measure.[77] One may measure only inaccurately with a utensil which is specifically used for measuring. An example of such a utensil is a measuring cup.[78] Scales and weights may not be used on Shabbos, even if one only intends to weigh something approximately.

One may measure on Shabbos for the purpose of a mitzvah. For example, one may determine if a cup holds the requisite *revi'is* for *Kiddush*. One may also measure when caring for a sick person, since one's efforts to heal him are considered a mitzvah.[79] One may measure when preparing food for babies although it is preferable not to measure exactly.

Building, spreading a cover for a roof, etc.

57.   It is prohibited to engage in any activity connected with building on Shabbos. This includes digging, leveling the ground, pouring concrete, erecting walls, driving in or removing nails, drilling holes, and installing doors and windows. Making or repairing a utensil is also not permitted. For more details, see the *melachah* of Building (*melachah* 34), above.

58.   It is prohibited to spread coverings or erect tents on Shabbos. This includes coverings which protect one from the sun, rain, mosquitoes, etc. This prohibition also applies to coverings which do not cover a walled area.[80]

If the covering is to form a roof, and it was at least a *tefach* wide before Shabbos, one may open it to its entire length on Shabbos. Any part of the covering that is rolled up or folded is not included in the *tefach* that must be open before Shabbos.[81]

59. It is prohibited to erect or unfold a partition on Shabbos. This prohibition applies if the partition is needed for halachic reasons, e.g. it turns an area into a private domain. Similarly, one may not erect a permanent partition, i.e. one that is firmly installed at the top and the bottom.

A partition or covering which may not be made on Shabbos, may not be taken apart or pulled down on Shabbos.[82]

An umbrella may not be used on Shabbos.[83]

A removable hood on a baby carriage should be attached to the carriage before Shabbos. It may then be opened and closed on Shabbos.

60. One may not remove doors or windows from their frames on Shabbos.
If a door or window came off or was removed, it may not be re-attached on Shabbos. Similarly, door or window handles may not be removed or attached on Shabbos.

Sweeping and washing floors

61. It is prohibited to sweep an earthen floor on Shabbos. This is because sweeping may level the ground, or fill existing holes. However, one may sweep a non-earthen floor (e.g. a tiled floor). If most of the houses in the area have earthen floors, one may not sweep his floor on Shabbos, even if it is not earthen.[84] One may not sweep with a straw broom or with one which is likely to have bristles break while sweeping.[85] This even applies to using such a broom on tile floors.

One may not wash floors on Shabbos.[86]

Personal grooming and medical needs

62. It is prohibited to cut, shave, or pluck out hair on Shabbos. This prohibition includes plucking out hair manually, without using an instrument.[87]

Fingernails may not be cut on Shabbos. This prohibition includes biting one's fingernails.[88] Similarly, one may not remove cuticles, or other skin around the nails.[89]

It is also prohibited to apply cosmetics to one's face, lips, eyes, or nails on Shabbos.[90]

63. One may not comb his hair on Shabbos in the same manner as he does during the week. One may only brush his hair lightly with a soft brush which does not pull out hairs. A special soft brush should be set aside for use on Shabbos.[91]

One may not braid or unbraid hair on Shabbos. This includes braiding hair by hand as well as with the help of a comb.[92] Similarly, one may not curl hair on Shabbos. One may part his hair by hand, but not with a comb or a brush.[93]

Washing up

64. On Shabbos, one may not wash his entire body, or even most of it, with warm water. One may use water that was heated before Shabbos to wash his face, hands and feet. If the water was heated on Shabbos, it may not be used at all.[94]

Although one may wash himself with cold water on Shabbos, halachic authorities write that it is customary to avoid doing so, so one does not accidentally squeeze water from his hair.[95]

The prohibition of using a bar of soap or a soap paste on Shabbos is cited in Section 37, above.

Swimming[96] or bathing in the sea or in a swimming pool is prohibited on Shabbos.

Caring for a baby

65. Normal baby care involves many activities, such as washing, and preparing and warming up food, which are likely to entail Shabbos transgressions. Therefore, it is essential to learn how to care for a baby correctly on Shabbos. Books are available which explain these halachos and provide practical advice.

When using cotton balls on Shabbos, one must be careful not to squeeze liquid from them, and not to spread liquid with them.

A *rav* should be consulted regarding whether one may open and close the adhesive strip on disposable diapers.

Taking medicine on Shabbos

66.   The *halachos* regarding when one may take medicine on Shabbos are
very involved. The *halachah* is different for different situations.[97] If
one knows in advance that medical care will be required on Shabbos, he
should consult a *rav* after receiving instructions from the doctor, regarding
how to administer the medications on Shabbos.

Shabbos laws are suspended if there is a possibility that the situation at hand
is life-threatening.

Pikuach nefesh (Saving a life)

The laws of Shabbos are suspended to save a human life. This rule applies
even if there is a doubt as to whether the person is in a life-and-death situation (this is called *safek pikuach nefesh*). It is up to each person to decide, as
honestly and realistically as he can, if he is in an actual, or a potential, life-
threatening situation that mandates suspending the laws of Shabbos.[98]

There are additional situations which our sages considered life-threatening. A
competent *rav* should be consulted regarding what these situations are, and
what procedure to follow in these situations.

One should minimize Shabbos transgression, as long as this will not obstruct
or delay life-preserving measures.

An ill person who is not in danger

An ill person whose life is not endangered, but who is confined to his bed, or
who suffers pains so that his entire body feels weak (e.g. a migraine headache), is called "an ill person who is not in danger." An ill person who is
not in danger is permitted to take medicine on Shabbos.

A young child is halachically considered an ill person who is not in danger.
Therefore, one may take care of a young child's health-related needs, in the
same way one would care for an ill person who is not in danger.

One who suffers from minor ailments

A person who feels a minor ache, like a minor sore throat or headache, is not
permitted to take medicine.

If a person is in such great pain that he has to lie down, or his whole body feels weak, then he is considered "an ill person who is not in danger."

Causing bleeding

It is forbidden to cause bleeding on Shabbos. One may not make a wound, even if the blood swells under the surface of the skin and does not come out (as in a bruise). Similarly, one may not press on a wound to cause it to bleed.

Plants and Trees

Climbing or making use of a tree

67. On Shabbos, one may not climb a tree or use it in any manner. For example, one may not put anything on or take anything off a tree. One may not climb a ladder which is leaning against a tree.[99]

One may not use anything extending from a tree, such as a stake sticking out of it. However, one may make use of an object attached to an object which extends from a tree. For example, one may put something into, or take something out of, a basket which was hung from a stake in a tree before Shabbos.[100] One may not remove the basket from the stake on Shabbos.

One should not place things whose use is permitted on Shabbos on a tree before Shabbos. This is to prevent the objects being taken off and used on Shabbos.[101]

68. One may touch a tree, as long as this will not cause the tree to move.[102]
If a tree is sturdy, and will not move if pressure is exerted on it, a person is permitted to gently lean against it. An exhausted person may not lean against a tree. This is because when an exhausted person leans against a tree, it is considered using it. One may not lean against a fragile tree which moves easily when it is leaned against.[103]

Cultivating the soil

69. All forms of gardening and working the land are prohibited on Shabbos. This includes plowing; sowing; watering; hoeing; weeding; picking flowers or fruit; spraying; uprooting unwanted grass; removing leaves and branches; covering seedlings in nurseries; and all other work done in connection with the ground, plants, or trees.[104] It is also forbidden to do any of these things for potted plants.

Flowerpots standing on the ground may not be moved from one place to another. It is also prohibited to take a flowerpot which is not standing on the ground and put it on the ground.[105]

It is best not to eat in a garden on Shabbos if water is being used, since it is almost inevitable that some water will be spilled on the soil.[106]

It is permitted to walk on grass on Shabbos. However, one should not run or walk quickly through tall grass. This is so one will not accidentally tear out grass.[107]

70. Fruit which fell from a tree on Shabbos may not be moved or eaten on Shabbos. Similarly, any fruit or vegetables found in a garden on Shabbos may not be moved or eaten because they may have become detached on Shabbos.[108] If it is clear that the fruits under a tree fell off before Shabbos, they may be picked up and eaten one at a time. They may not be gathered together, since it is prohibited to gather fruits on Shabbos (see *melachah* 4, above).

One may not put flowers in water on Shabbos. Similarly, one may not add or change the water in a vase of flowers on Shabbos.[109]

The Prohibition of Trapping on Shabbos

Riding an animal and riding in a wagon

71. Trapping animals is not permitted on Shabbos. This prohibition applies to animals which are commonly trapped, such as birds and wild animals, as well as to animals which are not commonly trapped, such as insects.

It is not permitted to ride animals on Shabbos. Similarly, one may not ride in a wagon pulled by an animal.

The prohibition to work one's animal

72.   One may not lead or prod an animal (even if the animal is not his own)
         by hand, with a stick, or even by making a noise, if this will result in the
animal doing one of the thirty-nine *melachos* forbidden on Shabbos.

The owner of an animal must ensure that his animal does not perform any
forbidden work on Shabbos, even if he does not initiate it. This *halachah* is
derived from the verse, "so that your ox and your donkey shall rest"
(*Shemos* 23:12).

Uvdin d'chol (Weekday affairs)

"Honor it [the Shabbos] by not going on your way, pursuing your business,
or speaking common talk" (*Yeshayahu* 58:13).

73.   Our sages added a number of prohibitions to the Shabbos laws. Their
         purpose was to prevent a person from inadvertently transgressing the
Torah prohibitions of Shabbos, and to prevent one from becoming involved
in weekday affairs, which would impair the spiritual and physical tranquility
necessary to experience the sanctity of Shabbos, and to show respect for the
holiness of Shabbos.

The prophet Yeshayahu stated:

> If you restrain your foot because of Shabbos, and you do not pursue your
> affairs on My holy day; if you call the Shabbos a delight, "His holy day ho-
> nored"; and you honor it by not going on your way, pursuing your business,
> or speaking common talk — then you shall delight in God, and I shall make
> you ride over the heights of the earth. (*Yeshayahu* 58:13-14)

Our sages derive from these verses three specific areas of activity which must
be avoided on Shabbos. These areas are in addition to those activities prohibited by the laws of Shabbos:

A. Going on one's way.

B. Pursuing one's affairs.

C. Speaking common talk.

These three things are included in the category of *uvdin d'chol*, "weekday affairs," which are prohibited on Shabbos.

Rushing around on Shabbos

74. The prohibition of "going on one's way" requires that one's stride on
Shabbos differ from his stride during the week. For instance, on Shabbos one should not run or take long strides as if he were in a hurry. People
tend to rush around during the week. The verse in *Yeshayahu* states, "Honor it
[Shabbos] by not going on your way." Therefore, we honor Shabbos by not
rushing around. Children who enjoy running and jumping are permitted to do
so on Shabbos.[110] Running to "tend to one's affairs" is prohibited, but running
to perform a mitzvah, e.g. running to synagogue, or to study Torah, is permitted.

Pursuing one's business

75. "Pursuing one's business" includes the prohibition to buy and sell things
on Shabbos. This prohibition also includes renting or leasing things out,
and hiring workers (even if no wages are mentioned).[111]

It is even prohibited for someone to walk to his fields, shop, or property on
Shabbos, if it is obvious that he is examining what work must be done, or
what items must be bought after Shabbos.

One may not walk to a place where activities which are forbidden on Shabbos
are done, if he intends to do an activity which may not be done on Shabbos
as soon as Shabbos is over. For example, one may not walk to a bus stop on
Shabbos so that he can travel as soon as Shabbos is over. Similarly, one may
not walk to his office on Shabbos so that he can begin to work right after
Shabbos.[112]

76. "Pursuing one's business" includes looking over one's accounts, and
reading professional journals and commercial advertisements. It also includes acquiring or transferring things to others by any act of acquisition
(known as *kinyan*), even without payment.

Gifts are not given on Shabbos because it resembles a business transaction.
However, gifts may be given to facilitate doing a mitzvah, or to enhance
the Shabbos.[113] One should consult a person proficient in Halachah regarding giving bar mitzvah gifts on Shabbos.

77. While "pursuing one's business" is prohibited, tending to religious affairs is permitted. Therefore, when one receives an *aliyah* on Shabbos, he may pledge to make a contribution to charity. One may also calculate sums of money that have been set aside for the purpose of a mitzvah.[114]

Speaking about activities prohibited on Shabbos; relating sad things

78. It is prohibited to talk about activities that are forbidden on Shabbos.
For example, one may not discuss his travel plans, or what he intends to write or buy.[115] Although talking about one's business is prohibited, thinking about it is permitted.

79. Although one may think about his business on Shabbos, one will enjoy Shabbos more if he feels as if all his work is completed before Shabbos begins. The *Mechilta* derives this from the verse in *parashas Yisro*, "Six days you shall work and do all your labor" (*Shemos* 20:9). The *Mechilta* explains, "Can a person complete all his labor in six days? Rather, the verse is implying that when one rests on Shabbos, he should feel as if all his work is completed."[116]

It is inappropriate to discuss sad things on Shabbos because it would detract from the Shabbos atmosphere. Shabbos should be dedicated to Torah study, and idle talk should be minimized. People who are busy earning their livelihood during the week are especially obligated to dedicate Shabbos to Torah study and spiritual growth.[117]

Exerting oneself on Shabbos

80. The prohibition of *uvdin d'chol* ("weekday affairs"), includes performing strenuous work on Shabbos, even if it is work that is not included in the thirty-nine *melachos* of Shabbos. For example, one may not carry a heavy load, or exert himself to gather fruit in a basket, if the fruits were scattered in the yard.

(Fruits that fell, and are scattered in a yard may not be gathered into a basket or container. However, they may be picked up one at a time and eaten, without being placed in a basket. If the fruits all fell in one place, they may be picked up and placed in a basket. If the fruits rolled in the dirt, they may only be picked up one at a time and eaten immediately [see also Section 70, above].[118])

Telling a non-Jew to do *melachah* on Shabbos

81. It is prohibited to tell a non-Jew to do *melachah* for a Jew on Shabbos. It
is also prohibited to instruct a non-Jew on Shabbos to do *melachah* after
Shabbos. Similarly, a Jew may not tell a non-Jew before Shabbos, to do
melachah for a Jew on Shabbos.

The *halachos* regarding when a non-Jew can be asked to do something on
Shabbos that a Jew may not do, are complex. There are ways in which one
is permitted to ask a non-Jew for his assistance. One should consult with
someone who is proficient in Halachah regarding these details.[119]

Laws of Eruvin
(Combining different domains)

82. The laws of *eruvin* are very detailed and complex. These *halachos* deal
with the prohibition of carrying objects from one halachic domain to
another, the prohibition of carrying an object four *amos* within a public domain, and the *halachos* of the four types of domains. The four types of domains are:

A. *Reshus ha-rabbim* — a public thoroughfare

B. *Reshus ha-yachid* — a private domain

C. *Carmelis* — an area which does not qualify as a *reshus ha-rabbim* or a
reshus ha-yachid

D. *Mekom petur* — an exempted space.[120]

Because of their many details, the laws of *eruvin* are only mentioned here in
general terms. One is advised to study these laws in depth, and when in
doubt, to consult a *rav*.

Reshus ha-rabbim (A public thoroughfare)

83. A *reshus ha-rabbim* includes streets which are at least sixteen *amos* wide
and are not covered by a roof. Intercity roads that are sixteen *amos*
wide are included in this category. Projections or depressions in a *reshus
ha-rabbim* which are less than three *tefachim* in height or depth are also considered a part of the *reshus ha-rabbim*. Some halachic authorities are of the

opinion that a thoroughfare must have 600,000 people pass through it daily to be considered a *reshus ha-rabbim*.

Reshus ha-yachid (A private domain)

84.   A *reshus ha-yachid* is a domain which measures at least four *tefachim* by four *tefachim*, and which is enclosed by a partition that is at least ten *tefachim* high. Any area which is ten *tefachim* higher or lower than its surrounding area (like a pit or a mound), and whose surface area is at least four *tefachim* by four *tefachim*, is considered a *reshus ha-yachid*. Any object (like a cupboard, crate, wagon, or car) which is standing in a *reshus ha-rabbim*, and is at least ten *tefachim* high, is considered a *reshus ha-yachid*. No objects may be transferred from the *reshus ha-yachid* (the cupboard, crate, wagon, or car), to the *reshus ha-rabbim* on Shabbos.

Carmelis

85.   A *carmelis* is an area which measures at least four *tefachim* by four *tefachim*, and which is enclosed by a partition of between three and nine *tefachim*. An area which is between three and nine *tefachim* higher or lower than the surrounding *reshus ha-rabbim* is considered a *carmelis*. Areas which do not qualify as a *reshus ha-rabbim* or a *reshus ha-yachid*, such as a field, the sea, a desert, and other open places, are also considered a *carmelis*.

A mekom petur (An exempted space)

A *mekom petur* is an area within a *reshus ha-rabbim* with a surface area of less than four *tefachim* by four *tefachim*, and which is at least three *tefachim* higher than its surrounding area.

There are different halachic opinions as to whether the rules of a *mekom petur* apply to an area with these dimensions which is within a *carmelis*.

According to the Chazon Ish, a *tefach* is 9.6 cm (3.8 inches). According to Rav Chaim Na'eh, a *tefach* is 8 cm (3.2 inches). An *amah* is equal to six *tefachim*. Therefore, according to the Chazon Ish, an *amah* is 57.6 cm (22.7 inches), and according to Rav Chaim Na'eh an *amah* is 48 cm (18.9 inches).

The prohibition of transferring from one domain to another

86. One may not transfer any object from one domain to another on Shabbos. This applies to a *reshus ha-rabbim*, a *reshus ha-yachid*, and a *carmelis*. This rule applies whether the object is carried by hand, in a pocket, or by any other means. This includes throwing the object, handing over the object, and pushing or pulling the object. Wearing clothes and jewelry is not considered carrying them. This *halachah* even applies to objects which are not *muktzeh* (forbidden to be moved on Shabbos). Objects which are *muktzeh* may not even be moved within a given domain, as will be explained below.

Carrying from a *mekom petur*

One may transfer objects from a *mekom petur* to a *reshus ha-rabbim* and to a *reshus ha-yachid*, and vice versa. One may not transfer objects from a *reshus ha-yachid* to a *reshus ha-rabbim* via a *mekom petur*, even if he leaves the object in the *mekom petur* before he passes it to the next domain.

Carrying four *amos* in a *reshus ha-rabbim* or a *carmelis*

One may not carry an object four *amos* within a *reshus ha-rabbim* or a *carmelis*, even if it will not be transferred to another domain.

Eruv chatzeros

87. The laws of *eruvin* (combining domains) explain how two domains may be combined into one by an *eruv chatzeros* ("mixing courtyards") or *shituf mevo'os* ("joining lanes"), to enable one to carry things between them. Because these *halachos* are extremely complicated, *eruvin* should only be made by experts in these *halachos*.

In many cities and towns, an *eruv* is set up, halachically changing the area into one domain. The *eruv* is made by creating "the shape of an entrance," i.e. two poles capped by a beam or a cord which is considered a partition. A network of such poles is set up around the population center. Additionally, bread which was acquired on behalf of the citizens of the area is kept in one citizen's home. By making an *eruv chatzeros*, residents are considered joint owners of the entire city, so that carrying within it becomes permitted. As mentioned above, the *halachos* concerning *eruvin* are very complex. Therefore, one should only rely on an *eruv* that was set up, and that is checked regularly, by an expert in the *halachos* of *eruvin*.

Jewelry

88.   Jewelry may be worn while going from one domain to another, or while walking four *amos* in a *reshus ha-rabbim*. However, the following conditions must exist: the jewelry must not be carried in one's hand or pocket. Rather, the jewelry must be worn in the same way that it is worn during the week, i.e. fastened to one's clothing or on one's person. A woman should not wear a piece of jewelry if she may take it off to show others. Similarly, one should not wear jewelry if it could fall off (for example, if the clasp is loose). This is because the person might pick up the jewelry that fell off, and carry it in his hand.[121] Because of these reasons, certain types of jewelry may not be worn when going from one domain to another on Shabbos. One should clarify these *halachos* with an expert.

Techum Shabbos (The *Shabbos* boundary)

89.   Another prohibition of Shabbos is *techum Shabbos* (the Shabbos boundary). On Shabbos, one may not walk more than two thousand *amos* from the city or population center. This rule applies whether or not one is carrying things.

An *eruv techumin* ("mixing boundaries") can be made, which enables a person to walk more than two thousand *amos* in one direction. Because of the many details involved, one should not make an *eruv techumin* without receiving guidance from an expert in these *halachos*.

The Prohibition of Muktzeh
(Objects which may not be handled on Shabbos)

90.   The term *muktzeh* means "set apart." Objects which are considered *muktzeh* may not be moved on Shabbos.[122]

The main categories of *muktzeh* are:

A. *Keli she-melachto l'issur* — an instrument normally used for work which is prohibited on Shabbos.

B. *Muktzeh me-chamas cheseron kis* — something of value which is normally used to do work which is prohibited on Shabbos, whose owner is particular about not using it for any other purpose.

C. *Muktzeh me-chamas gufo* — something which is not food (either for
people or for animals), and which has no specific purpose on Shabbos (e.g.
pebbles or dust).

D. *Basis l'davar ha-assur* — something which is not intrinsically *muktzeh*,
but which has something *muktzeh* on top of it.[123]

The Rambam writes:

> Our sages forbade moving certain items on Shabbos as they are moved during
> the week. Why did they decree this prohibition? They deduced that if the
> prophets commanded that one's stride on Shabbos be different from one's
> stride during the week, and that one's conversation on Shabbos be different
> from one's conversation during the week, then surely the items that one
> moves on Shabbos should be different from the items that he moves during
> the week. Thus, Shabbos should not be like a typical weekday, on which
> one lifts objects, and fixes them inside or outside his home, etc. Since he is
> inactive at home, he may seek to occupy himself rather than rest. He
> would thus nullify the entire reason for Shabbos, which is stated in the
> Torah: "In order that he rest." (*Hilchos Shabbos*, Chapter 24:12)

The Rambam lists additional reasons for the prohibition of *muktzeh* there.

Keli she-melachto l'issur

91.   A *keli she-melachto l'issur* is an object which is used to do *melachah* that
         is prohibited on Shabbos. This category includes: writing implements;
matches; building tools like a hammer, saw, and nails; and kitchen utensils
like a sieve, grater, sifter, and empty pots which are not ordinarily used for
food storage and their lids.

92.   A *keli she-melachto l'issur* may not be moved on Shabbos. The only ex-
         ceptions to this rule are if the object is needed for a use that is permitted
on Shabbos, or one needs the place where it is lying. An example of a *keli she-
melachto l'issur* that can be moved for a use that is permitted on Shabbos is a
hammer which can be used to crack nuts. However, if one has a nutcracker, or
any other suitable tool which is not *muktzeh*, one should use it instead of the
hammer. An example of a *keli she-melachto l'issur* that can be moved if one
needs its place is a hammer lying on a table where one wishes to eat, or

on a chair on which one wishes to sit. In these situations, one may move the *keli she-melachto l'issur* to another place.

Muktzeh objects included in the following categories may not be moved, even if it is for a use which is permitted on Shabbos, or if their place is needed.

Muktzeh me-chamas cheseron kis

93. *Muktzeh me-chamas cheseron kis* is something of value which is normally used to do work that is prohibited on Shabbos, whose owner is particular about not using it for any other purpose because the object would be damaged. Examples of things which would be included in this category are typewriters, candlesticks, cameras, and securities. Merchandise which the owner will not use because he intends to sell it is also included in this category.

Muktzeh me-chamas gufo

94. *Muktzeh me-chamas gufo* is something which is neither a utensil nor a food, such as; stones, sand, pits, coins, and tokens. Things which are not edible when they are raw are also included in this category, such as flour, uncooked beans, and raw potatoes. Foods whose consumption are forbidden by the Torah are also included in this category.

Basis l'davar ha-assur

95. A *basis l'davar ha-assur* is an object on which or in which the owner, or somebody else with the owner's knowledge, put a *muktzeh* object before Shabbos. If the *muktzeh* object is still in or on the non-*muktzeh* object when Shabbos begins, the non-*muktzeh* object becomes *muktzeh* for the entire Shabbos. It may not be moved, even if the *muktzeh* object is removed or falls off on Shabbos. For example, a desk drawer which contains money or tools is considered a base for the *muktzeh* objects, and therefore may not be opened.

The *halachah* is different if, at the beginning of Shabbos, the object held both *muktzeh* and non-*muktzeh* objects. If the objects that are not *muktzeh* are more important to the owner (e.g. if he needs to use them on Shabbos), and the *muktzeh* objects cannot be shaken off, the "base" may be moved.

The *halachos* of *muktzeh* are numerous and complex. Due to the frequency with which they are encountered, one is advised to study these *halachos* and their practical applications thoroughly.

Cases in which it is permitted to move *muktzeh* objects

96. Splinters and glass fragments which may cause injury may be removed.[124] Similarly, if peels and bones remain on the table after a meal, and one finds it repulsive for them to remain there until the end of Shabbos, one may remove them.

Permitted ways to move *muktzeh* objects

97. **Moving a *muktzeh* object by blowing it:** One may move a *muktzeh* item by blowing on it. For example, one may blow money bills off the table.

Moving a *muktzeh* object indirectly: One may move a *muktzeh* object by pushing it with another object. This method of moving an object is halachically termed *"tiltul min ha-tzad."* One may only use this method if his intention is not to move the *muktzeh* object.

For example, one may take a garment which is not *muktzeh*, even if in the process a *muktzeh* garment will be moved. One may take a book even if some coins will be moved in the process.

One may not move a *muktzeh* object through indirect means if he is really intending to move the *muktzeh* object.

Moving a *muktzeh* object with one's body: According to the *Mishnah Berurah*, one may move a *muktzeh* object with a limb other than his hand. For example, one may kick the *muktzeh* object with his foot, etc. The Chazon Ish, however, forbids moving *muktzeh* in this way.

Chapter Twenty-One

Preparations That Should Be Done before Shabbos

1.   This chapter lists preparations which should be done before Shabbos, so as to prevent the possibility of desecrating Shabbos. Each person should add other preparations to this list which are necessary to help him personally observe Shabbos in the proper spirit, in full compliance with its *halachos*.

2.   Food whose preparation requires grinding, mixing two substances into one indistinguishable mass, or squeezing juice, must be prepared before Shabbos.

3.   All cooking and baking must be done before Shabbos. Foods which one wants to serve warm on Shabbos should be placed on a source of heat after they are cooked, and before Shabbos starts. The source of heat that is used should be covered with a metal sheet.

4.   All the hot water needed for drinking and food purposes on Shabbos must be boiled in advance. The water should be kept hot in a kettle or urn placed on the source of heat, as mentioned in Section 3, above.

5.   Tea essence should be prepared before Shabbos for use on Shabbos. Using uncooked teabags or tea leaves on Shabbos may involve the prohibition of cooking.[1]

6.   Fruits and vegetables which are mixed with dirt and other unwanted matter should be washed before Shabbos. There is a *halachic* opinion that washing fruits under running water is included in the prohibition of "Selecting".[2]

7   It is preferable to open cans, food packages, milk containers, wine bottles and soda bottles before Shabbos. For more details, see Chapter 20, Section 32.

8.　　Tithes (*terumos* and *ma'asros*) should be separated before Shabbos.[3] It is
　　　　forbidden to separate tithes on Shabbos and *Yom Tov*. If, on *erev
Shabbos* or on *erev Yom Tov* one remembers that he did not separate tithes
from the food that he plans to eat on Shabbos or *Yom Tov*, he can separate
them on Shabbos or *Yom Tov* if he recites a special stipulation while it is still
daytime. See Chapter 37, Section 19, for the text of the stipulation, as well as
a discussion regarding how to separate tithes.

9.　　Some people use a timer to turn lights on and off at preset times on
　　　　Shabbos. The timer must be set before Shabbos.

The light bulb that turns on when the refrigerator is opened must be discon-
nected before Shabbos. There are different halachic opinions concerning when
an electric refrigerator can be opened on Shabbos. According to some halachic authorities, it can be opened at any time. According to other halachic
authorities, the refrigerator may only be opened when the motor is already
running, so that the motor will not start running when the refrigerator is
opened. (If the refrigerator has automatic defrost, one must clarify when it
may be closed.)

10.　Toilet paper must be cut before Shabbos, since it is prohibited to tear it
　　　　on Shabbos.[4]

11.　Objects which are *muktzeh* (i.e. may not be moved on Shabbos) should be
　　　　put away before Shabbos. This applies to money, writing utensils, and
many other articles, some of which are listed in Chapter 20, Sections 90-97.

These objects should not be left in places which are used on Shabbos, such as
in pockets, on chairs or tables, in kitchen drawers, etc., to prevent them from
being moved on Shabbos.

If a man uses the same *tallis* for Shabbos and weekdays, he should remove his
tefillin from the *tallis*-bag before Shabbos, so he will not move them on Shabbos.

12.　It is a mitzvah to check the pockets of the clothes that one will wear on
　　　　Shabbos. This is to ensure that they do not contain anything *muktzeh*,
and that one will not accidentally carry an item into a *reshus ha-rabbim* on
Shabbos.[5]

13.   If there is a baby in the house, everything needed for his care should be prepared before Shabbos in ample amounts, e.g. cooked or mashed food, diapers, etc.

14.   If one knows that medical treatment will be necessary on Shabbos (i.e. for an illness or a wound), one should ask a *rav* how to comply with the doctor's instructions on Shabbos.

15.   When *Yom Tov* precedes or follows Shabbos, or when *Yom Tov* is observed for two consecutive days, candles for the second day should be prepared before Shabbos begins. On these days, it is prohibited to melt the bottom of a candle so it will stand up straight in the candlestick, or to prepare the wick by temporarily lighting it (*Mishnah Berurah* 514 (18, 25)).

16.   As Shabbos draws near, one should gently urge his family to complete the Shabbos preparations. Our sages state, "One should say three things in his home on *erev Shabbos*, before it gets dark: Have you separated *ma'aser* (tithes)? Have you made an *eruv*? Then light the candles!" (*Shabbos* 2:7).

Every person should make those preparations, aside from the ones mentioned in this chapter, that will help him observe and enjoy Shabbos to its fullest. Every Jew can experience the pleasure, tranquility and holiness that encompasses Shabbos. Preparing for Shabbos, and being proficient in its *halachos*, will enable one to enjoy this day, which is truly "A reflection of the world to come, a day of tranquility and repose."

Part Four: Festivals and Special Days in the Jewish Calendar

The following chapters discuss the laws and customs of the festivals, *Rosh Chodesh* (the beginning of the lunar month), the various fast days, and other special days. The general *halachos* that apply to every festival (*Yom Tov*) and the *halachos* that apply to *Rosh Chodesh* are discussed first. These are followed by a detailed discussion of each *Yom Tov*.

One should study the *halachos* pertaining to each *Yom Tov* in the weeks preceding it, as well as on the *Yom Tov* itself. To achieve a more profound and meaningful observance of the *Yom Tov*, one should study the special significance of the festival and the insights associated with it. There are many books available which discuss these topics.

Annual halachic calendars are available which note the Torah Readings for each Shabbos and *Yom Tov*, the special *mitzvos* for each *Yom Tov*, and other pertinent information. Many synagogues hang these calendars on their wall. It is advisable to read it to learn many important details about the special days in the Jewish calendar.

Chapter Twenty-Two

The Halachos Pertaining to Yom Tov

The dates of the festivals

1. The laws in this chapter apply to the following *Yamim Tovim*:

   * Rosh Hashana, which begins on the first and second of Tishrei.

   * Succos, which begins on the fifteenth of Tishrei. (The sixteenth through the twenty-first of Tishrei are *Chol Ha-mo'ed Succos*, the intermediate days of the holiday.)

   * Shemini Atzeres (also called Simchas Torah), which begins on the twenty-second of Tishrei.

   * Pesach, which begins on the fifteenth of Nissan. (The sixteenth to the twentieth of Nissan are *Chol Ha-mo'ed Pesach*, the intermediate days of the holiday.)

   * Shavuos, which begins on the sixth of Sivan.

   The *halachos* pertaining to Yom Kippur, which are different from those of the other *Yamim Tovim*, are discussed in Chapter 28. The *halachos* pertaining to *chol ha-mo'ed* are discussed in Chapter 29. The *halachos* pertaining to the second day of *Yom Tov* observed outside of Israel are discussed in Sections 2-4, below.

The second day of *Yom Tov* in the Diaspora

2. Outside of Israel, an additional five days of *Yom Tov* must be observed each year. These days are called *Yom Tov sheini shel galuyos*, "the second day of *Yom Tov* in the Diaspora." These additional days occur on the second day of Succos (the sixteenth of Tishrei), the day after Shemini Atzeres (the twenty-third of Tishrei), the day after the first and the seventh day of Pesach (the sixteenth and twenty-second of Nissan), and the day after Shavuos (the

seventh of Sivan).[1] In the Diaspora, the day of *Yom Tov* which follows She-mini Atzeres is called Simchas Torah. In Israel, Shemini Atzeres and Simchas Torah are celebrated on the same day.

Jews living outside of Israel must observe the first day and second day of *Yom Tov* in exactly the same way.[2]

3.   The first and second days of Yom Tov are fully independent. Therefore, nothing may be prepared or cooked on the first day of *Yom Tov* for the second day.

One may only light candles for the second day of *Yom Tov* after the first day of *Yom Tov* is over. This is after three stars appear. (See Section 7, below, regarding how to light a fire on *Yom Tov*.)

If the second day of *Yom Tov* is on Friday, an *eruv tavshilin* is made on Wednesday, before the first day of *Yom Tov* begins (see Sections 13-17, below, for details). An *eruv tavshilin* allows one to prepare food on Friday for Shabbos, and to light the Shabbos candles before sunset. (See the timetable at the end of Chapter 16 for information regarding when to light candles for Shabbos.)

4.   The *halachos* regarding how the second day of *Yom Tov* is observed by one who lives outside of Israel, but who is spending *Yom Tov* in Israel, an Israeli who is abroad for *Yom Tov*, or someone who resides alternately in Israel and abroad, are complex.[3] These people should consult a *rav* regarding whether they may perform *melachah* on the second day of *Yom Tov*, should recite the holiday service, wear *tefillin*, join a *minyan* and receive *aliyos* to the Torah. Below are a few pertinent *halachos*.

A person from abroad who is presently living in Israel, but who intends to return to the Diaspora, must observe the prohibition of work on the second day of *Yom Tov*, and must recite the *Yom Tov* prayers. Similarly, he is required to recite *Kiddush*, partake of two holiday meals, and add *Ya'aleh V'yavo* in *Birkas Ha-mazon*.

An Israeli who is temporarily abroad during *Yom Tov* may not do prohibited work on the second day of *Yom Tov*. However, he dons his *tefillin*, and recites the weekday prayers privately at home, and then goes to the synagogue to hear *Kaddish*, *Kedushah*, etc.[3]

The Prohibition of Doing Melachah on Yom Tov

5.   Most *melachos* prohibited on Shabbos are also prohibited on *Yom Tov*. The *Yamim Tovim* should be devoted to relaxation, festival joy and spiritual rejuvenation.

Since the laws of *Yom Tov* are similar to those of Shabbos, they are only discussed briefly here. For a more in-depth discussion, see Chapters 20 and 21.

6.   Examples of *melachos* that are prohibited on *Yom Tov* are: laundering; wringing; cutting hair; shaving; cutting fingernails and toenails; writing and erasing; turning on or off electrical lights; driving a car (including starting and turning off the engine); using a telephone; and gardening.[4]

Some people mistakenly think that it is permissible to turn on lights on *Yom Tov*. It must be stressed that this is an error, and that turning lights on or off is prohibited.

There are some *melachos* that may be done on *Yom Tov* that may not be done on Shabbos. It must be noted that those *melachos* that may be done on *Yom Tov*, may only be done for *Yom Tov*. Some examples are discussed in the following sections.

Laws Regarding Fire and Cooking on Yom Tov

Transferring fire

7.   It is prohibited to light a match, a cigarette lighter, or the like on *Yom Tov*.[5] One may only light a fire from an existing fire. For example, one may light a candle or match from a burning flame. This new flame can be used to light other fires. (It is advisable to have a candle that burns throughout the day, from which one can light other candles.)

Smoking

Some halachic authorities prohibit smoking on *Yom Tov*. Other halachic authorities permit smoking for those who are accustomed to it. Smokers must be careful not to extinguish the flame that was used to light the cigarette or to shake off the cigarette's ash with their fingers, or by any other means. Similarly, one may not extinguish the cigarette when he has finished smoking it. This is because extinguishing a fire is prohibited on Yom Tov.[6]

Some people erase the printed letters on cigarettes before Yom Tov to avoid "erasing" the letters on Yom Tov when smoking the cigarette.

The prohibition to extinguish a flame

It is prohibited to extinguish or lower a flame on Yom Tov.[7] A burning match or candle should be carefully laid down and so it will extinguish itself.

Baking and cooking on Yom Tov

8. It is permitted to bake and cook on Yom Tov if the food is needed for that day. This is derived from the verse, "Only that which is needed for eating may alone be done" (Shemos 12:16). There are many halachos regarding cooking and baking foods on Yom Tov, when their taste would not be diminished if they were prepared in advance.[8] One should receive guidance regarding cooking on Yom Tov for persons who publicly desecrate Shabbos.

A fire may be enlarged for cooking, but may not be extinguished.

It is prohibited to cook on Yom Tov for the next day, even if the following day is also a Yom Tov, i.e. the second day of Yom Tov observed in the Diaspora, or the second day of Rosh Hashana. Regarding cooking for Shabbos on a Yom Tov which occurs on Friday, see the laws of eruv tavshilin in Sections 13-17, below. Guidance should be received regarding cooking for people who publicly desecrate Shabbos.

The prohibition to use electrical appliances on Yom Tov

Although food may be cooked on an electric stove and hot plate, it is prohibited to switch it on and off. Whether the temperature may be raised, depends on how the electric stove functions. Similarly, one may not turn on or off any electrical appliance on Yom Tov.

Squeezing, mixing, and grinding

9. Fruits and vegetables may not be squeezed on Yom Tov, even if the juice is needed for that day.[9]

10.   The *melachah* of mixing may be done on *Yom Tov* if the food will be
            eaten that same day. Because the *halachos* regarding sifting flour on
Yom Tov are complicated, one should sift his flour before *Yom Tov*. Since
we do not measure things on *Yom Tov*, one should estimate the amount of
flour needed for the dough.[10]

Whether or not one may grind food on *Yom Tov* depends on the particular
situation. Some of the laws are as follows:

It is permissible to grind a baked food that one plans to eat that day, if its
ingredients had been ground previously.

A food that is not of vegetable origin (such as meat, fish, and eggs) may be
mashed with a fork. However, if this food needs to be ground in a grinder,
this should be done before the holiday.

Spices may be ground with a mortar and pestle on *Yom Tov*. This is because
the quality of ground spices diminishes with time. The spices may not be
ground in a grinder.[11] The same rule applies to other produce that would
rot or lose flavor if it were ground before the holiday.

Selecting on *Yom Tov*

11.   The laws of selecting on *Yom Tov* are different from the laws of select-
            ing on Shabbos. (See Chapter 20, Sections 27-31 for details regarding
selecting on Shabbos.)

On Shabbos one may only select for immediate use. On *Yom Tov* selecting is
even permitted for later in the day, as long as it is for use on *Yom Tov*.

On Shabbos, when permitted, selecting must only be done by hand. On *Yom
Tov* one may select with utensils which are not specifically for selecting.

On Shabbos one may only select the wanted part of the mixture. On *Yom
Tov* one must remove the part that requires the least exertion. If separating
the food from the unwanted matter is difficult because there is less unwanted
matter than food, or if the food consists of tiny particles which are hard to
sort out, then one may remove the unwanted matter from the food. Similarly, if it is more difficult to select the unwanted matter from the food,
one should remove the food from the unwanted matter.[12]

The *halachos* pertaining to: carrying from one domain to another, *muktzeh*, and *techum Shabbos*

12.   On *Yom Tov*, it is permitted to carry objects that are needed for that day from a *reshus ha-yachid* to a *reshus ha-rabbim*, and vice versa.[13] One may also carry these objects in a *reshus ha-rabbim*. Objects which are not needed for *Yom Tov* may not be carried from one domain to another, or carried in a *reshus ha-rabbim*. (These rules apply to places where there is no *eruv*.)

Muktzeh objects may not be moved on *Yom Tov*.[14] One may not leave the *techum Shabbos* on *Yom Tov* (For more detailed discussion regarding carrying from one domain to another and *techum Shabbos*, see Chapter 20, Sections 82-89.)

The prohibition to move *muktzeh* is discussed in greater detail in Chapter 20, Sections 90-97. One may move *muktzeh* objects to facilitate eating. For example, if the key to a cabinet that contains food is located among *muktzeh* objects, one may take the key from there. When possible, it is preferable to move *muktzeh* objects in an unusual way (for example, with the back of one's hand).

Eruv Tavshilin
(Combining the cooking done for Shabbos on Yom Tov with the cooking done for Shabbos before Yom Tov)

13.   It is prohibited to cook or bake anything on *Yom Tov* that is not needed that same day. However, if *Yom Tov* is on Friday, it is permitted to cook or bake on that day for Shabbos, if an *eruv tavshilin* was made before *Yom Tov*.[15]

The concept of an *eruv tavshilin* is that one is "combining food" that was prepared for Shabbos before *Yom Tov* started, with the food being prepared on *Yom Tov* for Shabbos. Thus, whatever food was prepared on *Yom Tov* for Shabbos is considered a completion of the food preparations done before *Yom Tov*. The cooking must be completed early enough before Shabbos, that if guests would arrive suddenly, the food could be served to them on *Yom Tov*.

14. The *eruv tavshilin* is made on the day before *Yom Tov*. One sets aside a piece of bread (e.g. a challah, a matzah, or a roll) and a cooked food which is usually eaten with bread (e.g. an egg, fish, or meat).[16] The piece of bread and the cooked food must be at least the size of a *k'zayis*, but preferably the size of a *k'beitzah*. (For the exact size of a *k'zayis* and a *k'beitzah*, see the Table of Measures at the end of Chapter 15.) One who wishes to fulfill the mitzvah of *eruv tavshilin* in the best way should use a whole loaf of bread and a large portion of meat or fish.[17]

15. After setting aside the bread and cooked food, one recites the blessing *asher kideshanu b'mitzvosav v'tzivanu al mitzvas eruv* ("Who sanctified us with His *mitzvos* and commanded us concerning the mitzvah of *eruv*").

After reciting the blessing, one recites a passage which is printed in some *Siddurim*, as well as in the *Machzor* (the special *Yom Tov* prayer book).[18] The passage is in Aramaic, and means: "By means of this *eruv* we will be permitted to bake, cook, wrap up food to keep it warm, kindle lights and prepare on *Yom Tov* all that we need for Shabbos — we, and all the Jews living in this city." One who does not understand Aramaic may recite the text in any language he understands.[19]

We mention in the text of *eruv tavshilin* that we are making the *eruv* on behalf of all the Jewish inhabitants of the city that forgot to make one themselves. One who intends to have his *eruv* exempt other people in the city should have another person, who is not halachically considered a member of his household, raise the bread and cooked food at least one *tefach*. (For the exact measure of a *tefach*, see the Table of Measures at the end of Chapter 15.) The person holding the bread and cooked food must intend to acquire it on behalf of all the Jews of the city. The person then gives the bread and cooked food back to the head of the household, who recites the blessing and the text of the *eruv*.[20] If one forgot to make an *eruv*, he should ask a *rav* if the conditions are present under which he may rely on the *eruv* that others made.

16. The bread and cooked food used for the *eruv* may not be eaten until all the preparations for Shabbos, including cooking, baking and candle-lighting, are completed. If they were eaten before that, one may no longer rely on this *eruv* to allow him to prepare on *Yom Tov* for Shabbos.[21]

It is commendable to use the bread from the *eruv* as one of the loaves for the first two meals of Shabbos, and to eat it during the third meal.[22]

17.   If *Yom Tov* is on Thursday and Friday (i.e. Rosh Hashana in Israel, or two consecutive days of *Yom Tov* outside of Israel), the *eruv tavshilin* is made on Wednesday (before *Yom Tov* begins), and the preparations for Shabbos are done on Friday, the second day of *Yom Tov*.[23]

Lighting the Candles

18.   *Yom Tov* candles are lit at night.[24]

The lit candles help create an atmosphere of peace and joy in the home. The candles also express the importance and reverence we ascribe to the *Yom Tov*. The general *halachos* regarding how to light candles are discussed in Chapter 16, Sections 9-18.

19.   Some women light the candles when *Yom Tov* begins, while others wait until later, when their husbands return from synagogue.

It is prohibited to kindle a new fire on *Yom Tov*. Therefore, one who lights candles after *Yom Tov* began must do so from an existing flame. Since extinguishing a fire is also prohibited, the match or candle which was used to light the *Yom Tov* candles should be carefully laid down and allowed to extinguish itself. On *Yom Tov* it is prohibited to melt the wax on the bottom of the candles so they will sit firmly in the candlesticks.

When *Yom Tov* is on Shabbos, the candles must be lit before sunset.

20.   When *Yom Tov* is on a weekday, many women have the custom to recite the blessing before lighting the candles, instead of lighting the candles first, as is done before Shabbos.[25]

The blessing recited when lighting the candles for *Yom Tov* is *asher kideshanu b'mitzvosav v'tzivanu l'hadlik ner shel Yom Tov* ("Who sanctified us with His *mitzvos* and commanded us to kindle *Yom Tov* lights").[26] Ashkenazic Jews then recite the blessing of *She-hecheyanu*. Sephardic Jews do not recite *She-hecheyanu* at this time. If the person lighting the candles will be reciting *Kiddush* on *Yom Tov* night, he does not recite *She-hecheyanu* both times. He only recites it during *Kiddush*.

21. When *Yom Tov* is on Shabbos, the woman first lights the candles (as is done on *erev Shabbos*), and then recites the blessings *l'hadlik ner shel Shabbos v'shel Yom Tov*, and *She-hecheyanu.*[27]

She-hecheyanu is not recited when lighting the candles on the last day of Pesach. This is because all seven days of Pesach are considered one festival, and the blessing was already recited on the first night. *She-hecheyanu* is recited when lighting candles for Shemini Atzeres, because it is an independent festival (and not part of Succos). Candles are lit on the second day of *Yom Tov* which is observed outside of Israel. Both *l'hadlik ner shel Yom Tov* and *She-hecheyanu* are recited when lighting the candles.[28]

The Yom Tov Prayers

22. The *Yom Tov* prayers express the profound significance of the festival as well as supplications appropriate to these holy days. The *Musaf* service is recited, and special sections are read from the Torah. There is a special prayer book for each *Yom Tov* called a *Machzor*. The *Machzor* has all the holiday services and additions in the proper order. More details concerning the special prayers for each *Yom Tov* are discussed in the chapter dealing with each particular *Yom Tov*.

One should familiarize himself with the *Yom Tov* prayers before reciting them. The first time one recites them on the festival, he should do so from a *Siddur* or *Machzor*.[29] Before reciting prayers which are recited rarely (such as *va-todi'einu*, which is recited when *Yom Tov* is on Saturday night), it is advisable to note the prayer's place in the *Siddur* or *Machzor* before one begins praying. This will help a person avoid searching for the prayer and having to interrupt the flow of his prayers.[30]

Honoring the Yom Tov and Rejoicing in It

23. *Yom Tov* must be accorded the same honor as Shabbos.[31] It is a mitzvah to bathe with warm water on *erev Yom Tov.*[32] It is customary for men to immerse themselves in the *mikveh* before Rosh Hashana, Yom Kippur, and the three festivals. The garments one wears on *Yom Tov* should be finer than those he wears on Shabbos. This is because one of the ways to fulfill the mitzvah of rejoicing on *Yom Tov* is by wearing beautiful clothes.[33] If one needs a haircut, it is a mitzvah to have it done before *Yom Tov*.

Further details concerning preparations for *Yom Tov* are discussed in Chapter 16, Sections 1-8 (these sections discuss the preparations for Shabbos).

24.   The Torah commands us, "You shall rejoice on your festival"(*Devarim* 16:14). This obligates one to rejoice on *Yom Tov*. The joy emanates from God's closeness to His people Israel, the immense spiritual heritage of our people, and the significance and sanctity of the festival.

Men, women, and children must rejoice and be happy on *Yom Tov*. As the festival approaches, a man should delight his wife with new clothes, and his children with sweets, nuts, etc., according to his means.[34]

25.   In *The Kuzari*, Rabbi Yehudah HaLevy explains the significance of rejoicing on *Yom Tov*. He stresses the importance of this mitzvah as a means by which the heart attains deep faith in God, and closeness and devotion to Him:

> Our Torah distinguishes between fearing, loving and rejoicing in God. A person is expected to approach the Almighty in each of these ways.
>
> Your submissiveness on fast days does not bring you nearer to God than your joy on Shabbos and *Yom Tov*, provided your joy emanates from an attentive and complete heart. Just like the supplications on fast days require meditation and total concentration, when you rejoice when doing a mitzvah, your joy should emanate from your love for the One Who decreed the mitzvah, and from the realization that He is benefiting you through it.
>
> You should feel as if you are the Almighty's guest, invited to His table to partake of His beneficence. You should thank Him with your whole being, and if your joy brings you to song and dance — this is the service of God which enables you to attain Godliness. (*The Kuzari* 2:50)

According to Rabbi Yehudah HaLevy, a person is capable of reaching great spiritual levels and the utmost closeness to God through joy. This is what the medium of joy on *Yom Tov* is supposed to accomplish.

The Yom Tov Meals

26.   At least two meals must be eaten on *Yom Tov*, one at night after *Ma'ariv*, and one during the day.[35]

Kiddush is recited over wine before these meals. The text for *Kiddush* is printed in *Siddurim* and *Machzorim*. (Regarding how much wine must be used for *Kiddush*, the prohibition to eat or drink before *Kiddush*, how to exempt others from *Kiddush*, who drinks the wine, the rule that *Kiddush* must be recited where the meal is eaten, as well as other details pertaining to *Kiddush*, see Chapter 17, Sections 9-19.)

27.   Before the meal, one washes his hands, and recites the blessing *al netilas yadayim*. *Ha-motzi* is then recited over two loaves of bread, like on Shabbos.

The *Yom Tov* meals should be celebrated with joy. It is a mitzvah to eat meat and drink wine (which gladdens a man's heart) on *Yom Tov*. Torah topics pertaining to the festival should be discussed, and *zemiros* should be sung. The meaning and sanctity of *Yom Tov* should be impressed upon all members of the household.

Ya'aleh V'yavo is added to *Birkas Ha-mazon*. *Ya'aleh V'yavo* is a prayer asking God to remember us and grant us blessing. In Chapter 12, Section 9, there is a table which illustrates how one should proceed if he forgot to recite *Ya'aleh V'yavo*.

Havdalah

28.   In the *Shemoneh Esreh* for *Ma'ariv* on *Motza'ei Yom Tov* (the night following the end of *Yom Tov*), the paragraph of *Attah chonantanu* is added to the blessing of *Attah chonen*. If one forgot to add *Attah chonantanu*, he does not repeat the *Shemoneh Esreh*.[36] For additional details regarding *Attah chonantanu*, see Chapter 19, Sections 3-4.

On *Motza'ei Yom Tov*, *Havdalah* is recited over a cup of wine. (The exact text is printed in the *Siddur* and *Machzor*.) If the *Yom Tov* was on a weekday, the blessings recited over the candle and the spices are omitted.[37] For additional details regarding *Havdalah*, see Chapter 19, Sections 7-13.

When *Yom Tov* is followed by Shabbos, *Havdalah* is not recited on *Motza'ei Yom Tov*. This is because the lesser sanctity of *Yom Tov* is being replaced by the greater sanctity of Shabbos, instead of by an ordinary weekday.

Chapter Twenty-Three

The Halachos Pertaining to Rosh Chodesh
(The first day of the lunar month)

The Jewish year

1. There are twelve months in the Jewish year. The months are set according to the new moon, beginning at the reappearance of the moon each month. A lunar month (i.e. the period between one new moon and the next) is twenty-nine days, twelve hours, and .734 of an hour. Therefore, some months have thirty days, and some only twenty-nine.

The months of Tishrei, Shevat, Nissan, Sivan and Av always have thirty days. Teves, Adar (when it is not a leap year), Iyar, Tammuz and Elul always have twenty-nine days. Cheshvan and Kislev vary — in some years both have twenty-nine days, in other years both have thirty days, and in some years, Cheshvan has twenty-nine days and Kislev has thirty days.

2. There are seven leap years within a nineteen-year cycle. The third, sixth, eighth, eleventh, fourteenth, seventeenth, and nineteenth years are leap years. A thirteenth month is added during a leap year — Adar II. In this case, Adar I has thirty days and Adar II has twenty-nine days.

The year 5758 was the first year of the 304th nineteen-year cycle since Creation.

The first day of each month is called *Rosh Chodesh* ("the head of the month"). When a month has thirty days, the thirtieth day of that month and the first day of the next month are both *Rosh Chodesh*. In this case, two consecutive days of *Rosh Chodesh* are celebrated.

Shabbos mevarchim (The Shabbos preceding Rosh Chodesh)

3.   On the Shabbos before every *Rosh Chodesh* (except for the Shabbos before Rosh Hashana), *Birkas Ha-chodesh* ("Blessing the Month") is recited before *Musaf*. During *Birkas Ha-chodesh* an announcement is made, informing the congregation which day (or days) will be *Rosh Chodesh*.[1] *Birkas Ha-chodesh* also includes a prayer that God grant us a month replete with blessing.

When reciting *Birkas Ha-chodesh*, it is commendable to know the exact time that the moon passes between the sun and the earth. This time (referred to as the *molad*) is listed in some calendars. In Ashkenazic congregations, it is customary to announce the *molad* before *Birkas Ha-chodesh*.

A special *haftarah* called *Machar Chodesh* is read when *Rosh Chodesh* falls out on Sunday.

Yom Kippur Katan

4.   *Rosh Chodesh* is a time of atonement for the Jewish nation. In the days of the Temple, special sacrifices were offered on *Rosh Chodesh* to atone for transgressions committed during the previous month.

Therefore, some people have the custom to fast on the day before *Rosh Chodesh*. Many people recite special supplications during *Minchah* on the day before *Rosh Chodesh*. These supplications are called, "The Service for *Yom Kippur Katan*." When *Rosh Chodesh* is on Shabbos or Sunday, the *Yom Kippur Katan* service is recited on the preceding Thursday.

The *Yom Kippur Katan* service is not recited on the day preceding *Rosh Chodesh* for the months of Tishrei, Cheshvan, Teves and Iyar.

Tachanun is not recited during *Minchah* on *erev Rosh Chodesh*.

The Special Prayers for Rosh Chodesh

Ya'aleh V'yavo

5.   *Ya'aleh V'yavo* is recited during *Shacharis*, *Minchah*, and *Ma'ariv* on *Rosh Chodesh*. *Ya'aleh V'yavo* is added to the *Shemoneh Esreh* during the blessing of *Retzei*.[2] The following table illustrates how one should proceed if he forgot to add *Ya'aleh V'yavo* during *Shemoneh Esreh*.

Forgetting *Ya'aleh V'yavo* on *Rosh Chodesh*[1,2]

The place where one realized his error	During *Ma'ariv* on the first or second day	During *Shacharis* or *Minchah* on the first or second day
Before mentioning God's Name in the blessing *Ha-machazir Shechinaso l'Tzion*	Recite *Ya'aleh V'yavo* and continue with *V'sechezenah*	Recite *Ya'aleh V'yavo* and continue with *V'sechezenah*
After mentioning God's Name in the blessing *Ha-machazir Shechinaso l'Tzion*, but before reciting the words *Ha-machazir Shechinaso l'Tzion*[3]	Finish the *Shemoneh Esreh* without reciting *Ya'aleh V'yavo*. Do not repeat the *Shemoneh Esreh*	Say *lamedeini chukecha*,[4] then recite *Ya'aleh V'yavo*, *V'sechezenah*, and the rest of *Shemoneh Esreh*
After reciting the blessing *Ha-machazir*, but before beginning *Modim*	Finish the *Shemoneh Esreh* without reciting *Ya'aleh V'yavo*. Do not repeat the *Shemoneh Esreh*	Recite *Ya'aleh V'yavo* here[5] and then continue with *Modim*
After beginning *Modim* but before finishing the *Shemoneh Esreh*	Finish the *Shemoneh Esreh* without reciting *Ya'aleh V'yavo*. Do not repeat the *Shemoneh Esreh*	Return to the beginning of *Retzei*, and repeat that part of *Shemoneh Esreh*, including *Ya'aleh V'yavo*
After finishing the *Shemoneh Esreh*[6]	Do not repeat the *Shemoneh Esreh*	Repeat the entire *Shemoneh Esreh*[7]

1. S.A. 422:1. 2. According to the *Mishnah Berurah* (422 [10]), one who is not sure if he recited *Ya'aleh V'yavo* must recite the passage again. (The assumption is that the person recited *Shemoneh Esreh* as he normally does, without reciting *Ya'aleh V'yavo*.) One who is certain that he intended to recite *Ya'aleh V'yavo*, but sometime after reciting *Shemoneh Esreh* cannot remember whether or not he actually recited the passage, does not have to repeat the *Shemoneh Esreh*. However, if one is not sure if he recited *Ya'aleh V'yavo* immediately after reciting *Shemoneh Esreh*, he must repeat the *Shemoneh Esreh*. 3. M.B. 422 (2). 4. This is (Tehillim 119:12) *Baruch Attah Hashem lamedeini chukecha*. By completing the sentence *Baruch Attah Hashem* with the final words of the verse (*lamedeini chukecha*), one recites a verse from *Tehillim* rather than mention God's Name in vain (see M.B. 422 [5]). 5. S.A. 422:1. See also 114:6, and M.B. there (32). 6. Finishing *Shemoneh Esreh* means having recited *Yehi ratzon* at the end of *Elokai netzor*. 7. There are different halachic opinions regarding how one should proceed if he remembers that he did not recite *Ya'aleh V'yavo* after he began reciting *Musaf* (M.B. 422 [4]). One should consult a *rav* regarding how to proceed in this situation.

6.   *Tachanun*[3] and *La-menatze'ach* (*Tehillim* 20, which is recited before *u'Va l'Tzion*) are not recited on *Rosh Chodesh*.[4]

Hallel

7.   *Hallel* is recited on *Rosh Chodesh*, after the *Shacharis Shemoneh Esreh*.[5]
Hallel is composed of chapters from *Tehillim* which praise God for the miracles He has performed, and for the benevolence He bestows upon the Jewish nation.

Two passages are omitted when reciting *Hallel* on *Rosh Chodesh*. These passages are *Lo lanu* ("Not to us") and *Ahavti* ("I love"). This abbreviated form of *Hallel* is referred to as "half-*Hallel*."

Before reciting *Hallel*, one recites the blessing *asher kideshanu b'mitzvosav v'tzivanu likro es ha-Hallel* ("Who sanctified us with His *mitzvos* and commanded us to recite the *Hallel*"). *Hallel* ends with the blessing *Yehalelucha Hashem Elokeinu* ("They will proclaim Your praise, Hashem, our God..."). One should make every effort to recite *Hallel* with a *minyan*.[6]

Sephardic Jews do not recite the blessings when reciting half-*Hallel*. They only recite the blessings when reciting the whole *Hallel*. (Whole *Hallel* is recited on festivals. This is discussed in the following chapters).[7]

8.   *Hallel* is recited while standing.[8] The leader recites whole *Kaddish* after *Hallel*. One must not talk while reciting *Hallel*.

One may interrupt half-*Hallel* at any point to answer Amen or *Amen Yehei Shemeh rabbah*. This is similar to the interruptions which are permitted during *Pesukei d'zimrah*. (For more details, see the table in Chapter 7, Section 29).

The Torah reading and *Musaf*

9.   *Hallel* is followed by the Torah Reading for *Rosh Chodesh*. The section read on *Rosh Chodesh* discusses the daily *tamid* offering and the *musaf* offerings for *Shabbos Rosh Chodesh* (*Bemidbar* 28:1-15).

Four men receive *aliyos*: a *Kohen*, a *Levi*, and two *Yisraelim*, in that order. (For more details regarding the Torah Reading, see Chapter 7, Sections 89-100.)

10.   *Ashrei, u'Va l'Tzion* and *Kaddish* are recited after the Torah Reading. The congregants remove their *tefillin* after *Kaddish*. One must not talk between *Kaddish* and *Musaf*. The entire congregation begins *Musaf* together. (The *Musaf* service is printed in the *Siddur*.)

After *Musaf*, the Leader recites the Leader's Repetition.[9]

The sacrifices which were offered in the Temple on *Rosh Chodesh* are mentioned in *Musaf*. *Rosh Chodesh* is a time for atonement. Sacrifices were offered in the Temple to atone for the people's sins. This is mentioned in the *Musaf* service, "You gave *Rosh Chodesh* to Your people, as a time of atonement for all their misdeeds, when they sacrifice before You appeasement offerings and rams for sin-offerings to atone for themselves."[10]

11. *Tehillim* 104 (*Barechi nafshi*) is recited on *Rosh Chodesh*. This passage mentions that God created the moon to facilitate the calculation of months and the dates of festivals.[11] In Israel, people who recite their prayers according to *Nussach Ashkenaz* recite *Barechi nafshi* instead of the *Shir shel yom* (the special chapter of *Tehillim* recited for each day of the week). Those who recite their prayers according to *Nussach Sephard*, as well as all those not in Israel, recite *Barechi nafshi* in addition to the *Shir shel yom*.

The laws of *Kiddush Levanah* are discussed in Chapter 19, Sections 5-6.

Rosh Chodesh meals

12. It is a mitzvah to prepare more food than usual for one's meal in honor of *Rosh Chodesh*. Some people fulfill this mitzvah by adding another course to the meal. This mitzvah also applies when *Rosh Chodesh* is on Shabbos.[12]

13. *Ya'aleh V'yavo* is recited in *Birkas Ha-mazon* on *Rosh Chodesh*. The laws regarding how one should proceed if he forgot to recite *Ya'aleh V'yavo* are listed in the table in Chapter 12, Section 9.[13]

14. It is prohibited to fast on *Rosh Chodesh*.[14] *Rosh Chodesh* is a holiday for women, given to them as a reward for refusing to donate their jewelry for the golden calf. Many women observe the custom of refraining from doing some of their household chores on *Rosh Chodesh*.[15]

Shabbos Rosh Chodesh

15. If *Rosh Chodesh* is on Shabbos, *Ya'aleh V'yavo* is added to the Shabbos version of the *Shemoneh Esreh* during *Ma'ariv*, *Shacharis* and *Minchah*.

Ya'aleh V'yavo is added in the blessing of *Retzei*. After *Shacharis*, two Torah scrolls are taken out. The *parashas ha-shavua* (the Weekly Torah Portion) is read from the first scroll. The section discussing the sacrifices for Shabbos and *Rosh Chodesh* is read from the second scroll. This section is read instead of the regular *maftir*.[16] A special *haftarah* is read for *Rosh Chodesh*. (For details regarding the Torah Reading, see Chapter 7, Sections 89-100.)

16.   The middle blessing in *Musaf* is different from that on a regular Shabbos. The blessing begins *Attah yatzarta*, and discusses both Shabbos and *Rosh Chodesh*. This blessing is printed in the *Siddur*, in the *Musaf Shemoneh Esreh* for Shabbos.[17]

One who erred and recited the usual *Musaf* for Shabbos, instead of the special one for Shabbos and *Rosh Chodesh*, should proceed as follows: One who realized his mistake before reciting the words *yiheyu l'ratzon imrei fi*, at the end of *Elokai netzor*, should return to *Attah yatzarta*, and recite *Musaf* from there. One who only realized his mistake after finishing the *Shemoneh Esreh* should recite *Musaf* again.

Chapter Twenty-Four

Rosh Hashana
(The Day of Judgment)

Erev Rosh Hashana (The day before Rosh Hashana)

1. *Erev Rosh Hashana*, the twenty-ninth of Elul, is the last day of the year.

   Repenting and performing good deeds on this day has special significance. Sincere repentance can correct one's past sins and help one end the year feeling spiritually uplifted and close to God. It also prepares one for the imminent Days of Judgment — Rosh Hashana, and the Ten Days of Repentance.

   One should try to spend *erev Rosh Hashana* studying Torah and repenting for his misdeeds. Some people have the custom to fast until after *Minchah* on *erev Rosh Hashanah*.[1]

2. On the morning of *erev Rosh Hashana*, a large number of *selichos* (penitential prayers) are recited.[2] The *halachos* concerning reciting *selichos* during the month of Elul are discussed in Chapter 35, Section 36.

   It is customary to annul one's voluntary commitments on *erev Rosh Hashana*. This is called *hataras nedarim*. This custom is observed so one will not commit the sin of not fulfilling his obligations. At the same time, we annul all future obligations, provided that one forgets to utter the annulment statement when the obligation is undertaken. Some people have the custom of annulling their obligations on the day before Yom Kippur. The text for *hataras nedarim* and a description of how it is done are found in *Siddurim* and *Machzorim*.

3. The shofar is not blown on *erev Rosh Hashana*. This is to differentiate between the shofar blasts which are customarily blown during the month of Elul, and those which we are commanded to blow on Rosh Hashana.[3] *Tachanun* is not recited during *Shacharis* and *Minchah* on *erev Rosh Hashana*. It, however, is still recited during the *selichos* before *Shacharis*.[4]

Preparations for the festival

4.   All the preparations usually done on the day before a festival are also
        done on *erev Rosh Hashana*. For example, clothes are prepared, haircuts
and baths are taken,[5] the home is tidied, etc. (for further details, see Chapter
22). By preparing as one does for other festivals, we demonstrate our confi-
dence in God's merciful judgment on Rosh Hashana.

It is customary for men to immerse themselves in a *mikveh* (ritual bath) on *erev
Rosh Hashana*, beginning from one hour before noon.[6] The reason for this is
to approach the Day of Judgment in purity. Some people observe the custom
of wearing white garments on Rosh Hashana.[7]

5.   Candles should be prepared on *erev Rosh Hashana* for both nights of
        Rosh Hashana. This is because it is prohibited to melt and press the
candles into candlesticks on a festival.

If Rosh Hashana is on Thursday and Friday, an *eruv tavshilin* must be made on
Wednesday. (For details regarding how to make an *eruv tavshilin*, see Chapter
22, Sections 13-17.)

Rosh Hashana

6.   Rosh Hashana is on the first and second days of Tishrei. All the *halachos*
        of *Yom Tov* apply to these two days, including the prohibition of doing
melachah and the additional *halachos* listed in Chapter 22.

Days of judgment

7.   The days of Rosh Hashana are days of judgment. On these days, God
        judges all of His creations and decides their future fate. The heavenly
judgment assesses a man according to his deeds, words and thoughts;
whether he lived according to the Torah, observed the *mitzvos*, and faithfully
served God or — God forbid — if he sinned and did not fulfill his purpose
and spiritual mission. God, Who alone can search out a person's heart and
mind, judges the entire world on these days.

Repentance atones for one's sins and brings a person close to his Creator. The
Rosh Hashana service has many sections which discuss God's sovereignty
over the world and His creations. A person becomes closer to God when

he realizes that God created, rules, and supervises the world. Repentance and an awareness of God's loftiness and sovereignty can change one's verdict for the better.

Rosh Hashana prayers

8.   The Rosh Hashana morning service is lengthy, usually lasting until midday. These prayers are printed in the *Machzor* for Rosh Hashana. Some *Machzorim* include commentaries and explanations on various facets of the prayers.

The main theme of the *Rosh Hashana Shemoneh Esreh* is God's sovereignty over His world. We pray that all mankind believe in God, fulfill His *mitzvos*, and serve Him wholeheartedly.

9.   The Leader's Repetition of the *Shemoneh Esreh* is followed by the Torah Reading. The prayers that are recited when the *sefer Torah* is taken out of the *Aron Ha-Kodesh* are printed in the *Machzor*. Two Torah scrolls are taken out on Rosh Hashana. On the first day of Rosh Hashana, the Torah Reading, which is read from the first *sefer Torah*, is the section beginning, "And God remembered Sarah" (*Bereshis* 21). *Maftir* is the section in *Bemidbar* 28, which discusses the sacrifices that were offered on Rosh Hashana. *Maftir* is read from the second *sefer Torah*. The Torah Reading for the second day of Rosh Hashana is *Akedas Yitzchak* (the Binding of Isaac; *Bereshis* 22). The *Maftir* is the same as on the first day.

Musaf

10.   Three special blessings are recited in the *Musaf Shemoneh Esreh*. These blessings are recited after the first three blessings and before the last three blessings. These blessings are called *Malchuyos* ("Kingship"), *Zichronos* ("Commemorations"), and *Shofros* ("Shofar Blasts").[8]

The blessing of *Malchuyos* discusses God's sovereignty over His world, and how all creations will accept His Kingship in the future, at the time of the Redemption. This blessing ends with the words *Melech al kol ha-aretz mekadesh Yisrael v'yom ha-zikaron* ("King of the universe Who sanctifies Israel and the Day of Remembrance").

The blessing of *Zichronos* emphasizes God's providence over His creations, and how He remembers the deeds of each one. This blessing includes a prayer requesting that God remember the merit of *Akedas Yitzchak*. This blessing ends with the words *zocher ha-bris* ("Who remembers the covenant").

The blessing of *Shofros* recalls the Giving of the Torah on Mount Sinai, and the sound of the shofar that was heard on that occasion. The blessing includes a request that we merit hearing the shofar blast heralding the Final Redemption. This blessing ends with the words *shome'a teru'as ammo Yisrael b'rachamim* ("Who hears with mercy the shofar blasts of His people Israel").

In Israel, the last blessing of the *Shemoneh Esreh* ends with the usual ending, *ha-mevarech es ammo Yisrael ba-shalom*, rather than with the alternate ending which is printed in many *Machzorim*.

11.   The Repetition of the *Musaf Shemoneh Esreh* includes the prayer *U'ne-saneh tokef* ("Let us express with awe"), which was written by Rav Amnon of Mainz. This moving prayer is recited by the congregation and the Leader with great awe. Sephardic Jews do not recite this prayer.

Aleinu L'shabe'ach is recited during the Leader's Repetition of *Musaf*. It is customary for the congregants to prostrate themselves when reciting the words *va-anachnu kor'im u'mishtachavim* ("We bend our knees and prostrate ourselves"). Before one falls on his knees, he should put a handkerchief or piece of paper on the floor, since it is prohibited to prostrate oneself on a stone floor.[9] Sephardic Jews do not observe this custom.

The Mitzvah To Blow the Shofar

12.   It is a mitzvah from the Torah to blow the shofar on the first day of Rosh Hashana.[10] Our sages ordained that the shofar be blown on the second day of Rosh Hashana as well.

A shofar is made from a ram's horn.[11]

The sound of the shofar has the power to arouse one's heart and provoke thoughts of repentance. This is what the Rambam writes:

> Although the blowing of the shofar is a Torah decree whose reason was not disclosed, we can discern a hint in it. It prompts us, "Wake up, you who are slumbering! Scrutinize your deeds and return to God! Remember your Creator — you, who forgot the truth of your existence by your involvement with the

life's futilities, which will not help you in any way. Search your souls! Improve your ways and deeds! Forsake your wickedness and worthless thoughts! (*Hilchos Teshuvah* 3:4)

Additional reasons for the mitzvah of blowing the shofar, as well as other topics related to this mitzvah are printed in some *Machzorim.*

How to fulfill the mitzvah of shofar

13.   Before the shofar is blown, special verses and prayers are recited by the one who blows the shofar, as well as by the congregation. These verses and prayers are printed in the *Machzor.*[12]

The mitzvah of blowing the shofar may only be fulfilled during the daytime.[13] Since women are exempt from positive *mitzvos* that are bound by a time limit, they are exempt from the mitzvah of shofar.[14] Nonetheless, most women fulfill this mitzvah, by coming to the synagogue to hear the shofar.

14.   The one who blows the shofar has to stand while blowing. He may not lean on a table or a pillar.[15]

15.   Blowing the shofar correctly involves knowledge of many details. The man who blows the shofar must be proficient in all these laws. He must also practice blowing the shofar sufficiently before the *Yom Tov.*[16] Every member of the congregation must listen to the shofar blasts carefully, while intending to fulfill the mitzvah of hearing the shofar.

Before blowing the shofar, the person recites the blessings, *asher kideshanu b'mitzvosav v'tzivanu lishmo'a kol shofar* ("Who has commanded us to hear the sound of the shofar") and *She-hecheyanu.* The congregation should listen attentively to the words of both blessings, and answer Amen after each one.

The one who blows the shofar recites *She-hecheyanu* on both days of Rosh Hashana. Sephardic Jews only recite *She-hecheyanu* on the first day. However, if the first day of Rosh Hashana is Shabbos, Sephardic Jews recite *She-hecheyanu* on the second day.[16*]

16.   One may not speak (unless it concerns the shofar blasts or the prayers) from when the blessings for the shofar are recited, until the last shofar blasts of the day. One may not speak for any reason whatsoever from when the blessings are recited until the first series of shofar blasts, which precede the *Musaf* service, are completed. One who spoke after the blessings were recited, but before the shofar was blown, must recite the blessings.[17]

17.   The shofar is blown on both days of Rosh Hashana. The shofar is not blown on Shabbos.[18] The shofar may not be moved on Shabbos, because it is *muktzeh*. When the first day of Rosh Hashana is Shabbos, the shofar is only blown on the second day. The second day of Rosh Hashana is never Shabbos. See Section 15, above, regarding when *She-hecheyanu* is recited.

The symbolic foods eaten during the meal

18.   It is customary to eat special foods which symbolize a good year during the first evening meal on Rosh Hashana.[19] Some of the special foods are:

Apple in honey. It is customary to eat apple dipped in honey. Before eating it, one recites: "May it be Your will to decree upon us a good and sweet year."

The head of a lamb, a ram, or a fish. It is customary to eat from the head of a lamb, a ram, or a fish. Before eating it, one recites: "May it be Your will that we shall be at the head and not at the tail."

Pomegranate. It is customary to eat a pomegranate. Before eating it, one recites: "May it be Your will that our merits be as numerous as (the seeds of) a pomegranate."

Jews from different countries and communities have other special foods which they serve on Rosh Hashana.[20]

19.   It is customary to eat the symbolic foods after reciting *ha-motzi*, and eating a piece of the challah.

Before eating a symbolic fruit, the blessing over fruit must be recited. In this case, the appropriate phrase is recited after the fruit is eaten, since one may not speak between reciting the blessing and eating the fruit.[21] If one of the seven species for which the Land of Israel is praised is among the symbolic fruits, the blessing should be recited over it instead of over a different fruit. (See Chapter 13, Section 5, for the laws regarding which blessing to recite first.) A separate blessing is not recited over the head of a lamb, a ram, or a fish, since they are included in *ha-motzi*.

Some people observe the custom of dipping the slice of challah into honey instead of salt.[22]

20. It is customary not to sleep during the day on Rosh Hashana. However, the Ari z"l (R. Yitzchak Luria, the famous kabbalist) permitted sleeping after midday. One who sits without studying Torah or praying is no better than one who sleeps.[23]

Tashlich

21. It is customary to recite *Tashlich* after *Minchah*, but before sunset, on the first day of Rosh Hashana. According to the *Mishnah Berurah*, if the first day of Rosh Hashana is Shabbos, *Tashlich* is recited on the second day.[24] Sephardic Jews, however, always recite *Tashlich* on the first day of Rosh Hashana. They must be careful not to take their *Machzor* to *Tashlich*, in places where it is forbidden to carry on Shabbos.

Tashlich is a compilation of supplications in which we express our desire to wash away all our sins, return to God, and live a life untainted by sin. The name *Tashlich* is derived from one of the verses which begins, *v'tashlich bimetsulos yam kol chatosam* ("and You will cast all their sins into the depths of the sea").

22. *Tashlich* is recited near the sea, a stream, a well, etc., or from a place where one of these can be seen. The Midrash recounts that when Avraham (Abraham) was on his way to sacrifice his son Yitzchak (Isaac), he crossed a stream whose waters threatened to drown him. Avraham cried out to God, "Rescue me, for the water has reached unto my soul!" By reciting *Tashlich* near water, we are recalling the merit of *Akedas Yitzchak*.

Some people observe the custom of shaking out the pockets of one's garments when reciting *Tashlich*. This symbolizes casting away our sins, and searching for ways to return to God.

Lighting candles and reciting *She-hecheyanu* on the second night of Rosh Hashana

23. Candles are lit on the second night of Rosh Hashana.

Before lighting the candles, the woman recites the blessings *l'hadlik ner shel Yom Tov* ("Who has commanded us to light the *Yom Tov* lights") and *She-hecheyanu*. Sephardic women do not recite *She-hecheyanu* when lighting

Yom Tov candles. (For more details regarding lighting candles on *Yom Tov*, see Chapter 22, Sections 18-21. For more details about reciting *She-hecheyanu* on the second night of Rosh Hashana, see Section 24, below.) *She-hecheyanu* is also recited during *Kiddush* on the second night of Rosh Hashana. If the person who lights the candles will also be reciting *Kiddush*, he only recites *She-hecheyanu* when reciting *Kiddush*.

24.   There are two opinions whether the Halachah requires one to recite *She-hecheyanu* on the second night of Rosh Hashana. Therefore, both the woman who lights the candles and the man who recites *Kiddush* should wear a new garment, or have a new fruit in front of him or her, when reciting the blessing. When reciting *She-hecheyanu*, the person must intend for the blessing to apply to the new fruit or new garment (which definitely require the blessing of *She-hecheyanu*), as well as to the *Yom Tov* candles or *Kiddush*. This way, all opinions allow one to recite the blessing. However, one recites *She-hecheyanu* even if he does not have a new garment or fruit available.[25]

25.   The candles are lit after stars appear in the sky on the second night of Rosh Hashana. This is because work may not be done on the first day of *Yom Tov* for the second. One must light the candles from an existing flame, since it is prohibited to kindle a new fire on *Yom Tov*. As is mentioned above, the candles for the second night of *Yom Tov* must be prepared before *Yom Tov* begins. One may not cut or melt candles to make them fit into candlesticks, or prepare the candles' wicks on *Yom Tov*.

The prayers for the second day of Rosh Hashana are printed in the *Machzor*.[26]

Chapter Twenty-Five

The Halachos Pertaining to Public Fast Days

This chapter discusses the Fast of Gedalya, as well as the other public fast days.

The purpose of fast days

1. The third of Tishrei, the tenth of Teves, the seventeenth of Tammuz and the ninth of Av are public fast days.[1] These days commemorate major tragic events which befell the Jewish people on these dates. (Each of these events is discussed below in the appropriate chapter.)

The laws pertaining to Yom Kippur and Tish'ah b'Av (which are more stringent than those of the other fast days) are discussed in Chapters 27, 28, and 35.

Ta'anis Esther, the Fast of Esther, is on the thirteenth of Adar. On this day, in the time of Mordechai and Esther, the Jews fought against their enemies. After fasting and repenting, the Jews were saved with God's help. Since that time, the thirteenth of Adar has remained a day of fasting and introspection.

If the date of a public fast day is on Shabbos, the fast is deferred to Sunday. The only exception is *Ta'anis Esther*, which is advanced to the preceding Thursday.[2] (Yom Kippur that falls on Shabbos is not pushed off.)

2. Fast days are intended as an opportunity for one to repent, improve his deeds, and make a spiritual reckoning. Commemorating the destruction, exiles, and suffering which befell our forefathers on these days should motivate us to return to God. Serving God with devotion can prevent further tragedies.

The Rambam writes:

> There are days on which all of Israel fast because of the tragedies which occurred on them, the purpose being to awaken our hearts and inspire us to

231

return to God. These days are to remind us of our misdeeds which resemble those of our forefathers' misdeeds — which caused our past and present sufferings. By remembering this, we shall be moved to improve ourselves, as it says, "And they shall confess their sin and the sin of their fathers" (*Vayikra* 26:40). (*Hilchos Ta'anis* 5:1)

Concerning the repentance of the inhabitants of Nineveh, the prophet states, "And God saw their deeds" (*Yonah* 3:10). Our sages comment, "It does not say, 'and God saw their sackcloth and their fasting,' but that He saw, 'their deeds,' i.e. that they had repented from their evil ways" (*Ta'anis* 16a). The main purpose of a fast is to improve one's deeds and to return to God wholeheartedly.

The following laws apply to all the public fasts. The only exceptions are Tish'ah b'Av and Yom Kippur, whose laws are discussed separately.

The prohibition of eating and drinking

3.   It is prohibited to eat or drink on a fast day.[3] If one ate or drank, he must nevertheless continue the fast. This rule applies whether the person ate inadvertently or on purpose.[4]

One should not rinse his mouth or brush his teeth on a fast day. Someone who is very uncomfortable when he does not rinse out his mouth should consult with a *rav*, regarding how he should proceed.[5]

4.   These fast days begin at dawn and end at night, with the appearance of the stars. One may only eat and drink until dawn, during the night preceding the fast. One may only eat if he woke up early before the fast began, if he had planned to rise before dawn to eat.[6]

5.   People who are sick do not fast, Women who are pregnant or nursing do not fast if they feel weak or the fast causes them to suffer. People who are not fasting should not eat more than is necessary for their health. This way these people share in the community's mourning.[7] Children should also not indulge in delicacies.

The special prayers recited on a fast day

6.   *Selichos* are recited after the *Shacharis Shemoneh Esreh*.[8] *Selichos* are supplications in which we beseech God to forgive our sins and redeem us from our sufferings. The prayer *Avinu Malkeinu* ("Our Father, our King") is

also recited after the *Shacharis Shemoneh Esreh*. *Selichos* and *Avinu Malkeinu* are printed in the *Siddur*.

7.   The Torah Reading for fast days is the section beginning *Va-yechal Moshe*, "and Moshe beseeched God" (*Shemos* 32). This section discusses returning to God, and includes the Thirteen Divine Attributes of Mercy, as well as other related topics.[9] Only men who are fasting may receive an *aliyah*.[10] See Section 9, below, regarding how to proceed if there are less than ten fasting men present.

8.   At *Minchah*, the Torah portion from the morning is read again, followed by the *haftarah*, which is the section beginning with the words *Dirshu Hashem b'himatz'o*, "Seek God where He may be found" (*Yeshayahu* 55). The *haftarah* also discusses repenting and becoming close to God.[11] Sephardic Jews do not read the *haftarah* on fast days.

Those who are fasting include the passage *Aneinu* ("Answer us") in the blessing of *Shema koleinu* during the *Minchah Shemoneh Esreh*. This passage is printed in the *Siddur*.[12] Sephardic Jews also recite *Aneinu* in the *Shacharis Shemoneh Esreh*.

Forgetting *Aneinu*[1]

When one realized his error	How to proceed
If one remembered before mentioning God's Name at the end of *Shema koleinu*	Return to the beginning of *Aneinu*, and recite the passage
If one remembered after mentioning God's Name at the end of *Shema koleinu*, but before taking the three steps back at the end of the *Shemoneh Esreh*[2]	Recite *Aneinu* after *Elokai netzor* at the end of *Shemoneh Esreh*
If one finished reciting *Shemoneh Esreh* and began taking the three steps back	Do not repeat the *Shemoneh Esreh*

1. S.A. 565:2.   2. Ibid. See *Sha'ar Ha-Tzion* (6). It is preferable to recite *Aneinu* before reciting *yiheyu l'ratzon*.

In Israel, if *Minchah* is recited shortly before sunset on a fast day, *Birkas Kohanim* is recited by those *Kohanim* who are fasting. Outside of Israel, where *Birkas Kohanim* is only recited on the festivals, the Leader recites the passage, *Elokeinu v'Elokei avoseinu barcheinu* ("Our God, the God of our fathers, bless us").[13] Sephardic Jews do not recite *Birkas Kohanim* during *Minchah* on a fast day.

The congregation recites *Avinu Malkeinu* after the *Minchah Shemoneh Esreh.*

The Leader recites *Aneinu* during the Repetition of the *Shacharis* and *Minchah Shemoneh Esreh. Aneinu* is added between the blessings of *Go'el Yisrael* and *Refa'einu.*[14]

When less than ten people in the *minyan* are fasting

9.   According to some halachic opinions *Aneinu* is only recited by the Leader between *Go'el Yisrael* and *Refa'einu* if ten men in the *minyan* are fasting. If there are less than ten men fasting, the Leader recites *Aneinu* during the blessing of *Shome'a tefillah.* According to other halachic opinions, the Leader recites *Aneinu* between *Go'el Yisrael* and *Refa'einu* if as few as seven men in the *minyan* are fasting.

If a fast is on Monday or Thursday, and at least six men present are fasting, the Torah Reading for fast days is read from a *sefer Torah* during *Shacharis.* However, if there are less than six men fasting, the regular Torah portion for that week is read from a *sefer Torah.*

There are two halachic opinions regarding reading from the Torah during *Shacharis* on days when the Torah is not usually read, and on any day during *Minchah.* According to one opinion, the congregation only reads from the Torah if there are ten men present who are fasting. The other halachic opinion is that the Torah may be read if there are seven men present who are fasting.[15]

The Fast of Gedalya

10.   The Fast of Gedalya is on the day after Rosh Hashana (the third of Tishrei).[16] When the third of Tishrei is on Shabbos, the fast is deferred to Sunday.

This fast was ordained to commemorate of the assassination of Gedalya ben Achikam, and the suffering which befell the Jewish people in its wake. The king of Babylonia had appointed Gedalya governor over the Jews remaining in the Land of Israel after the Destruction of the First Temple (c. 420 BCE). After Gedalya was assassinated, the remaining Jews fled into exile where thousands of them were killed.

All the laws pertaining to fast days mentioned in this chapter apply to the Fast of Gedalya.

Chapter Twenty-Six

The Ten Days of Repentance

The mitzvah of *teshuvah* (repentance)

1.   The first ten days of the year from Rosh Hashana through Yom Kippur are especially set aside for the mitzvah of *teshuvah*.[1]

Although it is a mitzvah to correct our misdeeds throughout the year, our obligation to do so is much greater at the beginning of the year. During these days, God is close to His people and waits for them to return to Him wholeheartedly. The prophet Yeshayahu referred to these days when he urged his fellow Jews, "Seek God while He may be found, call upon Him while He is near" (*Yeshayahu* 55:6).

2.   The three stages of *teshuvah* are:

A) sincere regret over one's past misdeeds.

B) forsaking one's sins and sincerely undertaking to never repeat the sin in the future.

C) verbally confessing that one has sinned.

Many books have been written discussing the mitzvah of *teshuvah*. Two of the most well known are the Rambam's *Hilchos Teshuvah* and *Sha'arei Teshuvah*, by Rabbeinu Yonah Gerondi.

3.   During the Ten Days of Repentance, one should dedicate more time to studying Torah, performing *mitzvos*, and giving charity. It is advisable for one to peruse books which will motivate him to correct his misdeeds and return to God.[2] One should observe voluntary halachic restrictions (*chumros*) during these days, even if he does not usually observe them. During the Ten Days of Repentance we pray to God to judge us mercifully. Therefore, during these days we fulfill our religious obligations more strictly than Halachah requires[3] (i.e. we ask God to "go beyond the letter of the law" and judge

us favorably, and we in turn "go beyond the letter of the law" in our mitzvah observance).

The prayers

4.   One should pray more than usual during the days between Rosh Hashana and Yom Kippur.[4] *Selichos* (penitential prayers) are recited shortly before daybreak. (There is a special book called *Selichos*, which contains all the *selichos*.) *Avinu Malkeinu* is recited after the *Shemoneh Esreh* for *Shacharis* and *Minchah*. *Selichos* and *Avinu Malkeinu* are not recited on the Shabbos between Rosh Hashana and Yom Kippur.[5]

5.   The following phrases are added to the *Shemoneh Esreh* during the Ten Days of Repentance (including Rosh Hashana and Yom Kippur):[6]

   * In the first blessing the sentence *Zachreinu l'chayim* ("Remember us for life") is added.

   * In the second blessing the sentence *Mi chamocha* ("Who is like You") is added.

   * The ending for the third blessing is changed from *ha-Kel ha-kadosh* ("the holy God") to *ha-Melech ha-kadosh* ("the holy King"). The reason for this change is that God is judging the entire world during these days, "and His Kingdom reigns over all."[7]

   * The ending for the paragraph *Hashivah shofteinu* is changed from *Melech ohev tzedakah u'mishpat* ("the King Who loves righteousness and justice") to *ha-Melech ha-mishpat* ("the King of justice").[8]

   * In the blessing of *Modim*, the sentence *U'chesov l'chayim* ("And inscribe for life") is added.

   * In the blessing of *Sim shalom*, the section *B'sefer chayim* ("In the Book of Life") is added.

All of these additions and changes are indicated in the *Siddur* by the small letters עשי"ת (Hebrew initials for *Aseres yemei teshuvah* — the Ten Days of Repentance) or ש"ת (Hebrew initials for *Shabbos Teshuvah* — the Shabbos that is during the Ten Days of Repentance).

6.   The text for *Kaddish* is changed during the Ten Days of Repentance. Instead of reciting *l'eila min kol birchasa* ("above all blessings") in the second half of *Kaddish*, one recites *l'eila u'l'eila mi-kol birchasa* ("exceedingly high above all blessings").[9] The words *oseh shalom* ("Who makes peace") in

Kaddish and at the end of the *Shemoneh Esreh* are changed to *oseh ha-shalom* ("Who makes the Peace"). Some congregations, however, do not make any changes in *Kaddish*.

Forgetting an Addition for the Ten Days of Repentance[1]

The passage which was omitted	When one realized his error	How to proceed
Zachreinu, Mi chamocha, U'chesov, B'sefer[2]	Before mentioning God's Name at the end of the blessing in which the passage appears	Return to the beginning of the addition and repeat the *Shemoneh Esreh* from there
	After mentioning God's Name at the end of the blessing[5]	Do not return to the beginning of the blessing (continue reciting the *Shemoneh Esreh*)
ha-Melech ha-kadosh[3]	After finishing the blessing but within the time of *toch kedei dibbur*[6]	Immediately say *ha-Melech ha-kadosh*
	After finishing the blessing, and after the time of *toch kedei dibbur* has passed	Repeat the *Shemoneh Esreh* from the beginning
ha-Melech ha-mishpat[4]	After finishing the blessing but within the time of *toch kedei dibbur*[6]	Immediately say *ha-Melech ha-mishpat*
	After finishing the blessing, and after the time of *toch kedei dibbur* has passed	Do not return to the beginning of the blessing[7] (Continue reciting the *Shemoneh Esreh*.)

1. If one cannot recall whether or not he recited a text change, he should assume that he did not recite it. One who is sure he intended to recite the *Shemoneh Esreh* with the appropriate change, but some time after praying cannot remember if he actually recited the *Shemoneh Esreh* correctly does not have to repeat the *Shemoneh Esreh*. However, if one is in doubt immediately after praying, he must repeat the *Shemoneh Esreh* (M.B. 114 [38]). 2. S.A. 582:5. 3. S.A. 582:1-2. 4. S.A. 118. 5. M.B. 582 (16). 6. *Toch kedei dibbur* is the amount of time it takes one to say the words *Shalom aleicha rebbe* (M.B. 206 [12]). 7. According to the *Shulchan Aruch* (582:1), if one remembered that he did not recite *ha-Melech ha-mishpat* before finishing the *Shemoneh Esreh* he should return to *Hashivah shofteinu* and repeat the *Shemoneh Esreh* from there. If one realized his error after finishing the *Shemoneh Esreh*, he must repeat the prayer.

The custom of *Kapparos*

8.   The custom of *Kapparos* is observed during the Ten Days of Repentance. Although some people perform *Kapparos* on *erev Yom Kippur*, it may be done at any time during the Ten Days of Repentance.[10] *Kapparos* expresses our great longing for God to forgive our sins and remove our guilt.

9.   One performs *Kapparos* as follows: One takes a chicken or money in his right hand, and recites the appropriate verses (these verses are printed in the *Siddur* and at the beginning of the Yom Kippur *Machzor*). The person waves the chicken or money around his head while reciting the sentence *Zeh chalifasi, zeh temurasi, zeh kapparasi* ("This is instead of me..."). While reciting these words, the person should reflect that what is being done to the chicken should actually be done to him, as punishment for his sins, and that only sincere repentance can annul any evil decrees.

After *Kapparos* is done the money is given to charity or the chicken is slaughtered. Although he is under great pressure during these days, it is important that the *shochet* (ritual slaughterer) does not slaughter when he is tired. If he does, he may slaughter improperly, and the chicken will not be kosher.

When one has sinned against his fellow man

10.   "Yom Kippur does not atone for sins committed by one man against another unless he has appeased him" (*Yoma* 85b). One must ask forgiveness from those whom he hurt with words or actions during the past year, so that these heavy sins will not effect his record when Yom Kippur arrives.[11]

If a person has money or an object which is not his, or which he acquired by unjust means, he must return it to its owner before Yom Kippur, or resolve to return it immediately after Yom Kippur. This is in addition to asking the owner's forgiveness.

11.   A person who is asked for forgiveness should not refuse. Rather, the person should forgive his friend wholeheartedly. Our sages teach us that one who overcomes his natural feelings and forgives another will have his own sins similarly forgiven by God.[12]

Shabbos Teshuvah

12.   The Shabbos during the Ten Days of Repentance is called *Shabbos Teshuvah* ("The Shabbos of Repentance"), or *Shabbos Shuvah*. The name *Shabbos Shuvah* is derived from the first verse of the week's *haftarah*: *Shuvah Yisrael ad Hashem Elokecha* ("Return Israel, unto God, your Lord" (*Hoshea* 14)). Most of the additions in the service which were mentioned in Section 5 above, are also recited during the Shabbos prayers.

In *Magen Avos* ("Shield of our fathers"), which is recited at the end of *Ma'ariv* on Friday night, *ha-Melech ha-kadosh* is recited instead of *ha-Kel ha-kadosh*.

It is customary for the *rav* to give a sermon in the synagogue on *Shabbos Teshuvah*, calling upon the congregation to correct their failings and dedicate themselves to serving God.

Chapter Twenty-Seven

Erev Yom Kippur
(The day before Yom Kippur)

1. The day before Yom Kippur (the ninth of Tishrei) is a day full of pre-parations for the holy day that follows it.

On this day, one should contribute generously to charity.[1] Every Jew should contemplate his spiritual state, and scrutinize his past year's deeds. One should determine if he has observed the Torah and *mitzvos* properly, and if he has fulfilled his spiritual mission. One should make a great effort to forgive all those who caused him anguish; by doing this he accrues great merit for himself.

Some people annul their vows (*hataras nedarim*) on *erev* Yom Kippur. For more details, see Chapter 24, Section 2.

Prayers

2. *Mizmor l'sodah* (in the *Pesukei D'zimrah*), *tachanun*, and *La-menatze'ach* (*Tehillim* 20, recited between *Ashrei* and *u'Va l'Tzion*) are omitted during *Shacharis* on *erev* Yom Kippur.[2] Sephardic Jews, however, recite *Mizmor l'sodah*.

3. The long *Viduy* (Admission of Guilt) is added at the end of the *Minchah* *Shemoneh Esreh*. This *Viduy* is printed in the Yom Kippur *Machzor*,[3] and is recited several times during the Yom Kippur service. The *halachos* regarding when one may interrupt to answer Amen, *Amen yehei Shemeh rabbah*, or *Kedushah*, while reciting *Viduy* are the same as when one may interrupt while reciting *Elokai netzor* during *Shemoneh Esreh*. These laws are discussed in Chapter 7, Section 41.

4. One must stand up whenever *Viduy* is recited. One may not lean on a table, bench, etc., if he would fall if the support were removed. It is

proper to recite *Viduy* with one's head bent in the same manner as at the beginning of *Modim*.[4]

While mentioning the sins listed in the *Viduy*, one should sincerely regret having sinned, and he should undertake not to repeat his sins in the future. As one mentions each sin, he should strike his heart with his fist, as if to say, "You made me sin."[5] *Minchah* is recited early in the afternoon on *erev Yom Kippur*.

The mitzvah to eat on *erev Yom Kippur* and other preparations for Yom Kippur

5. It is a mitzvah to eat more than usual on *erev Yom Kippur*. Our sages say that whoever eats on *erev Yom Kippur* (the ninth of Tishrei) and fasts on Yom Kippur (the tenth or Tishrei), is rewarded as if he fasted on both days.[6] One of the reasons for eating more on *erev Yom Kippur* is to prepare for the fast.

Heavy foods are not eaten on *erev Yom Kippur*. The reason for this is that it is difficult to fast after eating these foods. Light, easily digested foods are eaten instead.[7]

6. It is a mitzvah for men to immerse themselves in a *mikveh* (ritual bath) on *erev Yom Kippur*. It is preferable to immerse oneself before reciting *Minchah* and *Viduy*.[8] One reason for this immersion is as an act of repentance. It is customary to immerse oneself three times.

7. The last meal before the fast (called the *se'udah ha-mafsekes*) should be completed some time before sunset. One must begin the fast while it is still daytime, since it is a mitzvah "to add from the ordinary to the holy." This concept also applies to the end of *Yom Kippur*. We continue fasting into the night, eating only a short while after the stars appear.[9]

8. If one plans to eat or drink after he finishes the *se'udah ha-mafsekes* (before the fast begins), it is best to consciously decide to do so, either quietly or by stating it out loud, before reciting *Birkas Ha-mazon*. Otherwise, one begins the Yom Kippur fast at the end of his meal.[10]

9. "Call the holy day of God — honored" (*Yeshayahu* 58:13). Our sages explain that this verse refers to Yom Kippur (*Shabbos* 119a). Although one does not enjoy food and drinks on this day, it is a mitzvah to honor it by wearing clean garments and illuminating the house with candles. Tablecloths should be put on the tables at home and in the synagogue in honor of Yom Kippur.[11] This should be done before nightfall.

Blessing the children and preparing for services

10. It is customary for fathers to bless their children before going to synagogue, since at that time the heavenly gates of mercy are open. The father's blessing includes a request for his children to be inscribed for a good life, that their hearts be filled with fear of God, and that they succeed in Torah study, as well as in all their endeavors. The text of this special blessing is printed in some *Machzorim*. This custom is primarily observed among Ashkenazic Jews.

11. A *tallis* is worn when reciting *Ma'ariv* on Yom Kippur. Men put on the *tallis* and recite the appropriate blessing before sunset.[12] Some people have the custom to wear white clothes on Yom Kippur, so they resemble angels. Similarly, some men have the custom to wear a white mantle (called a *kittel*) on Yom Kippur.[13]

The congregants should go to synagogue early, so they can prepare themselves for prayer. Many people recite *Tefillah Zakah* before reciting *Kol Nidrei*. *Tefillah Zakah* includes an admission of one's sins, as well as other prayers. *Tefillah Zakah* is printed in many *Machzorim*.

Lighting candles

12. Candles are lit before Yom Kippur begins. Jewish calendars often list the exact time to light candles in various cities. Candles are lit between eighteen and forty minutes before sunset, depending upon the local custom. It is very important not to light candles late.

The woman first lights the candles, and then recites the blessing *asher kideshanu b'mitzvosav v'tzivanu l'hadlik ner shel Yom Ha-Kippurim* ("Who sanctified us with His *mitzvos* and commanded us to light Yom Kippur candles").[14] Then the woman recites *She-hecheyanu*. If Yom Kippur is on Shabbos the blessing *l'hadlik ner shel Shabbos v'shel Yom Ha-Kippurim* ("to light candles for Shabbos and Yom Kippur") is recited.

It is customary among Ashkenazic Jews for husbands to light a candle before Yom Kippur begins that will burn until the fast is over. A *yahrtzeit* candle is also lit for the sake of the souls of deceased parents.[15]

Chapter Twenty-Eight

Yom Kippur
(The Day of Atonement)

1.　Yom Kippur, the tenth of Tishrei, is a holy day designated for spiritual growth and becoming close to God. The Yom Kippur services emphasize the obligation to repent and return to a life of scrupulous mitzvah observance, integrity, and purity of heart.

The sanctity of Yom Kippur is so great that, together with repenting, it can atone for a person's sins. The day's special prayers, if recited with concentration, can inspire a person to repent and resolve to improve his deeds.

The *halachos* regarding the prohibitions to do work and the five afflictions (which are discussed below) apply to the night of Yom Kippur, as well as to the day.[1]

Prohibition of work

2.　"The tenth day of the seventh month shall be a holy assembly for you. You shall afflict your souls and you shall not do any work" (*Bemidbar* 29:7). All activities which are prohibited on Shabbos are also prohibited on Yom Kippur. (For details regarding these *halachos*, see Chapters 20-21.)

On Yom Kippur it is prohibited to do activities related to food preparation. In this way, Yom Kippur differs from the other festivals.[2]

As mentioned above, one is supposed "to add from the ordinary to the holy" on Yom Kippur. Therefore, one is prohibited to do work a short while before sunset.

The five afflictions

3. The Torah commands us to afflict ourselves in five ways on Yom Kippur. Yom Kippur begins before sunset, and lasts until after the stars appear the following night.

The following are the five ways we are commanded to afflict ourselves on Yom Kippur:

4. A. It is prohibited to eat or drink even the smallest quantity of food or drink.[3] One may not brush his teeth or rinse his mouth.[4]

Children should fast part of the day from the time they are nine or ten years old. How many hours they should fast depends on their health.[5] Similarly, children should be taught not to wash, anoint, or wear leather shoes on Yom Kippur. (The other afflictions are discussed in detail below.)[6]

5. B. It is prohibited to wash up on Yom Kippur. One may wash his fingers until the knuckles when he rises in the morning and after he has relieved himself. One should not intend to derive any pleasure from this washing.[7] *Kohanim*, however, pour water on their hands until the wrists before reciting *Birkas Kohanim*.[8]

6. C. It is prohibited to anoint oneself on Yom Kippur. This includes applying cosmetics, ointments, or oil to any part of the body.[9]

7. D. It is prohibited to wear leather shoes or sandals on Yom Kippur. This rule even applies to shoes which are only partially leather. For example, if the sole, upper part, or straps are made of leather, the shoes may not be worn on Yom Kippur.[10]

E. Marital relations are prohibited on Yom Kippur. A husband and wife must observe the same laws of separation as when the wife has her monthly period,[11] including the prohibition for a husband and wife to touch each other.

Life-threatening situations

8. The restrictions of Yom Kippur are suspended when it is necessary to save a human life. An ill person whose life would be endangered by fasting must eat and drink on Yom Kippur.[12]

The *halachos* regarding how to eat on Yom Kippur if Halachah requires it are complex. For example, one must eat less than a certain amount at one time, and one must pause after eating this amount. If one knows before Yom Kippur that he has a medical problem, he should consult a *rav* concerning how to proceed on Yom Kippur.

The Yom Kippur Prayers

9.   The order of the prayers, Torah Readings, and *Viduyim* for Yom Kippur are printed in the *Machzor*. The following are a few of the highlights of the Yom Kippur service.

Kol Nidrei

Yom Kippur night is called "*Kol Nidrei* night," for the first prayer of this holy day. *Kol Nidrei* is a declaration by the congregation that they are annulling their vows. Two Torah scrolls are taken out of the *Aron Ha-Kodesh*. The two men holding the scrolls stand at the right and left of the Leader.[13] Different communities have different customs regarding *Kol Nidrei*, and the number of Torah scrolls taken out for the service. *Kol Nidrei* is recited before sunset. After *Kol Nidrei*, the Leader and the congregation recite the blessing of *She-hecheyanu*. The congregation should complete the blessing before the Leader so that they can answer Amen to his blessing.[14] If a woman recited *She-hecheyanu* when she lit the candles, she should not recite it again.

10.   The prayers and liturgical songs of Yom Kippur discuss God's exaltedness, and His sovereignty over the world. The verse *Baruch Shem kevod Malchuso l'olam va-ed* ("Blessed is the Name of His Kingdom for ever") in *Kerias Shema*, which is recited quietly all year round, is recited aloud on Yom Kippur. The angels recite this verse when they sing God's praises. Since the Jews resemble the angels on this holy day,[15] they too recite this verse aloud.

Viduy

11.   *Viduy* is recited during every *Shemoneh Esreh* on Yom Kippur, as well as during each Leader's Repetition. *Viduy* includes a list of sins, and a prayer that God pardon us and accept our repentance for having transgressed these sins. The text of *Viduy* is printed in the Yom Kippur *Machzor*.

The Torah reading

12.   After *Shacharis*, two Torah scrolls are taken out of the *Aron Ha-Kodesh*. The section at the beginning of *parashas Acharei Mos* (*Vayikra* 16) is read from the first scroll. This section discusses the High Priest's Yom Kippur service in the Temple, and the death of Aharon's two sons. The *Zohar* states that anyone who feels grief and sheds tears over the death of Aharon's two sons, will have his transgressions pardoned by God. This is because one who sheds tears upon reading this passage is contemplating, "If such righteous men (i.e. Aharon's sons) were punished (so severely) for their sins, what fate awaits lesser individuals?" Thus, the person will be motivated to repent.[16]

Maftir is read from the second Torah scroll. The *maftir* is a passage in *Bemidbar* 48 which discusses the sacrifices which were offered in the Temple on Yom Kippur.

Yizkor and *Musaf*

13.   Before *Musaf*, the memorial prayer *Yizkor* is recited on behalf of deceased relatives. At this time one pledges to give charity in their memory.[17] (One should make sure to fulfill this vow after Yom Kippur.) Those individuals whose parents are alive leave the synagogue when *Yizkor* is recited. Sephardic Jews do not recite *Yizkor*.

14.   The prayer *U'nesaneh tokef*, composed by Rav Amnon of Mainz, is included in the Repetition of the *Musaf Shemoneh Esreh* on Yom Kippur. (*U'nesaneh tokef* is also recited on Rosh Hashana.) Sephardic communities do not recite this section.

A description of the High Priest's Yom Kippur service in the Temple is included in the Repetition of the *Musaf Shemoneh Esreh*. When the words, "and the *Kohanim* and the people standing in the Temple Court fell on their faces," are recited, the Leader and the congregation prostrate themselves. (These words appear several times in the section.) It is also customary to prostrate oneself when reciting the words, "we bend our knees and bow down before the King of kings," during *Aleinu L'shabe'ach*. A handkerchief or paper should be placed on the floor as it is forbidden to prostrate oneself on a stone floor.[18] Some Sephardic communities do not observe this custom on Yom Kippur.

Minchah

15.   The Torah is taken out during *Minchah*. The Torah Reading is the section in *Vayikra* 18 which discusses prohibited marriages. The *haftarah* is
the *Book of Yonah*.[19]

The *Book of Yonah* discusses repentance and returning to God. The narrative
relates how Yonah tried to run away from God so he would not have to ad-
monish the inhabitants of Nineveh to repent, as God had commanded him.
The fate that befell Yonah demonstrates that man cannot escape God, and
that God's Providence encompasses everyone. One has no choice in life
but to return to God.[20]

Ne'ilah

16.   The final prayer recited on Yom Kippur is *Ne'ilah* (lit. "locking"). This
prayer is recited at the time when our fate for the following year is
being sealed. This last prayer, in which we plead before God for a good verdict, is recited with great awe and fear. *Ne'ilah* is begun when the sun is at the
top of trees, i.e. a period of time before sunset.[21]

Ne'ilah ends with the recitation of *Shema Yisrael* and other verses, followed by
one shofar blast.[22] The shofar is blown at the end of Yom Kippur to symbolize the departure of the *Shechinah* (God's Presence). This is similar to what
happened at Mount Sinai, when the shofar was blown when the *Shechinah*
departed. This is derived from the verse, "When the shofar is blown, they
may go up the mountain" (*Shemos* 19:13).

Motza'ei Yom Kippur (the night after Yom Kippur)

17.   The congregation recites a weekday *Ma'ariv* after the stars appear. The
paragraph of *Attah chonantanu* is recited during the blessing of *Attah
chonen* in the *Shemoneh Esreh*, just as on *Motza'ei Shabbos*. Since one must
"add from the ordinary to the holy," work may not be done and food may
not be eaten for a short while after the stars have appeared.[23]

There are two halachic opinions regarding when to recite *Kiddush Levanah*
(the blessing over the moon) in the month of Tishrei. Some people do not
recite *Kiddush Levanah* until *Motza'ei Yom Kippur*. Others recite *Kiddush
Levanah* during the Ten Days of Repentance.[24] The laws of *Kiddush
Levanah* are discussed above, in Chapter 19, Sections 5-6.

After finishing the Yom Kippur service, the congregation should leave the synagogue joyfully, confident that their sins were forgiven, and that they were inscribed for a good year. The Midrash states that on *Motza'ei Yom Kippur* a divine voice announces, "Go eat your bread with joy, and drink your wine with a glad heart, for God has already accepted your deeds" (*Koheles* 9:7).

18. The first blessing recited during *Havdalah* on *Motza'ei Yom Kippur* is *borei peri ha-gafen*, which is recited over a cup of wine. This is followed by the blessing *borei me'orei ha-esh*, which is recited over a candle which burned all *Yom Kippur* (or a candle which was lit from such a candle).[25] The final blessing is the blessing of *Havdalah*, *ha-mavdil bein kodesh l'chol* ("Who separates between the holy and the ordinary").

The blessing over spices is not recited on *Motza'ei Yom Kippur*. If Yom Kippur was on Shabbos, the blessing over spices is recited, as after every Shabbos. Sephardic Jews do not recite the blessing over spices after Yom Kippur that is on Shabbos.[25*]

One may only eat and drink on *Motza'ei Yom Kippur* after hearing *Havdalah*. For an overview of the *halachos* pertaining to *Havdalah*, see Chapter 19, Sections 7-12.

One should eat and feel happy on *Motza'ei Yom Kippur*. One should start building his *succah* that very night, so that he goes from one mitzvah to another. By starting to build a *succah* immediately after finishing the Yom Kippur service, one demonstrates how beloved God's *mitzvos* are to him.[26]

It is customary is for people to attend synagogue earlier than usual on the morning following Yom Kippur.

Chapter Twenty-Nine

Succos, Shemini Atzeres and Simchas Torah

1. The festival of Succos lasts seven days, from the fifteenth to the twenty-first of Tishrei.

The first day of Succos is a *Yom Tov*. All the *halachos* discussed in Chapter 22 are observed, including the prohibition of work. (Outside of Israel, the sixteenth and twenty-third of Tishrei are observed as second days of *Yom Tov*.) The sixteenth (seventeenth outside of Israel) to the twenty-first of Tishrei are *Chol Ha-mo'ed*, the intermediate days of the festival. The *halachos* pertaining to *Chol Ha-mo'ed* are discussed in Sections 52-58, below. The *halachos* pertaining to Shemini Atzeres (and Simchas Torah), which is on the twenty-second of Tishrei, are discussed in Sections 63-69, below.

Commemorating the Exodus from Egypt

2. The Torah commands us to dwell in a *succah* (hut) throughout the holiday of Succos. The *succah* recalls the Clouds of Glory in which God enveloped the Israelites when they left Egypt. The Torah states, "During these seven days, you shall live in *succos*. Everyone among the Israelites shall live in *succos*. This is so your future generations will know that I had the Israelites live in *succos* when I brought them out of the land of Egypt" (*Vayikra* 23:42-43).

The Exodus from Egypt is one of the foundations of our belief in God, Who chose us from all the nations, and gave us His Torah. Many of the *mitzvos* which we observe on Pesach and Succos, as well as some *mitzvos* observed during the year, commemorate the Exodus from Egypt. In this way, the beliefs which are derived from this foundation of our faith are etched indelibly in our minds.

3.   The *Tur Orach Chayim* states:

> The *succos* mentioned by the Torah, in which the Israelites lived, were the
> Clouds of Glory with which God surrounded them, to remind them of His
> wonders and miracles. Although we went out of Egypt in the month of Nis-
> san, we were not commanded to make a *succah* at that time of the year, be-
> cause the weather is mild, and many people camp out in tents and huts
> then. Therefore, it would not be apparent that we are living in *succos* because
> of God's command. God therefore commanded us to make *succos* in the month
> of Tishrei, during the rainy season. At that time, everyone leaves his summer
> home, and returns to his house, but we leave our houses to go live in a *succah*.
> This demonstrates that we do so because it is our King's command. (*Tur Orach
> Chayim*, Section 625)

When living in the *succah*, one should remember that the reason we were
commanded to live in a *succah* is to commemorate the Exodus from Egypt
and the Clouds of Glory which surrounded the Israelites in the Sinai wilderness. These clouds protected them from the desert heat and the beating sun.[1]

The three festivals

4.   Succos, Pesach, and Shavuos are the three festivals when the entire Jew-
        ish nation made a pilgrimage to Jerusalem and offered special sacrifices
in the Temple.

These pilgrimages greatly elevated the nation's spiritual level. The sacrificial
service in the Temple, the encounter with great Torah scholars, and the exalted spiritual atmosphere that pervaded Jerusalem brought the entire nation
closer to their Father in Heaven.

Building the *succah*

5.   The *succah* must be erected under the open sky. Trees, or parts of a
        building may not protrude over it.[2] If possible, one should complete
his *succah* on the day after Yom Kippur.[3]

6.   A *succah* must have at least three walls. If one is unable to build three
        complete walls he should consult a *rav* regarding how to proceed, since
the *halachos* pertaining to this situation are very detailed.[4] It is preferable for a
succah to have four walls.

7.   The walls of the *succah* may be made from any material,[5] provided that
        it is firm. If cloth or curtains are used for the walls, they must be

stretched tight and tied down so the wind will not move them. In this case, it is recommended to stretch ropes, or stand up bamboo canes or boards, at intervals of less than three *tefachim* along the perimeter of the *succah* frame.[6]

8.   A *succah* must measure at least seven *tefachim* by seven *tefachim*.[7] Each of its walls should be at least ten *tefachim* high.[8] (According to the Chazon Ish, a *tefach* is 9.6cm (3.8 inches). According to Rav Chaim Na'eh, a *tefach* is 8cm (3.2 inches)).

The *s'chach* (The roof of the *succah*)

9.   The roof of the *succah* is made of materials that grow from the ground (such as branches) that have been detached from their place of growth. It may not be made from substances that can become ritually impure. (This disqualifies whole or broken wooden utensils, parts of furniture, ladders, crates, etc.,[9] as well as fruits and vegetables.[10])

Thus, there are three general rules regarding the *s'chach*:

A. It must have grown from the ground.

B. It must be detached from its place of growth.

C. It must be incapable of becoming ritually impure.[11]

Today, one can buy reusable *s'chach*. One type of reusable *s'chach* is a woven mat, which is made especially for this purpose. When buying this type of *s'chach*, one must be sure it has rabbinical certification. There are many halachic details pertaining to this type of *s'chach*.[12]

10.   The *s'chach* may only be laid on the *succah* after the walls are erected. If the *s'chach* was laid on the poles of the *succah* before the walls were erected, the *succah* is invalid, and may not be used. The technical term for this disqualification is *ta'aseh v'lo min he-asuy*.[13]

11.   The *s'chach* should not be directly supported by an object which can become ritually impure, such as metal posts, ladders, etc. However, if this was done the *succah* is nonetheless valid, and may be used.[14]

The *s'chach* must be at least ten *tefachim* above the floor of the *succah*.[15] If even a few of its leaves or branches hang less than ten *tefachim* above the floor of the *succah*, the *succah* is invalid, and may not be used.

12.   Most of the *succah* must be covered with *s'chach*. The roof must provide the *succah* with more shade coming from the roof than sunlight. (The

halachic term for this is "its shade is greater than its sun."[16]) The s'chach must
be spread over the succah in such a way that there is no uncovered space three
or more tefachim wide.[17]

Making use of the succah's walls,
s'chach and decorations

13.   It is customary to decorate and beautify the succah as an expression of
       one's love for the mitzvah, and of his understanding of its importance.

The succah's s'chach, walls, and decorations may not be used for any purpose
during the eight days of the festival (i.e. seven days of Succos, and Shemini
Atzeres).[18] Outside of Israel, the succah and its decorations may not be used
for any purpose until after Simchas Torah, which is the day after Shemini Atzeres (the twenty-third of Tishrei).[19]

This rule only applies when one wishes to use the succah or its decorations in
a manner unbefitting the succah's sanctity. For example, one may not remove
a plank from the wall, or take down a decoration. One may however, lean or
rest something against the succah. Similarly, one may hang something from
the succah.[20]

If the succah or one of its decorations fell down, it may not be used for any
other purpose throughout the festival.[21] The succah and its decorations may
not be moved on Shabbos and Yom Tov. This is because they are considered
muktzeh. A succah is not muktzeh on Chol Ha-mo'ed. Therefore, if a succah fell
apart, it may be erected and repaired, and its decorations may be hung again
during Chol Ha-mo'ed. As mentioned above, the succah and its decorations
may not be used in any other way during the festival.[22]

14.   The s'chach and walls of the succah are considered accessories to the
       mitzvah of succah. Therefore they must be treated with respect.
When one dismantles his succah after the festival, he may not throw any
part of it out if it will be stepped on, or otherwise be abused.[23]

The mitzvah to live in a succah

15.   "You shall live in succos seven days" (Vayikra 23:42). It is a mitzvah to
       live in a succah during the seven days of Succos. This means that the
succah should be one's home during the seven days of Succos.[24] One should
eat, drink, and sleep in his succah. One should not even take a short nap out-

side the *succah*.[25] One should also study Torah in the *succah*. However, if one has difficulty concentrating on his studies while in the *succah* he may study elsewhere.[26]

One may eat a snack outside of the *succah*. Halachically, a snack is less than a *k'beitzah* of bread and pastries, as well as large quantities of fruits and drinks. One is considered praiseworthy if he does not even eat these items outside of the *succah*.[27] For the exact measure of a *k'beitzah*, see the Table of Measures at the end of Chapter 15.

16.   If one eats more than a *k'beitzah* of a food made from one of the five types of grain (for example, bread, cake, etc.) on Succos, one recites the blessing *asher kideshanu b'mitzvosav v'tzivanu leishev ba-succah* ("Who sanctified us with His *mitzvos* and commanded us to live in a *succah*"). This blessing is recited in addition to the specific blessing which one recites over the food.[28]

17.   If one recited the blessing *leishev ba-succah* before eating, and did not leave the *succah* before eating another meal, he does not recite the blessing again. Similarly, if one recited the blessing *leishev ba-succah*, and then left the *succah* intending to return immediately, he does not recite the blessing again.[29]

One is exempt from eating and sleeping in a *succah* if doing so will cause suffering.[30] For example, if rain is leaking into one's *succah* to such an extent that if that much rain would leak into his house he would leave it, he is no longer obligated to eat and sleep in the *succah*. (The one exception to this rule is the first night of Succos, as is discussed below.)

18.   Women are exempt from the mitzvah of *succah*, since it is a positive mitzvah which is bound by a time limit.[31] Children should be taught to observe this mitzvah from the age of five or six. One should not give a child food, or tell a child to eat outside of the *succah* if, according to Halachah, the food must be eaten in the *succah*.[32]

19.   Out of respect for the mitzvah of *succah*, one should not bring pots or cooking utensils which are usually not brought to the table into the *succah*.[33]

Special *halachos* pertaining to the first night of Succos

20.   On the first night of Succos one is required to eat at least a *k'zayis* (and preferably more than a *k'beitzah*) of bread in the *succah*. This bit of bread must be eaten before *chatzos ha-laylah*,[34] within a time span of *kedei achilas pras*.[35] Outside of Israel, this also applies on the second night of Succos. ("*Chatzos ha-laylah*" is the time exactly between sunset and sunrise. One should check with a *rav* regarding the exact time of *chatzos ha-laylah* in his location. For the exact measure of a *k'zayis*, *k'beitzah*, and *kedei achilas pras*, see the Table of Measures at the end of Chapter 15.)

One should not eat bread or foods made from any of the five grains on *erev Succos* (the fourteenth of Tishrei), from the beginning of the fourth *sha'ah zemanis* after midday (i.e. nine *sha'os zemanios* after daybreak). This is so the first *k'zayis* of bread eaten in the *succah* will be eaten with an appetite.[36] (*Sha'os zemanios* are defined in Chapter 7, Section 26.)

21.   Before the meal, *Kiddush* is recited over a cup of wine. The text of *Kiddush* includes the blessing *leishev ba-succah* (the complete text of *Kiddush* is printed in the Succos *Machzor*). This blessing is not repeated when eating the bread, since fulfilling the mitzvah of *Kiddush* exempts one from having to recite the blessing.

22.   After the first night of the festival (and the second night of the festival outside of Israel), any time one eats a *k'beitzah* or more of bread, he must do so in the *succah*. However, one may eat less than a *k'beitzah* of bread, or any quantity of fruit, outside of the *succah*. As mentioned above, one who fulfills his religious obligations more strictly than is required by Halachah, and eats everything in a *succah*, is blessed.[37]

23.   If it rains on the first night of Succos, one must delay his meal until the rain stops enough for him to enter the *succah*. One must recite *Kiddush* and eat at least one *k'zayis* of bread in the *succah*. This *halachah* is subject to various details which should be clarified with a person who is proficient in Halachah.[38]

Arba'ah Minim
(The four species)

24.   "And on the first day you shall take for yourself the fruit of a citron tree, palm branches, myrtle branches and willows of the brook" (*Vayikra* 23:40). It is a mitzvah to take the Four Species on each day of Succos, except for Shabbos. The Four Species are: an *esrog* (citron), a *lulav*

(a palm branch), three *hadassim* (myrtle branches), and two *aravos* (willow branches).

25.   Each one of the Four Species has its own set of *halachos*.[39] One must have great expertise to be able to determine if his set of species completely conforms to Halachah. Certain disqualifications only apply for the first day of Succos, while others apply for the entire festival. It is important to have one's set of species checked by a person who is proficient in these *halachos*, to be sure that they are kosher.

The main points to check when examining the Four Species are discussed briefly below.

The *esrog*

26.   The *esrog* must not be the result of grafting. Many *esrog* trees are grafted onto lemon trees. These grafted *esrogim* are often sold, and are difficult to distinguish from non-grafted *esrogim*. Therefore, one must carefully check out the source of one's *esrog*. A grafted *esrog* can usually be detected by its shape, seeds, etc. However, one cannot determine if an *esrog* is valid by relying on these signs. An *esrog*'s validity must be established by tradition, i.e. the *esrog* should come from a citrus grove that has been known for generations to have trees which are not grafted. One should purchase an *esrog* with a certificate from a reliable organization guaranteeing the *esrog*'s pedigree.

All parts of the *esrog* must be intact. This includes the fruit, its stem (called the *oketz*) and the protuberance at the end of the fruit (called the *pittom*). There are strains of *esrogim* available without a *pittom*. The *pittom* from these *esrogim* fall off while they are still on the tree. These *esrogim* are kosher.

One should check the *esrog* for spots and *chazazis* (uncommon lumps caused by disease or rot), which would invalidate the *esrog*.

Several factors are taken into account when determining if a spot invalidates an *esrog*. These factors include:

*   the color of the spot (black spots are the most serious);

*   the location of the spot (a single spot on the *chotem*, the sloping part of the *esrog* leading to the head, invalidates the *esrog*);

* the number of spots (less than two or three spots on the rest of the *esrog* do not invalidate it);

* the size of the spot (if it's easily visible to the naked eye).

One is advised to have one's *esrog* checked by a person who is an expert in these *halachos*.

27. The *esrog* should be at least a *k'beitzah* in size (according to the Chazon Ish, a *k'beitzah* is 100cc, which is 3.38 fl oz). Israeli *esrogim* must have tithes separated from them, or they are not valid for use. (The various tithes are discussed in Chapter 37.) One must inquire about this detail from the seller.

28. A beautiful *esrog* is one that:

* is clean of any spots;

* has a bumpy surface;

* has a recessed *oketz* (stem);

* resembles a tower (i.e. broader at its base and gradually narrowing towards the top);

* has a *pittom* (protuberance) that is exactly opposite the *oketz*.

The *lulav* (The palm branch)

29. The *lulav* must be straight, and not bent to the front or sides. (If the *lulav* is bent backwards, towards the spine, it may be used.) The *lulav* should be green, and not dried out. No part of its top should be broken off.

30. The uppermost leaf of the *lulav* is called the *teyomes*. The *teyomes* must be a double leaf (like all normal palm leaves, which are two leaves joined together at the spine). If the *teyomes* is a single leaf, the *lulav* is invalid, and may not be used.

Similarly, if the two leaves of the *teyomes* are not attached, the *lulav* is invalid, and may not be used. Some people are careful not to use a *lulav* if even a tiny part of the *teyomes* is separated. Other people are more lenient, and will use a *lulav* if the *teyomes* has separation of up to one *tefach* long.

If the leaves of the *teyomes* are split, however slightly, and they fork apart, the *lulav* is invalid. One must be particularly careful about this detail, because it is a common flaw, and because even a tiny forking split in the *teyomes* disqualifies the *lulav*. Similarly, the leaves of the *teyomes* must not be dry, or even slightly broken.

Some people are also careful not to use a *lulav* if the two leaves on either side of the *teyomes* are split and look like two separate leaves.

31.   The spine of the *lulav* must be at least four *tefachim* long. (For the exact measure of a *tefach*, see the Table of Measures at the end of Chapter 15.) The top leaves which grow above the spine are not included in the four *tefachim*.

The *hadassim* (The myrtle branches)

32.   Each *hadass* branch must be three *tefachim* long. The branch's top leaves are not included when measuring the three *tefachim*. One must make sure that most of the leaves on the *hadass* branch grow in clusters of three leaves, with the leaves of each cluster growing out of the branch at the same height. When a *hadass* branch has leaves growing in this manner, it is called *meshulash*. If one of the three leaves is higher than the others, or if the leaves grow in pairs, the *hadass* is invalid.

33.   The *hadass* branch should not be dry. It is especially important that the upper leaves are not dry. Similarly, the top of the branch should not be broken. If some of the leaves fell off the *hadass* branch, and two leaves remain at each level, a *rav* must be consulted regarding whether the branch may still be used.

The *aravos* (The willow branches)

34.   Each *aravah* branch must be three *tefachim* long. The branch's uppermost leaf is not included in the three *tefachim*.

The top of the *aravah* branch should not be broken. The branch should not be dry, and most of its leaves should not be cracked. Similarly, most of the leaves should not have fallen off the branch, nor should they be hanging by a thread.

Some people are particular that there be a fresh leaf growing at the top of the branch. This leaf is called a *livluv*.

35.   The Four Species should be meticulously cared for throughout the festival, so that they do not wither or become damaged. The *esrog* is generally wrapped in flax, and the other species are kept fresh by placing their

stems in water, wrapping them in a wet towel, placing them in an airtight plastic sheath, etc.

The Mitzvah of Taking the Lulav

How to tie the species together

36.   The *lulav* is tied together with three *hadassim* on its right and two *aravos* on its left. The three species must be tied together before *Yom Tov*, since one may not tie a tight knot on *Yom Tov*.[40] The spine of the *lulav* must be at least one *tefach* higher than the *hadassim* and *aravos* (the *lulav's* top leaves are not included in this *tefach*). The *hadassim* should be a little higher than the *aravos*. The *lulav* should have three ties around it; however, the top *tefach* of the *lulav* should not be tied.[41]

How to fulfill the mitzvah

37.   The mitzvah of taking the *lulav* is performed once on every day of Succos, except for Shabbos.[42]

This mitzvah is performed during the day. One may take the *lulav* any time during the day, starting at sunrise. This mitzvah may not be performed at night. If a person will be leaving home early, and will not have the opportunity to take the *lulav* later that day, he may perform the mitzvah after dawn.[43] One may not eat before performing this mitzvah.[44]

38.   One fulfills the mitzvah by taking the *lulav* with the *hadassim* and *aravos* in his right hand, and the *esrog* in his left. The *esrog* is held with the *pittom* facing down. The person holds the *lulav* and *esrog* together so that they touch. The person then recites the blessing *asher kideshanu b'mitzvosav v'tzivanu al netilas lulav* ("Who sanctified us with His *mitzvos* and commanded us to take the *lulav*").

Immediately after reciting the blessing, the person turns the *esrog* around so the *pittom* is facing up. The Four Species are then shaken in the manner described in Section 39, below.[45]

The mitzvah of taking the *lulav* is only fulfilled when the Four Species are held in the same manner in which they grow. Since the blessing must be recited immediately before the mitzvah is performed, we hold the *esrog* with the *pittom* facing down[46] until after the blessing is recited. This way, one must only turn the *esrog* around in order to fulfill the mitzvah after reciting the blessing.[47]

She-hecheyanu is recited on the first day of Succos (before turning the *esrog*). If the first day of Succos is Shabbos, *She-hecheyanu* is recited on the second day of the festival.[48]

One should stand while reciting the blessing and fulfilling the mitzvah.[49]

When and how to shake the Four Species

39.   One shakes the Four Species after reciting the blessings over them. The Four Species are also shaken during *Hallel*, while reciting the verses: *Hodu la-Hashem ki tov* ("Thank God for He is benevolent"), and *Ana Hashem hoshiah na* ("We beseech You, God, to save us"). The *lulav* is shaken to the east, the south, the west, the north, up, and down.

According to the *Mishnah Berurah*, the *lulav* should be shaken as follows: One should stand facing east, holding the *lulav* in his right hand, with the spine towards him, and holding the *esrog* in his left hand, touching the *lulav*. First one should shake the Four Species towards the east, and then return them to his body, opposite his heart. He does this three times. While shaking the Four Species, the leaves of the *lulav* should shake a little. The *lulav* is then shaken in the same manner towards the south (i.e. to the person's right). One does not have to look towards the direction he is shaking his *lulav*. However, he must point his *lulav* towards the correct direction. One then points the top of his *lulav* over his shoulder towards the west, then to the north, and finally up and down. Each time the Four Species are shaken in the manner described above.

It is customary not to point the top of the *lulav* downwards. When one shakes the *lulav* downwards, he should continue to hold the *lulav* facing up, and move it down and up. When shaking the *lulav* towards the south, west, and north, one must always change directions towards the right (i.e. one should always shake his *lulav* first towards the east, then towards the south, then towards the west, and finally towards the north).[50]

Many communities have their own customs regarding how to shake the Four Species. Each person should observe his community's customs.

In view of the many details connected with this mitzvah, it is advisable to receive instruction regarding how to tie the species together, how to shake the species, etc., from a person who is proficient in these *halachos*.

40.   Women are exempt from the mitzvah of *lulav* since it is positive a mitzvah bound by a time limit. However, many women do perform this mitzvah. Sephardic women do not recite the blessing before shaking the Four Species, since their custom is not to recite a blessing when performing a mitzvah from which they are exempt.

The Four Species are not shaken on Shabbos. The Four Species are considered *muktzeh*, and may not be moved on Shabbos.[51]

Halachos of the Four Species which only apply on the first day of Succos

41.   One must own his set of Four Species to fulfill the mitzvah of taking the Four Species on the first day of Succos. (Outside of Israel, this rule also applies on the second day of Succos.) One has not fulfilled his obligation if he borrowed a set of Four Species from someone else.[52] This *halachah* is derived from the verse, "And you shall take for yourselves on the first day" (*Vayikra* 23:40). Similarly, there are stricter *halachos* regarding what types of blemishes disqualify the Four Species on the first day of Succos (and, outside of Israel, on the second day as well). For example, an *esrog* may not be used on the first day of Succos if even the smallest bit is missing.

42.   If one does not own the Four Species, he must receive them as a gift from someone else in order to fulfill the mitzvah (i.e. the owner must intend to transfer the ownership of the Four Species to the receiver, and the receiver must intend to acquire them from the owner). Merely borrowing the Four Species does not suffice.[53]

There is a halachic principle that, "a gift which was given with the condition that it be returned is still considered a gift." Therefore, if a person received a set of the Four Species as a gift from the owner on condition that they will be returned after fulfilling the mitzvah, the Four Species are considered the person's in the interim, and he can fulfill his obligation with them.[54]

On the first day of Succos, a person should not give his Four Species to a child who is younger than thirteen years old, if an adult needs to use the Four Species after him. The reason for this is that according to Halachah a child cannot transfer ownership to others. Therefore, no adults will be able to acquire the Four Species from the child in order to fulfill their obligation.[55]

Outside of Israel, where the second day of the festival is observed in exactly the same manner as the first day, one must not give his Four Species to a child on the first day of Succos at all. (As explained above, a child cannot transfer ownership others. Therefore, the adult will be unable to fulfill the mitzvah on the second day of Succos.)

General Laws of Succos

Yom Tov

43. The first day of Succos (the fifteenth of Tishrei) is a *Yom Tov*. All the *halachos* pertaining to *Yom Tov* discussed in Chapter 22 apply to it, including the prohibition of work.

Outside of Israel, the second day of Succos (the sixteenth of Tishrei) is also a *Yom Tov*. This day is called "the second day of *Yom Tov* in the Diaspora."

44. On *Yom Tov*, it is prohibited to wrap the *hadassim* and *aravos* in a wet towel to prevent them from withering, since this may involve the *melachos* of Laundering and Squeezing. If the *hadassim* and *aravos* were taken out of a vase of water, they may be put back in it, but the water may not be changed.[56] As mentioned above, the Four Species are *muktzeh*, and may not be moved on Shabbos.

On *Chol Ha-mo'ed*, it is a mitzvah to keep the *hadassim*, *aravos*, and *lulav* fresh by changing the water they are kept in.[57]

"The season of our rejoicing"

45. Succos is called the "Season of our Rejoicing." It is a mitzvah to be happy and rejoice on the festival.

In the days of the Temple, great celebrations were held in Jerusalem on Succos. These celebrations were called *Simchas Beis Ha-sho'evah* ("The Rejoicing of the Water-drawing"). Every day of the festival, water was drawn from the Shiloach well near Jerusalem, and poured on the altar. The greatest scholars of the nation, as well as the huge crowds that had made the pilgrimage to Jerusalem, accompanied this service with dancing and singing. The rejoicing was so extraordinary that our sages declared, "Whoever has not seen The Rejoicing of the Water-drawing has never seen true rejoicing in his life" (*Succah* 51b).

It is customary to commemorate these celebrations by reciting many hymns and praises during the evenings of *Chol Ha-mo'ed Succos*. Among those which are recited are the fifteen chapters of *Tehillim* which begin with the words *Shir ha-ma'alos* (*Tehillim* 120-134). These passages were recited in the Temple during the Rejoicing of the Water-drawing.

The festival prayers

46. The text of the festival prayers are printed in the *Machzor* for Succos.

After *Shacharis*, *Hallel* is recited. The entire *Hallel* is recited on all the days of Succos (unlike *Rosh Chodesh*, when two sections are omitted).

One recites the blessing *asher kideshanu b'mitzvosav v'tzivanu likro es ha-Hallel* ("Who sanctified us with His *mitzvos* and commanded us to read the *Hallel*") before reciting *Hallel*. Sephardic Jews recite the blessing *ligmor es ha-Hallel* ("to complete the *Hallel*") when reciting the entire *Hallel*.[58]

The Four Species are held while reciting *Hallel*, and are shaken while reciting the verses *Hodu la-Hashem* and *Ana Hashem hoshiah na*, as mentioned above.

One may not talk while reciting *Hallel*.[59]

47. It is customary to read *Koheles* (*Ecclesiastes*) before the Torah Reading on the Shabbos during Succos. In some congregations, *Koheles* is read from a kosher parchment. In some of these congregations, two blessings are recited before *Koheles* is read. The two blessings are *al mikra megillah* and *Shehecheyanu*.[60] *Koheles* was written by King Solomon. In it he declares that this world and all its pleasures are futile. The scroll ends with this conclusion: "The end of the matter after everything is heard is to fear God and observe His commandments, as this is the totality of man."

48.　　The Torah is read on each day of Succos. Each day's section discusses the sacrifices offered in the Temple on that day, as well as other themes pertaining to Succos. Each day's Torah reading and *maftir* are printed in the *Machzor*.

Musaf is recited after the Torah Reading. The *Musaf* service corresponds to the *Musaf* sacrifice that was offered in the Temple each day of Succos.

49.　　Throughout Succos, *Ya'aleh V'yavo* is recited during the third blessing of *Birkas Ha-mazon*. There is a table in Chapter 12, Section 9, which illustrates how to proceed if one forgot to recite *Ya'aleh V'yavo* during *Birkas Ha-mazon*.

Hoshanos

50.　　On each day of Succos, special supplications are recited. These supplications are called *Hoshanos*, because the words *hosha na* ("Please save!") are repeated many times in the course of the prayer. A different chapter of *Hoshanos* is recited each day. All the *Hoshanos* are printed in the *Siddur* and *Machzor*.[61] The *halachos* pertaining to the *Hoshanos* which are recited on Hoshana Rabbah, the last day of Succos, are discussed in Sections 59-61 below.

A Torah scroll is taken to the *bimah* (the table in the center of the synagogue) when *Hoshanos* are recited. The congregants circle the *bimah* carrying their Four Species while reciting the *Hoshanos*. This is called *hakafos*. These *hakafos* commemorate the *hakafos* people made around the altar in the Temple.

51.　　On Shabbos, the *Aron Ha-Kodesh* is opened at the time when *Hoshanos* would normally be recited. However, no Torah scroll is taken out, and there are no *hakafos*. In the Temple, there were no *hakafos* on Shabbos either.[62]

Chol Ha-mo'ed
(The intermediate days of Succos)

52.　　The last six days of Succos (the sixteenth to the twenty-first of Tishrei) are *Chol Ha-mo'ed Succos*. (As mentioned above, the sixteenth of Tishrei is the second day of *Yom Tov* outside of Israel. Therefore, outside of Israel *Chol Ha-mo'ed Succos* is the last five days of Succos.)

53. It is a mitzvah to rejoice on *Chol Ha-mo'ed*.[63] Similarly, one should honor these days by eating nicer meals, wearing beautiful and clean garments, etc. Although one is not obligated to eat bread on *Chol Ha-mo'ed* (unlike *Yom Tov*, when at least two meals must be eaten with bread), it is a mitzvah to eat bread with the morning and evening meals.[64] *Chol Ha-mo'ed* should be a time of Torah study and spiritual rejuvenation.

On each day of *Chol Ha-mo'ed*, *Hallel* and *Musaf* are recited, and the *Torah* is read. The prayers and Torah Readings for *Chol Ha-mo'ed* are printed in the *Machzor*.[65]

54. *Ya'aleh V'yavo* is added in the *Shemoneh Esreh* of *Shacharis*, *Minchah* and *Ma'ariv*. Before one prays, one should familiarize himself with this addition and its *halachos*. The table below illustrates these *halachos*.

Forgetting *Ya'aleh V'yavo* in *Chol Ha-mo'ed* Prayer[1,2]

The place where one realized his error	How to proceed
Before mentioning God's Name in the blessing *Ha-machazir Shechinaso l'Tzion*	Return to *Ya'aleh V'yavo* and continue reciting the *Shemoneh Esreh* from there
After mentioning God's Name in the blessing *Ha-machazir Shechinaso l'Tzion*,[3] but before concluding the blessing	Say *lamedeini chukecha*,[4] then recite *Ya'aleh V'yavo*, *V'sechezenah*, and the rest of *Shemoneh Esreh*
After reciting the blessing *Ha-machazir Shechinaso l'Tzion*, but before beginning *Modim*	Recite *Ya'aleh V'yavo*[5] and then recite *Modim*
After beginning *Modim* but before finishing the *Shemoneh Esreh*	Return to the beginning of *Retzei* and repeat the *Shemoneh Esreh* from there
After finishing the *Shemoneh Esreh*[6]	Repeat the entire *Shemoneh Esreh*[7]

1. *S.A.* 422:1.   2. According to the *Mishnah Berurah* (422 [10]), one who is not sure if he recited *Ya'aleh V'yavo* must recite the passage again. (The assumption is that the person recited *Shemoneh Esreh* as he normally does, without reciting *Ya'aleh V'yavo*.) One who is certain that he intended to recite *Ya'aleh V'yavo*, but some time after reciting *Shemoneh Esreh* cannot remember whether or not he actually recited the passage, does not have to repeat *Shemoneh Esreh*. However, one who is not sure if he recited *Ya'aleh V'yavo* immediately after reciting *Shemoneh Esreh* must repeat the *Shemoneh Esreh*. M.B. 114 (38).   3. *M.B.* 422 (2).   4. This is *Tehillim* 119:12: *Baruch Attah Hashem lamedeini chukecha*. By completing the sentence *Baruch Attah Hashem* with the final words of the verse (*lamedeini chukecha*), one recites a verse from *Tehillim* rather than mention God's Name in vain (see *M.B.* 422 [5]).   5. *S.A.* 422:1. See also 114:6, and *M.B.* there (32).   6. Finishing the *Shemoneh Esreh* means having recited *Yehi Ratzon* at the end of *Elokai netzor*.   7. There are different halachic opinions regarding how one should proceed if he remembers that he did not recite *Ya'aleh V'yavo* after he began reciting *Musaf* (*M.B.* 422 [4]). One should consult a *rav* regarding how to proceed in this situation.

55. *Ya'aleh V'yavo* is recited in *Birkas Ha-mazon* after all meals eaten on *Chol Ha-mo'ed*. The table in Chapter 12 ,Section 9, illustrates how one should proceed if he forgot to recite *Ya'aleh V'yavo* in *Birkas Ha-mazon* on *Chol Ha-mo'ed*.

The prohibition of doing *melachah* on *Chol Ha-mo'ed*

56. Some activities are prohibited on *Yom Tov* and permitted on *Chol Ha-mo'ed*. Other activities are prohibited on *Chol Ha-mo'ed*. One should not take the prohibition of work on *Chol Ha-mo'ed* lightly by doing more than is permitted. Our sages speak against this in very grave terms.[66]

There are many *halachos* regarding what activities are prohibited or permitted on *Chol Ha-mo'ed*. The Halachah is often different for different situations. The *halachos* mentioned below define in a general way what activities are permitted. One is advised to study these *halachos* in more depth.

A person should not compare his situation to any of the cases mentioned below. Each case must be decided by a competent authority.

Types of work permitted on *Chol Ha-mo'ed*

57. Any work which is done to prepare food for the holiday is permitted. Examples of such work is grinding, squeezing, lighting a fire, cooking, baking, separating tithes, etc.[67]

Work indirectly needed for food preparation

Appliances and utensils which are needed to prepare food for the holiday may be repaired on *Chol Ha-mo'ed*. This includes refrigerators, mixers, etc. These items may be repaired because they are needed for food preparation.

If the utensils can be used without repairing them, they should not be repaired on *Chol Ha-mo'ed*. One may only repair utensils that are directly involved in food preparation. Utensils which indirectly facilitate food preparation, such as a ladder (to reach food on a high shelf) or a car (to help purchase food), are not included in this ruling.

One may perform any work to prevent a financial loss. In this context, "financial loss" does not include the loss of potential profit. Rather, it refers to an actual loss.[68] One who must work on *Chol Ha-mo'ed* to prevent a financial loss, should do the least amount of work possible.[69]

One may not create a situation where he will suffer a financial loss if he does not work on *Chol Ha-mo'ed*. One who knows before *Yom Tov* that he will have to complete work on *Chol Ha-mo'ed* to prevent a financial loss, should complete the work before *Yom Tov*. One may not set aside work with the intention of completing it on *Chol Ha-mo'ed*.[70]

58. A person is permitted to do work necessary for the holiday. One may also do this type of work for others, provided he does not charge for the service.

If the person doing the work is an amateur, he may do the work in the usual manner. However, if he is a professional, he should do the work a little bit differently than he normally does. This is called doing something with a *shinuy*. For example, one may mend a torn garment if it is needed for the holiday. If the person mending the garment does not know how to sew, he may mend the garment in the usual manner. However, if the person mending the garment knows how to sew well, the person must mend the garment with a *shinuy*. There are many additional details pertaining to this *halachah*. It is advisable to study the *halachah's* practical applications.[71]

One may take care of his personal hygiene, such as bathing, etc., on *Chol Ha-mo'ed*. One may also address his health and medical needs on *Chol Ha-mo'ed*.

It is a mitzvah to have a haircut and cut one's nails on *erev Yom Tov* in honor of *Yom Tov*. However, one may not have a haircut or shave on *Chol Ha-mo'ed*.[72] Ashkenazic Jews do not cut their nails on *Chol Ha-mo'ed*. However, if one cut his nails on *erev Yom Tov*, he may cut them again on *Chol Ha-mo'ed*.[73]

It is prohibited to wash clothes on *Chol Ha-mo'ed*. However, one may wash clothes for little children who are constantly soiling themselves.[74]

One may not buy or sell things on *Chol Ha-mo'ed*. One may only sell objects that will lose their value if one waits until after the festival to sell them. (This is an example of incurring financial loss. See Section 57, above.) Items needed for the festival may also be bought or sold. These *halachos* are very detailed.[75]

Writing is prohibited on *Chol Ha-mo'ed*. However, any information that is needed for the festival, or which may be forgotten if it is not written down — and it involves a real loss for that person — may be written down. When corresponding with a friend on *Chol Ha-mo'ed*, it is customary to write the letter with a *shinuy*.[76]

Hoshana Rabbah

59.   The last day of *Chol Ha-mo'ed* (the twenty-first of Tishrei) is called Hoshana Rabbah. This day is considered the last of the Days of Awe. This is the day on which man's heavenly judgment is finally sealed.

Some men observe the custom to remain awake studying Torah the entire night of Hoshana Rabbah. Many of those who observe this custom study a special book, called *Tikkun Leil Hoshana Rabbah*, which contains special topics to study on this night.

On Succos the world is judged regarding how much rain will fall that year. Hoshana Rabbah is the last day of Succos, when the verdict is finalized. Therefore, some customs reflecting the Day of Judgment are observed on Hoshana Rabbah. For example, the one who leads the community in prayer dons a white *kittel*.[77]

60.   *Shacharis* on Hoshana Rabbah is longer than usual. *Mizmor l'sodah* (which is recited during the week) as well as the chapters of *Tehillim* which are added on Shabbos are recited during *Pesukei D'zimrah*. However, the chapter beginning with the word *Nishmas* is not recited.[78]

The *Hoshanos* recited on Hoshana Rabbah are printed in the *Machzor*. Torah scrolls are taken out, and the congregation circles the *bimah* seven times while holding the Four Species and reciting the *Hoshanos*. It is customary to untie the *lulav* for these *hakafos*.

61.   The last chapters of the *Hoshanos* are prayers for water. When these *Hoshanos* are recited, the Four Species are set aside, and five *aravah* branches tied with a *lulav* leaf are taken. One shakes the branches while reciting these *Hoshanos*. One beats the branches on the floor five times when he reaches the words *Kol mevasser* at the end of the *Hoshanos*. The branches are then beaten on an object like a table or bench to remove their leaves.[79] It is not necessary to remove all the leaves. This custom, called *Chibut aravah*, is enhanced if the *aravah* branches are long and beautiful.

62.   One must eat in the *succah* until the end of Hoshana Rabbah. One takes leave of the *succah* after eating his last meal in it. Some people recite a special prayer when they leave the *succah* for the last time. This prayer is printed in some *Machzorim*.[80]

Shemini Atzeres

63.   Shemini Atzeres immediately follows the seven days of Succos. Shemini Atzeres is on the twenty-second of Tishrei.[81]

Although it immediately follows Succos, Shemini Atzeres is a separate festival. One does not sit in the *succah* (see Section 69 regarding the halachah for one who does not live in Israel), nor does one take the Four Species. *She-hecheyanu* is recited during *Kiddush* and when lighting the candles. (Some Sephardic Jews do not recite *She-hecheyanu* when lighting the candles. See Chapter 22, Section 20.) *Tefillas geshem*, the prayer for rain, is recited on Shemini Atzeres. *Tefillas geshem* is also discussed in Section 67, below. All the festival prayers are printed in the *Machzor*.

Shemini Atzeres is a *Yom Tov*, and all the *halachos* pertaining to *Yom Tov*, including the prohibition of work mentioned in Chapter 22, apply to it.

Simchas Torah (Rejoicing over the Torah)

64.   In Israel, Simchas Torah and Shemini Atzeres are celebrated on the same day.

A portion of the Torah is read in the synagogue every Shabbos. In the course of the year, the entire Torah is read. The last portion, *V'zos ha-berachah*, is read on Simchas Torah. Upon completing *V'zos ha-berachah*, the reader immediately begins reading from *Bereshis*, starting the cycle anew. The community rejoices at having completed the whole Torah.

65.   In the evening and morning of Simchas Torah, all the Torah scrolls are taken out of the *Aron Ha-Kodesh*. Congregants hold the scrolls while circling the *bimah* seven times amidst dancing and singing in honor of the Torah.

The *Mishnah Berurah* writes that there is great merit to rejoicing and dancing in honor of the Torah. One should be visibly excited while rejoicing in honor of the Torah. This is derived from *Shmuel II*, where it is related that King David, "with all his energy danced and twirled before God" (*Shmuel II*

6:16). According to tradition, the Ari z"l stated that he merited his high spiritual level due to the immense joy he felt while performing *mitzvos*. It is related that the Gaon of Vilna danced before the Torah scrolls on Simchas Torah with all his strength.[82]

66. After *Shacharis* on Simchas Torah, three scrolls are taken out for the Torah reading. *V'zos ha-berachah* is read from the first scroll. It is customary for every man to receive an *aliyah* on Simchas Torah. Therefore, *V'zos ha-berachah* is repeated from the beginning until the words *me'onah Elokai kedem* ("in the Eternal God is shelter"),[83] until every man has received an *aliyah*. It is also customary for all the boys to receive one *aliyah* together. This *aliyah* is called *kol ha-ne'arim* ("all the youths"). After the Torah portion is read, the boys are blessed with the verse *Ha-mal'ach ha-go'el osi* ("The angel who rescues me," *Bereshis* 48:16). The man who receives the last *aliyah* in *V'zos ha-berachah* is called the *Chasan Torah* ("the Bridegroom of the Torah").

The beginning of *Bereshis* is read from the second scroll. The man who receives this *aliyah* is called the *Chasan Bereshis* ("the bridegroom of *Bereshis*"). The *maftir*, which is read from the third scroll, discusses the sacrifices offered in the Temple on Shemini Atzeres as well as other themes related to the day.

After the Torah readings, the *Yizkor* prayer is recited for the elevation of the souls of deceased relatives. (See Chapter 28, Section 13, for more details.) Sephardic Jews do not recite *Yizkor*.

Tefillas geshem (The prayer for rain)

67. An announcement is made before *Musaf* that *Mashiv ha-ruach u'morid ha-gashem* ("Who makes the wind blow and brings the rain") should be recited during the prayers. *Tefillas geshem*, the Prayer for Rain, is also recited on Shemini Atzeres. When reciting this prayer, we praise God's mightiness in bringing rain, and we beseech Him to send the seasonal rains during the winter.[84]

68. *Mashiv ha-ruach u'morid ha-gashem* is recited during the second blessing of *Shemoneh Esreh* from when *Tefillas geshem* is recited (or when the announcement is made to recite *Mashiv ha-ruach*) on Shemini Atzeres. It is recited during the second blessing of the *Shemoneh Esreh* until *Musaf* on the first day of Pesach.

In Israel, the summer version of the blessing of *Bareich aleinu* ("Bless for us") in the weekday *Shemoneh Esreh*, is recited until the seventh of Cheshvan. Outside of Israel, people start reciting *Mashiv ha-ruach* sixty days after *tekufas Tishrei*. For a more detailed discussion about *Mashiv ha-ruach* and the winter version of *Bareich aleinu* see Chapter 7, Sections 53, 56, and 57.

Outside of Israel

69. Outside of Israel, one eats in the *succah* on Shemini Atzeres, which is the twenty-second of Tishrei. The blessing of *leishev ba-succah* is not recited (because it is not clear if this day is considered the seventh day of Succos).[85] The twenty-third of Tishrei is the second day of *Yom Tov* in the Diaspora, when Simchas Torah is observed. The *halachos* for the second day of *Yom Tov* in the Diaspora are discussed in Chapter 22, Sections 2-4.[86] In Israel, the twenty-third of Tishrei is *isru chag* (the day following the festival). Outside of Israel, the twenty-fourth of Tishrei is *isru chag*.[87]

Chapter Thirty

Chanukah

The Chanukah miracle

1. The eight days of Chanukah begin on the twenty-fifth of Kislev.

The Rambam explains the reason for this holiday:

> During the Second Temple period, the Greek kings issued decrees against Israel calculated to abolish their religion. They did not allow them to study Torah and keep *mitzvos*, and they seized their property and their daughters. They entered the Temple, breached its walls and defiled its consecrated parts. The Jews were greatly oppressed by them until the God of our fathers had compassion on them and saved them. The sons of the Hasmonean High Priests overcame and killed the Greeks, and rescued the Jews from their hands. They appointed a king from among the priests, so that kingship returned to Israel for more than two hundred years until the destruction of the Second Temple.
>
> It was on the twenty-fifth of Kislev that the Jews overcame and destroyed their enemies. When they entered the Temple, they only found one little vessel of pure oil, only sufficient for one day. When they lit the Temple Menorah, the oil continued to burn for eight days, until they were able to obtain pure oil.
>
> Therefore, the sages in those days decreed that, beginning on the twenty-fifth of Kislev, there be eight days of rejoicing and praise. On every evening of these eight nights, candles are lit at the entrances of the homes to publicize the miracle. These are the days that are called Chanukah. (*Hilchos Chanukah* 3:1-3)

2. The name Chanukah is an acronym for the Hebrew words *chanu kaf heh*, "they rested on the twenty-fifth" (*chanu* means, "they rested," and the letters *kaf* and *heh* have the numerical value of 20 and 5, respectively). This refers to the Jews' victory over their enemies. The name Chanukah also means "dedicated." During those days, the Temple and the altar were rededicated, and purified from the defilement caused by the Greeks.

The Chanukah prayers

3.   Chanukah is a holiday of praise and thanksgiving to God. The para-
        graph of *Al ha-nissim* ("For the miracles") is added in the *Shemoneh
Esreh* (during the blessing of *Modim*), and in *Birkas Ha-mazon* (during the blessing of *Nodeh Lechah*).[1] When reciting this prayer we praise God and give
thanks to Him for the Jews' deliverance from the Greeks' decrees.

The table in Chapter 12, Section 9 illustrates how one should proceed if he
forgot to recite *Al Ha-Nissim* during *Birkas Ha-mazon*.

4.   Whole-*Hallel* is recited all eight days of Chanukah[2] during *Shacharis*. We
        also read from the Torah every day of Chanukah. The section read is
from *Bemidbar* 7, and discusses the dedication of the altar in the Tabernacle.
This section is read because the Tabernacle was completed on the twenty-
fifth of Kislev.[3] Two Torah scrolls are taken out on the Shabbos during Chanukah. The weekly Torah portion is read from the first scroll, and a special
maftir for Chanukah is read from the second scroll.

Tachanun and *La-menatze'ach* (the passage before *u'Va l'Tzion*) are not recited
on Chanukah. Some people recite *Tehillim* 30, *Mizmor shir chanukas ha-bayis
l'David*, as the hymn of the day (*Shir shel yom*). This is the psalm that King
David composed in honor of the Temple's dedication.

5.   The table on the following page describes how to proceed after forget-
        ting *Al ha-nissim*.

Lighting Chanukah Candles

6.   On each of the eight days of Chanukah, candles are lit to recall the
        miracle of the oil. All family members assemble for the lighting, in
order to publicize the miracle.[4]

One candle is lit on the first day of Chanukah. Every day a candle is added to
the previous day's number so that eight candles are lit on the eighth day of
Chanukah.[5]

7.   It is customary for each member of the family to light his own Chanu-
        kah candles. The only exception to this rule is the wife, who fulfills her
obligation with her husband's candles. If a number of people are lighting their
candles in one place, each one's candles should be in a separate area, so that

the number of each person's candles can be clearly seen. A child who is old enough to light candles should be allowed to do so.[6] Among Sephardic Jews it is customary for one family member to light candles for the entire family.[7]

The Chanukah candles

8. Some people enhance the mitzvah by using olive oil instead of candles. This is because the miracle in the Temple occurred with olive oil.[8]

The candles or wicks must be arranged in a straight line. There must be at least the width of a finger between each candle. One may not use a candle made from braided wicks. Similarly, one may not put a number of wicks in a bowl of oil if there is no separation between them. In these cases, the candles resemble a torch or flaming fire, which may not be used to fulfill this mitzvah.[9]

Forgetting *Al Ha-Nissim* While Praying

The place where one realized his error	How to proceed
If one remembered before mentioning God's Name in the blessing *ha-tov shimcha* at the end of *Modim*	Return to the beginning of *Al ha-nissim* and continue reciting the *Shemoneh Esreh* from there[1]
If one remembered after mentioning God's Name in the blessing *ha-tov shimcha* at the end of *Modim*, but before finishing the *Shemoneh Esreh*	Continue reciting the *Shemoneh Esreh* until the verse *Yiheyu l'ratzon* at the end of *Elokai netzor*, and then recite: *Yihi ratzon milfanecha she-ta'aseh lanu nissim v'nifla'os k'shem she-asisah la-avoseinu ba-yamim ha-hem ba-zeman ha-zeh* ("May it be Your will to perform miracles and wonders for us as You performed for our fathers in those days at this time.") on Chanukah continue: *Bi-mei Matissyahu...* ("In the days of Matissyahu...") on Purim continue: *Bi-mei Mordechai v'Esther...* ("In the days of Mordechai and Esther...")[2]
If one finished the *Shemoneh Esreh*	Do not repeat the *Shemoneh Esreh*

1. S.A. 682:1 (for Chanukah) and 693:2 (for Purim).   2. M.B. 682 (4).

9.   It is prohibited to use the light from the Chanukah candles. Therefore, a
       separate candle, called the *shamash*, is lit. The *shamash* is used to light
the other candles. The *shamash* must be separated from the other candles,
either by placing it a little bit away from the other candles, or by placing
it a little bit higher than the other candles. This is so one can see how
many Chanukah candles were lit that night.[10]

Where and when to light

10.   The Chanukah candles should be lit by the entrance of one's house, if
       the entrance faces a public domain. This is to publicize the Chanukah
miracle. The candles must be lit in the place where they are to remain, rather
than being lit inside the house and taken outside later.[11] The candles should be
placed within a *tefach* of the entrance. If the entrance has a *mezuzah*, the candles should be placed to the left of the doorway, opposite the *mezuzah*.[12] If
one does not have an entrance which faces a public domain, the candles
should be lit on a windowsill that can be seen from the street.

11.   The candles must be at least three *tefachim* above the ground. It is a
       mitzvah to place them less than ten *tefachim* above the ground. How-
ever, if the candles are placed higher than ten *tefachim*, one has fulfilled the
mitzvah.

Anyone living in a place which is higher than twenty *amos* from the street
should ask a *rav* where to light Chanukah candles. (See the Table of Measures at the end of Chapter 15, for the exact measure of a *tefach* and an *amah*.)

12.   The Chanukah candles are lit at nightfall. One halachic opinion is that one
       should light the candles at sunset, and the other halachic opinion is that
one should light the candles when the stars appear.[13] One who did not light his
candles at either of these times can light them any time during the night, as
long as members of the family are awake and present at the lighting.[14]

13.   The candles (or oil) must burn for at least half an hour after the stars
       appear. This rule applies whenever the candles were lit.[15] If one lights
with oil, he must make sure he has enough oil to burn the required amount of
time when he lights his flames. One may not add oil after the flames have
been lit.

The candles must be set up so the wind will not extinguish them while they
are burning.[16]

How to light

14.   Before lighting his Chanukah candles, one recites the blessings, *asher kideshanu b'mitzvosav v'tzivanu l'hadlik ner shel Chanukah* ("Who sanctified us with His *mitzvos* and commanded us to light the Chanukah candle"), and *she'asah nissim la-avoseinu ba-yamim ha-hem ba-zeman ha-zeh* ("Who performed miracles for our fathers in those days at this time"). On the first night of Chanukah, the blessing of *She-hecheyanu* is also recited. Sephardic Jews have a slightly different ending for the first blessing. Instead of reciting *l'hadlik ner shel Chanukah*, they recite *l'hadlik ner Chanukah*.[17]

15.   On the first night of Chanukah, one lights a candle on the far right side of his Menorah. On the second night, two candles are lit. One candle is placed on the far right side of the Menorah, and the second candle is placed to the left of the first candle. The candle on the left is lit first. On each consecutive night, a candle is added to the left. The candle on the extreme left is always lit first, followed by the other candles. The candles are lit from left to right.[18]

According to a different halachic opinion, if one lights his Chanukah candles near a doorway, the candle which is nearest to the doorway is lit first. For example, when the Chanukah candles are placed at the left of the entrance, the right candle should be lit first, followed by the other candles, going towards the left (i.e., the candle which is added for that night is lit first). There are other customs regarding how to light the Chanukah candles.[19]

16.   On each day of Chanukah, *Ha-neros ha-lalu* ("These lights") is recited. One begins reciting this hymn after the first candle is lit, and completes the hymn while lighting the other candles.[20] After the candles have been lit, the hymn *Ma'oz tzur* ("A stronghold, the Rock of my salvation") is sung. *Ha-neros ha-lalu* and *Ma'oz tzur* are printed in the *Siddur*. Sephardic Jews recite *Mizmor shir chanukas ha-bayis l'David* (*Tehillim* 30) instead of *Ma'oz tzur*.

Additional laws

17.   Chanukah candles are lit in the synagogue between *Minchah* and *Ma'ariv* to publicize the miracle. The Menorah is placed at the southern wall, and the candles are arranged from east to west. One can not fulfill his obligation by watching the Chanukah candles being lit in the synagogue. Therefore, one must return home and light his own Chanukah candles.[21]

18.   A person who is not in his own home for the night, and either his wife
is not lighting candles in their home, or he is not married, can fulfill the
mitzvah of Chanukah candles in one of two ways. The best way is for the
person to light his own Chanukah candles. Alternatively, the person can fulfill his obligation when his host lights the Chanukah candles. In this case,
either the guest gives his host a token sum to purchase a part in the candles, or the guest can receive his part as a "gift" from the host (this is done
through an act of *kinyan*, i.e. a halachic transfer of property). In this case,
the guest must listen and answer Amen when his host recites the blessings.

If a guest has a room for himself, with a window (or door) facing a public
domain, he must light his own Chanukah candles.[22]

One who is visiting his friend at night may not light Chanukah candles at his
friend's home if he is not planning to sleep at his friend's house, and if he lives
in that city. In this case he must return home to light his Chanukah candles.

Lighting Chanukah candles on
Friday and *Motza'ei Shabbos*

19.   On Friday, the Chanukah candles are lit before the Shabbos candles. On
Friday the Chanukah candles must burn for a longer time than during
the week (i.e. from some time before sunset until half an hour after the
stars appear). Therefore, one must use longer candles or more oil than
usual. The standard colored candles are not long enough to be used on Friday.

It is proper to recite *Minchah* before lighting the Chanukah candles.[23]

20.   When lighting the Chanukah candles on Friday, one must make sure
that opening the door will not allow the wind to extinguish the candles. If this is a problem, one must erect a partition before Shabbos to prevent the wind from extinguishing the candles.[24]

21.   On *Motza'ei Shabbos*, Chanukah candles are lit after Shabbos has ended.
Some people light them after *Havdalah*, and others light them before
Havdalah. If one who lights his Chanukah candles before *Havdalah* forgot
to recite *Attah chonantanu* in the *Shemoneh Esreh*, he must recite "*Baruch ha-
mavdil bein kodesh l'chol*," before lighting the Chanukah candles.[25] If possible, the candles or wicks for the Menorah should be prepared on Friday
for *Motza'ei Shabbos*, so one will be able to light them immediately after
nightfall.

Chanukah customs

22.   Women observe the custom not to do work for the half hour that the candles are lit as a reminder not to use the candles for any purpose. This custom is observed specifically by women, because one of the Chanukah miracles occurred through a woman, Yehudis, the daughter of the High Priest Yochanan.[26]

It is customary to eat dairy dishes on Chanukah. This custom originates with Yehudis. Yehudis fed the Greek army commander cheese to make him thirsty, and then wine to intoxicate him. When the Greek commander fell asleep, Yehudis decapitated him, the result being that his forces fled. In this way, the Jews were saved.[27]

Asarah b'Teves
(The tenth of Teves)

23.   On the tenth of Teves, King Nebuchadnezzar of Babylonia lay siege to Jerusalem. This siege was the first of many tragedies which befell the Jews, and which ended in the Destruction of the First Temple and the Babylonian exile.[28]

The Destruction of the Temple has a profound effect on the Jewish nation to this day. It caused the loss of our people's bountiful spiritual blessings, the lack of which has been keenly perceptible throughout the generations.

24.   All the laws pertaining to public fasts apply to the tenth of Teves. For example, one may not eat or drink from dawn until night, *selichos* are recited, the Torah is read, and *Aneinu* is added in the *Shemoneh Esreh*.[29] (For more details regarding these laws, see Chapter 25.)

A public fast should be utilized for introspection, self-improvement, and repentance. The *Chayei Adam* writes:

> Every man and woman is obligated to reflect upon his deeds and return to God; indeed, this is the main purpose of a fast. Concerning the people of Nineveh, it is written, "And God saw their deeds, that they had repented from their evil ways" (*Yonah* 3:10). Our sages comment on this, "It does not say that God saw their sackcloth and their fast, but that He saw their deeds" (*Ta'anis* 22). (*Chayei Adam*, Section 133)

For additional information about the purpose of fast days, see Chapter 25, Section 2.

Tu bi-Shevat
(The fifteenth of Shevat)

25. Tu bi-Shevat is the beginning of the year for trees. This date determines which year the fruits of the trees belong to regarding the *mitzvos* of the Land of Israel (*orlah, neta reva'i, terumos, ma'aser*, etc.). Fruits which reached the stage of growth known as *chanatah* before Tu bi-Shevat belong to the former year, while those which reached that stage after Tu bi-Shevat belong to the next year.

One must not separate tithes which pertain to one year for fruits from another year.

The tithes which must be separated change in the course of the seven-year *shemittah* cycle. (*Shemittah* is the sabbatical year when land must lay fallow.) In the first, second, fourth and fifth years of the cycle, *ma'aser sheini* is separated from the crops, and in the third and sixth years of the cycle, *ma'aser ani* is separated. (The next *shemittah* years are 5761, 5768, and 5775.)

26. Tu bi-Shevat also determines the new year for *orlah* and *neta reva'i*.
 Fruits which grew during the first three years after a tree was planted are *orlah*, and may not be eaten. Fruits which ripen after Tu bi-Shevat of the tree's fourth year are *neta reva'i*. Fruits that ripen after Tu bi-Shevat of the tree's fifth year are no longer *neta reva'i*.

For more details concerning the laws of the *mitzvos* that apply to the Land of Israel, see Chapter 37.

27. It is customary to eat fruits for which the Land of Israel is praised on Tu bi-Shevat. This is an expression of our love for the Land of Israel, and the *mitzvos* that apply to it.[30]

Tachanun is not recited on Tu bi-Shevat.

Chapter Thirty-One

The Month of Adar

1. "When Adar comes, joy increases." The whole month of Adar is infused with the joy resulting from the great miracle which happened to the Jews in the time of Mordechai and Esther. In those days the entire Jewish people were in danger of being annihilated due to Haman's decree. God rescued the Jews from their oppressor, and turned their despair into joy and gladness.

2. In a lunar leap year there are two months of Adar (Adar I and Adar II). During a lunar leap year, the laws of Purim as well as the other laws pertaining to the month are observed during Adar II. However, *tachanun* and *La-menatze'ach* (the psalm recited before *u'Va l'Tzion*) are not recited on the fourteenth and fifteenth of Adar I.[1]

The *arba parashiyos* (The four sections)

3. A special section is read for *maftir* on the four *Shabbosim* from the Shabbos preceding *Rosh Chodesh Adar* until *Rosh Chodesh Nissan*. This special *maftir* is read instead of the usual one. These special sections discuss subjects related to these weeks.[2] Two Torah scrolls are taken out on each of these four *Shabbosim*. The weekly Torah portion is read from the first scroll, and the special *maftir* is read from the second scroll. If *Rosh Chodesh Adar* or *Rosh Chodesh Nissan* is on one of these *Shabbosim*, three scrolls are taken out. The weekly portion is read from the first scroll, the portion for *Rosh Chodesh* is read from the second scroll (see Chapter 23, Section 9), and the special *maftir* (*Parashas Shekalim* on *Rosh Chodesh Adar* or *Parashas Hachodesh* on *Rosh Chodesh Nissan*) is read from the third scroll.[3]

4. *Parashas Shekalim (Shemos 30:11-16)* is read on the Shabbos before *Rosh Chodesh Adar* (or on *Rosh Chodesh Adar* itself, if *Rosh Chodesh* is on Shabbos).[4] In the time of the Temple, everyone contributed a half-shekel to help pay for the public sacrifices. Announcements were made on *Rosh Chodesh Adar* to remind the people to bring their half-shekel contribution to the Temple.

The *haftarah* is from *Melachim II* 11, and discusses the people's contributions towards the maintenance of the Temple during the First Temple Era.

5.   *Parashas Zachor* (*Devarim* 25:17-19) is read on the Shabbos preceding Purim. It discusses how the nation of Amalek attacked the Israelites when they left Egypt. Haman, the Jews' archenemy in the Purim story, was a descendant of Amalek.[5]

The *haftarah* for *Parashas Zachor* is from *Shmuel I* 15, and begins with the words, "I remember that which Amalek did..."

It is a mitzvah from the Torah to hear *Parashas Zachor*. Both the Reader and the congregation must intend to fulfill this mitzvah when *Parashas Zachor* is read in the synagogue.[6]

According to some halachic authorities, women are obligated to listen to *Parashas Zachor*.

6.   *Parashas Parah* (*Bemidbar* 19:1-22) discusses the process through which one who came into contact with a corpse was purified in the time of the Temple. The process included using ashes from a *parah adumah* ("red heifer").[7] In the time of the Temple, it was a mitzvah to purify oneself before the festivals so one could enter the Temple and partake of the sacrifices. *Parashas Parah* is read during these weeks in anticipation of Pesach.

The Israelites slaughtered and burned the first red heifer in the Sinai wilderness. This was done just before the month of Nissan, so they would be able to purify themselves right after the Tabernacle was erected. This enabled the Israelites to offer their Pesach sacrifices. When we read this *parashah* we express our longing for God to purify us and allow us to merit once again serving Him in the Temple.

According to some halachic opinions it is a mitzvah from the Torah to read *Parashas Parah*.[8]

The *haftarah* for this Shabbos is from *Yechezkel* 36, and begins with the words, "And I shall sprinkle over you pure water."

7.   *Parashas Ha-chodesh* (*Shemos* 12:1-20) is read on the Shabbos preceding Rosh Chodesh Nissan (or on *Rosh Chodesh* itself, if *Rosh Chodesh* is on Shabbos).[9] This section states that the month of Nissan is the first month of the year. This section also discusses the *halachos* pertaining to the Pesach

sacrifice. The *haftarah* for *Parashas Ha-chodesh* is from *Yechezkel* 45, and begins with the words, "In the first month on the first day..."

Ta'anis Esther
(The Fast of Esther)

8. In the time of Mordechai and Esther, the Jews assembled to defend themselves from their enemies on the thirteenth of Adar. On that day the Jews fasted and prayed to God for deliverance. We, too, fast on this day, which is called *Ta'anis Esther*. *Ta'anis Esther* helps us realize that when one returns to God wholeheartedly, God takes notice of him, and listens to the prayers he recites amidst his suffering, just as He did in the days of Mordechai and Esther.[10]

9. The laws pertaining to *Ta'anis Esther* are similar to those of the public fast days. These include the prohibition to eat and drink from dawn until night, reciting *selichos* (supplications), reading from the Torah, and adding *Aneinu* in the *Shemoneh Esreh*. These laws are discussed in Chapter 25. The Rambam's words concerning the purpose of a public fast day, i.e. repentance, are quoted there at length.

Commemorating the half-shekel

10. When there was a Temple, all male Jews contributed half a shekel to help pay for the purchase of the public sacrifices. Announcements were made in the month of Adar reminding the people to donate their half-shekel.

Today, this mitzvah is commemorated by contributing money for the poor. The word *terumah* ("gift") is mentioned three times in *Parashas Shekalim* (*Shemos* 30:11-16). Therefore it is customary to contribute three coins whose name includes the word "half" (e.g. three half-dollars). The money is donated in the synagogue, either on *Ta'anis Esther* before *Minchah*, or on Purim night before reading the Megillah.[11]

It is customary for fathers to contribute this same amount for each of his children. A father who once contributed on behalf of his child must continue to do so every year.[12]

Purim

11.   The name Purim comes from the word *pur* ("lot"). This refers to the lot
which Haman cast to determine the date on which to annihilate the
Jews. In His great compassion, God saved the Jews and turned their distress
into a great salvation.

The fourteenth of Adar was set as a day of feasting and joy, and thanksgiving
to God for His deliverance. (The fifteenth of Adar, Shushan Purim, is discussed in Section 22, below.)

Reading the Megillah

12.   *Megillas Esther* (the *Book of Esther*) describes the events surrounding Haman's decree against the Jews, and the manner in which God saved His
people. The Megillah is read as an expression of our gratitude to God for His
kindness towards His people. One can learn how God conducts His world,
and how He supervises each of His creations individually, from the Megillah.

The Megillah is read twice, once at night and once in the morning.[13] A kosher
scroll which was written on parchment, must be used.[14]

13.   Women are obligated to hear the Megillah. The *mitzvos* of Purim are
positive *mitzvos* which are bound by a time limit. Nevertheless,
women must observe these *mitzvos* since the women were also included in
the decree of annihilation, and in the miraculous salvation.[15]

14.   One must hear every word when the Megillah is read. If one did not
hear a few words, he should immediately read them from the text in
front of him, or recite them by heart.[16] In this case, one must recite the Megillah until he reaches the word the Reader is reciting. This is because one
must read every word of the Megillah in the correct order. One must not
talk when the Megillah is being read.[17]

15.   Three blessings are recited before reading the Megillah: *asher kideshanu
b'mitzvosav v'tzivanu al mikra Megillah* ("Who has commanded us to
read the Megillah"), *she'asah nissim la-avoseinu ba-yamim ha-hem ba-zeman
ha-zeh* ("Who performed miracles for our fathers in those days at this
time"), and *She-hecheyanu*.[18] Sephardic Jews only recite *She-hecheyanu* before
reading the Megillah at night.

When reciting the blessings and reading the Megillah, the Reader must intend to exempt all the listeners, and those who are listening must intend to fulfill the mitzvah of reading the Megillah. After reading the Megillah at night, *Asher heini* ("Who brought to naught") and *Shoshanas Ya'akov* ("The Rose of Ya'akov") are recited. Sephardic Jews recite other hymns as well. These hymns are printed in the *Siddur*.

When one recites (or listens to) the blessing of *She-hecheyanu* before the morning Megillah reading, he should intend for it to apply to the other special *mitzvos* of the day as well. These *mitzvos* include sending gifts of food to friends and eating the Purim feast.[19] Sephardic Jews, who do not recite *She-hecheyanu* in the morning, should have this intention when reciting *She-hecheyanu* at night.

The blessing *ha-rav es riveinu* ("Who pleads our cause") is recited after the Megillah is read with a *minyan* (i.e. when ten men are present).[20] This blessing is printed in the *Siddur*.

The Megillah is called the "letter of Purim" (*Esther* 9:26).[21] Therefore, it is customary for the Reader to fold the Megillah like a letter (i.e. one section on top of the other) before beginning to read from the scroll. Those who follow along in a scroll during the Megillah reading do not have to do this.

Al ha-nissim and the Torah reading for Purim

16.   The section *Al ha-nissim...Bi-mei Mordechai* ("For the miracles...In the days of Mordechai") is added in the blessing of *Modim* in the *Shemoneh Esreh*,[22] and in *Nodeh Lechah* in *Birkas Ha-mazon*. The table in Chapter 30, Section 5 illustrates how one should proceed if he forgot to recite *Al ha-nissim* in the *Shemoneh Esreh*. The table in Chapter 12, Section 9 illustrates how one should proceed if he forgot to recite *Al ha-nissim* in *Birkas Ha-mazon*.

V'Attah Kadosh ("You are the Holy One") is recited after the Megillah is read at night. If Purim is on Saturday night, one recites *Vi-hi no'am* ("May God's pleasure") before *V'Attah Kadosh*.[23]

Haman was a descendant of Amalek. Therefore, *Va-yavo Amalek* ("And Amalek came;" *Shemos* 17:8-16) is read from the Torah before the morning Megillah reading.

Tachanun and *La-menatze'ach* before *u'Va l'Tzion* are omitted on Purim and Shushan Purim.

Mishloach manos (sending gifts of food) and *matanos l'evyonim* (gifts to the poor)

17.   It is a mitzvah to send gifts of food to fellow Jews. These gifts are called *mishloach manos*. This mitzvah increases friendship and fellowship among Jews. One fulfills the mitzvah by sending at least two types of foods that are ready to be eaten (i.e. foods which do not require any further cooking, etc.) to another person. Drinks may also be sent.[24]

It is best to send the *mishloach manos* with a messenger instead of bringing it oneself.[25]

18.   It is a special mitzvah to give gifts to the poor on Purim. This mitzvah is called *matanos l'evyonim*. One fulfills this mitzvah by giving gifts to at least two poor people (i.e. giving one gift to each of the two poor people). The gift should either be money or food.[26]

The Rambam writes:

It is preferable for a person to give many gifts to the poor rather than to make an extravagant meal or send many portions of food to his friends, for there is no greater and more wonderful joy than gladdening the hearts of the orphans, widows, proselytes and the poor. The one who brings joy to these unfortunate people emulates God of Whom it says, "He revives the spirit of the humble and invigorates the heart of the contrite ones" (*Yeshayahu* 57:15). (*Hilchos Megillah* 2:17)

19.   Women are also obligated to observe the *mitzvos* of *mishloach manos* and *matanos l'evyonim*. A man should send his *mishloach manos* to a man, and a woman should send hers to a woman.[27]

20.   One must fulfill these *mitzvos* during the day.[28] If one spends Purim in a place where there are no poor people, he may give the money to a poor person after Purim.[29]

The Purim feast

21.   Purim is a "day of feasting and joy." It is a mitzvah to make a festive meal during the daytime.[30] It is customary to begin the meal after *Minchah*. One must make sure that most of the meal is eaten during the day. If the meal lasts into the night, *Al ha-nissim* is still recited in *Birkas Ha-mazon.*[31]

The Purim meal is celebrated amidst unbounded joy, with more wine served than usual. Our sages said, "One must drink (wine) on Purim until he cannot distinguish between 'Blessed be Mordechai' and 'Cursed be Haman.' "[32]

During this meal one should praise and thank God for His deliverance and compassion during the time of Haman's decree. It is proper to study Torah before the meal begins. Our sages comment: "The Jews had light, and gladness, and joy, and honor" (*Esther* 8:16). " 'Light,' this refers to Torah."[33]

Shushan Purim

22.   In cities which were surrounded by a wall in the time of Yehoshua (Joshua), Purim is celebrated on the fifteenth of Adar, as it was in Shushan, the capital of Persia. An example of such a city is Jerusalem. In Shushan, the Jews overcame their enemies and celebrated their deliverance one day later than in all other places.

All the *mitzvos* of Purim which are observed on the fourteenth of Adar in other places, are observed in Jerusalem on Shushan Purim.[34]

23.   If Shushan Purim is on Shabbos, the *mitzvos* of Purim are observed over three days. (This is called *Purim Meshulash.*) On Friday (the fourteenth of Adar), the Megillah is read and gifts are given to the poor; on Shabbos (the fifteenth of Adar), *Al ha-nissim* is recited, and *Va-yavo Amalek* is read after the weekly Torah portion from a second Torah scroll; and on Sunday (the sixteenth of Adar), the festive meal is eaten, and the *mishloach manos* are sent. The laws pertaining to *Purim Meshulash* are discussed in greater detail in more comprehensive compendia of Jewish law.[35]

24.   One who travels on Purim from a city that did not have a wall in the time of Yehoshua (nearly all cities fall into this category) to a city that did have a wall in the time of Yehoshua (e.g. Jerusalem), or vice versa, should consult a *rav* regarding how to observe Purim on both days. The *halachos* in this case are complex. Various details determine whether a person is required to celebrate Purim on the fourteenth or the fifteenth of Adar. For example, where the person is in the evening of the fourteenth (or the fifteenth) of

Adar, where he intends to be when the morning dawns, when he intends to return to the first location, etc. A person must explain all the relevant details to a *rav*, so a halachic ruling may be reached in his case.

25.   Those who live in a city where Purim is celebrated on the fourteenth of Adar do not recite *tachanun* and *La-menatze'ach* (the chapter from *Tehillim* recited before *u'Va l'Tzion*) on Shushan Purim. These people should enjoy a more festive meal than usual, but they do not recite *Al ha-nissim* or observe the other *mitzvos* of Purim.

Chapter Thirty-Two

The Month of Nissan and the Halachos Pertaining to Chametz

1.   *Tachanun* is not recited during the entire month of Nissan.[1] (For a complete list of the days when *tachanun* is not recited, see Chapter 7, Section 87.)

2.   There is an ancient custom dating from Talmudic times to supply the poor with matzahs for Pesach. This custom is called *Kimcha d'Pischa* ("Flour for Pesach"). The *Kimcha d'Pischa* fund is the means through which the poor are supplied with all their festival needs. Every Jew must contribute towards the fund in his town.[2]

Shabbos Ha-gadol ("The Great Shabbos")

3.   The Shabbos preceding Pesach is called *Shabbos Ha-gadol*. This name commemorates the great miracle which occurred on that Shabbos. On the Shabbos before leaving Egypt, the Israelites took lambs in preparation for offering their Pesach sacrifices. Although the lamb was an Egyptian deity, the Egyptians were unable to prevent the Israelites from, or retaliate against the Israelites for, taking the lambs.[3]

The name is also derived from the concluding verse of the *haftarah*, "Behold I will send you Eliyahu the prophet, before the coming of the great and fearful day of God" (*Malachi* 3:23). (Malachi was the last of the prophets.)

4.   On *Shabbos Ha-gadol*, the *rav* speaks in the synagogue about the *halachos* of Pesach and other related topics.

Since the miracles surrounding the Exodus began on this Shabbos, some people observe the custom to read part of the *Hagadah* after *Minchah*. (The *Hagadah* is the special guide to the Seder night which is read during the Seder meal.) The section that is read begins with the words *Avadim hayinu*

288

("We were slaves"), and ends with the words *l'chaper al kol avonoseinu* ("to forgive all of our sins"). Some communities do not observe this custom.

The Prohibition of Chametz (leavened bread) on Pesach

5.   The Torah commands us not to eat *chametz*, not to derive benefit from *chametz*, and not to own *chametz* throughout Pesach. These prohibitions are derived from the verse, "No *chametz* shall be seen in your possession. No leaven shall be seen in all your territories" (*Shemos* 13:7).

6.   Flour made from one of the five kinds of grain (wheat, barley, rye, oats, and spelt) which comes into contact with water becomes *chametz* if it is not baked within eighteen minutes. Sometimes dough can become *chametz* in less than eighteen minutes; for example, when the dough is kneaded in a warm room.

All food products made from flour are considered *chametz* if they were not certified as being kosher for Pesach. It is assumed that the products became *chametz* while being produced. See Sections 19-24, below, for the laws regarding kosher for Pesach food products.

7.   The prohibition of eating *chametz* on Pesach impresses the great miracle of the Exodus in our minds. When it came time for the Redemption on the fifteenth of Nissan, the Israelites had to leave Egypt very quickly. Therefore, the dough they had prepared for the journey did not have time to rise, and had to be baked into matzahs. When we eat matzahs and avoid *chametz*, we commemorate in a tangible way our miraculous redemption from Egypt, as well as God's great power and show of strength through which He redeemed us. The prohibition of *chametz* on Pesach highlights how our nation suddenly went from darkness to radiance, and how between the two there was not even time for the dough to rise!

The *halachos* pertaining to Pesach are numerous, and one is advised to study them in detail. They are summarized below.

The following preparations must be done before Pesach in order to avoid transgressing the grave prohibition of *chametz* on Pesach.

Bedikas chametz and Biur chametz
(Checking the house and getting rid of the chametz)

8.   In the days preceding Pesach, the whole house should be thoroughly
       cleaned, and all *chametz* should be removed. Whatever *chametz* is
needed until Pesach (i.e. food and drinks, as well as cooking utensils used
with *chametz*) should be kept in one place.[4]

9.   One must check his house for *chametz* on the night before *erev Pesach*
       (the fourteenth of Nissan), right after the stars appear. One should
not begin working on something from half an hour before the stars appear,
until one has finished checking the house for *chametz*. Similarly, one may
not eat a meal before checking for *chametz*. However, one may eat fruit or
less than a *k'beitzah* of bread.[5]

How to check the house for *chametz*

10.   The house is checked by the light of a single candle. It is preferable to
       use a wax candle.[6] One should not use a torch or a braided candle.

11.   Before one begins to check, he recites the blessing *asher kideshanu
       b'mitzvosav v'tzivanu al biur chametz* ("Who sanctified us with His
mitzvos and commanded us to get rid of the *chametz*"). The text of the blessing uses the word *biur* (destruction), because the purpose of the search is to
remove and destroy any *chametz* left in the house.[7]

One should begin checking for *chametz* immediately after reciting the blessing. Every place where *chametz* is likely to be found in one's home must
be checked by candlelight. One should check closet shelves, clothing pockets
(including those of children), cellars, attics, and any utensil which is used to
hold *chametz*. One should also examine the cracks and crevices of every
place that is checked.[8]

12.   One should not speak between reciting the blessing and beginning the
       search. It is best not to discuss matters unrelated to the search until one
finishes looking for *chametz*. This is to avoid being distracted and not conducting a thorough search. One who discussed matters unrelated to the
search between reciting the blessing and beginning the search must repeat
the blessing. One who spoke after he started the search does not repeat
the blessing.[9]

13.   Some people observe the custom of placing ten pieces of bread in different spots around the house before beginning the search. These pieces are gathered during the search. One should not just "search" the house for these ten pieces of bread. Rather, one must check the entire house well. It is a good idea to wrap each of the ten pieces of bread, so no small pieces, which will be hard to locate and remove, fall off. Some people are particular that each piece of bread be less than a *k'zayis* in size.[10]

14.   All *chametz* which is found while checking the house is set aside in a secure place. All *chametz* which will be eaten after the search should also be kept separate. Whatever *chametz* remains is burned in the morning.[11] (Burning the *chametz* is discussed in detail in Sections 28-29, below.)

Additional laws

15.   One who has a store, office, kiosk, warehouse, car, etc. where *chametz* may have been brought in the course of the year, must search these places for *chametz*. The blessing of *biur chametz* is only recited once, even if one has many places to check.[12] The time it takes to travel between two places that have to be checked is not considered a break which would require a new blessing.

16.   One who will not be at home on the night before *erev Pesach* (he may be traveling, etc.), is still required to check for *chametz*. He should appoint someone else to search for and nullify the *chametz* in his place. This person recites the blessing on the required night before searching for the *chametz*. After conducting the search, he recites the nullification text with the following change, "All *chametz* and leavening which exists among the belongings of so-and-so..." In addition to the search and nullification performed by this person, the owner must also recite the nullification text, regardless of where he is.

One who leaves his home less than thirty days before Pesach and has not appointed someone to search his home for *chametz* the evening before *erev Pesach*, must conduct the search himself on the night before he travels. In this case, the person does not recite the blessing before conducting the search.[13] The person nullifies the *chametz* after the search.

One who did not check for *chametz* the night before *erev Pesach* must check as soon as he remembers. This applies if the person remembers on *erev Pesach*, on

Pesach itself, or after Pesach. The reason for checking after Pesach is to pre-vent transgressing the prohibition of benefiting from *chametz she-avar alav ha-Pesach* (*chametz* which was in a Jew's possession on Pesach). No blessing is recited when one searches for *chametz* after Pesach.

One who finds *chametz* in his house or possession on *Chol Ha-mo'ed Pesach* (the intermediate days of Pesach), must burn it immediately. If the *chametz* is found on *Yom Tov* or *Shabbos Chol Ha-mo'ed*, it should be covered with a utensil and burnt immediately after nightfall.

Bittul chametz (Nullifying the chametz)

17.   After checking for *chametz*, one nullifies the *chametz* by deciding that it is valueless to him, and by renouncing ownership of it.[14]

One then recites the special text for nullifying the *chametz*. This is called *bittul chametz*. The text of *bittul chametz* is printed in the *Siddur* and at the beginning of the *Hagadah*. The text of *bittul chametz* is in Aramaic. If one does not under-stand Aramaic, he should say, "Any *chametz* or leaven which is in my posses-sion, which I have not seen and have not destroyed, shall be nullified and regarded like the dust of the earth."[15] See Section 28, below, for details re-garding nullifying the *chametz* on the following morning (*erev Pesach*).

Selling chametz to a non-Jew

18.   *Chametz* which one finds difficult to burn, as well as food products which may contain *chametz*, can be sold to a non-Jew by a *rav*.[16] The person who wants to sell his *chametz* signs a document of authorization, and appoints the *rav* as his agent to sell his *chametz*. Then the *rav* sells the *chametz* to a non-Jew, so that the *chametz* no longer belongs to a Jew. All the *chametz* that was sold to a non-Jew should be placed in one special closed off area for the entire holiday.

One may sign the document of authorization and transfer his *chametz* to the *rav* a few days before Pesach. On *erev Pesach*, from the fifth *sha'ah zemanis* onwards, it is prohibited to use *chametz* in any way. One can no longer sell his *chametz* to a non-Jew, and any such sale is invalid.

Kosher for Pesach Food Products and Utensils

Food products

19.   Bread, cakes, biscuits, wafers, ice cream cones, noodles, soup nuts, beer, etc. are definitely *chametz* since they are made from grain that was mixed with liquid, and allowed to sit for more than eighteen minutes while being processed.

Many other products which are not *chametz* may have been mixed with *chametz*. Even if the ingredients listed on the package do not include one of the five kinds of grain, or any of the many extracts and additives manufactured from grain, one may not assume that the product is free from *chametz*.

20.   When buying or eating food, one should not rely on a stamp or label that only has the words, "Kosher for Passover." One should only buy products bearing both the stamp of a reliable *kashrus* organization, and the words, "Kosher for Passover." There are products which may appear unproblematic at first glance. These products could contain ingredients made from *chametz*, or may have been manufactured in utensils, machines, or ovens in which *chametz* products were produced.

21.   Matzahs can also be *chametz*. One should be careful only to use matzahs and matzah flour produced in a factory that has reliable *kashrus* supervision. One should find out which factories are included in this category from an expert in this area.

Matzah which was baked from dough that was folded over may be *chametz*. Therefore, such matzah may not be eaten on Pesach. It is advisable to check the packages of matzahs before the holiday to make sure they contain no such matzahs.[17]

Some people eat handmade matzahs on Pesach. The whole process involved in making these matzahs, including kneading and cutting the dough, is done manually.

22.   Ashkenazic Jews observe the custom not to use rice or legumes (like beans, peanuts, soy oil, etc.) on Pesach. Observance of this custom is obligatory for Ashkenazic Jews.[18]

Some Sephardic Jews do not eat rice either. Everyone must observe whatever custom the previous generations of his family observed. Those who use legumes or rice on Pesach have to check and clean them carefully before Pesach, to be sure that no *chametz* is mixed in with them.

Salted peanuts and seeds are likely to be *chametz* since the salt is frequently stuck to the seeds with flour.

Kosher for Pesach tableware and cookware

23. Utensils such as bowls, pots, cutlery, cups, and tablecloths, which were used during the year with *chametz* products, may not be used on Pesach. This is because *chametz* absorbed by these utensils may be emitted and absorbed by the Pesach food they are now being used with.

It is recommended to set aside special utensils to be used on Pesach. If this is not possible, one may kasher (i.e. render kosher) the utensils that he uses during the year. Kashering eradicates any traces of *chametz* which were absorbed by the utensils, so that they are like new.

24. The *halachos* pertaining to kashering utensils are numerous, and the methods of kashering (e.g. immersion in scalding water, blowtorching, etc.) vary according to the kind of utensil and how it was used (e.g. for frying, cooking, baking, hot or cold foods, etc.). Not all utensils can be kashered.[19]

Below is a brief discussion of some of these *halachos*.

25. Utensils used for cooking or with hot foods, like pots and cutlery, must be kashered with boiling water. These utensils must be cleaned very well before kashering. After cleaning the utensils, one must examine them to ascertain that there is no dirt or rust in any of the crevices. Then, the utensils may not be used for at least 24 hours, after which they are immersed in boiling water. Many communities provide public kashering facilities before Pesach.

Utensils used to heat food without water being added (e.g. pans used for baking, roasting, etc.) are kashered by heating them until they glow from the heat.

Porcelain or ceramic utensils that were used for hot foods cannot be kashered. If they were used in a different way, a *rav* must be consulted.

One must clean his dentures carefully before Pesach. Some people are careful not to eat or drink hot *chametz* food for 24 hours before cleaning them, and then to pour hot water (from a first vessel) over the dentures after cleaning them. One should be careful not to damage his dentures when pouring hot water over them.

26.   Kitchen counters and sinks, stovetops and ovens, dishwashers, blenders, etc. must all be kashered if one intends to use them for Pesach. Each one of these items has its own set of requirements for kashering, which must be meticulously observed. Many people do not use any oven that was used for *chametz*. This is because it is very difficult to thoroughly clean and kasher an oven.

When kashering utensils, one should consult with a person who has practical experience in this area. One should finish kashering his utensils before the beginning of the fifth *sha'ah zemanis* on *erev Pesach*. After this hour, the *halachos* regarding the kashering process are much more complex.

The Halachos Pertaining to the Fourteenth of Nissan

27.   On *erev Pesach*, *chametz* may only be eaten until the end of the fourth *sha'ah zemanis*.[20] In Israel, this is around nine o'clock in the morning, standard time. Every year the local rabbis announce the exact time to their congregations. One should take note of this announcement.

Burning and nullifying the *chametz*

28.   All *chametz* which remains in our possession in the morning is burned.
      After burning the *chametz*, the text of *bittul chametz* is recited. The text recited in the morning differs slightly from that which was recited the night before. The original text is in Aramaic, and is printed in the *Siddur*. If one does not understand Aramaic, he should recite the text in English: "Any *chametz* or leaven which is in my possession, that which I saw and that which I didn't see, that which I burned and that which I didn't burn, shall be nullified and regarded like the dust of the earth." The text of *bittul chametz* recited the previous night only mentioned *chametz* that was not discovered. The text recited in the morning nullifies all *chametz*, i.e. *chametz* which the owner is aware of as well as *chametz* which the owner is not aware of. One should concentrate on the words he is reciting, intending to wholeheartedly nullify the *chametz*.[21]

29. It is prohibited to have any benefit from *chametz* after the fifth *sha'ah zemanis*. This means that after this time one may not feed his animals *chametz*, sell *chametz* to a non-Jew, etc. One must burn and nullify his *chametz* before the end of the fifth *sha'ah zemanis*, because one cannot nullify his *chametz* once he is prohibited to benefit from it.

Rabbis usually announce the latest time to nullify one's *chametz* to their congregations. In Israel, this time is approximately 10:15 A.M., standard time.

When Erev Pesach Is on Shabbos

30. If *erev Pesach* (the fourteenth of Nissan) is on Shabbos, special rules apply regarding searching for *chametz*, burning the *chametz*, eating the Shabbos meals, etc. Books have been written discussing this situation. The main *halachos* are briefly mentioned below. When this situation occurs, one should clarify how to observe these *halachos* in a practical way.

The search for *chametz* is performed on the night of the thirteenth of Nissan, i.e. Thursday night. Before beginning the search, one recites the blessing *al biur chametz*. After the search, the *chametz* is nullified, as is done every year.

The *chametz* is burned on Friday morning (see Section 28, above). The *chametz* to be eaten on Friday and Shabbos is set aside in a special place. One must be careful not to spread the *chametz* through the house when eating it.

Services are held early on Shabbos morning so that the Shabbos meals will be finished before the latest time when *chametz* may be eaten.

It is best to prepare kosher for Pesach foods for the Shabbos meals in kosher for Pesach (or disposable) pots and pans, and to serve the food on disposable dishes. Some people eat the *challah* in one place, and then eat the rest of the Shabbos meal (which is kosher for Pesach) in another part of the same room, on disposable dishes. Other people eat the meal on chametz dishes, but make sure that the food is not the type that will stick to the dishes. After the meal, the *chametz* dishes are wiped clean and then stored with *chametz* dishes that were already put away for Pesach.

Although it is preferable to eat bread as part of the third meal on Shabbos, *chametz* may not be eaten in the afternoon on *erev Pesach*. Therefore, some people divide the Shabbos morning meal into two. They eat part of the meal, and then recite *Birkas Ha-mazon*. After waiting half an hour, these people perform *netilas yadayim* and recite *ha-motzi* again. They then eat the second part of the meal. (Halachically, the second part of the meal is a separate meal, and counts as the third Shabbos meal.) One must finish the second half of the meal before the time when *chametz* may no longer be eaten.

One must be very careful that no *chametz* crumbs remain after the meal is finished. The floor should be swept. Any leftover *chametz* should be crumbled and washed down a drain.

The *chametz* must be nullified after the fourth *sha'ah zemanis*, as on an *erev Pesach* that occurs on a weekday.

Minchah is recited early, and a third meal consisting of Pesach foods, vegetables, fruits, etc. is eaten. Matzah may not be eaten on *erev Pesach*.[22]

Working on Erev Pesach

31. Work such as sewing new garments, laundry, etc. may not be done on *erev Pesach* after midday. One may mend garments after midday if they will be worn on Pesach, and only need minor repairs. If one needs a haircut, he should have it done before midday. Similarly, one should cut his nails before midday. However, if one forgot to cut his nails before midday, he may cut them later in the day.[23]

32. *Mizmor l'sodah (Tehillim* 100) is omitted during *Shacharis* on *erev Pesach*, as well as during *Chol Ha-mo'ed*.[24] Sephardic Jews recite *Mizmor l'sodah* on these days.

Ta'anis bechorim (The fast of the firstborn)

33. *Erev Pesach* (the fourteenth of Nissan) is a fast day for all firstborn sons. This fast commemorates the miracle that occurred during the tenth plague, when all the firstborn Egyptian children died, and the firstborn Israelite children were not harmed. All firstborn sons must fast, including one who is his mother's firstborn, even if he is not his father's firstborn. It is customary for the father to fast instead of his firstborn son, until the son is thirteen. Daughters who are the firstborn do not fast.[25]

A firstborn son is permitted to eat if he is taking part in a *seudas mitzvah*. It is customary for firstborn sons to join in a *siyum* (the celebration at the completion of a Talmudic tractate) or a *bris* on *erev Pesach* after *Shacharis*. After eating this meal, the firstborns are permitted to eat throughout the day.

Preparations for the festival

34.   It is a mitzvah to have a haircut and cut one's nails in honor of the festival (these things should be done before midday, as mentioned in Section 31, above). One should bathe, dress in holiday clothes, and do all the other preparations mentioned in Chapter 16, Sections 1-8, and in Chapter 22, Sections 23-24.[26]

One may not eat matzah on *erev Pesach*. This is so one will eat the matzah with an appetite on Pesach night.[27] Some people observe the custom not to eat matzah from *Rosh Chodesh Nissan* until Pesach. Other people observe the custom not to eat matzah from thirty days before Pesach until Pesach.

35.   One may not eat anything upon which the blessing *borei minei mezonos* is recited after nine *sha'os zemanios* (i.e. from the beginning of the fourth *sha'ah zemanis* after midday) on *erev Pesach*. This is so one will fulfill the mitzvah of eating a *k'zayis* of matzah at the Seder with an appetite. Fruits and vegetables may be eaten, but not in amounts that will leave one feeling full when Pesach arrives.[28]

36.   After *Minchah*, it is proper to study the *halachos* pertaining to the Pesach sacrifice. Many *Machzorim* and *Siddurim* have a *Seder Korban Pesach* which includes these *halachos*. Since the Temple no longer exists, and we are not able to offer sacrifices, God accepts our studying of these *halachos* in their stead.[29]

Preparations for the Seder

37.   The table is prepared for the Seder (the special meal eaten on the first night of Pesach) on *erev Pesach*. The seder plate with all its special holiday items, as well as the pillows and chairs which will be used by all those participating in the Seder, are arranged. The table should be as festive as possible (it should be set with beautiful tableware, etc.). This demonstrates the freedom from Egyptian slavery that we are celebrating on this night.[30]

It is best if all the preparations for the Seder are done on *erev Yom Tov*, so that everything is ready when the family returns from the synagogue at night. Those preparations which may not be done on *Yom Tov* must be done on *erev Yom Tov*.

38. Listed below are some of the preparations which should be done on *erev Yom Tov* for the Seder:

* Wine should be prepared for the "Four Cups." It is a mitzvah to use red wine.[31]

* Celery or another vegetable should be set aside for *karpas*.[32]

* *Maror* (bitter herbs) must be prepared for the mitzvah of eating *maror*. If romaine lettuce is used for *maror*, the leaves must be checked on *erev Pesach*. Each leaf must be held up to the sun or a strong light, and checked for tiny insects and worms which are forbidden to be eaten. The inspection must be very careful and thorough because the insects are often the same color as the leaves. Therefore, it is very hard to distinguish the insects from the leaves.[33] Today, there is lettuce available which bears rabbinic certification that it was grown under special insect-free conditions. If possible, one should use lettuce (and other leafy vegetables) that bears this type of rabbinic certification.

If horseradish (*chazeres*) is used as *maror*, it must be grated so that it is edible. Some people grate it at night right before the Seder so that the bitter taste does not dissipate. However, if Pesach is on Shabbos one may not grate the horseradish on the night of the Seder because it is prohibited to grate food on Shabbos. In this case, the horseradish must be grated before Shabbos, and then covered so it retains its bitter taste.[34]

* *Charoses* is a mixture of chopped fruits which commemorates the mortar used by the Israelites when doing slave labor in Egypt. It is prepared from fruits to which the Jews are compared in the Scriptures, such as almonds and other types of nuts, apples, pomegranates, and figs. Red wine and spices such as cinnamon and ginger are also added to the mixture.[35]

* Salt water is made. The *karpas* is dipped in salt water before being eaten.[36]

* The *zeroa* (a roasted bone from meat) is prepared to commemorate the Pesach sacrifice, and a cooked egg is set aside to commemorate the *Chagigah* sacrifice (a special festival sacrifice). These sacrifices were offered in the Tem-

ple on Pesach.[37] Many communities (all Ashkenazic communities, as well as several Sephardic ones) observe the custom not to eat roasted meat on the Seder night.[38] This is why the *zeroa* is not eaten from the Seder plate.

Details of the items which are placed on the seder plate, as well as how they should be arranged, are printed at the beginning of the *Hagadah* (the special guide to the Seder night).

Chapter Thirty-Three

Pesach

Commemorating the Exodus from Egypt

1. Pesach lasts seven days, from the fifteenth to the twenty-first of Nissan. Outside of Israel, an extra, eighth day is observed. This day is called *Yom Tov sheni shel galuyos* (the extra day of *Yom Tov* in the Diaspora).

The Israelites left Egypt on the fifteenth of Nissan. The Exodus from Egypt is one of the foundations of Jewish faith, and the source of our conviction that the Jews are God's Chosen People. After gaining freedom from slavery, the Israelites stood at Mount Sinai and received the Torah.

There are many *mitzvos* connected with Pesach. These *mitzvos* instill in us faith in God, Who took us out from slavery to freedom, as well as other special values which are connected to the holiday.

2. The first day of Pesach (the fifteenth of Nissan) is a *Yom Tov*. The *halachos* of candlelighting, prayers, and the prohibition of work which apply to *Yom Tov* are discussed in Chapter 22.[1]

After *Ma'ariv*, whole-*Hallel* is recited. The prayers recited on Pesach are printed in the Pesach *Machzor* (holiday prayer book).[2]

Outside of Israel, the sixteenth of Nissan is also a *Yom Tov*. It is the second day of *Yom Tov* which is observed in the Diaspora. The second day of *Yom Tov* must be observed exactly like the first day of *Yom Tov* (see Chapter 22, Sections 2-4).[3]

The Seder Night

3.   The first night of Pesach is called *Leil Ha-Seder* ("the Seder night"). Out-
        side of Israel, a second Seder is held on the second night of Pesach. All
the *halachos* pertaining to the Seder apply to both nights.[4]

Women must observe all the *mitzvos* of the Seder, although women do not
recline.[5] If a woman is not able to hear the entire *Hagadah*, she must at
least hear *Kiddush*, and the section beginning, "Rabban Gamliel says, whoever did not say these three things on Pesach," until after they drink the second cup of wine. Women must also try their best to hear the recitation of the
Ten Plagues.[6]

The *Pesach Hagadah* is a step-by-step guide to the Seder rituals. Some of the
mitzvos which are observed on this night are listed below.

Retelling the story of the Exodus

4.   We fulfill the mitzvah of discussing the Exodus by reading the *Hagadah*.
        It is an important mitzvah to discuss the slave labor which our fore-
fathers did in Egypt, and how God performed great miracles when taking
them from slavery to freedom. We discuss the Exodus so we will be
moved to thank God for the kindness He has done for our forefathers and
for us. Discussing the Exodus instills faith in God and encourages belief in
His providence over every individual person. The story of the Exodus re-
minds us that God chose us as His people, so that we will sanctify His
Name throughout the world. The *Hagadah* relates, "The more one discusses
the Exodus from Egypt, the more one is to be praised."

5.   The emphasis on the Seder night is to explain these concepts to one's
        children. The aim is to impress the values of Jewish faith upon them,
and to teach them how to observe the *mitzvos* of Pesach.

6.   One should arouse the children's interest and encourage them to take
        note of all the different and special customs of this night. The children
should be encouraged to ask questions about all aspects of the Seder. One
should try to keep his children awake, at least until after the section, "We
were slaves unto Pharaoh." is read. Some people give their children nuts to
help keep them awake. The children recite a special section of the
Hagadah which begins with the words *Ma nishtanah* ("Why is this night different?"). This section is composed of questions concerning some of the spe-

cial customs of Seder night. The parents should answer the children, explaining the reasons for the customs.

The four cups of wine

7.   During the Seder, we drink four cups of wine. Each cup corresponds to an expression of redemption mentioned in the Torah in the section discussing the Exodus.[8]

Each of the four cups must contain at least a *revi'is* of wine. According to the Chazon Ish, a *revi'is* is 150 cc (5. 07 fl oz), and according to R. Chaim Na'eh, a *revi'is* is 86cc (2.9 fl oz).

If the cup being used only holds one *revi'is*, it is preferable to drink the entire cup of wine (for each of the four cups). If one is not able to drink the entire cup of wine, he can fulfill the mitzvah by drinking most of the wine in the cup. One must drink the entire fourth cup of wine, so that the *berachah acharonah* (*al ha-gefen v'al peri ha-gefen*) can be recited after it. There is a halachic opinion that one must drink most of the wine in the cup, even if the cup holds more than a *revi'is*. Therefore, if one does not want to drink a large quantity of wine, he should use a cup that only holds a *revi'is*. This way, one will avoid relying on a more lenient halachic opinion (i.e. that one may fulfill the mitzvah by only drinking most of a *revi'is* of wine even if the cup being used holds much more than a *revi'is*).[9]

Karpas

8.   Before eating the *karpas*, one performs *netilas yadayim* without reciting the blessing *al netilas yadayim*. One takes less than a *k'zayis* of *karpas*, dips it into salt water (or vinegar), recites the blessing *borei peri ha-adamah*, and eats the *karpas*. When reciting this blessing, one should intend to include the *maror* which will be eaten later in the evening.[10]

When the word *karpas* is written backwards in Hebrew it is read פרך 'ס, sixty (myriad) hard labor. This is a hint to the 600,000 Jews who did slave labor in Egypt.

9.   Three matzahs, one on top of the other, are placed on the Seder table. After eating the *karpas*, the one who is leading the Seder breaks the middle matzah into two parts. He puts the larger part aside for the *afikoman* (the *halachos* pertaining to the *afikoman* are discussed in Section 15, below).

The mitzvah to eat matzah

10. The Torah requires every person to eat at least a *k'zayis* of matzah on the first night of Pesach.[11] According to the Chazon Ish, the amount of matzah that should be eaten is 50 cc (1.7 oz), while according to R. Chaim Na'eh, a *k'zayis* of matzah is 27 cc (.91 oz). Before Pesach, one should find out exactly how much matzah comprises a *k'zayis*, so he is sure he eats the required amount.

It is a special mitzvah to eat matzah on the night of the Seder. One should use *shemurah matzah* (matzah made from one of the five grains which was kept dry from the day it was reaped) for the Seder.[12] Many people use handmade *shemurah matzah* for the Seder. One should remember that he is eating matzah specifically to fulfill the mitzvah.

11. Before eating the matzah, one performs *netilas yadayim* and recites the blessing *al netilas yadayim*. Two blessings are recited over the matzah. The first blessing is *ha-motzi*, and the second blessing is *asher kideshanu b'mitzvosav v'tzivanu al achilas matzah* ("Who has sanctified us through His commandments and has commanded us to eat matzah"). One must eat a *k'zayis* of matzah within the time of *kedei achilas pras*. According to the Chazon Ish, this is between two and nine minutes. (See the Table of Measures at the end of Chapter 15.)

12. Before reciting the blessings, the one who leads the Seder takes the three matzahs that are in front of him, with the half-matzah between the other two (the half-matzah is the matzah which was broken earlier, with one part set aside for the *afikoman*). He then recites *ha-motzi* and *al achilas matzah*, and takes one *k'zayis* from the top matzah and another *k'zayis* from the broken matzah. He eats both pieces of matzah together.[13] The one who leads the Seder should intend to exempt all those present with his blessings. All those present must answer Amen to his blessings, while intending to fulfill their obligation to recite the blessings. The one leading the Seder gives each person two *k'zeisim* of matzah. (If each person has his own three matzahs, he takes two *k'zeisim* from his own matzahs.) Everyone must eat the matzah within the time of *kedei achilas pras*.

Any time that matzah is eaten on Pesach other than the Seder night, the only blessing recited is *ha-motzi*. The blessing *al achilas matzah* is only recited on the Seder night.

Maror (Bitter herbs)

13.   A *k'zayis* of *maror* is eaten to commemorate the slave labor through which the lives of the Israelites were embittered in Egypt. Romaine lettuce or horseradish is used for *maror*. As mentioned earlier, if romaine lettuce is used, it must be thoroughly checked for insects and worms.

One dips the *maror* in *charoses* before eating it. Then one shakes the *charoses* off so it does not neutralize the bitter taste of the *maror*. Before eating the *maror*, one recites the blessing *asher kideshanu b'mitzvosav v'tzivanu al achilas maror* ("Who sanctified us with His *mitzvos* and commanded us to eat bitter herbs").[14]

Korech (The *maror* sandwich)

14.   After eating the *maror*, a *k'zayis* of the bottom matzah and a *k'zayis* of *maror* are taken and eaten together. Hillel the Sage, who lived during the Second Temple Era, ate a sandwich made of matzah, *maror*, and the Pesach sacrifice. The sandwich we eat commemorates the Temple and the sandwich that Hillel ate. This sandwich is referred to as *korech* in the *Hagadah*.

One should not speak from when he recited *ha-motzi* until after he has eaten the *korech*. The blessings recited over the matzah and *maror* also include *korech*.[15]

The *afikoman*

15.   Everyone present eats a *k'zayis* of matzah after the meal. This *k'zayis* of matzah is taken from the *afikoman* (the half-matzah that was set aside at the beginning of the Seder). If the *afikoman* is not large enough for each person to have a *k'zayis*, it is supplimented with other *matzah shemurah*.[16]

The *afikoman* commemorates the Pesach sacrifice which was offered in the Temple. One ate the Pesach sacrifice after eating the meat from the other festival sacrifices and the festival meal. One should remember that he has to eat the *afikoman*, so he will not eat too much during the meal and be too full at the end of the meal.[17] It is best to eat two *k'zeisim* of matzah for the *afikoman* — one *k'zayis* commemorates the Pesach sacrifice, and one *k'zayis* commemorates the matzah which was eaten with it.[18]

The *afikoman* must be eaten before *chatzos ha-laylah*. "*Chatzos ha-laylah*" is the time exactly between sunset and sunrise. In Israel *chatzos ha-laylah* is often around 11:40 P.M. standard time. (The exact time is listed in annual Jewish calendars.)

16. Nothing may be eaten after the *afikoman*.[19] After drinking the fourth cup of wine no other drinks may be taken. The only exceptions to this rule are water and tea.[20]

Additional laws

17. Except for the mitzvah of eating *maror*, men recline towards their left (in the manner of free men) while performing all the *mitzvos* of the Seder night (e.g. drinking the four cups of wine, eating the matzah, etc.). It is preferable to eat the meal in this position too.[21]

18. In the course of reciting the *Hagadah*, one comes across many *mitzvos*, customs, and Jewish concepts. In view of the many details, one is advised to receive guidance from an expert regarding how to lead the Seder.

The *Tur* (*Orach Chayim* 481) writes, "One is obligated to spend the entire night occupied with the laws of Pesach, and recounting the story of the Exodus, and the miracles that God did for our forefathers — until sleep overcomes him." The *Hagadah* also states, "The more one relates about the Exodus, the more he is to be praised."

The first night of Pesach is called *leil shimurim* ("the night when God watches the Jews"). Therefore, only two passages of *Kerias Shema al ha-mittah* ("The *Shema* recited before retiring") are recited. One is the passage which begins with the words *Shema Yisrael*, and the other passage is the blessing of *Ha-mapil* ("Who lets sleep fall"). All the other passages, which are petitions for God to watch us, are omitted.[22]

The Prayer for Dew

19. The Prayer for Dew is recited on the first day of Pesach (the fifteenth of Nissan). This prayer is recited either before *Musaf* or during the Leader's Repetition of *Musaf*. Beginning with this service, the words *Mashiv ha-ruach u'morid ha-gashem* ("Who blows the wind and sends down rain") are omitted during the second blessing of the *Shemoneh Esreh*. The words *Mashiv ha-ruach u'morid ha-gashem* are recited again beginning with the *Musaf* service on Shemini Atzeres (which is on the twenty-second of Tishrei). In Israel, as well as in some other communities, the words *Morid ha-tal* ("Who brings

down the dew") are recited during the period that *Mashiv ha-ruach u'morid ha-gashem* is omitted.

Another change is made in the weekday *Shemoneh Esreh*. In the blessing of *Bareich aleinu*, the words *v'sein berachah* (bestow blessing) are recited instead of *v'sein tal u'matar li-verachah* ("and bestow dew and rain for a blessing").

Immediately before *Musaf* on the first day of Pesach, someone in the synagogue announces that the congregation is to begin reciting *Morid ha-tal* in place of *Mashiv ha-ruach*. In those congregations where it was not announced, and where the Prayer for Dew was not recited before *Musaf*, the congregation recites *Mashiv ha-ruach* during *Musaf*. In this case, the congregation only begins omitting *Mashiv ha-ruach* with the Leader's Repetition of the *Musaf Shemoneh Esreh*.[23]

Chapter 7, Sections 56 and 57, have tables illustrating how one should proceed if he recited *Mashiv ha-ruach* instead of *v'sein tal u'matar*, or vice versa.

Chol Ha-mo'ed

20. The second through the sixth days of Pesach (the sixteenth through the twentieth of Nissan) are *Chol Ha-mo'ed*. Outside of Israel, *Chol Ha-mo'ed* is the third through sixth days of Pesach (the seventeenth to the twentieth of Nissan). *Chol Ha-mo'ed* is the intermediate days of *Yom Tov*.[24] These days are dedicated to spiritual inspiration and rejoicing. Certain types of work may not be done during *Chol Ha-mo'ed*. *Chol Ha-mo'ed* is discussed in greater detail in Chapter 29, Sections 52-58.

Two sections are omitted when reciting *Hallel* on the last six days of Pesach. These are the sections that begin with the words *Lo lanu* ("Not for us") and *Ahavti* ("I loved"). This abridged form is called half-*Hallel*. (Half-*Hallel* is also recited on *Rosh Chodesh*.) Sephardic Jews do not recite a blessing when reciting half-*Hallel*. They only recite a blessing when reciting whole-*Hallel*, which is recited on the first day of Pesach, as well as on the other festivals.

21. *Song of Songs* is read before the Torah reading on the Shabbos during Pesach. This book from the Scriptures describes, in allegorical form, God's love for Israel. *Song of Songs* is read on Pesach because the Exodus from Egypt, which was accompanied by great miracles and wonders, was an expression of God's love for Israel.

Song of Songs is classified as a Megillah. Therefore, if *Song of Songs* is read from a kosher scroll, some congregations recite the blessings *al mikra Megillah* and *She-hecheyanu* before reading from it.[25] Both the Reader and the listeners should intend for the listeners to fulfill their obligation to recite the blessings by listening.

The Seventh Day of Pesach

22. The seventh day of Pesach (the twenty-first of Nissan) is a *Yom Tov*.
Outside of Israel, the following day (the twenty-second of Nissan) is *Yom Tov* as well. For details regarding the laws pertaining to *Yom Tov*, see Chapter 22.

The entire festival of Pesach is considered one unit. The *She-hecheyanu* which was recited at the beginning of Pesach includes the seventh day of Pesach as well. Therefore, one does not recite *She-hecheyanu* when lighting the candles and reciting *Kiddush* on the seventh day of Pesach.

On the seventh day of Pesach (the twenty-first of Nissan), the Red Sea split and the Israelites crossed to the other side on the dry seabed. The Torah reading for this day (*Shemos* 14-15) describes the splitting of the Red Sea, and includes the *Song of the Sea* which the Israelites sang when they were saved.

Yizkor is recited before *Musaf* on the seventh day of Pesach. (*Yizkor* is a prayer recited in memory of one's deceased relatives.) Sephardic Jews do not recite *Yizkor*. (For more details regarding *Yizkor*, see Chapter 28, Section 13.)

The day following Yom Tov is *isru chag* of Pesach.[26]

Chametz which was in a Jew's possession during Pesach

23. *Chametz* which was in a Jew's possession during Pesach may never be eaten, sold, or used in any way. (See Chapter 32, Section 18 regarding selling *chametz* to a non-Jew before Pesach.) One must make sure not to transgress this prohibition when purchasing *chametz* after Pesach.[27]

Chapter Thirty-Four

Sefiras Ha-Omer
(The counting of the omer)

The mitzvah of counting the *Omer*

1. "And you shall count for yourselves, from the day following the festival when you brought the *omer* as a wave-offering, seven complete weeks. You shall count until the day after the seventh week, when there will be a total of fifty days" (*Vayikra* 23:15-16).

It is a mitzvah to count the days from the second day of Pesach (the sixteenth of Nissan) until the festival of Shavuos.[1] This mitzvah is called *Sefiras Ha-omer*, after the *omer*-offering which was offered in the Temple on the second day of Pesach.

The *Sefer Ha-Chinnuch* (*Mitzvah* 306) explains that the main reason why the Israelites were redeemed from Egypt was to receive the Torah and to observe its *mitzvos*. Every year we count the days from when the Exodus occurred (on Pesach) until the day the Torah was given to the Israelites (on Shavuos) to show how much we revere and long for that day.

How to fulfill the mitzvah

2. The mitzvah of counting the *omer* is performed every evening after *Ma'ariv*, from the second night of Pesach until the night before Shavuos.[2] One may not count before nightfall. The proper time for counting is after the stars are visible. If one counted earlier, he should count again after the stars appear. One should not begin a meal nor begin working from half an hour before the stars appear, until one has counted the *omer*. One may begin eating if someone is appointed to remind him afterwards to count. In all cases, one may eat fruit or less than a *k'beitzah* of bread.[3]

One recites the blessing *asher kideshanu b'mitzvosav v'tzivanu al sefiras ha-omer* ("Who has commanded us to count the *omer*"), and counts the days and the weeks which have passed since the count began. (Each day's calculation, as well as prayers which are customarily recited after counting *Sefiras Ha-omer*, are printed in the *Siddur*.) The blessing and the calculation are recited while standing.[4]

3.   It is best to count *Sefiras Ha-omer* early in the evening. If one did not count *Sefiras Ha-omer* early in the evening, he may recite the blessing and count anytime during the night.[5] If one forgot to count during the night, he may count during the day. In this case one counts *Sefiras Ha-omer* without reciting the blessing, and then continues to count with the blessing for the remaining nights.

One who forgot to count *Sefiras Ha-omer* at night, and did not remember to count it during the following day, continues to count the following nights without reciting a blessing. The same rule applies to one who made a mistake and said the wrong number when he counted (and therefore did not fulfill the mitzvah). In this case (when one cannot count *Sefiras Ha-omer* with a blessing), one should try to hear another person recite the blessing. The person listening to the blessing must answer Amen, thereby intending to be exempted from making a blessing. The person reciting the blessing must intend to exempt the other person with his blessing. Then both the person who listened to the blessing and the person who recited the blessing count that day's correct number.

One who is not sure whether he counted *Sefiras Ha-omer* one night, continues counting the rest of the nights with a blessing.[6]

4.   One who counts *Sefiras Ha-omer* at night without reciting a blessing may no longer recite a blessing that evening.[7] Therefore, if a person is asked, "What is the *omer* count for today?" he should be careful not to answer with that day's count. Rather, the person should answer, "Yesterday was so-and-so many days." This way, he will still be able to recite a blessing when counting that night's *Sefiras Ha-omer*. One should answer in this manner from sunset until after he has counted *Sefiras Ha-omer* that night. This problem is very likely to arise on Lag ba-Omer (the thirty-third day of the *omer*; see Section 6 below), since one may inadvertently answer, "Tonight is Lag ba-Omer," before having recited that night's count.

Customs which are observed during *Sefiras Ha-omer*

5. Twenty-four thousand disciples of Rabbi Akiva died during the days of *Sefiras Ha-omer*. Some laws of mourning are observed to commemorate those bitter days when Torah study was greatly diminished in the world.

During the days of *Sefiras Ha-omer*, men do not shave, men and women do not cut their hair, and marriages are not performed. One may make an engagement party during these days,[8] although one should not dance during the days of *Sefiras Ha-omer*.[9] One may recite *She-hecheyanu* if the occasion arises (e.g. if one is eating a new fruit for the first time).[10]

Days when the laws of mourning are observed

6. There are various customs regarding which days the laws of mourning (not shaving, not having haircuts, etc.; see Section 5, above) are observed. Some people observe the laws of mourning from the beginning of *Sefiras Ha-omer* until the morning of Lag ba-Omer. Sephardic Jews observe this custom, although they wait until the morning of the thirty-fourth day of the *omer* (an additional day) before completing the period of mourning.

Other people observe the mourning period from *Rosh Chodesh Iyar* (beginning from the thirtieth of Nissan) until three days before Shavuos (the morning of the third of Sivan). Still other people observe this period from the second of Iyar until Shavuos. Each person should observe his community's custom.[11]

If *Rosh Chodesh Iyar* is on a Shabbos, one may have a haircut on Friday, in honor of Shabbos being *Rosh Chodesh*.[12]

Lag ba-Omer (the eighteenth of Iyar) is the thirty-third day of the *Sefiras Ha-omer* (the numerical value of the Hebrew word *lag* is 33). Rabbi Shimon bar Yochai, the author of the *Zohar*, died on Lag ba-Omer. *Tachanun* is not recited on this day (see Chapter 7, Section 87). The plague that claimed the lives of Rabbi Akiva's disciples finally ceased on Lag ba-Omer. Therefore, it is customary to rejoice on this day.[13]

The *Zohar's* commentary on *Parashas Ha-azinu* relates that on the day Rabbi Shimon bar Yochai passed away, he revealed deep secrets from the Torah to his disciples, and the world was filled with a luminous light of infinite delight.

The sun did not set until Rabbi Shimon had revealed everything he was permitted to reveal, and then his soul departed to Heaven.

It is customary to rejoice on Lag ba-Omer, the day Rabbi Shimon passed away. Some people observe the custom to light many candles in the study halls, to light bonfires under the sky, to study Rabbi Shimon's teachings, and to sing songs composed in his honor.

The Festival of Shavuos

7.   The festival of Shavuos is on the sixth of Sivan (see Section 13, below, regarding the second day of *Yom Tov* which is celebrated in the Diaspora). This festival's name is derived from the seven weeks of *Sefiras Ha-omer* which are counted between Pesach and Shavuos. The word for weeks in Hebrew is *shavuos.*

All the laws of *Yom Tov* apply to Shavuos, including the prohibition to perform work, reciting special prayers, etc. (These laws are discussed in detail in Chapter 22.)

The festival of Shavuos celebrates our receiving the Torah. Seven weeks after our forefathers left Egypt, they stood at the foot of Mount Sinai and accepted the Torah. The entire nation comprehended the secret of the ministering angels when they declared as one, "We shall do and we shall obey."

Beginning with the Revelation at Mount Sinai, the Torah has been passed down from generation to generation. Each generation, including the present one, has lived their lives according to the Torah's dictates.

8.   Many people celebrate receiving the Torah on Shavuos by remaining awake and studying Torah throughout the night. Many of those who observe this custom study an anthology of special Torah selections arranged specially for this night.

There is a *safek halachah* (a doubt regarding what the *halachah* is) regarding whether a person who was awake all night must recite the blessings *al netilas yadayim, Elokai neshamah, ha-ma'avir sheinah,* and *Birchos Ha-Torah.* (This issue is discussed in detail in Chapter 3, Section 10.)

It is customary to commemorate the Giving of the Torah by decorating the house and the synagogue with greenery and plants.[14]

The festival prayers

9. The festival prayers, including whole-*Hallel*, the Torah Readings, *Yizkor*, *Musaf*, etc. are printed in the Shavuos *Machzor*.[15] Sephardic Jews do not recite *Yizkor*. *Ya'aleh V'yavo* is recited during *Shemoneh Esreh* (except for the *Musaf Shemoneh Esreh*), as well as during *Birkas Ha-mazon*. Chapter 12, Section 9, has a table illustrating how one should proceed if he forgot to recite *Ya'aleh V'yavo* during *Birkas Ha-mazon*.

10. The *Book of Ruth* is read on Shavuos. One reason we read the *Book of Ruth* is because King David, who was a great-grandson of Ruth the Moabite, was born on Shavuos.

The *Book of Ruth* is classified as a Megillah. When the *Book of Ruth* is read from a kosher parchment, some congregations recite the blessings *al mikra Megillah* ("Who has sanctified us with His *mitzvos* and commanded us to read the Megillah"), and *She-hecheyanu*.

The *Book of Ruth* describes Ruth the Moabite's devotion to God. It relates how Ruth left her people and her homeland, and joined the Jewish people. Ruth married Boaz the Judge from Bethlehem, who was the greatest sage of that generation.

11. Two Torah scrolls are taken out of the *Aron Ha-Kodesh* on Shavuos. The section which discusses the Giving of the Torah and the Ten Commandments is read from the first scroll. This section is from *Parashas Yisro*. The section which discusses the laws of Shavuos is read from the second scroll. This section is from *Parashas Pinchas*, and begins with the words *U'v'yom ha-bikkurim*. The Aramaic poem *Akdamos* is read out loud after the *Kohen* is called up to the *bimah* for the first *aliyah*, but before the Torah is read. This poem extols the Almighty and praises the Torah. (*Akdamos* is printed in many *Machzorim*.) Some communities do not read *Akdamos*.

Dairy foods

12. It is customary to eat dairy foods on Shavuos. Some people eat foods with honey with the dairy meal. This is derived from the verse, "Honey and milk under your tongue" (*Shir Ha-Shirim* 4:11). This verse is a metaphor for the words of the Torah.

One must follow the procedure mentioned in Chapter 36, Section 28, when eating meaty foods after dairy foods.

13.   Outside of Israel, the seventh of Sivan is the second day of Shavuos. All the laws of *Yom Tov* apply to the second day of Shavuos. (The second day of *Yom Tov* is discussed in detail in Chapter 22, Sections 2-4.) The *Book of Ruth* is read and *Yizkor* is recited on the second day of Shavuos, rather than on the first day. In Israel, the seventh of Sivan is called *isru chag Shavuos*.

Chapter Thirty-Five

Shiv'ah Assar b'Tammuz and Tish'ah b'Av
(The seventeenth of Tammuz and the ninth of Av)

Shiv'ah Assar b'Tammuz

1.   Throughout the ages, many tragedies befell the Jewish nation on the
      seventeenth of Tammuz. The Tablets on which the Ten Command-
ments were written were broken after the Giving of the Torah, the *tamid*-
sacrifice ceased being offered before the Destruction of the Temple, the
walls around Jerusalem were breached by the enemy, a Torah scroll was
set on fire, and an idol was erected in the Temple.[1]

The memory of these tragedies always remains with the Jewish people.
Therefore, this day was set aside for contemplating one's ways, improving
one's deeds, and returning to God, to prevent such tragedies from recur-
ring. The Rambam's words regarding devoting fast days to returning to
God are cited in Chapter 25, Section 2.

2.   All the laws pertaining to public fast days mentioned in Chapter 25 are
      observed on Shiv'ah Assar b'Tammuz (e.g. one may not eat and drink,
selichos are recited, the Torah is read, *Aneinu* is added to the *Shemoneh Esreh*,
etc.).

Yemei bein ha-Metzarim — The Three Weeks between *Shiv'ah Assar b'Tammuz* and *Tish'ah b'Av*

3.   The three weeks from the seventeenth of Tammuz until Tish'ah b'Av
      (the ninth of Av) are called *yemei bein ha-metzarim* ("days in straits").
This name is derived from the verse in *Eichah* (*Lamentations*), "All her perse-

315

cutors overtook her in the straits" (*Eichah* 1:3). This verse describes the Destruction of the Temple.

The *haftarah* for each Shabbos during these three weeks discusses the tragedies and punishments which will befall the Jewish people because of their sins. These *haftaros* are called *gimmel d'pur'anusa* ("a trilogy on punishment").[2]

The laws of mourning are observed to commemorate the Destruction of the Temple during these three weeks.

The laws of mourning observed during *yemei bein ha-metzarim*

4.   Marriages are not performed from the seventeenth of Tammuz until after the ninth of Av. Some Sephardic communities only observe the laws of mourning from *Rosh Chodesh Av* until after Tish'ah b'Av.[3] Although one may become engaged during these three weeks, engagements may not be celebrated with a festive meal from *Rosh Chodesh Av* through Tish'ah b'Av. One may celebrate an engagement by eating cakes, candies, etc., since this is not considered a meal.

5.   *She-hecheyanu* is not recited over a new fruit or a new garment during these three weeks. These three weeks are a time of punishment. Therefore, it is customary to refrain from situations which require reciting *She-hecheyanu*. One who has the opportunity to eat a new fruit should wait until Shabbos to recite *She-hecheyanu* and eat the fruit.[4] One recites *She-hecheyanu* for a mitzvah which cannot be deferred (e.g., circumcision, redeeming the firstborn), even if the mitzvah is done on a weekday. Similarly, one who has a new fruit which will not keep until Shabbos, and which will be unobtainable after Tish'ah b'Av, may recite *She-hecheyanu* and eat it on a weekday.[5] Sephardic Jews follow the Ari's custom, and do not even recite *She-hecheyanu* on Shabbos during these three weeks.

6.   One may not have a haircut or shave during these three weeks. Sephardic Jews do not have haircuts or shave from the beginning of the week in which Tish'ah b'Av occurs (rather than for the entire three-week period).[6]

The nine days from *Rosh Chodesh Av* until Tish'ah b'Av

7.   Rejoicing is minimized from *Rosh Chodesh Av* until Tish'ah b'Av. The mourning over the Destruction of the Temple is intensified during

this period.[7] New clothes may not be sewn or purchased during this period. This applies even if one only intends to use the clothes after the ninth of Av.[8]

8.   Clothes may not be washed, ironed, or taken in to be dry cleaned from *Rosh Chodesh Av* until after Tish'ah b'Av. This rule applies even if one only intends to wear the clothes after Tish'ah b'Av.[9] It is customary to wash little children's clothes during this period, because they are constantly being soiled.[10]

Freshly laundered clothes should not be worn during these nine days. One may wear clothes that were worn for a short while before *Rosh Chodesh Av*. One may wear freshly laundered clothes on the Shabbos that occurs during these nine days. Sephardic Jews only observe the restrictions regarding washing and ironing clothes, and wearing freshly laundered clothes, during the week of Tish'ah b'Av.

9.   One should not bathe from *Rosh Chodesh Av* until after the ninth of Av even in cold water. One may wash his face, hands and feet in cold water.[11] One may remove dirt and perspiration with cold water. For health and medical reasons one may bathe even in hot water.[12]

Men who immerse themselves in the *mikveh* every *erev Shabbos*, no matter how busy they are, may immerse themselves in cool water on the *erev Shabbos* preceding the ninth of Av. Sephardic Jews only refrain from bathing during the week of Tish'ah b'Av.

There are various customs regarding cutting one's nails during the week of Tish'ah b'Av. If the ninth of Av is on Shabbos, one may cut his nails on Friday in honor of Shabbos.[13]

10.   It is customary not to eat meat or foods that have been cooked with meat, and not to drink wine during these nine days. A sick person may eat meat.[14]

It is permitted to eat meat at a *se'udas mitzvah*, such as the meal following a circumcision or when redeeming a firstborn.

Havdalah is recited over a cup of wine on the *Motza'ei Shabbos* between *Rosh Chodesh Av* and Tish'ah b'Av. If a young child who knows the significance of reciting blessings but who is not old enough to understand the mourning over the destruction of the Temple is present, he should drink most of the cup of wine. If a child of this age is not present, the one who recites *Havdalah* drinks the wine.[15]

Shabbos Chazon

11.   The Shabbos before Tish'ah b'Av is called *Shabbos Chazon*. This name is derived from the *haftarah*, which begins with the words *Chazon Yeshayahu ben Amotz* ("The vision of Yeshayahu, son of Amotz"; *Yeshayahu* 1:1). This prophecy severely rebukes the Israelites for their sins.

It is permitted to wear Shabbos clothes, eat meat and drink wine on this Shabbos.[16]

Erev Tish'ah b'Av

12.   A small meal (the *se'udah ha-mafsekes*) is eaten shortly before the fast of Tish'ah b'Av begins. Only one cooked food may be eaten at this meal. One may eat more than one uncooked food, like vegetables and cheese, at this meal.

Some people eat a hard boiled egg dipped in ashes for this meal. This meal is eaten while sitting on a low chair or the floor, to demonstrate our mourning for the Destruction of the Temple.[17]

Three men should not eat the *se'udah ha-mafsekes* together, as this would obligate them to recite *Birkas Ha-mazon* together. Rather, each person should sit separately and recite *Birkas Ha-mazon* alone.[17*]

One must stop eating a short while before sunset, because that is when the fast begins. Similarly, one must take off his leather shoes at that time, because leather shoes may not be worn on Tish'ah b'Av.

13.   On *erev Tish'ah b'Av* after midday some people only study those sections of Torah which may be studied on Tish'ah b'Av.[18] (This is discussed in Section 26, below.)

14.   If Tish'ah b'Av is on Sunday, the preceding Shabbos is observed in the usual manner (one may eat meat, drink wine, etc.). The only difference is that the third Shabbos meal must be completed a little while before sunset. When reciting *Ma'ariv* in the synagogue on *Motza'ei Shabbos*, the Leader says *Baruch ha-mavdil bein kodesh l'chol*, and then removes his shoes before reciting *Barechu*. The congregation removes their shoes after reciting *Barechu*. One may not touch his shoes with his hands during the service.

Tish'ah b'Av

15.   On the ninth of Av terrible catastrophes befell the Jewish nation. The *Kitzur Shulchan Aruch* relates:

> The spies sent by Moshe had returned [bringing an evil report of the Land of Israel, and this caused] the Israelites to weep in vain on that night. It was therefore decreed upon our forefathers that they would not enter the Land of Israel. It was also decreed that this day would be a day of weeping for the Jewish people. On this day, both the First and Second Temples were destroyed, the town of Betar was captured and its tens of thousands of Jews killed, and Turnus Rufus plowed the area of the Temple and its environs, fulfilling the verse, "Zion shall be plowed like a field" (*Yirmeyahu* 26:18; *Michah* 3:12). (*Kitzur Shulchan Aruch* 121:5)

These tragedies profoundly influenced all future generations, because when the Temple was destroyed we lost our greatest fount of spirituality. The laws of mourning that we observe on Tish'ah b'Av are accompanied by a longing for the Temple to be rebuilt and for the Final Redemption to take place speedily in our times.

16.   The laws of Tish'ah b'Av are more stringent than those of the other public fast days (with the exception of Yom Kippur).

When the ninth of Av is on Shabbos, the fast is deferred until Sunday.[19]

The five afflictions

17.   One must fast from sunset on Tish'ah b'Av night until when the stars appear on the following evening.[20] One must observe the same five afflictions that are observed on Yom Kippur.[21] These are:

18.   A. One may not eat or drink at all. An ill person who must eat and drink should consult a *rav* regarding how to proceed on Tish'ah b'Av.[22]

One may not brush his teeth or rinse his mouth on Tish'ah b'Av.

A person who is a heavy smoker, who is bothered by not smoking, may smoke privately (but not in public) after midday.[23]

19.   B. One may not bathe, wash his face, etc. One may only wash his fingers up to the knuckles (i.e. one may not wash his palms) when performing *netilas yadayim* upon arising, or when washing his hands after relieving himself.[24]

20.   C. One may not use any soap or apply any fragrance to himself on
Tish'ah b'Av. This includes applying cosmetics, oils, and soaps to any
part of the body.

21.   D. One may not wear leather shoes or sandals.

22.   E. Marital relations are forbidden on Tish'ah b'Av. A husband and wife
may not even touch each other.

Additional laws

23.   One may not sit on a chair, bench, etc., from when the fast begins (in
the evening) until midday the following day. One may only sit close to
the ground on a low stool, etc.[25] Similarly, one should sleep less comfortably
than usual. For example, one who usually sleeps with two pillows should
sleep with one pillow on Tish'ah b'Av.[26]

24.   It is customary not to do work on Tish'ah b'Av until midday. This is so
one's attention will not be diverted from his mourning for the destruction of the Temple. One may do things which do not divert his attention
from his mourning, e.g. turning on lights, making knots, etc.[27]

25.   One may not greet another person on Tish'ah b'Av. If a person is
greeted by someone who does not know the *halachah*, he may respond
in a subdued tone with a downcast countenance.[28]

Studying Torah on Tish'ah b'Av

26.   Studying Torah gladdens the heart. This is derived from the verse, "The
statutes of God are righteous, gladdening the heart" (*Tehillim* 19:9).
Rejoicing is prohibited on Tish'ah b'Av. Therefore, one may only study
the following sections of the Torah, which discuss the Destruction of the
Temple and mourning: the *halachos* pertaining to Tish'ah b'Av, the *Book of
Iyov, Eichah*, the chapters in *Yirmeyahu* describing the Destruction of the Tem-
ple (one should skip the verses of consolation), the third chapter of tractate
Mo'ed Katan (which discusses the *halachos* of mourning), and pages 55b-58a
in tractate *Gittin*, which discuss the Destruction of the Temple and the
Jews' subsequent exile from the Land of Israel.[29]

When studying these sections, one should only learn their simple meaning,
and not engage in the enjoyable Talmudic exegesis with its usual provoking
questions and answers.

The Prayers for Tish'ah b'Av

The night of Tish'ah b'Av

27.   On Tish'ah b'Av night *Ma'ariv* is recited quietly, in the manner of mourners. *Eichah* is read after *Ma'ariv*. Written by the prophet Yirmeyahu, *Megillas Eichah* is an elegy describing the Destruction of the Temple.[30] The blessing *al mikra Megillah* is recited when *Megillas Eichah* read from a kosher scroll in the synagogue.[31]

28.   *Kinos* (lit. "Elegies") are recited after *Eichah* is read. *Kinos* are a compilation of prayers and poems which express our mourning for the Destruction of the Temple and the subsequent exiles and tribulations. These prayers and poems are compiled in a special book called *Kinos for Tish'ah b'Av*. One who is not praying with a congregation should recite *Eichah* and *Kinos* by himself.

On Tish'ah b'Av night, *Eichah* and *Kinos* are read by the light of a few candles (or a dim light).[32]

The *paroches* (the curtain on the *Aron Ha-Kodesh*) is removed from the *Aron Ha-Kodesh*. Some congregations do not observe this custom.[33]

Shacharis

29.   Men do not put on their *tallis* and *tefillin* during *Shacharis* on Tish'ah b'Av. (In some communities men put on their *tallis*.) The Leader recites *Aneinu* during the Repetition of the *Shemoneh Esreh*, between the blessings of *Go'el Yisrael* and *Refa'einu*. The Torah reading is from *Devarim* 4, and begins with the words, "When you shall beget children." The *haftarah* is from *Yirmeyahu* 8, and is read with the same mournful cantillation as *Megillas Eichah*. *Kinos* are recited after *Shacharis*, until close to midday. After *Kinos*, *Megillas Eichah* is read a second time. No blessing is recited before *Eichah* is read for the second time.

Tachanun is not recited on Tish'ah b'Av. The verse *Va-ani zos berisi* ("As for me, this covenant") is omitted when reciting the prayer *u'Va l'Tzion*.

Minchah

30.   During *Minchah*, *tallis* and *tefillin* are worn, and the sections which were omitted during *Shacharis* are recited. Half-*Kaddish* is recited after *Ashrei*, followed by the Torah reading for a fast day. (The Torah reading for fast days is discussed in Chapter 25, Section 8.)

31. Two sections are added to the *Minchah Shemoneh Esreh* on Tish'ah b'Av. The section beginning with the word *Nachem* ("Console") is added during the blessing *Boneh Yerushalayim*, and the section beginning with the word *Aneinu* is added during the blessing *Shema koleinu*. One who forgot to recite *Nachem* during the blessing of *Boneh Yerushalayim*, may recite it during the blessing of *Retzei*. In this case the person does not recite the blessing which concludes *Nachem* (*menachem Tzion u'voneh Yerushalayim*), but continues with the section of *V'sechezenah*. One who recited the *Shemoneh Esreh* without reciting *Nachem* does not repeat the *Shemoneh Esreh*.[34] The table in Chapter 25, Section 8 illustrates how one who forgot to recite *Aneinu* should proceed. Sephardic Jews recite *Aneinu* during *Shacharis* as well as during *Minchah*.

Additional laws

32. The Temple began burning on the ninth of Av, and continued burning into the tenth of Av. Therefore, some of the laws of mourning are observed until midday on the tenth of Av. The following things are not done until midday on the tenth of Av: bathing for pleasure, laundering clothes or linens, having a haircut, shaving, eating meat, and drinking wine.[35] These things may be done after midday on the tenth of Av.

When Tish'ah b'Av is on Thursday, one may bathe on Friday morning in honor of Shabbos. When the ninth of Av is on Shabbos and the fast is deferred to Sunday, one may partake of wine and meat on Monday morning.

33. When Tish'ah b'Av is on (or is deferred to) Sunday, one does not recite *Havdalah* on *Motza'ei Shabbos*. In this case, one recites the blessing *borei me'orei ha-esh* when he sees a lit candle on *Motza'ei Shabbos*. *Attah chonantanu* is recited during the *Ma'ariv Shemoneh Esreh*, as on every *Motza'ei Shabbos*. One who wants to do work before reciting *Ma'ariv*, or who did not recite *Attah chonantanu*, must recite the words *baruch ha-mavdil bein kodesh l'chol*. *Havdalah* is recited over a cup of wine on *Motza'ei Tish'ah b'Av* (Sunday night), but the blessings *borei me'orei ha-esh* and *borei minei vesamim* are not recited.[36]

The Month of Elul

34.   Elul is the month of mercy and forgiveness, especially conducive for returning to God. After the Israelites made the Golden Calf in the wilderness, Moshe ascended Mount Sinai. This was on *Rosh Chodesh Elul*. Moshe stayed on Mount Sinai for forty days, until Yom Kippur. The Israelites fasted and repented that entire time, until Yom Kippur, when God forgave them. This period of time, beginning with *Rosh Chodesh Elul*, was set aside as a time of mercy and forgiveness. The month of Elul is a period of preparation for the Ten Days of Repentance (see Chapter 26). During this period it is customary to give more charity and do more good deeds than usual, as well as to take time for spiritual introspection.

35.   There are many hints to the special atmosphere of the month of Elul in the Hebrew letters of the word Elul.

According to the Ari z"l, Elul is alluded to in *Shemos* 21:13: "ואשר לא צדה **ו**האלקים **א**נה **ל**ידו **ו**שמתי לך מקום אשר ינוס שמה" ("If a man did not lie in wait, but God allowed it to happen to him, then I will appoint you a place to which he shall flee"). The first letters of the fifth through eighth words in this verse spell "Elul." This verse discusses the Cities of Refuge. Someone who unintentionally killed another person had to flee to one of these cities. The month of Elul serves the same function in a spiritual sense — God accepts and gives refuge to those who flee from their sins. (This verse also intimates that one should repent for sins done unintentionally.)

The word Elul is also alluded to with the first letters of the fourth to seventh words in *Devarim* 30:6: "ומל ה' **א**ת **ל**בבך ואת **ל**בב זרעך" ("And God will circumcise your heart and the heart of your progeny"). Similarly, the word Elul is alluded to with the first letters of the first four words of *Shir HaShirim* 6:3: "**א**ני **ל**דודי **ו**דודי **ל**י" ("I am my beloved's and my beloved is mine"), as well as with the first letter of the words in *Esther* 9:22: "**א**יש **ל**רעהו **ו**מתנות **ל**אביונים" ("portions to one another and gifts to the poor"). These verses hint that one should correct his deeds, pray, and give more charity than usual in Elul.

Selichos

36.   During Elul, *selichos* (special supplications asking God to forgive our sins) are recited. All the *selichos* recited on various days during the year are compiled in a special book called *Selichos*.[37] One must recite *al netilas yadayim* and *Birchos Ha-Torah* before reciting *selichos* in the morning.[38] One who did not have time to recite the other blessings normally recited in the morning before *selichos*, may recite them after reciting *selichos*.

We usually begin reciting *selichos* on the *Motza'ei Shabbos* before Rosh Hashana. However, *selichos* must be recited at least four days before Rosh Hashana. Therefore, if Rosh Hashana is on Thursday or Shabbos, *selichos* are recited from the *Motza'ei Shabbos* preceding it, while if Rosh Hashana is on Monday or Tuesday, *selichos* are recited from the *Motza'ei Shabbos* a week earlier. Sephardic Jews begin reciting *selichos* immediately after *Rosh Chodesh Elul*.

One who recites *selichos* without a *minyan* does not recite the Thirteen *Middos* (the Thirteen Divine Attributes) which begin, "God, God, Almighty, compassionate and gracious..." or the Aramaic sections at the end of *selichos*.

L'David Hashem ori v'yishi

37.   *L'David Hashem ori v'yishi* (*Tehillim* 27) is recited after *Shacharis* and *Ma'ariv* throughout the month of Elul. In Israel, this passage is recited every day from *Rosh Chodesh Elul* until Hoshana Rabbah (which is the twenty-first of Tishrei). Outside of Israel, this passage is recited until Shemini Atzeres (which is the twenty-second of Tishrei). *Tehillim* 27 discusses faith in God and trust in His salvation. According to the *Midrash Shocher Tov*, Rosh Hashana, Yom Kippur and Succos are all alluded to in this chapter of *Tehillim*, as follows: "The Lord is my light" refers to Rosh Hashana, "and my salvation" refers to Yom Kippur, and "He shall hide me in a *succah*" refers to Succos.

Blowing the shofar

38.   A shofar is blown after *Shacharis* during the month of Elul. The shofar's blast has the power to make a person tremble, arousing him to repent. The prophet declares, "Shall a shofar be sounded in the city, and the people not be afraid?" (*Amos* 3:6).[39] The shofar is not blown on Shabbos. Sephardic Jews blow the shofar while reciting *selichos*.

The laws and customs pertaining to *erev Rosh Hashana* (the twenty-ninth of Elul) are discussed in Chapter 24, Sections 1-3.

Part Five: Kashrus and Other Selected Topics

The chapters in this section discuss selected topics related to keeping kosher, and the *halachos* which pertain to agriculture in the Land of Israel (due to its special sanctity there are special *mitzvos* pertaining to produce grown in the Land of Israel). This is followed by a discussion of various *mitzvos* which are frequently encountered in daily living, such as *mezuzah*, *sha'atnez*, shaving, Torah study, and *mitzvos* pertaining to human interrelations. This section closes with the laws of mourning.

This book does not discuss all areas of Jewish law. These topics are discussed in the following sections of the *Shulchan Aruch: Yoreh De'ah, Even Ha'ezer,* and *Choshen Mishpat.* A large portion of *Orach Chayim,* the first section of the *Shulchan Aruch,* is discussed in the preceding sections of this book.

Chapter Thirty-Six

Kashrus

The importance of keeping kosher

1.   The laws of *kashrus* have always been one of the foundations of the Jewish people. The Torah lists numerous admonitions against eating non-kosher foods.

Besides being a Torah transgression in itself, eating and drinking non-kosher food has other consequences — it causes the sanctity of a man's soul to wane. A man's fear of God, his love of the Torah and its *mitzvos*, and delicate inner perceptions of faith in God and yearning for holiness are all likely to be affected.

The *Mesilas Yesharim* states:

> The forbidden foods defile a man's heart and soul until God's holiness withdraws from him. This is how our sages explain the verse, "and you will become defiled by them"(*Vayikra* 11:43): "Do not read [the verse to mean] 'become defiled by them,' but rather [read the verse as meaning] 'become stunted by them' [i.e. both words are spelled the same in Hebrew, but have different pronunciations]." This sin renders a man's heart insensitive to true knowledge and the spirit of wisdom that God bestows on the righteous. This is derived from the verse, "because it is God Who gives wisdom" (*Mishlei* 2:6). The person remains materialistic and boorish, immersed in the crass existence of this world. Forbidden foods are worse in this respect than all other prohibitions because they enter a person's body and become part of his flesh. Anyone possessed of sense will regard forbidden food like poison, or like a food into which poison was mixed. Would anyone partake of such a food — even if only the slightest doubt existed that the poison had been mixed in? (*Mesilas Yesharim*, Chapter 11)

There are many diverse laws of *kashrus*. One should consult a *rav* whenever a question arises.

Purchasing Kosher Food Products

The complexity of food products

2.   In previous generations, food products were made with familiar ingre-
      dients. Most foods were prepared at home, or close to home, and peo-
ple knew what ingredients were in every product. For this reason, *kashrus*
supervision was easier. Due to the development of the food industry, food
products such as processed foods, canned goods, bread, baked goods, candies, soft drinks, etc. contain numerous additives. These include various extracts, preservatives, and food colorings, many of which are not listed
among the ingredients. Many of these additives are made from non-kosher
animal products. Consumers have no way of knowing every ingredient in
each product, and if every ingredient is kosher. In addition to this, many factories manufacture food using a steam system which encompasses the entire
factory. Thus, food products which are intrinsically kosher can be rendered
non-kosher because they were heated with steam in which non-kosher
foods were processed.

Examples of common *kashrus* concerns

Listed below are some examples of food products which are likely to contain
non-kosher ingredients if there is no *kashrus* certification:

> *Bread*: Bread may contain fats, enhancers and leavening agents. These
> additives may be derived from animal sources. Therefore, the bread
> may not be kosher. In some places, the flour may contain insects if it
> was not sifted in accordance with Jewish law.

> *Chocolate and candies*: These may contain non-kosher fats, extracts, non-
> kosher wine, mammalian gelatin, non-kosher milk, and other ingredients
> derived from non-kosher animals.

> *Canned foods*: These may contain preservatives and acids of animal ori-
> gin.

> *Cakes*: These may contain non-kosher fats and wine, mammalian gelatin,
> glycerin, milk powder, etc., many of which may be halachically problem-
> atic.

> *Raisins*: These are sometimes smeared with non-kosher fat.

These concerns apply to all food products available today. Even products which seem unquestionably kosher may include non-kosher substances.

Competent *kashrus* supervision

3.   Due to the development of the food industry, *kashrus* supervision has become a complicated and responsible job.

Therefore, in addition to being proficient in Halachah and possessing fear of God and a profound sense of responsibility, the *kashrus* supervisor must have in-depth understanding of the various stages and processes of food production and chemistry. The *kashrus* supervisor must also maintain close contact with scientists, manufacturers of raw materials and extracts, and their suppliers.

Serious halachic errors are likely to occur without high-quality *kashrus* supervision. It is extremely important to only use those products which have reliable supervision. Today there are excellent *kashrus* organizations operating in Israel and abroad which certify a wide selection of food products. Before certifying a product as kosher, these organizations subject the product to stringent investigation. In most cases the symbol or name of the certifying *kashrus* organization is printed on the food package. *Kashrus* certification is known as *hashgachah*.

It is not practical to present a list of reliable *kashrus* organizations in this book, since the situation may change over time. Each person must keep current in his knowledge of *kashrus*. Rabbis and others who are knowledgeable in this area are usually able to provide guidance.

Precautions when buying food

4.   In some sectors of the food industry, misrepresentation, and even outright deception, occurs regarding the *kashrus* of products. Food manufacturers and retailers may try to deceive the public. Therefore, one may not rely on the word "kosher" when it appears by itself on the signs of shops, stalls, and food packages.

One must ascertain that the product is truly kosher by asking reliable people, checking that the *kashrus* certificate which is displayed in the store is signed and valid for that date, and checking the product's wrapper for a *kashrus* organization's stamp.

Kosher Meat

Kosher animals

5.   The Torah tells us which animals and fowl may be eaten and which are
       prohibited. Today we eat only those kinds of fowl and animals which
we know were eaten by our parents in previous generations.

Shechitah (Ritual slaughter)

6.   Poultry and animals must be slaughtered according to Halachah. They
       may only be slaughtered by a God-fearing *shochet* (ritual slaughterer).
The *shochet* must be an expert in the requisite *halachos* and an experienced
slaughterer. He must possess a certificate of authorization from a Rabbi,
which attests to his expertise in this area.

If an animal was not slaughtered precisely according to Halachah, it is considered *nevelah* ("carrion") and may not be eaten.

It should be noted that even if the animal was slaughtered properly, its meat
may not be eaten until it is kashered by salting or broiling. Meat markets may
sell meat that was slaughtered according to Halachah, but which was not yet
kashered. This meat must be kashered before one can eat it. The details regarding how to kasher meat and poultry are discussed in Sections 9-14,
below. One should only buy meat and poultry that are certified kosher by
a reliable authority.

Tereif

7.   The word *tereif* literally means "torn," although it is commonly used as a
       synonym for non-kosher. Sometimes an animal or fowl is diseased or
wounded (e.g. it may have a broken bone or an internal defect in some
part of its body). Some of these illnesses and wounds render the animal or
fowl *tereif* even if it was slaughtered according to Halachah.

Meat from an animal whose lungs were clear of adhesions is called *glatt*. It is
advisable to only eat meat which is *"glatt* kosher," because generally, the
kashrus level of non-*glatt* meat may be substandard. This also applies to processed meats such as hot dogs and salami. Therefore, it is important to only
buy meat which is labeled *"glatt* kosher."

Most of the poultry sold today are chickens which were fattened artificially and slaughtered young. This process increases the chances of diseases and internal defects that were uncommon in the past, when poultry was raised naturally.

Today, there is a high incidence of diseases affecting the sinews and lungs of chickens. Supervisors of reliable *kashrus* organizations are aware of these problems.

If one notices anything unusual in the animal or fowl, such as a defect, a broken limb (even one which has already healed), or any sign of a malady or a wound, he should consult a *rav* to determine if the animal is kosher.

Chickens, turkeys, and geese that are fattened artificially are routinely given injections in the neck. These injections may puncture the esophagus and render the birds unkosher. Reliable *kashrus* organizations check for this halachic problem.

Nikkur (Removing the thigh sinew and the forbidden fat)

8.   The thigh sinew (*gid ha-nasheh*) and the fat from certain areas must be removed from animals, as it is forbidden to eat these parts. (This does not apply to fowl.) Great expertise is required to know which parts are prohibited, and how to remove them. The person who is qualified to do this is called a *menaker*. This process must also be supervised by a *rav*.

One can only be sure that the *nikkur* (the removal of the non-kosher parts) was done according to Halachah if he purchases meat from a God-fearing and trustworthy butcher. One should not buy meat from butchers who do not have reliable *kashrus* certification because *nikkur* may not have been done (not to mention doubts as to whether the meat itself is kosher). One should bear in mind that the punishment specified by the Torah for eating forbidden fats is *kares*, Divine excision. A *kashrus* organization's stamp is not necessarily a guarantee that *nikkur* has been done on fresh meats. Reliable *kashrus* organizations ensure that forbidden fats were not mixed in processed meats (such as hot dogs, salami, etc.).

The margin of error when doing *nikkur* of the thigh sinew is significant. Therefore, many people do not eat any meat from the hind part of the animal (where *nikkur* is performed). In the United States, the hind part of the animal is not used at all.

The Prohibition of Eating Blood

Kashering meat and liver

The Torah forbids eating the blood from animals or fowl. Blood is extracted from meat by either salting or broiling the meat.

Salting must take place within three days

9.   Meat must be salted within three days (seventy-two hours) from when the animal was slaughtered. If the meat was immersed in water within three days from when the animal was slaughtered, the meat must be salted within three days (seventy-two hours) from when it was immersed. If the meat was not salted within this time, it may no longer be kashered by salting.

Broiling meat extracts blood even if more than three days have passed (the *halachos* of kashering meat by broiling it are discussed in Sections 17-19, below). Such meat that was kashered by broiling should not be cooked afterwards.

It is preferable not to leave meat for three days without being salted to avoid the possibility of the meat being salted after that time, and being cooked rather than broiled.

How To Kasher Meat by Salting

Below is a brief description of how to salt meat or poultry. However, one should not salt meat without first being shown how to do it from an expert in these *halachos*.

Preparations before rinsing the meat

10.   The following preparations must be done before rinsing fowl. The stomach, heart, liver, intestines, and preferably the lungs are removed. The

stomach is cut open and emptied. The veins are removed from the neck, and the claws of the feet are removed. The chicken's head is also cut off. It is also customary to cut the edges of the wings and the knee joints.

Fowl must be opened well so they can be salted inside.

Liver (from fowl as well as from other animals) can only be kashered by broiling, as is discussed below.

Certain animal limbs

Blood tends to pool in the inner cavities and veins of certain parts of the animal. One should receive instruction from a person proficient in Halachah concerning how to prepare these parts for kashering.

These parts include the head (which together with the brain, must be cut in a specific way before the kashering), the tongue, the neck (which contains many veins), the heart (blood pools in its cavities), the esophagus and windpipe (they must be cleaned carefully and the interior must also be salted), the lungs (its branches must be cut), the udder (which contains milk), and the feet (the hooves must be cut off).

The liver, spleen, kidneys, intestines, crop, omasum, and reticulum of animals are covered with fat membranes which may not be eaten. Before kashering these organs, one must make sure that *nikkur* was performed and the forbidden parts removed.

Soaking the meat in water and the first rinsing

11. Meat must be rinsed thoroughly with water when it is ready to be kashered. This removes surface blood, and cleans and softens the meat, allowing the subsequent salting to effectively draw out blood. One must check all sides of the meat for blood clots; any that are found should be rinsed with water and removed. If there is red discoloration (i.e. due to a wound), that area must be cut off before the meat is soaked.

Frozen meat must thaw before it may be kashered. It can be thawed in a warm room or by indirect heat, but not by pouring hot water on it.

12. The meat should be soaked in water for half an hour. The entire piece of meat must be covered with water. The meat may not be cut from the

time it is soaked until after the last rinsing which follows the salting. The utensil the meat is soaked in may not be used for other food.

Meat that was left in the water for twenty-four hours may not be eaten. This meat may not be kashered at all, not even by broiling.

Hot water and very cold water may not be used for soaking meat. If the water is very cold, one must wait until it is no longer very cold before placing the meat in it.

Salting the meat

13.   The meat is left a short while after being soaked to allow the water to drip off. This prevents the salt from being absorbed immediately after being sprinkled on the meat. However, the meat should not be dry when it is salted. The meat must be wet enough for the salt to stick to the meat and extract the blood from it.

The meat is salted on a surface (e.g. a board) where the blood will be able to flow off. The surface should be slanted or perforated, and should not have a depression where blood can accumulate. (One must observe many more details if the meat is salted on a level surface without holes.)

The salt must be sprinkled all over the meat or fowl i.e. on the sides as well as inside and outside, so that no spot is left without salt. One must make sure to salt any cuts or cavities as well.

When the piece being salted has a cavity (i.e. the inside cavity of fowl and large pieces of meat), it should be placed with the cavity facing downwards after it is salted. This enables the blood to drip off, and prevents it from accumulating within the cavity.

The salt used for salting should not be as fine as table salt (fine salt will be absorbed immediately without extracting the blood), unless no other salt is available. Similarly, the salt used should not be very coarse. Bones that have been separated from the meat should be salted and placed on the kashering board separately.

Unsalted meat should not be placed together with meat being salted. Similarly, meat that has already been salted should not be placed together with meat that is being salted.

The salt must be left on the meat or fowl for one hour. The salt should not be left on the meat or fowl for more than twelve hours.

The final rinsing

14. After the meat or poultry was salted for an hour, one shakes off the salt and rinses it well three times with water that isn't hot. The meat or poultry must be rinsed on all sides. This completely removes the salt. If one rinses off the salt in a container of water rather than under running water, the water in the container must be changed, and the container must be rinsed out between each of the three rinses. The meat should not be put in a utensil (without water) until it is rinsed.

Eggs inside the chicken

15. Eggs which were found in a slaughtered hen must be kashered just like the hen — by soaking in water and salting. The membrane should be removed before the eggs are kashered. Even if an egg with a hard shell is found in the chicken, it is customary to kasher it by soaking and salting. The eggs should not be salted with the hen.

Eggs which were found inside a hen are considered meat products and may not be eaten together with milk products. It is customary to observe this rule even when the eggs have a hard shell.

Buying kosher meat today

16. Today, meat markets sell meat and poultry which have already been kashered, and which are ready to be cooked. One should make sure these meat products have a reliable and responsible *kashrus* certification. There are large slaughterhouses and meat production plants where thousands of chickens are slaughtered and kashered each day. These plants' *kashrus* supervision must be comprehensive and thorough. This is one reason why it is so important to have an excellent and reputable *kashrus* organization supervising the entire process.

If the butcher kashers the meat in his shop, one must make sure that the butcher can be relied upon to properly observe all the *halachos* pertaining to kashering. One can be sure of this if he is supervised by a reliable *kashrus* organization.

Beef and chicken liver that is sold with kashered meat has not been kashered. Liver can only be kashered by broiling it over a fire. Therefore, when a person buys kashered chicken or meat, he must remember to kasher the liver that comes with it.

Kashering Liver by Broiling

17.   Animal and poultry liver contains such a large amount of blood that it cannot be extracted by salting. Therefore, liver can only be kashered by broiling. (Meat may also be kashered by broiling.)

Liver should not be left in water for twenty-four hours before it is kashered.

One should only kasher liver after being shown how to do it by someone with experience.

How to broil the liver

18.   First, the liver is rinsed well to remove the surface blood. Then it is laid on a metal grid (or a spit) over a flame and salted lightly. The liver must be broiled immediately after being salted.

Both sides of the liver should be broiled over the fire until the outer layer dries out. If the liver (or meat, if it is being kashered by broiling) was frozen, broiling it over the fire may singe the outside while the inside is still raw. Therefore, one should check the liver after it was broiled to be sure that the inside is not raw. However, one should not stick a kosher knife in the liver since the inside may not be broiled enough yet (i.e. the liver may not be kosher yet).

The liver should be removed from the metal grid or the broiling spit immediately after it is broiled. It is then rinsed three times in water to remove the blood that still remains on the surface.

Additional laws

19.   One may not cook liver in a frying pan or pot before it has been kashered over a flame. Similarly, the liver may not be placed on aluminum foil when it is being kashered. If one broiled liver that was not yet kashered in the utensils mentioned above (instead of on a spit or metal grid), the liver may not be eaten, and the utensils may not be used until they have been kashered.

Whole animal livers that were not cut up into pieces and will be cooked after being broiled, must be kashered slightly differently. A crisscross cut is made in the liver so that its inner blood vessels will be opened. The cut side of the liver is placed face down on the grid (i.e. with the cut side towards the fire) to let the blood drip off. When this side has been broiled, the liver is turned over and the other side is broiled. Chicken livers that will be cooked after being broiled should have the bile duct and part of the liver removed before broiling. Sephardic Jews always cut the liver this way before kashering it.

Meat or liver which was not kashered within seventy-two hours of the animal's slaughter may be kashered by broiling. In this case the same procedure is followed as when kashering liver. However, in this case, the meat should not be cooked after being broiled.

It is preferable not to have the meat sit for three days without being salted. This is to avoid the possibility of accidentally salting and cooking the meat rather than broiling it.

Blood in eggs

20. It is forbidden to eat blood which is found in chicken eggs and in the eggs from other types of fowl. If the blood is from a developing chick, the entire egg may not be eaten. This is often the case with fertilized eggs. Where the blood is located in the egg helps determine whether the blood is from a developing embryo. Today, most eggs which reach the consumer market are not fertilized eggs, and blood that is found in them is not from a developing chick. Therefore, one may remove the blood and eat the egg. Nevertheless, some people discard the entire egg.

When preparing cakes or other foods with eggs, each egg should be poured into a separate utensil and checked to be sure that it does not contain blood. (If the egg was poured directly into the cake batter or food, and blood was found in it, it would be very difficult to separate the egg from the rest of the food.) A *rav* must be consulted if a fertilized egg with a blood spot was added to cake batter or food that already had other eggs added to it.

Hard boiled eggs may be eaten without being examined.

A peeled egg that was left overnight should not be eaten.

Blood from one's gums

Human blood is not included in the Torah prohibition against ingesting blood. Our sages prohibited ingesting human blood because it looks like forbidden blood. One may swallow blood from a cut in his mouth. If one bit into food and then saw blood from his gums on it, that blood may not be eaten.

Fish

Permitted and prohibited kinds of fish

21.   All fish which have fins and removable scales are kosher, and may be eaten. Fish which do not have fins or scales are not kosher and may not be eaten. Fish do not require slaughtering or salting.

All fish which have scales also have fins. However, there are many forbidden kinds of fish which have fins but no scales. If one finds scales on a fish or on a piece of a fish, he can be sure the fish is kosher.

It should be emphasized that many shops and markets carry non-kosher fish. One must be especially careful when buying fish fillet or ground fish, etc., because one cannot see whether or not the fish had scales. Therefore, one must not buy any part of a fish unless he can verify that it is truly kosher.

Cans of fish may contain non-kosher fish whose flesh (and name) may be similar to kosher fish.

22.   The eggs from non-kosher fish are also prohibited. Caviar, for example, is usually made from non-kosher fish eggs. Therefore, it is usually not kosher.

Unlike the blood from animals and fowl, the blood of kosher fish is not prohibited. However, fish blood that has accumulated in a bowl should not be used because people may think that the blood is from animals or fowl. However, one may use the blood if it contains some scales, since this shows that it comes from fish.

Seafood

23.   Fish which have fins and scales are the only types of seafood which are permitted to be eaten. All the other seafood is referred to by the Torah as *sheretz ha-mayim* (literally, "those that swarm in the water"), and is prohibited. This prohibition includes oysters, snails, crabs, shrimps, etc.

Dairy and Meat Foods

This section provides a general overview of the *halachos* of meat and milk. These *halachos* apply to one's everyday life. Therefore, one should study them thoroughly. One is advised to learn how to run a kosher kitchen in which the laws of milk and meat, as well as the other laws of *kashrus*, are strictly observed from a person knowledgeable in this area.

Meat and milk and their by-products

24.   Meat and poultry (and all products which are made from them, like sausages) may not be eaten together with milk (or any milk products such as cheese and butter).

Many products contain additives derived from milk or meat which are added during the food's production. Such products are considered either dairy or meat. For example, many candies, bittersweet chocolates, and pastries contain milk derivatives, and soup mixes often contain animal derivatives. Often, these additives are not listed among the ingredients. For this reason, it is essential to only use products which bear a reliable *kashrus* certification. This guarantees the kosher consumer that, when necessary, products are explicitly marked as meat or dairy.

There are products which contain both dairy and meat derivatives. These products may not be eaten, and one may not derive any benefit from them whatsoever. Infant formula sometimes contains both dairy and meat derivatives. One must always ascertain the *kashrus* of every food product he is using.

Pareve (neither dairy nor meat)

25.   Foods and drinks which do not include milk or meat products are called "pareve." These foods may be eaten with either dairy or meat foods.

Many products with rabbinical supervision bear the word *pareve* or a statement that they may be eaten with either milk or meat.

Waiting between meat and milk

26. One must wait six hours after eating meat, poultry, or their derivatives, before eating dairy products. (Some communities wait a different amount of time between meat and dairy.) This rule applies if one ate foods which had been cooked with meat or dairy products, even if he did not eat the actual meat or dairy product.

Children should be trained to wait between eating meat and milk. The amount of time the children wait should be lengthened gradually, as they get older.

If one found meat between his teeth six or more hours after eating meat, he should remove it and clean his mouth by eating something like a piece of bread, and rinse his mouth with a drink. Then he may eat dairy foods.

27. If one ate a pareve food that was cooked in a clean meat pot (i.e. there was no meat residue inside the pot), he may eat dairy food afterwards (i.e. without waiting the usual amount of time). Similarly, one may eat a pareve food that was cooked in a clean dairy pot immediately after eating meat.

Sharp foods like onions, garlic, horseradish, hot spices, etc. which were cut with a meat knife may not be eaten with dairy foods. Similarly, if sharp foods were cut with a dairy knife, they may not be eaten with meat foods.

Waiting between milk and meat

28. One does not have to wait between drinking milk or eating dairy foods and eating meat. (The only exception to this rule is hard, aged cheese.) However, one should clean his mouth by eating bread and taking a drink. One should also wash his hands to clean off any dairy residue that might remain.

After eating cheese that was aged for six months, one must wait six hours until he may eat meat. [There is an opinion that today's yellow cheeses are similar to aged cheese with regard to this *halachah*, and require a six-hour wait.]

All dairy foods, as well as any crumbs left on the table from the dairy meal, must be cleaned off the table before eating a meat meal. This is to ensure that no dairy products are accidentally eaten with the meat meal. A meat meal should not be eaten on the same tablecloth that was used for a dairy meal.

Eating meat and dairy at one table

29. If two people who are acquainted with each other are eating at one table when one is eating meat and the other dairy, they must place some kind of marker between them. The marker is to remind them not to partake of each other's food, and not to drink from the same cup or eat from the same loaf of bread. For example, an object not usually placed on a table should be placed between them, or each one should have his own place mat.

The prohibition to mix meat and milk

30. The Torah prohibitions regarding mixing meat and milk include cooking meat and milk together, even if one does not intend to eat the mixture afterwards.

It is also forbidden to derive any benefit from milk and meat that was cooked together. One must throw away such a mixture, and not feed it to animals, nor sell or give it to a Jew or a non-Jew, etc.

Meat and dairy doughs

31. One may not make a dairy dough for bread or for a pastry which is normally eaten as a side dish, because it may accidentally be eaten with meat. Likewise, one may not make dough with animal fat, lest it be eaten with diary foods or drinks.

One may only make a dough with milk or animal fat if the finished baked product has a special shape to alert people that the dough was made with milk or meat. It is also permissible to make the dough with milk or animal fat if the amount prepared is only sufficient for one day's meals. A larger amount of baked goods made from a dough containing milk or animal fat that do not have a special shape may not be eaten.

Meat and dairy utensils

32. It is prohibited to use the same utensils for dairy and meat. Therefore, every Jewish home must have two sets of tableware and cookware, one for dairy and one for meat. The pots, pans, cutlery, plates, cups, etc. used for dairy meals may not be used for meat meals.

One should have different colors or patterns for his meat and dairy kitchenware. This is to prevent the meat and dairy utensils from becoming mixed up. If all of one's utensils are of the same color and pattern, one should make an identifying mark on the dairy utensils. It is advisable to have some pareve utensils as well, like knives for cutting bread, fruits, vegetables (especially for sharp foods like onions), etc.

33. It is easier to observe the laws of *kashrus* if there are two kitchen sinks, one for dairy and one for meat.

If there is only one sink in the kitchen, it is not kosher, since both dairy and meat foods are poured into it. Therefore, dishes may not be soaked directly in the sink, but must be washed in running water above the sink, or one may use separate dishpans for soaking and washing meat and dairy dishes.

It is also easier if there are separate kitchen counters for milk and meat.

The *halachos* pertaining to mixing meat and dairy also apply to ovens and dishwashers. One who wishes to bake a cheesecake, roast meat, etc., in an oven should receive instructions regarding how to use the oven without making it dairy or meaty.

One must make sure that dairy and meaty foods do not touch or drip on each other. Therefore, one must be careful when putting dairy or meaty foods in the refrigerator, etc.

Meat and milk foods which became mixed; kitchenware which became unkosher

34. If a dairy utensil was used for meat, or vice versa, a *rav* should be consulted concerning the status of both the utensil and the food. In some cases, the utensil is not kosher, and may not be used until it is kashered. (Kashering utensils is discussed at the end of this chapter.)

Before speaking to the *rav*, one should take note of the following details: was the food hot or cold, how much food was involved, was a sharp food involved, and when was the utensil last used with a dairy food (if it is a dairy utensil) or with meat (if it is a meaty utensil) before the error occurred (i.e. was the utensil heated with food within the last twenty-four hours).

35. A *rav* should also be consulted if dairy and meaty utensils were mixed up, and one does not know which are which. Similarly, one must consult with a *rav* if any quantity of milk or a milk product spilled into a meaty food, or vice versa. In all cases, one must inquire about the status of the foods involved as well as that of the utensils.

Fish

36. Fish is not considered meat. Therefore, it may be eaten with milk and dairy foods. However, many Sephardic Jews, as well as some Ashkenazic Jews, do not eat fish with milk or milk products.

When eating fish and meat during the same meal, one should make a separation between them. This is done by eating a piece of bread or some other food, and taking a drink of something other than water. Fish and meat may not be eaten together because our sages determined it to be unhealthy.

Fish and meat may not be cooked together, or put together in the same utensil. After eating fish, the cutlery and plates must be rinsed before they may be used for meat.

The Prohibition against Eating Crawling Animals

37. The Torah commands us: "Do not make yourselves despicable with all kinds of crawling creatures, and you will not become defiled with them and be coarsened by them. For I am Hashem your God, and you shall be holy because I am holy, and you shall not defile yourselves with all kinds of creeping things which swarm on the ground" (*Vayikra* 11:43-44).

The prohibition against consuming insects, worms, etc. is referred to in halachic literature as *issur tola'im*. These *halachos* are discussed in the *Shulchan Aruch, Yoreh De'ah* 84.

38. As the verses above state, failure to avoid consuming insects defiles the soul and dulls the spiritual refinement which leads a person to emulate God's ways. On the other hand, when one refrains from eating insects he sanctifies his soul and becomes closer to God.

39.   Various insects are sometimes found in food products. One must make
           sure he does not eat the insects together with the food, so as to avoid
transgressing this most severe prohibition.

Examining food

40.   Insects may be found in almost every kind of food. This section dis-
           cusses how to examine those foods which are frequently infested by
insects and worms. The general rules for examining food mentioned here
are applicable for others kinds of food as well.

It should be noted that different foods are likely to be infested by insects and
worms in different places. One should check with someone who is familiar
with the situation in his locale, regarding which foods are likely to be infested.

41.   Some fruits and vegetables are frequently infested with insects during
           the summer. The produce should be examined for worms if there is a
soft or spoiled area on its surface.

Worms are more likely to infest fruits or vegetables at the end of the season.
Greater care should be taken then.

42.   Scale insects are sometimes found on citrus fruit peels, and may not be
           eaten. This insect can be detected by the round or elongated black and
brown spots it secretes on the citrus peel to conceal its body. While peeling
the fruit the scales may inadvertently be moved onto the fruit. If they were,
they must be removed before the fruit may be eaten.

43.   Peas, beans, chickpeas, peanuts, and lentils should be examined for in-
           sects, insect eggs and worms. If they are soaked in water for a long
time, it is easier to examine them for worms and the holes left by worms.
There are several effective methods to check for worms in legumes. It is advisable to receive instructions regarding how to check legumes.

Rice should be spread on a white surface, and one should check between the
grains for moth caterpillars, which are white (and which produce cobwebs) or
for black or brown beetles (weevils). (Stains on grains of rice are not a sign of
infestation, and so the grains themselves do not have to be examined.)

44.   Leafy vegetables and herbs such as lettuce, cabbage, cauliflower, pars-
           ley, dill, scallion, mint, etc. are very difficult to check for insects. Each
leaf must be held up to the sunlight or another source of strong light and

examined meticulously. Some of the insects that infest these leaves are so tiny that only a trained eye will notice them. Some insects are difficult to see because they are the same color as the leaves.

Today there are many types of leafy vegetables which are grown under special greenhouse conditions, which prevent insect infestation. It is preferable to buy vegetables which were grown under these conditions, since it is very hard to clean leafy vegetables which were grown in the usual way.

Even leafy vegetables which were grown under these special greenhouse conditions should be washed well. One must make sure that the vegetables he buys which were grown in greenhouses have a reliable *kashrus* certification.

45. Dried fruits such as figs, prunes, dates, etc. must also be examined. They must be opened and examined for worms.

Fruit or vegetable preserves are sometimes infested as well. Therefore, one must check to make sure any fruits or vegetables (whether they are fresh, dried or preserved) he eats are not infested. Each fruit or vegetable should be examined individually.

46. Flour in most areas must be sifted well and examined for any worms or insects. Even flour that is pre-sifted should be sifted before being used. This is because the flour can become infested if it is stored after being sifted. A flour sifter with a very fine mesh should be used to prevent insects from passing through the sifter.

47. Fish sometimes have worms between their scales and inside the head. Worms multiply greatly in untreated fish pools, penetrating the fish's skin. This is especially true of carp pools, although it applies to other types of fish pools as well. A fish's scales and skin must be cleaned well. Similarly, one must discard the intestines and scrape or rinse the cavity well. If worms were found in the head, the head should not be eaten.

48. Items such as noodles, cookies, rice, chocolate, candies, dried fruit, etc. which have been stored for a long time should be thoroughly checked for signs of infestation. These signs include nibbling marks, crumbs, and thin threads in between layers of package wrappings.

Warmth facilitates insect breeding. Storing foodstuffs in cool or chilled places helps prevent infestation. Insects are likely to spread from infested food to non-infested food stored nearby. Similarly, small flies are likely to fall into packages or containers of food that are left open. It is best to store food in well sealed packages and containers.

As mentioned above, observing the mitzvah not to consume insects brings one closer to God. This is derived from the verse, "and you shall be holy because I am holy" (*Vayikra* 11:44). This topic is discussed in greater detail in the volume of *Iturei Halachah* which discusses *kashrus*.

Non-Jewish Bread, Cooked Foods, Dairy Products and Wine

The following sections only discuss the main points of these *halachos*. When one encounters these issues, he should study the *halachos* in depth.

Non-Jewish bread

49.   Our Sages prohibited eating bread baked by a non-Jew (*pas akum*), even if the bread which does not include any non-kosher ingredients. (It should be noted that there are many *kashrus* issues involved with any food prepared by a non-Jew.)

There is a halachic difference between bread baked by a non Jew in a bakery for commercial purposes (*pas palter*), and bread baked by a non-Jew for non-commercial purposes to be used in his home. The *halachah* is stricter regarding the latter.

In places where there is no Jewish baker, it is the custom of some communities to buy bread from a non-Jewish bakery (after ascertaining that the bread is kosher). Some communities allow commercial bread even where Jewish bread is availble. Bread baked by a non-Jew not for commercial sale may not be used unless there is absolutely no kosher, Jewish bread available in the area.

If a Jew was involved (in even a small way) in the baking, the bread is not considered *pas akum* and may be eaten. The Jew's role may be as trivial as lighting the oven.

If a bakery is owned by a Jew but operated by non-Jewish workers, and the Jew does not participate in the baking, besides being *pas palter*, the bread is considered *bishul nachri*, "food cooked by a non-Jew," and may not be eaten. It is therefore especially important that a Jew be involved (in even a small way) in the actual baking. The *halachos* of *bishul nachri* are discussed in the following section.

If non-Jewish bread is glazed with eggs, some consider the glaze to be *bishul nachri* and do not allow the glaze to be eaten.

If one travels to a place where it is not possible to obtain kosher food, he should take along sufficient quantities to eat from. If a person must spend an extended period of time in a place where Jewish bread is not available, he should consult with a *rav* regarding how to proceed.

It should be noted that many pita bakeries in Israel are owned by Arabs. Aside from being *pas palter*, pita from these bakeries may also contain non-kosher ingredients. Therefore, one should always look for reliable *kashrus* certification when buying pita.

Food cooked by a non-Jew

50. It is prohibited to eat food that was cooked by a non-Jew (*bishul nachri*). This prohibition applies even if the food does not contain forbidden ingredients.

Even if the food was cooked by the non-Jew specifically for a Jew (e.g. a non-Jewish cook who works for a Jewish family), one may not eat the food if a Jew did not participate in cooking it.

If a Jew participated in the cooking, the food is no longer considered *bishul nachri*. According to the *Shulchan Aruch*, this condition can be fulfilled by a Jew placing the food on the fire. However, according to the Rema, it is sufficient for the Jew to turn on the oven. (For further details, see *Shulchan Aruch, Yoreh De'ah* 113:7.)

This *halachah* applies only to foods which are of a quality that would be served at the table of kings and only if the foods are not eaten raw. Foods which are also eaten raw, which were cooked by non-Jews, are not considered *bishul nachri*, and may be eaten even if they would be served at the table of kings. Therefore, the prohibition of *bishul nachri* does not apply to an apple or to a carrot, but does apply to eggs.

Non-Jewish milk

51. Milk which is milked by a non-Jew without Jewish supervision is called
chalav akum. It is forbidden to drink *chalav akum*. However, if a Jew
supervises the milking, the milk is not considered *chalav akum*. It is preferable
for the Jew to check the milk can before the milking begins to make sure it
contains no non-kosher milk.

Many people rely on the halachic opinion which allows consumption of non-
Jewish milk in countries where the law prohibits commercial producers from
mixing milk from non-kosher animals with cow's milk.

Cheese produced by a non-Jew is also prohibited, even if it contains no non-
kosher ingredients. One may only eat cheese with a reliable *hashgachah*.

Powdered milk produced outside of Israel is made from non-Jewish milk.
Many food products contain powdered milk (for example, milk, ice cream,
chocolate, candies, etc.). Therefore, it is advisable to consult with a *rav* concerning how these *halachos* pertain to these products.

Non-Jewish wine

52. Wine that is made or touched by a non-Jew is prohibited. Therefore,
one should not send wine with a non-Jewish messenger unless the bottle is closed with two seals. Grape juice is halachically the same as wine.

Wine touched by a Jew who publicly desecrates Shabbos is also prohibited.
Therefore, wine must have two seals when it is being transferred and handled
by Jews who are not observant.

One should be aware that many food products, such as liquor, cognac, candies, chocolates, etc. may contain wine. The prohibition against drinking
non-Jewish wine is one of the reasons why it is important to only buy
these products if they bear the certification of a reliable *kashrus* organization.

Wine that was cooked may be touched by a non-Jew without becoming prohibited.

Tevilas Kelim
(Immersing utensils in a mikveh)

53.   Utensils used with food often require immersion in a *mikveh* before their
initial use. Whether or not a utensil requires immersion depends upon
the type of utensil, and the material the utensil is made from.

Food utensils made by or purchased from a non-Jew must be immersed in a
mikveh before they can be used. (A *mikveh* is any body of water which fulfills
certain halachic specifications.) It is assumed that utensils manufactured outside of Israel were made by non-Jews. Therefore, they require immersion.
Food utensils produced by a company jointly owned by Jews and non-
Jews must be immersed in a *mikveh*.

Utensils which have contact with food require immersion. For example, the
following utensils require immersion: tableware (plates, cups, cutlery, etc.),
food storage containers (e.g. bottles or boxes used to store bread, sugar, vegetables, wine, etc.), cookware (pots, baking tins, pans, ladles, roasting spits,
etc.), mixer pieces that come in contact with food, serving dishes, etc.

A utensil which was made by a non-Jew and was used for non-kosher food
requires both kashering and immersion. First, the utensil must be kashered
and then it must be immersed in a *mikveh*.

Which materials require immersion

54.   Utensils made of metal or glass require immersion with a blessing.
Glazed earthenware, china, and porcelain require immersion without a
blessing. Utensils made of wood, ivory, stone, or unglazed clay do not require immersion. Plastic utensils do not require immersion, although some
go beyond the letter of the law and immerse them without reciting the blessing. Disposable aluminum pans do not require immersion.

Cans, jars, or bottles (that were made by non-Jews) which contained food (e.g.
coffee jars) should be immersed without a blessing before being used again.

Disposable plates, bowls, and cutlery (which are thrown away after they are
used) do not require immersion.

55.   Some utensils must be immersed in a *mikveh*, although a blessing is not
recited when they are immersed. Examples of these are: utensils used
while the food is still inedible (e.g. kneading utensils, a meat-grinder, a slaugh-

tering knife, etc.), utensils which are only used to store food, but which are not used for preparing or eating food, and which are not used as serving dishes. An exception to this rule are glass bottles which are used for storing drinks. A blessing is recited when immersing these bottles.

In view of the many types of utensils which we use, it is often unclear if certain utensils require reciting a blessing when they are immersed. Therefore, one should clarify the *halachah* whenever he is unsure how to proceed. There are books which discuss these *halachos* in detail.

How to immerse utensils

56.   Before immersing a utensil one must remove all dirt, rust and adhesive labels, as well as the glue from the labels. Nothing may come between the utensil and the water. Therefore, the entire utensil (including cracks in the place where the handles are attached, etc.) must be examined to make sure it is completely clean.

Before immersing the utensil, one recites the blessing *asher kideshanu b'mitzvosav v'tzivanu al tevilas keli*. If more than one utensil is immersed, one ends with the words *al tevilas kelim*. ("Who sanctified us with His *mitzvos* and commanded us to immerse the utensil(s).")

The blessing is recited outside the room with the *mikveh*. The person enters the room of the *mikveh* immediately after reciting the blessing, and immerses the utensils. If the *mikveh* is only used for immersing utensils (and is not used for people), one recites the blessing next to the *mikveh*.

57.   The water from the *mikveh* must completely cover the utensil. Not even a tiny part of the utensil may remain uncovered. If half of the utensil was immersed, and then the second half was immersed, it is as if the utensil was not immersed at all.

The water must touch the entire utensil at one time. Therefore, the utensil should either be let loose for an instant or held loosely while being immersed. One must make sure that the water touched the inside and outside of the utensil at one time. When one immerses a utensil with a narrow neck (like a bottle), he must wait until it is completely filled with water.

Immersing New Metal
Utensils in Boiling Water

58. Some manufacturers coat new metal cooking utensils with non-kosher fat. This problem may arise with aluminum and stainless steel utensils. Therefore, many halachic authorities require kashering new metal utensils before they can be used. One can kasher these utensils by immersing them in boiling water.

If the utensil was made by or bought from a non-Jew, it is immersed in boiling water before being immersed in a *mikveh* (as mentioned in Section 53, above). Utensils that bear a *kashrus* organization's label certifying that they were not greased with non-kosher fat do not need to be kashered.

Before immersing the utensil in boiling water, all adhesive labels must be removed, and the utensil must be completely clean. It is advisable to receive help immersing the utensil from a person who is experienced in this area. At the very least, one should receive advice from such a person regarding how to immerse the utensil.

Kashering Utensils

59. A utensil that became not kosher (for example, a dairy utensil that was used for meat) may not be used until it is kashered. Some utensils cannot be kashered. If they become not kosher, they may no longer be used for cooking or serving food.

In addition to the *halachos* pertaining to the actual kashering, there are various *halachos* concerning how to clean and prepare utensils to be kashered. An expert in these *halachos* should be consulted when kashering utensils.

60. The goal of kashering utensils is to remove whatever food flavors were absorbed into the utensil. The utensil is then halachically like a new utensil. There are different methods of kashering for different types of utensils. The method of kashering required depends upon how the utensil was used. For example, a utensil that was used for cooking is kashered by being immersed in boiling water, while a utensil used for roasting is kashered by being heated to a very high temperature. These *halachos* have many details.

Chapter Thirty-Seven

Mitzvos Dependent
upon the Land of Israel

The Land of Israel (*Eretz Yisrael*) is holier than other lands. God chose this land as the special dwelling place for His Divine Presence (the *Shechinah*). Produce grown in *Eretz Yisrael* is also endowed with holiness. Therefore, the Torah commands the Jewish people to observe numerous *mitzvos* which apply to agriculture in the Land of Israel. These *mitzvos* are called "*mitzvos* which are dependent upon the Land of Israel." One of these *mitzvos* is the mitzvah of separating tithes from produce grown in *Eretz Yisrael*. In Hebrew, this is called separating *terumos* and *ma'asros*.

In the introduction to his book *Sha'arei Tzedek*, the *Chochmas Adam* writes about the obligation to be familiar with the practical applications of the *mitzvos* which are dependent up on the Land of Israel:

> If a man were to enter a king's palace and not be aware of the accepted modes of behavior, he would be risking his life. This is all the more so in the case of one who wishes to dwell in the Holy Land and is not familiar with the special *mitzvos* which must be observed there... . Of such a person, it is written, "Who sought this from you, to trample My courtyards" (*Yeshayahu* 1:12). (*Sha'arei Tzedek*, Introduction)

The *Sefer Ha-Chinnuch* explains one of the reasons for this mitzvah:

> Since the whole world belongs to God, it is proper that a man should remember his Creator [when enjoying] His blessings, especially grain, wine, and oil, which are man's basic foodstuffs. Therefore, it is proper for man to remember his Creator by reciting a blessing before eating, and by setting aside part of [his harvest] for God's servants, the *Kohanim*, who occupy themselves with the Divine service. (*Sefer Ha-Chinnuch*, Mitzvah 507: separating *terumah*)

The Prohibition of Tevel

An explanation of various concepts

1. Before giving a step-by-step discussion of how to separate the various tithes, first the *halachos* of the different types of tithes are discussed.

Produce grown in Israel from which tithes (*terumos* and *ma'asros*, i.e. *terumah gedolah, ma'aser rishon, terumas ma'aser,* and *ma'aser sheni* or *ma'aser ani*) have not yet been separated, is called *tevel. Tevel* is an acronym for the Aramaic words *tav lo,* which mean "not good," because the produce may not be eaten or used in certain ways until *terumos* and *ma'asros* have been separated. This rule also applies to *Kohanim* and *Levi'im.*

When one does not know whether or not *terumos* and *ma'asros* have been separated from produce, the produce is called *safek tevel* (possible *tevel*). *Terumos* and *ma'asros* must be separated from *safek tevel.*

Tithes are separated from *safek tevel* in the same manner as from food that is definitely *tevel.* The only difference is that one does not recite the blessing when separating tithes from *safek tevel.* (This is discussed in greater detail below.)

It is forbidden to eat or use *tevel* in ways that some of it becomes consumed. So too, one may not consume any product that contains an ingredient of *tevel.* Therefore, one may not use juices, oils, powders, extracts, canned goods, etc., until *terumos* and *ma'asros* have been separated from them.

* *Tevel* may not be fed to one's animals.

* Seeds from *tevel* may not be planted.

* Oil made from *tevel* may not be used for lighting or heating.

* Oil made from *tevel* may not be used as an ingredient in creams and ointments.

One may not sell or give a present of fruits, vegetables, or their by-products if *terumos* and *ma'asros* were not separated from them, because the buyer may mistakenly assume that the seller had already separated *terumos* and *ma'asros.*

2. First, *terumah gedolah* is separated from the produce. In the days of the Temple, *terumah gedolah* was given to a *Kohen.* People who are not *Kohanim* are not allowed to eat it.

Today, *Kohanim* are not allowed to eat *terumah gedolah* because they are ritually impure. Therefore we do not give our *terumah gedolah* to *Kohanim*. Only a tiny amount of produce is separated for *terumah gedolah*.

Terumah gedolah must be buried. If it is too difficult to bury it, one should wrap it well and throw it in the garbage. *Terumah gedolah* may not be left around the house because someone may eat it by mistake.

Terumah that was separated from a liquid must be poured out, preferably on the ground (but not in a degrading place). If it is difficult to pour liquid *terumah* on the ground, it may be poured down a drain.

3.   After the *terumah* has been separated, a tenth of the remaining produce is separated. This tithe is called *ma'aser rishon* ("the first tithe").

After *terumas ma'aser* has been separated, *ma'aser rishon* may be eaten by anyone. *Terumas ma'aser* is discussed in Section 4, below.

In the days of the first Temple, *ma'aser rishon* was given to a *Levi*. Today, when separating *ma'aser rishon* from *safek tevel*, it is customary for the owner to eat the *ma'aser rishon* himself. Some people give *ma'aser rishon* that was separated from produce that is definitely *tevel* to a *Levi*.

4.   A tenth of the *ma'aser rishon* is separated for *terumas ma'aser* (i.e. one-hundredth of the entire produce). As with *terumah gedolah*, only a *Kohen* may eat *terumas ma'aser*.

In the days of the Temple, the *Levi* would separate a tenth from his *ma'aser rishon* and give it to a *Kohen*. Today, *Kohanim* cannot eat *terumas ma'aser* because they are ritually impure.

Today, *terumas ma'aser* is separated from *ma'aser rishon*, but it is not given to a *Kohen*. Instead, it is either buried or wrapped well and then disposed of in the same manner as the *terumah gedolah*.

5.   *Ma'aser sheni* ("the second tithe") is separated from produce grown during the first, second, fourth, and fifth years of a seven-year cycle. The seventh year of the cycle is *shemittah*, the Sabbatical year. The years 5761 (2000-1), 5768 (2007-8), and 5775 (2014-5) will be *shemittah* years. (The mitzvah of *shemittah* is discussed in greater detail in Sections 29-32, below.) One must separate one-tenth of the produce that remains after *ma'aser rishon* has been separated, for *ma'aser sheni* (this is about 9 percent of the entire produce).

In the days of the Temple, one ate *ma'aser sheni* in Jerusalem, when he was ritually pure. If it was too difficult to bring the produce to Jerusalem (because of the distance), the produce's special sanctity was transferred to coins. Since the produce no longer had any special sanctity, it could be eaten anywhere. This is referred to as, "redeeming produce with money." The money which acquired the produce's sanctity was brought to Jerusalem, and used solely for buying food which was eaten there in lieu of the original *ma'aser sheni*.

Today, since we do not have a Temple, and we are unable to ritually purify ourselves, we are not permitted to eat *ma'aser sheni*. Therefore, we redeem *ma'aser sheni* with a coin. This procedure is described in Section 6, below. (There are special *halachos* pertaining to redeeming *ma'aser sheni* within areas of Jerusalem which were sanctified during the Temple era.)

6. A coin or several coins (but not paper money) should be set aside in a secure place to be used for redeeming *ma'aser sheni*.

Ma'aser sheni is redeemed with a coin whose value equals that of a *perutah*, i.e. a coin whose value is equivalent to .025 grams of silver.

One coin can be used to redeem *ma'aser sheni* until the value of the produce redeemed equals the value of the coin. Since the exact number of times a given coin can be used to redeem *ma'aser sheni* is dependent upon various factors, it is important to clarify the status of one's coin with an expert in these *halachos*.

Other *halachos* that apply to this coin include: what to do with the coin after it was used the maximum number of times, the *halachos* of *perutah chamurah*, etc.

One who uses Israeli produce regularly can subscribe to the Fund for the Redemption of *Ma'aser Sheni*. Members of the Fund separate *ma'aser sheni* and recite the text as usual. Members redeem their *ma'aser sheni* with coins maintained by the Fund, instead of with coins kept at home. Members of the Fund receive complete instructions regarding how to observe this mitzvah. This arrangement allows for easier observance of this mitzvah. (The Fund's current address is: The Fund for the Redemption of *Ma'aser Sheni*, P.O.B. 50100, Jerusalem, Israel 91501. The American branch is located at: 540 Fifth Street, Lakewood, NJ, tel. (908) 905-6725, fax (908) 942-0001.)

7.   One separates *ma'aser ani*, "the poor man's tithe," from produce grown
           during the third and sixth years of the seven-year *shemittah* cycle.
Ma'aser ani is one-tenth of the produce that remains after *ma'aser rishon*
was separated. *Ma'aser ani* is given to the poor. *Ma'aser ani* is about 9 percent of the total produce.

Ma'aser ani may be eaten by anyone.

One who separates tithes from produce that is *safek tevel* must separate
ma'aser ani, but does not have to give this tithe to the poor.

The table on the following page describes separating tithes.

Preparing produce for tithing

8.   All the fruits, vegetables, and other products from which tithes will be
           separated must be gathered in one place.

When there are several packages of the same type of food, one should open
the wrappers and place the packages next to each other.

One should make sure that the fruits, vegetables, and other food products are
not moved while reciting the text. One should be especially careful that the
liquids do not shake.

Separating the tithes

9.   Tithes are separated and the text printed below is recited. One should
           recite the text in a language he understands. One designates a quantity
and a specific location for the various tithes when he recites this text. One
separates a little more than one one-hundredth of each type of produce,
and places the bit separated next to the food it was separated from. One
must be careful not to separate less than the required amount.

Before separating tithes from *tevel*, one recites the blessing *asher kideshanu
b'mitzvosav v'tzivanu l'hafrish terumos u'ma'asros* ("Who has sanctified us
with His *mitzvos* and has commanded us to separate tithes"). One does not
recite a blessing when separating tithes from *safek tevel*. After separating
the tithes one recites the following text:

> The part on the northern side of that which has been separated, which is in
> excess of one one-hundredth, I hereby designate as *terumah gedolah*. [If one
> separates tithes from several types of produce at one time, he adds, "each

Separating Tithes

Which tithe	During the Temple Era		Today	
	Amount to be separated	**The halachah**	**Amount to be separated**	**The halachah**
Terumah gedolah	According to the Torah any amount; the *Chachamim* recommended three amounts: a generous amount = 1/40; an average amount = 1/50; a stingy amount = 1/60	Given to a *Kohen*	Any amount	It is buried or wrapped well and then disposed of
Ma'aser rishon	One-tenth of what remains after *terumah gedolah* is separated	Given to a *Levi*	One-tenth of what remains after *terumah gedolah* is separated	Remains in owner's possession and may be eaten by anyone (some give *ma'aser rishon* separated from definite *tevel* to a *Levi*)
Terumas ma'aser	One-tenth of that designated as *ma'aser rishon* (i.e. 1% of the original amount)	Given to a *Kohen*	One-tenth of that designated as *ma'aser rishon* (i.e. 1% of the original amount)	It is buried or wrapped well and then disposed of
Ma'aser sheni (separated during the first, second, fourth and fifth years of the *shemittah* cycle)	One-tenth of what remains after separating *ma'aser rishon* (i.e. about 9% of the original amount)	Either it is brought to Jerusalem and eaten there, or its sanctity is transferred to a coin which is brought to Jerusalem and spent on food which is eaten there.	One-tenth of what remains after separating *ma'aser rishon* (i.e. about 9% of the original amount)	It is redeemed with a *perutah*
Ma'aser ani (separated during the third and sixth years of the *shemittah* cycle)	One-tenth of what remains after separating *ma'aser rishon* (about 9% of the original amount)	It is given to the poor	One-tenth of what remains after separating *ma'aser rishon* (about 9% of the original amount)	*Ma'aser ani* separated from food that is definitely *tevel* is given to the poor. If it is separated from *safek tevel*, anyone may eat it.

one from its own kind."] I hereby designate the remaining one one-hundredth which has been separated as well as nine one-hundredths on the northern side of the produce, [each one from its own kind] as *ma'aser rishon*.

That one one-hundredth which is separated that I have designated as *ma'aser rishon*, I hereby designate as *terumas ma'aser* [each one from its own kind].

I hereby designate the southern side of the produce as *ma'aser sheni*. I am hereby redeeming the *ma'aser sheni* and an additional fifth (25 percent) thereof with the value of a *perutah* on the coin that I have designated for redeeming *ma'aser sheni* and *reva'i*. If (the *ma'aser sheni*) is not worth a *perutah*, it and the additional fifth shall be redeemed at its value.

If the produce is required to have *ma'aser ani* separated from it, I hereby designate the southern side [each one from its own kind] as *ma'aser ani*.

If (the food) is *reva'i*, it and its fifth (25 percent) shall be redeemed with the value of a *perutah* on the coin which I have designated for redeeming *ma'aser sheni* and *reva'i*.

An explanation of the text

10.   Text: "The part on the northern side of that which has been separated, which is in excess of one one-hundredth, I hereby designate as *terumah gedolah* [each one from its own kind]."

Explanation: By reciting this passage, one designates the amount in excess of 1 percent, that is on the northern side of what has been separated, as *terumah gedolah*. One may separate tithes from several types of produce simultaneously. In this case one should separate a little more than 1 percent from each type of produce and add the words, "each one from its own kind" to the text.

Text: "I hereby designate the remaining one one-hundredth which has been separated as well as nine one-hundredths on the northern side of the produce, [each one from its own kind] as *ma'aser rishon*."

Explanation: By reciting this passage, one designates *ma'aser rishon* in two places: one-tenth of the *ma'aser rishon* is designated as the 1 percent that has been separated, and the remainder (the other nine-tenths) is designated on the northern side of the produce that has not been separated.

Text: "That one one-hundredth which is separated that I have designated as *ma'aser rishon*, I hereby designate as *terumas ma'aser* [each one from its own kind]."

Explanation: By reciting this passage, the one one-hundredth which was separated and designated as part of *ma'aser rishon* is now designated as *terumas ma'aser*.

Text: "I hereby designate the southern side of the produce as *ma'aser sheni.*"

Explanation: By reciting this passage the southern side of the produce is designated as *ma'aser sheni*.

Text: "I am hereby redeeming the *ma'aser sheni* and an additional fifth (25 percent) thereof with the value of a *perutah* in the coin that I have designated for redeeming *ma'aser sheni* and *reva'i.*"

Explanation: By reciting this passage, one redeems the *ma'aser sheni* with a coin that he has set aside for this purpose. This means that the *ma'aser sheni's* sanctity is transferred to the coin. This procedure is explained in greater detail in Section 1, above. A fifth here means 25 percent, which is a fifth after it is added in.

If one knows that the produce is from a year when one is required to separate *ma'aser ani*, he substitutes the text for *ma'aser ani* (see below) for the text of *ma'aser sheni*. If one does not know what year the produce is from he recites both texts. In this case, the southern one-tenth is conditionally designated as either *ma'aser sheni* or *ma'aser ani*.

Text: "If the produce is required to have *ma'aser ani* separated from it, I hereby designate the southern side [each one from its own kind] as *ma'aser ani.*"

Explanation: If the produce is from a year when it is required to separate *ma'aser ani*, the southern side of the produce is designated as *ma'aser ani* (instead of *ma'aser sheni*). The final part relating to *revai* will be explained in Section 28.

The blessings

11.   Before separating tithes from *tevel*, one recites the blessing *asher kideshanu b'mitzvosav v'tzivanu l'hafrish terumos u'ma'asros* ("Who has sanctified us with His *mitzvos* and has commanded us to separate tithes").

Generally, when one purchases fruits and vegetables at the market or in a store, it is not known whether tithes have been separated. Therefore, one must separate tithes in the manner discussed above. However, one does not recite a blessing since the tithes may have already been separated. One only recites the blessing if he is certain that tithes have not been separated, e.g. if the fruits and vegetables are straight from the field or garden.

One recites the blessing *asher kideshanu b'mitzvosav v'tzivanu al pidyon ma'aser sheni* ("Who has sanctified us with His *mitzvos* and has commanded us to redeem *ma'aser sheni*") before redeeming *ma'aser sheni* with a coin. If one is not sure whether *ma'aser sheni* has been separated from the produce (e.g. he bought the produce in the market), or if he is not sure that this produce was grown during a year when *ma'aser sheni* must be separated, he recites the text without reciting the blessing.

The procedure following tithing

12.   The little more than 1 percent of produce which was separated and designated as *terumah* may not be eaten or used in any way by anyone because it has been sanctified. Today, *Kohanim* are not given this portion because it is also forbidden to them. Since *terumah* may not be thrown away in a degrading manner, it must be buried or wrapped up and then disposed of.

If the *terumah* is a liquid (e.g. wine, juices, etc.), it must be poured out. It is preferable to pour the *terumah* on the ground because it is considered less degrading than pouring it down a drain.

Utensils which contained liquid *terumah* should be rinsed before they are used, so that one will not accidentally drink any *terumah* remaining in the utensil.

After one has separated the necessary tithes, the rest of the produce (which amounts to a little less than 99 percent of the original quantity) may be eaten.

13.   The mitzvah to separate tithes from produce before eating or deriving benefit from the produce, and the mitzvah of giving the tithes to a *Kohen*, *Levi*, or the poor, are independent of each other.

As mentioned above, today *terumah* and *terumas ma'aser* are not given to *Kohanim*. This is because *Kohanim* may not eat these tithes due to their ritual impurity, as well as for other reasons.

The portion of food that is *ma'aser* remains in the owner's possession and may be eaten by anyone. Some people give *ma'aser rishon* that has been separated from food that is definitely *tevel* to a *Levi*.

Ma'aser ani that is separated from produce that is definitely *tevel* is given to the poor.

Additional laws

14. Tithes may not be separated from produce grown in one year for produce grown in another year. There are many criteria used to determine which year of the *shemittah* cycle the produce belongs to, including: the type of plant, the plant's stage of development at Rosh Hashana or at Tu bi-Shevat, when it was harvested, etc.

When one is not sure to which year a fruit belongs (i.e. whether *ma'aser sheni* or *ma'aser ani* must be separated), one adds, "and if [it is a year when] *ma'aser ani* must be separated, the *ma'aser ani* shall be on the southern side," after reciting, "*ma'aser sheni* is on the southern side..."

It is preferable to always recite this phrase to avoid erring regarding what year the produce belongs to.

According to the Chazon Ish, if one does not have the complete text for separating tithes, and he does not know the text by heart, he may recite the following short version instead: "I hereby separate all the *terumos* and *ma'asros* and redeem all the *ma'aser sheni* and *reva'i* according to the *halachah*, as it is written in the text located (state where the text is located or written, e.g. in a certain *Siddur*)."

Aside from the change in the text, a person in this situation separates the tithes in the usual manner. He separates a little more than one one-hundredth of the food, he must have a special coin for redeeming *ma'aser sheni*, etc.

15. One may not separate tithes from one type of produce in order to permit another type of produce to be eaten. For example, one may not separate a piece of tomato for use as a tithe for cucumbers. However, one variety of produce may be used as a tithe for another variety of the same type of produce. For example, green grapes may be used as a tithe for red grapes.

It is not clear whether citrus fruits (lemons, grapefruits, oranges, etc.) are halachically considered the same type of produce. Therefore, one should not separate tithes from one type of citrus fruit for another type. If one did this, he must separate tithes again from each type of citrus fruit without reciting the blessing.

One may not use produce which is exempt from tithing (e.g. tithes have already been separated from this produce) for tithing produce which is *tevel*. Similarly, one may not use produce which is *safek tevel* for tithing produce which is definitely *tevel*, or vice versa.

If one buys produce that is *safek tevel* in two different stores, or if one buys produce that is *safek tevel* that was delivered to the store by two different distributors, tithes must be separated from each batch of produce separately. This is because some of the produce may be exempt from tithing (i.e. its tithes may have already been separated), while the rest of the produce may be obligated in tithing (i.e. its tithes have not yet been separated).

16.	The produce and the tithes being separated must be close to each other when the tithes are being separated. The halachic term for this is *min ha-mukaf*, i.e. adjacent, or near each other. If several unpackaged foods are in the same room, they are considered *mukaf* even if they are not touching. If the food is in several uncovered containers, the containers should be touching and the tithes should be placed with them. If the containers are closed, they should be opened.

When tithing several types of food at once, each type of food should be placed in a separate group.

If one separated tithes without fulfilling the requirement of *min ha-mukaf*, he has nevertheless fulfilled the mitzvah. If one cannot separate tithes *min ha-mukaf*, he should ask a *rav* how to proceed.

Tithes should be separated from produce before it is cooked, so the pots do not absorb food that is *tevel*.

If produce was cooked before tithes were separated, one should intend to include the *tevel* absorbed by the pots when separating the tithes. In this case, one should separate the tithes on the same day the food was cooked.

If one used a knife to slice or peel sharp vegetables (like onions or radishes) that are *tevel*, one should intend to include the *tevel* absorbed by the knife when separating the tithes.

17. Only the owner of the produce or his appointee may separate tithes.

A guest may separate tithes from his personal serving if his host does not mind. If the food is *safek tevel*, the guest may separate tithes from his personal serving even if his host objects. Before tithing, the guest should lift his serving, intending to halachically acquire it. If the person cannot wrap up the tithes he should leave them (the tithes) at the side of his plate.

Children may not separate tithes. If a boy in his thirteenth year (i.e. not yet thirteen), or a girl in her twelfth year (i.e. not yet twelve) separated tithes from food, one should consult with an expert in these *halachos* regarding the food's status. This age (the year before a child is obligated to observe *mitzvos*) is called *mufla samuch l'ish*.

18. One does not have to separate tithes from fruit that grew wild. Similarly, one does not have to separate tithes from fruit that was cultivated by a non-Jew and owned by a non-Jew at the time of its final processing. One must separate tithes from the fruit if it belonged to a Jew during either of these two stages.

What is considered, "final processing," depends on the produce involved.

"Final processing" is the last stage of harvesting (e.g. placing the fruit in boxes).

"Final processing" for grapes and olives which were cultivated to produce wine and oil is when the wine and oil are produced.

One may not assume that fruits and vegetables sold by a non-Jew were grown by a non-Jew. Therefore, one may not assume that this produce is exempt from tithing. One must clarify this situation to determine whether or not tithes must be separated.

Many Israeli food products are sold abroad. Jews who live outside of Israel must be certain that tithes have been properly separated from these products, so as to avoid transgressing the prohibition of *tevel*. Produce grown outside of Israel, whose final processing took place in Israel, must have tithes separated from them.

19.   It is forbidden to separate tithes on Shabbos or *Yom Tov*. Therefore, one should make every effort to separate the tithes beforehand.

One who has *tevel* in his home before Shabbos or *Yom Tov* and does not have time to separate tithes from it, can recite the text in the future tense (as printed below) on Friday or *erev Yom Tov*. Then, he may separate the tithes on Shabbos or *Yom Tov*.

When one follows this procedure, he must recite the usual text again when actually separating the tithes (the text is cited in Section 9, above). One must be careful not to move the bit that was separated, since it is *muktzeh*. (The laws of *muktzeh* are discussed in detail in Chapter 20.)

This method of tithing may only be done if the food was in one's possession before Shabbos or *Yom Tov*.

The text recited on Friday or *erev Yom Tov* is:

> I shall separate later a little more than one one-hundreth of the produce. The amount in excess of one one-hundreth on the northern side of the separated part shall be *terumah*. [If one will separate several types of produce at one time, he adds, "each one from its own kind".] The remaining one one-hundredth together with nine similar parts on the northern side of the food shall be *ma'aser rishon* (each one from its own kind). That one one-hundredth which I will have designated as *ma'aser* shall then be designated as *terumas ma'aser* (each one from its own kind). The southern side of the food shall be designated as *ma'aser sheni* (each one from its own kind). It and an additional fifth thereof shall be redeemed on a *perutah* with the coin which I set aside for redeeming *ma'aser sheni*. If (the *ma'aser sheni*) is not worth a *perutah*, it shall be redeemed with an additional fifth thereof at whatever its value is. And if *ma'aser ani* [has to be separated instead], *ma'aser ani* shall be designated on its southern side (each one from its own kind).

Clearing out the *ma'asros*

20.   One is obligated to clear out all *ma'asros* on *erev Pesach* of the fourth year of the *shemittah* cycle and on *erev Pesach* of the *shemittah* year.

Whoever has *tevel* or *safek tevel* in his house from the first, second, or third years of the *shemittah* cycle on *erev Pesach* of the fourth year of the *shemittah* cycle, must separate tithes from it. Similarly, whoever has *ma'asros* that must be given away, must distribute them according to Halachah. One must also redeem his coin for redeeming *ma'aser sheni* and *reva'i* with a *perutah*. This *perutah* must then be destroyed or thrown into the sea.

One is also obligated to clear out *ma'asros* on *erev Pesach* of the *shemittah* year. In this case, the *ma'asros* are from produce grown during the fourth, fifth, and sixth years of the *shemittah* cycle.

Separating Challah

21. It is a mitzvah to separate a bit of dough that was made with flour from one of the five grains (wheat, spelt, oats, barley, rye). This bit of dough is called *challah*. One must not eat any baked goods (e.g. bread, cake, matzah, matzah meal, cookies, etc.) if *challah* has not been separated from them. Baked goods are considered *tevel* before *challah* has been separated.

The mitzvah of separating *challah* is derived from the verse, "You must separate the first portion of your dough. It must be separated like *terumah* that is taken from the threshing floor" (*Bemidbar* 15:20). The *Sefer Ha-Chinnuch* cites the following as one of the reasons for the mitzvah of *challah*:

> Since life is sustained through food, and most people subsist on bread, God wished to give us the merit to do a mitzvah which we would constantly be fulfilling through our bread. As a result of observing the mitzvah, a blessing will rest upon our bread and we will receive a merit for our souls. In this way, the dough provides sustenance for our bodies and our souls. Another reason (for this mitzvah) is so God's servants, the *Kohanim*, who are constantly involved in serving Him, can be supported by the *challah* without expending any effort. Whereas they must toil to winnow and grind the *terumah* which is separated from the grain, here they receive their requirements without any inconvenience whatsoever. (*Sefer Ha-Chinnuch, Mitzvah* 385)

Challah should be separated when the dough is made. If *challah* was not separated when the dough was made, it may be separated after the dough is baked.

Challah must be separated from dough that was made in *Eretz Yisrael*. This rule even applies when the dough's flour was made from grain imported from abroad. Our sages decreed that the mitzvah of *challah* must also be observed outside of Israel. This even applies when the dough's flour was made from grain grown outside of Israel.

In Israel, the baked goods must not be eaten before *challah* has been taken, whereas outside of Israel one may eat baked goods even before *challah* was taken as long as one leaves over a piece from which the *challah* will be taken.

How to separate *challah*

22.   One separates a bit of dough and declares, "This is *challah*." (Details regarding when to recite the blessing, etc., are discussed below.)

The piece of dough separated for *challah* should be the size of an olive. If the piece of dough is smaller than an olive, one has nonetheless fulfilled the mitzvah. There are times when one may not be sure whether or not *challah* was separated from dough or baked goods. In this situation, some people separate a very small amount for *challah*.

The piece of dough which was separated may not be eaten. Rather, it must either be burned or wrapped up and placed in the garbage. The piece of dough should not be thrown away in a degrading manner.

The piece of dough separated for *challah* should not be burned in an oven when other food is baking.

When separating the piece of dough, one recites the blessing, *asher kideshanu b'mitzvosav v'tzivanu l'hafrish challah min ha-isah* ("Who has sanctified us with His *mitzvos* and commanded us to separate *challah* from the dough"). One then declares, "This is *challah*." Some people recite the blessing *l'hafrish challah*, instead of *l'hafrish challah min ha-isah*.

According to the Chazon Ish, one only recites the blessing when separating *challah* from dough containing at least 4.32 lt. or 2.25 kg. (5 lbs.) of flour. According to Rav Chaim Na'eh, one only recites the blessing if the dough contains at least 2.5 lt. or 1.66 kg. (3.65 lbs.) of flour.

If the dough contains 1.2 kg. (2.6 lbs.) of flour (but does not contain the amount of flour stated above), one separates a bit of dough and declares, "This is *challah*," but does not recite the blessing. There is no obligation to separate *challah* from dough containing less than 1.2 kg. (2.6 lbs.) of flour.

If the dough will be cooked or fried, but not be baked, (for example, dough prepared for making pasta), *challah* is separated without reciting a blessing.

A woman has first priority when performing the mitzvah of separating *challah*. If there is no woman in the house, a man performs the mitzvah.

A child who is not yet bar or bas mitzvah should not separate *challah*.

Additional laws

23. If one is not certain that *challah* was separated from commercial baked goods purchased in a store or bakery, he must separate *challah* before eating the baked goods. The baked goods may not be eaten until *challah* has been separated.

As mentioned above, when one is not sure whether or not *challah* was separated from baked goods (e.g. if one purchases baked goods and is not certain that *challah* was separated), he must separate *challah* without reciting the blessing. In this situation the person only declares, "This is *challah*."

24. If a person places several batches of dough or baked goods in a container, and each individual batch does not contain enough flour to necessitate separating *challah*, but together they contain the amount of flour required for separating *challah*, the container joins them together into one group. In this case the owner must separate *challah* from the dough or baked goods. This rule does not apply if the owner does not want the different types touching and mixing together.

If one received baked goods from several people (or bought various commercial baked goods), and is not sure if *challah* was separated from all of them, he must separate a piece of *challah* from each baked good. In this situation, one may not separate *challah* from one of the baked goods and exempt the others. This is because if that baked good already had *challah* separated from it, it cannot exempt foods from which *challah* has not yet been separated.

25. It is customary for women to bake challahs on Friday from dough which contains enough flour to require separating *challah*.

There are two reasons for this custom. One reason is to honor Shabbos by making especially festive foods, and the other reason is to enable women to fulfill the mitzvah of separating *challah* on *erev Shabbos*.

Challah may not be separated on Shabbos. The *halachah* concerning separating *challah* on Shabbos is the same as the *halachah* concerning separating tithes on Shabbos. (This prohibition, as well as the permitted way to separate tithes on Shabbos, are discussed in detail in Section 19, above.)

The *halachah* is different outside of Israel. Outside of Israel, one may eat baked goods even if *challah* was not separated. In this case, on Shabbos one must leave over a piece of the baked good. *Challah* must be separated from that piece on *Motza'ei Shabbos*. It should be noted that *challah* is separated from the piece left over, but the entire piece should not be designated as *challah*.

As is the case on Shabbos, *challah* may not be separated on a *Yom Tov*. However, a dough that was prepared on *Yom Tov* may have *challah* separated from it on *Yom Tov*.

The piece of *challah* that was separated on *Yom Tov* is *muktzeh*. Therefore it may not be moved after it is set down. The dough may not be burned on the *Yom Tov*, since burning the dough is not a necessity for *Yom Tov*.

Orlah and Neta Reva'i

26. The Torah states: "When you come to the Land [of Israel] and plant any food tree, you shall reckon the fruit as *orlah*; for three years [the fruit] shall be *arelim* and may not be eaten. Then, in the fourth year, all [its] fruit shall be sanctified for giving praise to God. In the fifth year, you may eat its fruit; that it [the tree] may increase its yield for you. I am the Lord your God" (*Vayikra* 19:23-25).

The first verse prohibits eating fruit grown during the first three years of a tree's life. These fruits are called *orlah*. The second verse states that fruit grown during the fourth year of a tree's life is imbued with sanctity, and must be used as a way of giving praise to God. These fruits are called *neta reva'i*. The third verse permits eating fruits grown any time from the tree's fifth year onward.

Orlah

27. Fruit which grew during the first three years of a tree's life may not be eaten or used in any way. For example, one may not smell the fruits, sell them to Jews or non-Jews, feed them to animals, etc.

The prohibition of *orlah* only applies to fruits. The leaves and branches from trees within their first three years may be used.

Orlah fruits are burned. If it is not possible to burn *orlah* fruits, they should be buried.

The prohibition of *orlah* applies to fruit grown by Jews and non-Jews.

The prohibition of *orlah* applies outside of Israel as well for fruits that one is certain that grew within the first three years after a tree was planted.

The prohibition of *orlah* applies to seedlings, as well as to mature trees that have been transplanted. The prohibition of *orlah* applies for the first three years after a tree was transplanted.

Branches stemming from a tree's roots or trunk, that emerge from the ground, are considered new plants. The prohibition of *orlah* applies to these branches for the first three years after they emerged from the ground. (This phenomenon is common among pomegranate trees.)

One should consult a halachic authority regarding how the *halachos* of *orlah* apply in the following cases:

* a tree that was transferred from one location to another when its roots were embedded in a clod of soil;

* a tree which was cut down and the remaining stump was less than a *tefach* high, which grew again.

There is a halachic opinion that if the majority of a certain type of fruit available on the market is not *orlah*, one may buy this fruit without *orlah kashrus* supervision. There is another opinion that even if only a small percentage available on the market is *orlah*, as long as it is more than a certain percentage one may not buy that fruit without *orlah kashrus* supervision.

The relevant percentage for each type of fruit may change from year to year, since new orchards are constantly being planted. It is essential to clarify these details with experts or to check the percentage tables that are publicized every year.

This is how years are calculated for *orlah*:

* A plant takes root fourteen days after being planted.

* Thirty days of a tree's first year is considered one complete year of *orlah*. For example, a tree planted any time up to 15 Av 5751 (i.e. it was in the ground for forty-four days before Rosh Hashana 5752), has halachically completed the first year of *orlah*. This is because the tree took root on 29 Av (fourteen days after it was planted). Another thirty days passed between 29 Av and Rosh Hashana, halachically completing the first year of *orlah*. The tree's second year begins with Rosh Hashana 5752. This tree's three years of *orlah* are completed at the end of 5753.

* Tu bi-Shevat (the fifteenth of Shevat) is the "New Year for trees." Therefore, all fruits that reach *chanatah* before Tu bi-Shevat 5754 are considered *orlah* for that year. (Some explain *chanatah* as the stage of development when the bud is discernible after the flower falls off, others explain it to be when the fruit is one-third grown.) Fruits that reach this stage of development from Tu bi-Shevat 5754 until Tu bi-Shevat 5755 are *neta reva'i* and must be redeemed before they may be eaten. (*Neta reva'i* is discussed in detail in the next section.)

* Fruits that reached the *chanatah* stage of development after Tu bi-Shevat 5755 are not restricted in any way, and may be eaten (after tithes are separated from them).

Neta reva'i

28. Fruit which grew during the fourth year after a tree was planted is called *neta reva'i*. In the days of the Temple, these fruits were brought to Jerusalem and eaten there.

If it was difficult to bring the fruit to Jerusalem (due to the distance), the fruit was redeemed with money. It was then permissible to eat the fruit anywhere, as its sanctity was transferred to the money. The money was then brought to Jerusalem and used to buy food, which was eaten there.

Today, these fruits may only be eaten after the fruits' sanctity has been transferred by redemption to a coin, similar to *ma'aser sheni*.

The text which is recited when separating tithes (cited in Section 9, above) specifies the redemption of *neta reva'i* after the redemption of *ma'aser sheni*.

Before redeeming fruits which are definitely *neta reva'i*, one recites the blessing *asher kideshanu b'mitzvosav v'tzivanu al pidyon neta reva'i* ("Who has sanctified us with His *mitzvos* and commanded us to redeem *neta reva'i*"). One recites the text for redeeming fruit immediately after reciting the blessing.

If one is not sure if fruit is *neta reva'i* (e.g. fruits bought in the market) he must redeem the fruit without reciting the blessing.

No blessing is recited when redeeming fruits grown outside of Israel. A majority opinion holds that most fruits (except for grapes) that are grown outside of Israel do not have to be redeemed.

The Shemittah Year

29.   "For six years you may sow your fields, prune your vineyards, and harvest your crops. But the seventh year is a sabbatical year for the Land. It is God's Sabbath during which you may not sow your fields or prune your vineyards" (*Vayikra* 25:3-4).

The Torah commands us to observe the *shemittah* year once every seven years. The *shemittah* cycle began after Yehoshua (Joshua) divided the Land of Israel among the twelve tribes.

The upcoming *shemittah* years will be 5761 (2000-1), 5768 (2007-8), and 5775 (2014-15).

Special *halachos* apply to cultivating land in Israel during *shemittah*. For example, not every type of work may be done in fields and gardens during *shemittah*. Different *halachos* also apply to fruits and vegetables which grew during *shemittah*. For example, which produce may be eaten, how fruits which possess the sanctity of *shemittah* may be purchased, clearing out fruits after the *shemittah* year ends, etc.

30.   We demonstrate our conviction that everything belongs to God by refraining from cultivating the soil and observing the other *halachos* pertaining to *shemittah*. "The earth and all that is in it is God's" (*Tehillim* 24:1). God is the One Who grants us the ability to enjoy the land's bountiful crops. Refraining from work every Shabbos demonstrates our conviction that God created the world in six days and rested on the seventh. Similarly, by refraining from working the land during the *shemittah* year we express our conviction that God created the world and that it all belongs to Him.

The *Sefer Ha-Chinnuch* discusses the mitzvah of *shemittah*:

> Among the underlying reasons for this mitzvah is that we should impress upon our hearts and visualize in our minds the renewal of the world — that God created the heaven and the earth in six days and He rested on the seventh day... . Just as we count the six days of the week and then observe a day of rest, so God commanded us to work the land for six years and let it rest during the seventh. By declaring all the produce that the land grows during [the seventh] year ownerless, man will be reminded that it is not nature or [the land's] inherent properties that make food grow but the Will of God. When He so desires, He commands man to declare his field ownerless.
>
> Another benefit of the mitzvah of *shemittah* is that one acquires the character trait of conceding to others that which is his. The truly generous person is one who gives to others with no expectation for compensation. Another benefit of this mitzvah is that it deepens one's trust in God. One who is able to abandon his land's produce and that of his father's land for an entire year and does so repeatedly every seven years, will never become miserly or lack trust in God. (*Sefer Ha-Chinnuch, Mitzvah* 84)

31. Books have been written which discuss the complex *mitzvos* and *halachos* of *shemittah*. These books discuss which forms of agricultural work are permitted and which are not; how to care for fields, plantations, gardens and plants during *shemittah*; how to handle the produce that grew during *shemittah* (which possess sanctity); which vegetables may not be eaten due to the prohibition of *sefichin*, etc.

Remission of debts at the end of *shemittah*

32. In addition to the agricultural laws of *shemittah* discussed above, there is also the mitzvah to cancel outstanding debts. This aspect of *shemittah* applies to those living in Israel, as well as to those living in the Diaspora. At the end of the *shemittah* year, a borrower is released from his obligation to repay his loan. Hillel the Sage instituted a special legal contract called a *prozbul*. A *prozbul* allows a creditor to collect the money owed to him. Halachic books which specifically discuss *shemittah* discuss the *halachos* connected with the remission of debts and *prozbul* in great detail.

This book provides a brief introduction to *shemittah*. When the *shemittah* year approaches, one should study its *halachos* thoroughly from a comprehensive text.

Kilayim
(The prohibition of crossbreeding different types of crops)

33. It is prohibited to crossbreed different types of trees or plants. It is also prohibited to sow different types of seeds next to each other without leaving a halachically specified distance between them. These *halachos* are called the Laws of *Kilayim*. Included in this category are the prohibitions of grafting different types of trees, sowing different types of seeds together, and planting vegetables in a vineyard.

This mitzvah is derived from the verse, "You shall not sow mixed seeds in your field" (*Vayikra* 19:19).

The *Sefer Ha-Chinnuch* writes:

> Among the underlying reasons for this mitzvah is that God created His world with great wisdom and understanding, giving every creation its perfect form. As the Torah relates about Creation, "And God saw everything that He had made, and behold it was very good" (*Bereshis* 1:31). Since He made everything perfectly suited to its purpose, He decreed that each species only produce food of its kind. The different species are not to be mixed with each other, lest they become lacking in perfection, whereupon He will then withhold His blessing from them. (*Mitzvah* 244)

> At the beginning of Creation, God fixed the natural properties for each species, so as to provide a benefit for mankind, and He commanded that each species should retain its properties. This is derived from the fact that the Torah always uses the phrase, "according to its type," when discussing the various creations in *Bereshis*. One who crossbreeds one species with another to bring about a third species has cancelled the special properties of the original two species. We may not do this, since it appears that we are trying to improve on God's perfect creation. (*Mitzvah* 62)

The basic *halachos* of *kilayim* are discussed below. Books dealing with the *mitzvos* that apply to the Land of Israel contain more comprehensive discussions of these *halachos*. Every question that arises must be clarified, either by consulting a *rav* or by researching the relevant issues.

Prohibited crossbreeding of trees

34. It is prohibited to graft one type of tree onto another. This includes grafting together two or more types of trees, two or more types of plants, or a tree with a plant.

It is prohibited to care for trees or plants which were crossbred with a different species. One may not water, weed, or hoe them. Furthermore, one is obligated to uproot these trees and plants.

Although it is prohibited to care for the plant, and it must be uprooted, its fruits are permitted to be eaten. (This *halachah* differs with regard to a vineyard, as is explained below.)

Kilei zera'im (Prohibited mixing of seeds)

35.   It is prohibited to sow two or more types of grains, legumes, or vegetables next to each other unless they are separated by the halachically required distance.

Plants which were sown in a prohibited way may not be cultivated. One may not weed, water, or care for the plants in any way. If seeds were sown too close together, one must either be uproot them or erect a partition ten *tefachim* high between the different types of seeds.

Although it is forbidden to cultivate a mixture of vegetables, the vegetables may be eaten.

A mixture of plants in a vineyard

36.   It is prohibited to sow seeds next to a vineyard unless they are separated by the halachically required distance. One may not even sow seeds under a branch of a grapevine that has grown far from the main vine.

Neither the plants nor the vines may be cultivated and they must be uprooted. The Torah prohibits eating and using the fruits of both the vines and the plants in any way. This prohibition is unique for *kilayim* in a vineyard.

It is permissible to plant different types of fruit trees close to each other or next to a grapevine.

General note

37.   The distance that must be left between different types of seeds depends on the types involved (e.g. whether they are grains, legumes, or vegetables) and the size of the plot involved. The distance required between seeds and a single grapevine is different than that required between seeds and a vineyard. (The exact distance required is specified in books on Jewish law that deal with the *mitzvos* that apply to the Land of Israel.)

Crossbreeding trees and mixing plants in a vineyard are forbidden outside of Israel as well. However, mixing vegetable seeds is permitted.

Chadash

38. It is forbidden to eat grain during the year in which it was grown. This prohibition applies to any of the five types of grain (wheat, barley, spelt, oats, and rye), that took root after the sixteenth of Nissan of that year. This grain is called *chadash*.

In the days of the Temple, grain that had taken root before the sixteenth of Nissan was allowed to be eaten after the *omer*-sacrifice was offered. (The *omer*-sacrifice was offered on the sixteenth of Nissan, the first day of *Chol Ha-mo'ed Pesach*.) Grain that took root after the sixteenth of Nissan was forbidden to be eaten until the sixteenth of Nissan of the following year.

Today, the new grain may be eaten from the seventeenth of Nissan. Grain that took root after the seventeenth of Nissan may not be eaten until the seventeenth of Nissan of the following year. Outside of Israel, the new grain may only be eaten from the eighteenth of Nissan.

One must verify with experts which grains are likely to be from the new crop (one should inquire about grain that is grown in Israel, as well as about grain that is grown abroad). In Israel, grains likely to be from the new crop are those which are imported during the winter months (for example, barley and oats).

Chapter Thirty-Eight

Miscellaneous Topics

This chapter briefly discusses miscellaneous halachic topics, including the prohibition of shaving with a razor, the prohibition of *sha'atnez*, and the mitzvah of studying Torah. One is advised to study these topics in greater detail and, when in doubt, to consult a *rav*.

Shaving

1. "Do not round off the hair on the sides of your head, nor should you shave off the edges of your beard" (*Vayikra* 19:27).

The Torah prohibits shaving with a razor blade. Each time a man shaves with a razor blade he transgresses five prohibitions from the Torah. In light of the frequency that men shave, and the severity of this prohibition, one must be very careful not to transgress it. It is permitted to shave with many electric shavers.

It is also prohibited for men to shave off their *pe'os* (the hair on the sides of the face above the beard). There are different halachic opinions regarding the exact perimeters of *pe'os*. Therefore, each man should consult with a person proficient in Halachah regarding this, to make sure he does not shave off any *pe'os*. *Pe'os* may not be removed with any type of implement. When men have a haircut, they must make sure that the barber does not cut their *pe'os* too short.

Sha'atnez
(A forbidden mixture of wool and linen)

2. "Do not wear a forbidden mixture of wool and linen" (*Devarim* 22:11).

It is prohibited to wear a garment which contains wool and linen threads. One wool thread in a linen garment, or one linen thread in a wool garment, is considered *sha'atnez*. Such a garment may not be worn or used to cover a person. This prohibition applies to all types of garments.

It is also prohibited to sit on upholstered furniture if the upholstery contains wool and linen threads.

3. Wool is used extensively in the garment industry in many types of cloth. Linen is frequently used as thread, lining for coats, cloth belts, etc. Since these two fibers are frequently used, one must examine every garment which may contain a mixture of wool and linen.

Sha'atnez laboratories have been set up in many Jewish communities. These laboratories examine garments and cloth to determine if they contain both wool and linen. The textile industry is so sophisticated that many similar types of cloth are produced. Often, even experts have difficulty determining if wool or linen threads are woven into the cloth. Therefore, it is best not to rely on tailors or shop owners who say that the clothes they are selling do not contain *sha'atnez*. Often, only a laboratory test can determine what type of threads are used. This is why it is essential to have a *sha'atnez* laboratory check every garment which may contain *sha'atnez*.

Mezuzah

4. "And you shall write them [on parchments affixed to] the doorposts of your house and upon your gates" (*Devarim* 11:20). It is a mitzvah to affix a *mezuzah* to the doorposts and gates of one's houses.

The *mezuzah* is a piece of parchment, on which two passages from the Torah are written. One is the passage beginning *Shema Yisrael* ("Hear O Israel"; *Devarim* 6:4-9), and the other is the passage beginning *V'hayah im shamo'a* ("If you shall hearken"; *Devarim* 11:13-21). These passages must be written with a special ink, in the special script used when writing *sifrei Torah*.

These passages discuss the essentials of faith in God, Divine Providence over His creations, and the Jewish nation's acceptance of God's sovereignty and the yoke of His *mitzvos*. Some people kiss the *mezuzah* when passing through a doorway, as a way of impressing these elements of faith upon themselves.

Affixing the *mezuzah*

5.   One must affix a *mezuzah* to his courtyard gate (if it has a lintel), to the doorpost of his house, and to the doorposts of all the rooms in his house (except for the bathrooms).

The *mezuzah* is affixed to the right doorpost (i.e. the doorpost on the right side of a person entering the room or house). The *mezuzah* is affixed to the top third of the doorpost, but not within a *tefach* of the lintel.

The *mezuzah* is rolled from its left to its right (e.g. one passage in the *mezuzah* is *Shema Yisrael...Hashem Echad*. The *mezuzah* is rolled from the word *Echad* towards the word *Shema*). It is customary to enclose the *mezuzah* in a special protective case to prevent it from becoming damaged.

6.   One recites the blessing *asher kideshanu b'mitzvosav v'tzivanu l'kebo'a mezuzah* ("Who sanctified us with His *mitzvos* and commanded us to affix a *mezuzah*") before affixing the *mezuzah*. The *mezuzah* is attached to the doorpost immediately after reciting the blessing. If a number of *mezuzos* are being attached at once, the blessing is only recited before attaching the first one. One should not discuss any other matter until all the *mezuzos* have been attached.

The *mezuzah* must be firmly attached to the doorpost and is therefore nailed to the doorpost from the top and bottom.

One should study the Halachah for various situations. For example, whether to affix a *mezuzah* to the doorpost of a room which measures less than four *amos* by four *amos* (e.g. a dinette), how to affix a *mezuzah* to the door of a balcony, on the corridor between two rooms, and to a room with a non-standard doorway (e.g. arched, slanted, etc.). The *halachah* for each case depends on the particulars of the situation. Therefore, it is best to consult a *rav* before attaching a *mezuzah* to a non-standard doorway.

If a doorway has no door, the *mezuzah* is attached without reciting a blessing.

A *mezuzah* must be halachically acceptable

7. Numerous *halachos* must be observed for a *mezuzah* to be acceptable.

Mezuzos which are not valid (i.e. they were not written according to *halachah*) are often sold. Therefore, one should only buy a *mezuzah* from a reliable, God-fearing person proficient in the *halachos* pertaining to *mezuzah*. Additionally, one should have a new *mezuzah* checked by an expert in the pertinent *halachos* before attaching it to the doorpost. (Often, *mezuzah* dealers are not familiar with all the *halachos* of *mezuzah*, and may inadvertently be selling invalid *mezuzos*.)

The *mezuzos* in one's house should be examined twice in seven years. One should have a scribe examine the *mezuzos* for any defects that may have occurred over the course of time (e.g. ink which came off the parchment, damage from moisture, etc.).

Torah Study

8. Torah study is the foundation upon which Torah and mitzvah observance is built. Torah study provides one with an awareness of his Creator as well as instruction regarding proper *mitzvah* observance. The reward for studying Torah is immeasurably great, as the Mishnah relates, "The study of Torah equals them all [the other *mitzvos*]."

Each and every Jewish man is obligated to study Torah. The Rambam writes:

> Every Jewish man is obligated to study Torah, whether he is poor or rich, healthy or sick, young or old or weak. Even if he is a pauper who lives off of charity and has to beg for his sustenance, even if he is occupied with [supplying the needs of] his wife and children, he must set aside time for Torah study during the day and at night, as it says, "You shall meditate in it by day and by night." (*Hilchos Talmud Torah* 1:8)

9. Torah study has many facets: the Written Law (comprised of the Torah, Prophets, Scriptures, and their commentaries); the Oral Law (the Mishnah, the Babylonian and Jerusalem Talmuds and their commentaries, and the Midrash); Jewish law (such as the *Shulchan Aruch* with the *Mishnah Berurah's* commentary, as well as that of others, the *Chayei Adam* and *Chochmas Adam*, the *Kitzur Shulchan Aruch*, the *Ben Ish Chai*, etc.); books of *mussar* (Jewish ethics); Jewish philosophy; and more.

It is extremely important to be proficient in the *halachos* that affect one's daily life, e.g. the *halachos* pertaining to prayers, blessings, Shabbos and festival observance, *kashrus*, etc. Clarity and proficiency in Jewish law is a prerequisite for living a complete Jewish life. Therefore, the highest priority should be given to studying Halachah.

Today, daily study programs are available for studying Mishnah, Talmud and Halachah. These programs help Jews throughout the world to study the same Mishnah, page of Talmud, or Halachah every day. In the course of a few years the participants in these programs study the entire Mishnah, Talmud, or the *Orach Chayim* section of the *Shulchan Aruch*.

10.　A man is obligated to study Torah for as long as he lives. All of one's free time must be dedicated to Torah study. This is derived from the verse in which God told Yehoshua, "You shall meditate in it by day and by night" (*Yehoshua* 1:8). In addition to utilizing all free time for Torah study, one must also have set times, both during the day and at night, for studying Torah. One must make every effort not to skip these set study sessions, even if he has other pressing affairs to attend to. Our sages state that one of the questions each person will be asked by the Heavenly Court will be, "Did you set aside times for Torah study?"

One who would like to be well versed in the study of Torah should find a teacher or a suitable framework which will aid his progress.

Bris Milah
(Circumcision)

11.　Our sages comment about circumcision (*bris milah*), that any mitzvah which the Jewish people accepted joyfully will be joyfully observed in every generation. Indeed, Jews have joyfully circumcised their sons in all places throughout the ages.

Most of the *halachos* pertaining to *bris milah* are observed by the *mohel* (the one who performs the circumcision). Some of the more important details are discussed below.

12.　Baby boys are circumcised when they are eight days old. Halachically, a new day starts with the onset of night. For example, a boy born on

Saturday night or on Sunday during the day is circumcised on the following Sunday.

A boy born on Shabbos (i.e. on Friday evening after dark, or on Saturday during the day) is circumcised on the following Shabbos. However, if the child was born by Cesarian section, he may not be circumcised on Shabbos. In this case the child is circumcised on the following Sunday (i.e. the ninth day after birth).

If a baby was not circumcised on the eighth day, he may not be circumcised on Shabbos. A *bris milah* may be deferred if, for example, the baby's health does not permit his being circumcised on the eighth day. In this case, a *rav* or the *mohel* must authorize the decision to defer the *bris milah*.

A *rav* must be consulted to determine the *halachah* if there is a doubt regarding what day the child must be circumcised. For example, a *rav* must be consulted if the child was born at dusk (between sunset and the appearance of the stars), or if the exact time of birth is not known.

The *bris milah* must be performed by an experienced and God-fearing *mohel* who is proficient in the pertinent *halachos*.

Pidyon Ha-Ben
(The redemption of the firstborn son)

13. The mitzvah of *pidyon ha-ben* is performed if the following three conditions exist:

A. The child is his mother's firstborn son, and the mother had no previous pregnancies.

B. The child was not born by Cesarian section.

C. The father is not a *Kohen* or *Levi*, and the mother is not the daughter of a *Kohen* or *Levi*.

A *rav* must be consulted in any unusual situation, such as if the mother is not sure if she had suffered a previous miscarriage, if the mother miscarried during the first trimester of pregnancy, if the child was delivered by forceps, etc.

The *pidyon ha-ben* is performed when the child is thirty days old. For example, if the child was born on Sunday (or Saturday night), he is redeemed on Tuesday after four weeks have passed.

A *Rav* must be consulted whenever it is unclear what day the *pidyon ha-ben* should take place (e.g. if the child was born at dusk, or the exact time of birth is not known).

A *pidyon ha-ben* is not performed on Shabbos or *Yom Tov*. If the child is thirty days old on Shabbos or *Yom Tov*, the *pidyon ha-ben* is performed on the following day.

This mitzvah is performed by a *Kohen*. The *Kohen* should be proficient in the *halachos* pertaining to *pidyon ha-ben*.

The text for the ceremony of *pidyon ha-ben* is printed in some *Siddurim*.

14.   If a child was not circumcised or redeemed at the proper time, he must be circumcised or redeemed at the first possible opportunity. An adult man who was not circumcised or redeemed is required to fulfill these *mitzvos* for himself. One in this situation should consult with a *rav* regarding how to fulfill these *mitzvos*.

Laws Pertaining to Kohanim

15.   God endowed the entire tribe of Levi, including the *Kohanim* (the paternal descendants of Aaron, who was a great-grandson of Levi), with a special sanctity.

After the Israelites made the Golden Calf, all the men from the tribe of Levi assembled before Moshe as the Torah relates, "Moshe stood up at the camp's entrance and announced, 'Whoever is for God, join me!' And all the *Levi'im* gathered around him" (*Shemos* 32:26). Not one *Levi* participated in the sin of making the Golden Calf. As a reward for their steadfast devotion to God, all *Levi'im* were granted special sanctity forever.

The tribe of Levi was assigned special spiritual tasks. The *Kohanim* offered the sacrifices in the Temple, and the *Levi'im* accompanied them in song. The *Levi'im* were also the nation's spiritual leaders and Torah teachers. This is derived from Moshe's blessing, "And to Levi, he said...'They shall teach Your law to Ya'akov and Your Torah to Israel. They shall place incense in Your presence and burn sacrifices upon Your altar'" (Devarim 33:8-11).

We await the Final Redemption when the Temple will be rebuilt. The Kohanim will once again fulfill their spiritual duties of serving God in the Temple in holiness and purity, and assisting the Jewish people to grow spiritually and approach their Father in Heaven.

The Kehunah (priesthood) passes from father to son. A Kohen is obligated to observe the special halachos that his status entails.

16. Listed below are the most common halachos that apply to Kohanim today.

   * It is a mitzvah for Kohanim to recite Birkas Kohanim, and to bless their fellow Jews when praying. Levi'im pour water on the Kohanim's hands before Birkas Kohanim. The halachos pertaining to Birkas Kohanim are discussed in Chapter 7, Sections 69-81.

   * Kohanim are given priority in all religious matters. This halachah is derived from the verse, "And you shall sanctify him" (Vayikra 21:8). An example of this practice is when a Kohen participates in a zimmun, it is he who leads the Birkas Ha-mazon. Levi'im are given precedence after Kohanim. This is derived from the verse, "And He gave it to the Kohanim, sons of Levi" (Devarim 31:9). An example of this practice is during Kerias Ha-Torah, when a Kohen always receives the first aliyah, and a Levi always receives the second aliyah.

   * A Kohen is forbidden to have contact with a corpse. This includes entering a house where there is a corpse, and approaching a grave. (For further details, see the Laws of Mourning, Chapter 39, Sections 21-23.) This halachah does not apply to the daughter or wife of a Kohen.

   * Due to his special holiness, a Kohen may not marry the following women:
       A **divorcee** (including his own wife whom he had divorced).

       A **convert** to Judaism.

       A **chalalah** (i.e., a woman born from a liaison between a Kohen and a woman who was prohibited to him).

There are other *halachos* regarding the women that a *Kohen* may not marry. For example, Halachah requires a *Kohen* who married a woman who is forbidden to him to separate from her.

  * As mentioned in Section 13, above, *Kohanim* and *Levi'im* are exempt from redeeming their firstborn son. Similarly, if the mother of a firstborn son is the daughter of a *Kohen* or a *Levi*, the parents are exempt from the mitzvah of *pidyon ha-ben*.

  * *Kohanim* and *Levi'im*, like all other Jews, are required to separate tithes from fruits and vegetables grown in Israel (as is discussed in Chapter 37). If a *Kohen* or *Levi* did not separate tithes from his fruits and vegetables, the produce remains *tevel*. Like all other Jews, *Kohanim* and *Levi'im* may not eat *tevel*. Similarly, *Kohanim* and *Levi'im* are required to separate *challah* from dough made with flour from one of the five grains. In Israel, no Jew, including *Kohanim* and *Levi'im*, may eat from baked goods until *challah* has been separated. The *halachos* pertaining to separating *challah* are discussed in Chapter 37, Sections 21-25.

The firstborn among animals

17.   "You must consecrate to God every firstborn male born among your cattle and flocks. Do not work with your firstborn ox and do not shear your firstborn sheep" (*Devarim* 15:19). Firstborn male calves, sheep, and goats which belong to a Jew have special sanctity. Firstborn male animals are one of the twenty-four gifts which were given to *Kohanim*. Many *halachos* apply to firstborn animals (e.g. one may not slaughter them, eat their meat, etc.). Today, when there is no Temple, and we do not give firstborn animals to *Kohanim*, it is customary to sell the mother cow, sheep, or goat to a non-Jew before she gives birth to her firstborn, and then buy back the mother and the firstborn. This way, the firstborn does not possess the special sanctity of a Jew's firstborn animal. Therefore, the *halachos* that pertain to a Jew's firstborn animal do not apply. In this way, one avoids accidentally transgressing these *halachos*. This sale is implemented with a special document.

It is advisable for anyone owning female livestock which is expecting its firstborn to contact a *rav* regarding implementing this sale, so as to avoid the many prohibitions involving a firstborn animal.

Halachos Pertaining to Interpersonal Relationships

"You must love your neighbor as yourself" (*Vayikra* 19:18). Man was created in God's image. The Torah commands every Jew to love his fellowman because every person is created in God's image. The group of *mitzvos* that regulate social relationships is called *mitzvos she-bein adam la-chavero* ("*mitzvos* between man and his fellowman"). These *mitzvos* are as fundamental as the *mitzvos* between man and God.

These *mitzvos* affect every area of life. The halachic details that apply to these *mitzvos* are numerous. However, these *mitzvos* are only discussed here briefly. When one has a question regarding any of these *halachos*, he should consult with an expert in this area.

Gemilus chasadim (Acts of kindness)

18.   It is a mitzvah to assist one's fellowman in all possible ways: through financial or other material support, giving helpful advice, offering encouragement, etc.

It is written in *Mishnah Pe'ah* that *gemilus chasadim* is one of the *mitzvos* for which a person is rewarded in this world, while the principal reward awaits him in the World to Come. Kind deeds and benevolent behavior towards others are the cornerstones of a society which lives according to the Torah and its ethical imperatives.

Gemilus chasadim encompasses many *mitzvos*. These include charity, providing for a bride, visiting the sick, consoling mourners, etc. Some of these *mitzvos* are discussed below.

Tzedakah (Charity)

19.   It is a mitzvah to give charity to the poor. This is derived from the verses, "Open your hand generously to him" (*Devarim* 15:8), and, "Let your brother live alongside with you" (*Vayikra* 25:36). We are commanded to help our fellow Jews by supplying their various needs.

There is great merit to acting charitably. The Torah states about Avraham, "For I know him, that he will command his children... to do deeds of charity" (*Bereshis* 18:19). God praised Avraham for instructing his children to act charitably.

The merit is even greater if one does the charitable act secretly, without any-one knowing about it.

Everyone, including those who are impoverished, is obligated to give charity. Everyone has to give charity according to his ability and income. The rich have to give more, and the poor have to give as much as they can.

Charity has to be given gladly, with a warm countenance. The Torah instructs us, "Do not feel bad about giving to him; since God your Lord will then bless you in all your endeavors, in whatever you do" (*Devarim* 15:10).

20.   One who made a verbal commitment to give a certain sum to charity must fulfill his commitment without delay. Similarly, one who pledged charity in synagogue (e.g. when he received an *aliyah*), must fulfill his pledge. He may not change the cause or delay giving the donation. Even a person who decided to donate a specific sum to charity without making a verbal commitment must carry out his decision.

In addition to assisting individuals so they can live at their normal standard of living, every person is obligated to support charitable organizations and Torah institutions. This support enables these institutions to accomplish their vital tasks and to expand the range of their activities.

Many people contribute one-tenth of all their earnings to these distinguished causes. The mitzvah to separate one-tenth of one's income and designate it for charity is called *ma'asar kesafim* ("tithing money").

Bikur cholim (Visiting the sick)

21.   It is a mitzvah to visit the sick. The purpose of this mitzvah is to de-termine what the sick person needs, to provide him with it, and to pray for the patient's speedy recovery. The visitor must speak gently and wisely to the patient, so as to relieve his worries and lift his spirits.

22.   If visits are not a nuisance or a bother to the patient, it is best to visit him often.

If the visit is difficult for the patient (e.g. he is very sick, or he cannot speak), the visitor should not enter the patient's room. In this situation one should only inquire about the patient's health and needs, and continue praying for the patient.

Gossip and slander

23. The Torah commands us, "Do not go around as a gossiper among your people" (*Vayikra* 19:16). This verse forbids us to gossip. One may not say, "Mr. X said such-and-such about you," or, "Mr. Y did such-and-such to you." This rule applies even if the details mentioned are true, and do not reflect negatively on the person being spoken about. Anything that is likely to result in hatred or dissension may not be said.

Lashon ha-ra (slandering someone) is an even greater sin than gossiping. The prohibition against slandering is included in the verse quoted above. Halachically, slander is anything derogatory which is said about others. Slander includes any words, tales, etc. which may cause loss, fear, sorrow, or shame to the person who is being spoken about. Halachically, slander may be something which is completely true. One who includes lies or exaggerations with the slander is called a *motzi shem ra* ("one who gives another a bad name"). The sin of *motzi shem ra* is far greater than that of slander.

One must avoid saying things which may cause slander to be spoken. For example, one should not praise a person in the presence of his enemies. One is forbidden to listen to gossip and slander. If one did hear gossip or slander, he may not believe it.

There are books which discuss these grave prohibitions in detail, such as *Chafetz Chaim*, *Shemiras Ha-Lashon*, and *Guard Your Tongue*. Abstaining from prohibited talk and relating positively to one's fellowman without looking for his faults and shortcomings, are the conduits that lead to a life of good deeds.

Lending money

24. "When you lend money to My people, to the poor man among you" (*Shemos* 22:24). It is a great mitzvah to lend money to a person in need. Lending money is one type of *gemilus chasadim*.

The Rambam classifies different types of charity. Helping a person whose financial situation has deteriorated by extending a loan to him is classified as one of the greatest types of charity. Extending a loan can save a person from bankruptcy or destitution.

There are various places where our sages mention the importance of extending loans, and laud those who extend loans. For example, our sages state that,

"One who extends a loan to a poor person in his hour of need is the one referred to in the verse, 'then you will call out, and God will answer' (*Yeshayahu* 58:9)." (*Sanhedrin* 76b)

There are priorities regarding to whom one should extend a loan: a poor person precedes one who is well-to-do; family members precede non-family members; residents of one's town precede residents of other places.

The prohibition to charge interest

25. "Do not take from him interest and increase, and you shall fear your God, and let your brother live with you. Do not give him your money with interest, and do not give him your food with increase" (*Vayikra* 25:36-37).

The Torah forbids us to extend loans to other Jews with interest payments. The Torah also forbids us to take out loans from Jews if there are interest payments due. It is also forbidden to accept anything of value or any form of benefit in return for extending a loan. (This applies while the loan is extended, as well as after the loan has been paid.) There are many complex *halachos* pertaining to paying and receiving interest. Therefore it is advisable to study these *halachos* well.

Due to the way business is transacted today, the prohibition to charge and pay interest is often transgressed. Interest payments are often a factor when dealing with contracts, payment obligations, pension funds, various insurance payments, etc. Therefore, it is very important to consult with a *rav* who is an expert in these *halachos* regarding any questionable situation that arises. The *rav* will be able to advise the person as to the halachically correct way to execute these business transactions.

One must also be careful not to transgress the prohibition to pay interest when purchasing items which will be paid for according to a payment schedule. Very often, the item's price depends upon whether the consumer pays cash or with some form of credit (credit cards, post-dated checks, etc.). The *halachah* sets forth clear guidelines regarding how to proceed in these situations. Similarly, there are detailed *halachos* regarding when it is permitted to pay for goods or services in advance, so as to receive the goods or services at a cheaper price.

In many situations it is permitted to set up a *heter iskah*. A *heter iskah* is a legal document through which the money is not given as a loan but rather as a combination of an investment and loan in the business deal that the one receiving the money is investing in. The investor then receives a percentage of the profits instead of receiving interest payments. It is very important to receive detailed instructions from an expert in this area regarding how to conduct business transactions without transgressing the severe prohibitions of collecting and paying interest.

There is another, related prohibition. This prohibition is referred to as *ribbis devarim*, paying interest with things rather than with money. For example, a debtor may not show any special honor to his creditor. Rather, the debtor may only honor the creditor in the same manner as when he did not owe his creditor money. There are additional details pertaining to *ribbis devarim*. It is advisable to familiarize oneself with these *halachos*.

Dinei Mamonos
(Halachos pertaining to business transactions)

26. The *halachos* pertaining to business transactions are discussed in detail in *Choshen Mishpat* (one of four parts the *Shulchan Aruch*). The *halachos* discussed in *Choshen Mishpat* pertain to all types of financial dealings, including all types of financial claims and fines.

Each person must be aware that the Torah's laws encompass any question or situation which may occur. Our obligation to lead lives according to the Torah's laws includes conducting our financial affairs totally in accordance with Halachah. Therefore, when any halachic question arises pertaining to one's financial affairs, or when any conflict arises relating to a financial issue, one must ascertain what the *halachah* is in the particular situation. Similarly, if one must seek outside mediation, he must do so through a rabbinical court, and resolve the issue according to Halachah.

Our sages teach us that, "Your friend's money should be as dear to you as your own" (*Avos* 2:17). This is an important principle, which guides us regarding safeguarding our fellow Jew's money. This principle includes acting responsibly, so as not to diminish another's funds. It is within this framework that we will briefly discuss a number of related topics.

Saving a person and his money, and returning lost property

27.   One who sees a person who is in danger or who is in a difficult situation must save the person. Saving a life is an incomparably great mitzvah, about which our sages comment, "Whoever saves one Jewish life, it is as if he saved the entire world." One is not required to endanger his own life to save another persons life.

Similarly, it is a great mitzvah for one who sees a person in danger of losing his money to save the money and to return it to its owner.

One who finds some possession with an identifying mark must return the object to its owner. However, one does not have to concern himself with objects which the owner set down intending to come back and retrieve (i.e. the objects were not lost).

There are many detailed *halachos* pertaining to returning lost property. Therefore, one must consult with a *rav* whenever one is unsure how to proceed.

Being careful to avoid harming others

28.   Each person is obligated to refrain from harming others directly or indirectly or causing them pain. This includes placing a stumbling block in front of someone (both a physical stumbling block, as well as offering inappropriate advice). This is derived from the verse, "do not place a stumbling block before a blind man" (*Vayikra* 19:14).

One is forbidden to cause someone else financial harm, even indirectly and even if he intends to pay for the damage. Similarly, one may not harm others or their possessions.

It is forbidden to throw pieces of glass or any type of object in a place where people walk. This is because passersby are likely to trip and get hurt.

It is forbidden to destroy food (i.e. to render it inedible), utensils, or anything from which people might derive benefit. This prohibition is known as *"bal tashchis."* This name is derived from the verse, *lo tashchis es eitzah li-nedo'ach alav garzen* ("do not destroy its trees by swinging an axe against them," *Devarim* 20:19).

The Torah explicitly forbids mistreating animals. The Torah only permits killing animals if people will derive some benefit from doing so. For example, one may slaughter fowl and other animals for food, or one may kill animals which endanger or bother people. However one may not harm animals in any way unless there is a truly justifiable reason.

Fencing off dangerous areas

29. The Torah states, "When you build a new house, and you shall make a fence for your roof" (*Devarim* 22:8). This verse clearly states that it is a mitzvah to build a fence around a roof which people go up on and use. This is due to the possibility that someone might fall from the roof. The fence must be at least ten *tefachim* high. The fence must also be sturdy enough to support a person leaning against it.

One is also obligated to build a fence around any area which is ten or more *tefachim* above the surrounding area, and which people use. Examples of such an area are balconies, stairwells, etc. Similarly, one must either cover or erect a fence around an open pit. Once again, this is to eliminate the possibility that someone might fall into the pit. This mitzvah is derived from the verse, "And you shall not place blood in your house" (*Devarim* 22:8). These words teach us that one must not allow potentially dangerous situations to exist on his property, so that he will not indirectly harm someone.

Respecting other people's property

30. It is forbidden to borrow someone else's possession without first receiving permission from the owner. This rule even applies if one intends to return the possession immediately after using it. If a person has someone else's property or money in his possession, he must return the property or repay the money.

One who borrows or rents an object must only use the object in the manner specified by the owner. Furthermore, the person may not lend the object to others without the owner's permission.

One who is renting or borrowing an object must be careful that the object is not harmed, lost, or stolen.

Any type of employee who works for others must perform his duties faithfully and honestly. Employees must be aware that their working hours are set aside solely for work. Furthermore, employees must make every effort to perform their duties well during all the hours for which they are paid by their employer.

"On that day you shall give him his wages"

31.   The Torah states, "On that day you shall give him his wages, and the sun shall not set upon him" (*Devarim* 24:15). This refers to a worker who finished working at sunrise or during the day before sunset. An employer is obligated to pay his employee on the same day the employee fulfills his duties. If the employee was hired for the day, and he completed his job that day, the employer must pay him before sunset of that same day. If the employee was hired to work at night, then the employee must pay him during the course of the night. This same rule applies regarding an employee who was hired on a weekly or monthly basis. If the employee completed his workweek during the day, the employer must pay him on that very day. If the employee's workweek ends during the night, the employer must pay him before the night is over.

If an employer arranges to pay his employees at a different set time, or if it is well known that the employer pays his employees on a certain day (e.g. the first of the month), this *halachah* does not apply. This is because the employees were aware of these conditions when they were hired.

The obligation to pay an employee on that same day or that same night also applies when taking an object from a craftsman or repairman (e.g. after the object was repaired). However, if a payment schedule was set up that did not require the person to pay for the service immediately, then the obligation to pay on that same day or night does not apply.

The *halachos* pertaining to negotiations

32.   When dealing with financial matters one is obligated to conduct his affairs honestly and in a straightforward fashion. One is forbidden to deceive, trick, or lie to the person with whom he is dealing.

The Torah clearly states, "and when you sell merchandise to your fellow, or buy merchandise from your fellow, do not aggrieve one another" (*Vayikra* 25:14). This verse mentions both the buyer and the seller. Both the buyer and the seller are obligated not to deceive the other one. Our sages state that the first question one is asked when called before the Heavenly Court is, "Did you buy and sell faithfully" (*Shabbos* 31a).

The prohibition of deceiving people applies to all financial dealings, including sales, rentals, contracting, barter, etc.

One may not deceive customers regarding the quality of his merchandise. For example, one may not paint old utensils so they appear new, mix inferior produce with more expensive produce and then sell the inferior produce at a high price, etc. Similarly, it is forbidden to advertise merchandise at prices which no longer apply.

One must think before he speaks and take responsibility for the words he utters. For example, a merchant who negotiated with a customer and agreed to sell him merchandise should not go back on his offer even before the sale was completed.

Weights and measures

33.   "Do not have two stones in your bag, a large one and a small one. Do not have in your house two ephahs, a large one and a small one" (*Devarim* 25:13-14). This verse teaches that a person's weights and measures must be absolutely correct. The verse, "you shall do no wrong in judgement, in measures of length, weight, or content" (*Vayikra* 19:35), teaches that it is forbidden to measure merchandise incorrectly.

These transgressions are very severe, and very difficult to atone for. One who sins in this manner generally does it repeatedly, and does not know whom he cheated, and to whom he owes money. Some halachic authorities maintain that one should not have incorrect weights or measures (or inaccurate instruments for weighing and measuring) in his house, even if the person does not intend to use them.

Modes of behavior within a group; improving one's character traits

34.   "You shall not hurt one another's feelings, and you shall fear your God" (*Vayikra* 25:17). This verse warns us not to hurt another person in non-physical ways, even if the other person will not suffer a financial loss as a result of our actions. One must behave in an honorable and upright manner. This includes not providing misleading information or lying.

It is also forbidden to embarrass another person or cause him pain. This rule applies to how one relates to his spouse and other family members, as well as to how one relates to non-family members. Our sages teach that, "one who embarrasses another person in public has no portion in the World to Come" (*Bava Metzia* 58b). This illustrates how severe a transgression it is to intentionally embarrass someone. It is also forbidden to call someone by a derogatory nickname, even if the person is accustomed to being called by that name.

35. One must refrain from speaking improperly. This includes refraining from cursing and using other improper language. Speaking in a refined manner helps purify one's soul and prevents a decline in one's spiritual level.

It is preferable not to make unnecessary promises or vows, since it is a serious sin not to fulfill a promise or vow.

One is obligated to foster positive character traits, such as modesty, compassion, happiness, philanthropy, etc. Possessing these character traits guarantees one a life of purity and integrity. On the other hand, one should avoid negative character traits, such as cruelty, anger, jealousy, bearing grudges, seeking revenge, laziness, conceitedness, and envy.

The Rambam sets forth a detailed program for improving one's character traits (*Hilchos De'os*, Chapters 1,2,3,5,6). The Rambam explains the positive aspects of various character traits, human attributes, and what one should embrace or distance himself from as he travels through life. One who studies these chapters thoroughly will be empowered to embrace an exalted life of purity lived according to the Torah's precepts.

The mitzvah to sanctify God's Name

36. It is a great mitzvah to sanctify God's Name. One who faithfully and wholeheartedly observes the *mitzvos*, even when self-sacrifice is required, is capable of sanctifying God's Name with every step he takes. Faithfully and modestly leading a life of Torah and mitzvah observance causes others to love those who study and observe the Torah. This is what the prophet Michah proclaimed in God's Name: "a man told you what is good and what God asks of you, just to do justice and acts of loving-kindness, and to walk modestly with your God" (*Michah* 6:8).

Chapter Thirty-Nine

The Halachos Pertaining to Mourning

A transient world and an eternal world

"Remember your Creator in your youth before the days of evil come upon you and those years arrive about which you will say, 'I desire them not.' The dust returns to the earth from where it came, and the spirit returns to God Who gave it" (*Koheles* 12:1-7).

Our world is transient. Suddenly one is summoned to stand before his Creator. Rabbeinu Tam remarks in *Sefer Ha-Yashar* (*Sha'ar* 12):

> This world is similar to an underground cave in the desert. Its occupant imagines that the cave is the total sum of existence, since he never saw all that exists outside of the cave. Were he to leave the cave, he would discover the existence of expansive lands, the sky, oceans, stars and heavenly bodies. A man in this world imagines that this is the only kind of existence. Were he to leave it, though, he would see the expanse of the World to Come, and would be thunderstruck by its awesomeness.

The World to Come is eternal, not transient. Reflecting upon both worlds, the words of the Mishnah are easily understood: "Rabbi Ya'akov says: This world is similar to a corridor leading to the World to Come. Prepare yourself in the corridor before you enter the palace" (*Avos* 4:21).

The words of the Mishnah teach that truly living wisely involves gathering the spiritual treasures of Torah and *mitzvos*. The following verse also teaches this lesson: "The wise will take with him *mitzvos*" (*Mishlei* 10:8). One fulfills his purpose in life by performing *mitzvos*. Thus, when one will present himself to his Creator he will have a treasure-trove full of eternal treasures and bountiful reward.

This chapter discusses the *halachos* which deal with a man's departure from this world and the *halachos* that apply to the deceased's close relatives.

Please note that only the most common *halachos* are discussed here. If any questionable or unusual circumstances arise, a *rav* must be consulted. There are many comprehensive books that discuss these *halachos* such as *Gesher Ha-Chaim* and *Penei Baruch*. These books provide a comprehensive, thorough discussion of this topic.

In addition to the general *halachos* discussed here, there are many customs pertaining to mourning. Different communities observe different customs. Each person should observe his community's customs.

The moment of death

1.   It is a great merit for a person to die while repenting for his sins. There-fore, a seriously ill person who does not know what the next day may bring should confess his sins in detail and repent wholeheartedly before his Creator. If the patient cannot confess verbally, he should confess in his heart. If the patient has difficulty confessing, one should read the *Viduy* in front of him. If the patient can only utter a few words, he should say, "If, Heaven forbid, I die, may my death atone for my sins."

2.   It is important for others to remind the ill person to confess. This should be done in a sensitive, wise way, so the patient will not become frightened or brokenhearted, and his health will not be adversely affected.

3.   When a person is nearing death, the people who are with him may not leave him. It is a mitzvah to be at a person's side the moment his soul departs.

Whenever possible, all medical care and efforts to save the person must be continued until there is no hope of saving him. However, one may not touch a dying person (unless one does so in an effort to save him), so as to avoid inadvertently hastening his death.

4.   At the moment the soul departs, those standing with the person recite the first verse of *Shema* (*Shema Yisrael Hashem Elokeinu, Hashem Echad*). Other verses are also recited.

The deceased may not be left alone. The person who remains with the deceased recites chapters from *Tehillim* and ensures that candles are constantly lit near the body. One may not eat in the same room as the deceased.

When a person dies, his relatives are required to observe the *halachos* of *aninus*. This period is followed by the period when the *halachos* of mourning are observed. These *halachos* are discussed according to the order in which they are observed.

Relatives for whom one is required to mourn

5.   There are seven relatives for whom one must mourn. They are one's:

A. father, B. mother, C. son, D. daughter, E. brother (this includes a half-brother), F. sister (this includes a half-sister), and G. spouse.

An infant that dies before he is thirty days old is not mourned.

Aninus

6.   One who is required to mourn is called an *onen* during the period before the deceased has been buried. The *halachos* of *aninus* apply to an *onen*.

The *onen* must occupy himself with his deceased relative's burial, ensuring that all the funeral arrangements are taken care of. He must honor the deceased and do everything possible to prevent an autopsy.

7.   The deceased's burial must not be unjustifiably delayed. (This is called *issur ha-lanas ha-mes*.) The funeral may not be postponed to another day unless the delay is done to honor the deceased, i.e. the extra time will allow for a more distinguished funeral. It is best to consult with a *rav* or the *Chevrah Kadisha* (Jewish burial society) concerning this matter.

8.   The halachos of aninus are as follows:

An onen may not join in a meal with friends, or take part in a celebration. Similarly, an onen may not eat meat or drink wine. An onen may not greet others.

An onen is forbidden to have a haircut, shave, bathe or apply body creams and lotions to himself (for more details, see Section 31, below), and may not do work.

An onen who will suffer a financial loss due to the interruption in his business during the week of mourning, or who has partnership obligations, should discuss the matter with a rav before the burial. This is because according to many, the halachos of mourning do not apply before the burial. Therefore, the rav can suggest halachic solutions to the problem at this time.

9.   An *onen* is exempt from observing *mitzvos* and reciting prayers and berachos such as: *Kerias Shema, Shemoneh Esreh, Birkas Ha-mazon*, etc. Although an *onen* is exempt from observing *mitzvos*, he may not transgress any prohibitions. An *onen* should perform *netilas yadayim* before eating a meal, but should not recite the blessing. Similarly, when an *onen* awakens in the morning, he should perform *netilas yadayim*.

10.   As soon as the grave is covered with earth, the mourner stops observing the *halachos* of *aninus* and begins observing the *halachos* of mourning. The mourner does not wear *tefillin* on the day of the burial. He dons them on the following day. If the burial does not take place on the day the deceased passed away, a *rav* should be consulted regarding how the *onen* should proceed.

11.   An *onen* is obligated to observe *mitzvos* on Shabbos. This is because funerals are not held on Shabbos, and an *onen* cannot make arrangements for the burial on Shabbos. An *onen* may eat meat and drink wine on Shabbos, but may not engage in marital relations.

The funeral

> When a person passes away, he goes alone. He is not accompanied by silver, gold, jewels, or pearls, (he is) only (accompanied) by his Torah study and good deeds, as it says, "When you go out, it shall guide you; when you lie down, it shall guard you, and when you awaken, it shall be your conversation." "When you go out, it shall guide you" - in this world; "when you lie down, it shall guard you" - in the grave; "when you awaken, it shall be your conversation" - in the World to Come. (*Avos* 6:9)

12.   Making a funeral is a distinguished mitzvah called *Chesed shel Emes*. This name is derived from the verse, "Do with me kindness and truth (*chesed v'emes*) and do not bury me in Egypt" (*Bereshis* 47:29). In this verse Ya'akov asked Yosef not to bury him in Egypt. As mentioned in Section 6, above, the relatives must honor the deceased by arranging a respectable burial for him.

One may not exceed the permitted expressions of sorrow during the funeral or the period of mourning. One may not cut his skin or face, or tear his hair out as an expression of his sorrow.

The burial is arranged by the *Chevrah Kadisha*, whose members explain to the mourners and family members how to conduct themselves. A few details are discussed below.

13. Those who join a funeral procession recite *Tehillim* 91, *Yoshev b'seser elyon*, which is called the "Psalm of Afflictions." Other appropriate passages may be recited instead, according to the local custom. They pray that God have mercy on the deceased and save him from punishment in the merit of his ancestors. Charity is given during the funeral.

One's behavior during a funeral should be appropriate for the solemn occasion. One should reflect upon the fact that a person's life is transient, and that when he dies he will have to give a reckoning for his deeds before the Heavenly Court. The Torah one studied and the *mitzvos* one observed during his life are the only possessions which will remain with him after he dies. These are the only things for which he will receive reward. "And let the living take it to heart."

14. One who approaches within four *amos* of the deceased must cover his *tzitzis*.

One who sees a funeral procession passing by should accompany it for at least four *amos*. According to some halachic opinions, after accompanying the procession for at least four *amos*, one must remain standing until the funeral procession is out of sight.

Tearing a garment

15. Those who are required to mourn the deceased must make a tear in their clothes. The members of the *Chevrah Kadisha* instruct the mourners how and when to tear their clothes.

Mourners are permitted to change their clothes before the funeral so as not to tear a garment that they do not want to tear.

The mourners recite the blessing, *dayan ha-emes* ("Who is the true Judge"), before tearing the garment.

The garment is torn while the mourner is standing. The garment is torn at the top of the collar, in the front. The garment is torn downwards; not sideways.

16. One who is mourning a parent tears his garment differently from one who is mourning another relative. One who is mourning his parent tears all his garments besides his outer coat and undershirt. (There are various halachic opinions regarding whether or not a *tallis katan* is torn.) The garment is torn on the left side, by hand.

One who is mourning a relative other than a parent (i.e. brother, sister, husband, wife, son, or daughter) only tears one *tefach* on the right side of one garment.

The accepted practice (when mourning a parent as well as when mourning other relatives), is for a member of the *Chevrah Kadisha* to begin the tear with a knife, and for the mourner to continue tearing the garment by hand. A woman begins to tear the garment for a woman mourner.

17. One who is mourning a parent must tear any garment he will be wearing during the week of mourning. The only exception is the garment worn on Shabbos.

One should ask an expert in Halachah when and how the torn garment may be mended. Out of consideration for her dignity, a woman may immediately sew the tear with crooked stitches or may pin the tear together.

The eulogy

> When Shmuel Ha-Katan [one of the *Tanna'im*] died, he was eulogized: "Kings die and leave their crowns to their sons. The wealthy die and leave their wealth to their sons. Shmuel Ha-Katan took all the treasures of the world and went away." (*Semachos* 8)

18. It is a mitzvah to eulogize the deceased before he is buried. The one delivering a eulogy expresses sorrow and grief over the loss of the deceased, and mentions the deceased's fine qualities and good deeds. It is a merit for the deceased if the listeners are inspired to repent and better themselves as a result of hearing the eulogy.

There are certain days and certain times during the year when eulogies are not delivered. In this case a *rav* or members of the *Chevrah Kadisha* present at the funeral will inform those attending how to proceed.

19.   After the grave is covered, those present recite the prayer *Tziduk Ha-din*
("Acknowledging the Judgment") and the mourners recite a special version of *Kaddish, Kaddish d'hu asid l'ischadeta. Tziduk Ha-din* is not recited on
days when *tachanun* is not recited or on Friday afternoon. Different communities observe different customs regarding which prayers are recited during
and after the funeral. The *rav* or members of the *Chevrah Kadisha* provide
guidance in these matters.

After the funeral

20.   After the funeral, the men who are present stand in two rows (at least
four *amos* from the graves) and recite the words *Ha-Makom yenachem
eschem b'soch she'ar avlei Tzion v'Yerushalayim* ("May the Almighty comfort
you among all those who mourn [the destruction of] Zion and Jerusalem")
as the male mourners pass between the two rows with their shoes removed. There are other customs concerning this rite.

One returning from a funeral or a cemetery must perform *netilas yadayim*
pouring the water on each hand three times. It is customary not to enter a
house before one washes his hands.

Tum'ah and *Kohanim*

21.   As mentioned in Chapter 38, Section 16, a *Kohen* may not become *tamei*
(ritually impure). Therefore, a *Kohen* may not enter a house where there
is a corpse, or approach a grave. However, it is a mitzvah for a *Kohen* to become *tamei* for a deceased relative.

22.   It is a mitzvah for a *Kohen* to become *tamei* for seven relatives. They are
his: A. father, B. mother, C. son, D. daughter (the latter two only if they
died thirty or more days after birth), E. paternal brother (but not his maternal
half-brother), F. paternal unmarried sister (in this case one should consult with
a *rav*), G. wife. These are not the exact same seven relatives for which every
Jew mourns.

23.   A *Kohen* may only become *tamei* for a deceased relative whose body is
whole and intact. According to some halachic opinions this rule only
applies if the deceased's body became incomplete at or after the moment
of death. According to other halachic opinions this rule applies to a body
that became incomplete while the person was alive.

A *Kohen* whose relative passed away should consult with a *rav* concerning how he should observe the *halachos* of mourning, e.g. if he may enter the cemetery during the funeral, etc.

Se'udas hav'ra'ah (Meal of consolation)

24. The mourner's first meal after the deceased is buried is called the *se'udas hav'ra'ah*, the meal of consolation. This meal should not come from the mourner's means. The mourner's neighbors should provide this meal. Women provide the meal for women mourners.

25. It is customary to offer the mourner round bread or cookies, peeled, hard-boiled eggs, and beans. This is because these foods do not have a "mouth," like a mourner whose grief has made him speechless. Another reason for this custom is that round foods symbolize mourning as rolling through the world.

A mourner who was not sent a *se'udas hav'ra'ah*, is not required to go hungry. He may eat his own food.

Shiv'ah (The one-week period of mourning)

26. The *halachos* of mourning apply as soon as the grave is covered with soil. Below, the *halachos* of mourning that apply during the *shiv'ah* (the first week following the burial) are discussed briefly. A number of these *halachos* also apply after the *shiv'ah*.

27. The mourner does not leave his house during the *shiv'ah*. A *minyan* gathers in the mourner's house, and the mourner recites his prayers there. If the only way the mourner can join a *minyan* is if he goes to synagogue (i.e. a *minyan* cannot be organized in his house), the mourner should consult a *rav* regarding how to proceed.

A mourner may not sit on a regular chair or bench. He may only sit close to the ground.

28. A mourner may not wear leather shoes or sandals. This *halachah* applies to shoes that have leather soles, as well as to those which only have leather uppers or straps.

A mourner may not greet others and inquire about their welfare, and others may not greet him.

29. Torah study gladdens the heart. This is derived from the verse, "The laws of Hashem are upright, they gladden the heart" (*Tehillim* 19:9). A mourner is prohibited to rejoice. Therefore, he may only study those sections of Torah concerning mourning. For example, the mourner may study the *Book of Iyov*, the sections of rebuke in *Yirmeyahu*, the third chapter of *Mo'ed Katan*, the *halachos* pertaining to mourning, etc. A mourner may also study ethical works which inspire one to repent and fear God.

30. A mourner may not launder or iron his clothes, nor may others do so for him. A mourner may not wear freshly laundered clothes and he certainly may not wear new clothes. However, if a mourner's clothes become dirty or sweaty, he may change them. The mourner's sheets and towels should not be washed or changed.

31. A mourner may not bathe, even with cold water. However, he may wash his face, hands, and feet with cold water. Washing with warm water is prohibited. This *halachah* applies to bathing for pleasure. However, a mourner may wash dirt off himself, or wash himself for health reasons.

A mourner may not apply lotions, oils, or perfumes to any part of his body. However, a mourner may use cleansing lotions to remove dirt or maintain his health.

32. A mourner is forbidden to have a haircut or to shave.

A mourner may not trim his nails. This rule applies to trimming his nails with any implement (e.g. a scissors, a nail clipper, etc.). However, a mourner may peel his nails with his hands. A mourner may also bite his nails.

A mourner may not have marital relations.

A mourner may not engage in business. A mourner may do housework, like baking, cooking, and cleaning.

33. The mirrors and pictures are covered in a mourner's home. A candle is lit throughout the *shiv'ah* for the benefit of the deceased's soul. The candle should remain lit on the Shabbos during the *shiv'ah*. The candle should be lit in the room where the deceased passed away. If this is not possible, the candle should be lit where the deceased lived.

34. A mourner does not publicly observe the *halachos* of mourning on the Shabbos during the *shiv'ah*. Therefore, he may wear leather shoes, change to Shabbos clothes (but not new clothes), and attend synagogue.

A mourner may not have marital relations on the Shabbos during the *shiv'ah*. In addition to studying those sections of Torah that are permitted during the *shiv'ah*, the mourner may review the weekly Torah portion twice and the *Targum* once.

35.   After *Shacharis* on the seventh day of the *shiv'ah*, those attending the *minyan* in the mourner's home recite the verse *Ha-Makom yenachem...* Then the mourner concludes the *shiv'ah*. There is a halachic rule that, "part of a day is considered like a whole day." In this case, the mourner sat *shiv'ah* for part of the seventh day, so he is permitted to end this seven-day period of mourning. For example, if the *shiv'ah* began on Monday (whether the deceased was buried Sunday night or sometime on Monday), the mourner ends his *shiv'ah* on Sunday morning, which is the seventh day after beginning this period of mourning.

Prayers recited during the *shiv'ah*

36.   It is a mitzvah to participate in a *minyan* at a mourner's home. A *sefer Torah* is brought to the mourner's home for *Kerias Ha-Torah*, which should be read at least three times during the *shiv'ah*. The mourners recite *Kaddish*, and the deceased's sons lead the services. Among Sephardic Jews the deceased's sons do not lead the services during the *shiv'ah*.

37.   At the end of *Shacharis* and *Ma'ariv* (some people include *Minchah*) in the mourner's home, *Tehillim* 49 is recited (this passage begins *La-mena-tze'ach li-venei Korach mizmor, shim'u zos*). On days when *tachanun* is not recited as well as on *Motza'ei Shabbos*, *Tehillim* 16 is recited instead (this passage begins *Michtam l'David shamereini Kel*). Sephardic Jews recite the *Hashkavah* at the end of the service.

38.   *Tachanun, Kel erech apayim,* and *La-menatze'ach mizmor l'David ya'ancha* are not recited in a mourner's home. According to some halachic opinions, the verse *Va-ani zos berisi* in *u'Va l'Tzion* is also not recited in a mourner's home. There are different customs regarding whether the *Birkas Kohanim* and *Hallel* (if the *shiv'ah* includes *Rosh Chodesh*) are recited in a mourner's home.

39.   *Mishnayos* are studied in the mourner's house after services, for the benefit of the deceased. It is customary to study chapters of *Mishnayos* which begin with the letters of the deceased's name, as well as *Mishnayos* 4-7 in Chapter 7 of Tractate *Mikva'os*. These four *Mishnayos* begin with the letters of the word *neshamah* ("soul"). If these *Mishnayos* are too difficult, other *Mishnayos* should be studied. (Studying any *Mishnayos* benefits the deceased.) It is customary to recite the prayer *Ana* after studying the *Mishnayos*. This prayer is printed in volumes of *Mishnayos*.

Some communities observe the custom to eulogize the deceased, and to deliver inspirational speeches in the mourner's house during the *shiv'ah*. Different communities observe different customs concerning the prayers and practices during the *shiv'ah*. One should consult with a *rav* regarding how to observe his community's customs.

Prayers and merits to elevate the deceased's soul

40. The Midrash relates that the merit of a son's *Kaddish* greatly assists a deceased parent in his heavenly judgment. Reciting *Kaddish* is a way of sanctifying God's Name. *Kaddish* is a request that God's Name be glorified and sanctified in the entire universe, and that everyone recognize His sovereignty and acknowledge Him. God's Name is sanctified when a son recites *Kaddish*. The son's *Kaddish* also increases merit for the deceased parent for whom it is being recited. If there is no son to recite *Kaddish*, *Kaddish Yasom* is recited by another male relative.

Mourners recite *Kaddish* for eleven months.

41. The deceased accrues additional merit when his son receives the *maftir aliyah* during *Kerias Ha-Torah* on Shabbos. The deceased also accrues merit when his son leads the service during his year of mourning, particularly the *Ma'ariv* service on *Motza'ei Shabbos*.

One does not lead the service on Shabbos or *Yom Tov* during his year-long period of mourning. Similarly, one does not lead the recitation of *Hallel* or *Musaf* for *Rosh Chodesh* during his year-long period of mourning. There are various customs regarding whether or not a mourner should lead any services on *Rosh Chodesh* (*Shacharis* until *Hallel*, *Minchah*, and *Ma'ariv*), during Chanukah, etc. One should observe the local custom.

42. One can honor his parents after their death, and accrue great merits in the eternal world on their behalf. The *Zohar* in *Parashas Bechukosai* teaches that when a child observes the Torah, he is honoring his parents. This is even true after their death. Thus, parents accrue merits in the spiritual world when their child observes *mitzvos* and performs good deeds.

Jewish sources relate that when a son intensifies his Torah study, his parents' souls accrue great merit. Similarly, a father receives great honor in the heavenly yeshiva when his son thinks of new explanations for Torah passages.

Comforting mourners

43. "It is preferable to go to a house of mourning than to go to a house of feasting, for this is the end of man and the living will take it to heart" (*Koheles* 7:2).

Comforting mourners is included in the mitzvah of *gemilus chasadim* (performing acts of loving-kindness). The Torah relates, "And it was after the death of Avraham that God blessed his son Yitzchak" (*Bereshis* 25:11). This verse hints to the mitzvah of comforting mourners.

44. One does not say "Hello" or "Good-bye" when entering or leaving a mourner's house. This is because mourners may not be greeted.

Visitors should not speak until the mourner begins a conversation. Visitors should encourage and console the mourner. Visitors should encourage the mourner to accept the heavenly decree with love.

When a visitor leaves a mourner he says, *Ha-Makom yenachem oscha b'soch she'ar avlei Tzion v'Yerushalayim* ("May the Almighty comfort you among all those who mourn [the destruction of] Zion and Jerusalem"). Some Sephardic Jews say *Min Ha-shamayim tenuchamu...* ("May Heaven comfort you...") instead of *Ha-Makom yenachem...*

45. One who did not comfort a mourner during the *shiv'ah* may express his condolences during the twenty-three-day period following the *shiv'ah* (this period is called the *sheloshim*). Similarly, one who meets a mourner during the *sheloshim* should express his condolences if he has not yet done so. (One who meets a mourner after the *sheloshim* only says, "May you be comforted.") One who is mourning his parent may receive condolences throughout the twelve months of mourning.

Sheloshim

46. The *sheloshim* continues after the *shiv'ah* ends, and lasts for 23 days.

The following *halachos* apply to the mourner during this period.

47. The mourner may not have a haircut or shave.

The mourner may not trim his nails with a nail scissors or any other implement. However, the mourner may peel his nails with his hands or bite them
with his teeth.

It is customary not to bathe for pleasure, even when using cold water. One
may bathe for health reasons, or to wash away sweat. Sephardic Jews do not
observe this custom, and bathe for pleasure after the *shiv'ah*.

Mourners should not wear freshly laundered and ironed clothes during the
sheloshim. A mourner may wear freshly laundered clothes that another person
wore for a short time. Sephardic Jews permit wearing freshly laundered
clothes after the *shiv'ah*.

48. A mourner does not take part in celebrations where there is music or
dancing (e.g. weddings, parties, etc.).

Although people should not greet a mourner and inquire about his welfare, a
mourner may inquire after the welfare of others. A mourner may reply if he
was greeted.

It is customary for a mourner to sit in a different place in the synagogue during the *sheloshim*. There are different customs concerning whether or not this
applies to Shabbos as well. The mourner should not take a seat closer to the
mizrach (eastern) wall in the synagogue.

The laws of mourning during holidays and *Yamim Tovim*

49. The holidays (Pesach, Shavuos, Succos, Rosh Hashana and Yom Kippur)
annul the *shiv'ah* or *sheloshim*. This means that one who is in the middle
of either his *shiv'ah* or *sheloshim* when one of the holidays begins, has that
period of mourning cut short. This rule applies if one began the period of
mourning a short while before the holiday started, as well as if the holiday
occurred in the middle of the period of mourning. For example, if the holiday
begins the evening after the mourner ends his *shiv'ah*, the *sheloshim* period is
annulled. This is because the mourner began the *sheloshim* period the morning
before the holiday began. Similarly if the mourner began the *shiv'ah* a few
hours or days before one of the holidays begins, the *shiv'ah* ends when the
holiday begins.

50. The holidays only annul a period of mourning which began before the
holiday started. If the period of mourning commenced after the holiday

started, the holiday does not annul it. For example, if the deceased was buried during *Chol Ha-mo'ed*, the *shiv'ah* begins after the holiday ends, and lasts for seven days. However, even though the *shiv'ah* begins after the holiday, the *sheloshim* is calculated from the day of the funeral.

When a holiday annuls the *shiv'ah*, the mourners should consult a *rav* regarding how to count the *sheloshim*, as these *halachos* are very detailed.

A recent report and a belated report

51. Halachically, a "recent report" is one which is received within thirty days of the occurrence. If one receives a recent report that a relative for whom he is required to mourn has passed away, he must observe all the *halachos* of mourning.

Halachically, a "belated report" is one which arrives more than thirty days after the occurrence. If one receives a belated report that a relative for whom he is required to mourn has passed away, he only observes the *halachos* of mourning for a short time. There are numerous *halachos* pertaining to a belated report. Therefore, one should consult a *rav* regarding how to proceed in this situation.

The twelve-month period of mourning

52. Most relatives are only mourned for one month. Parents, however, are mourned for twelve months. Twelve months of mourning are even observed during a leap year (a Jewish leap year has thirteen months).

53. One who is mourning his parents does not cut his hair, even after the *sheloshim*. The mourner may cut his hair when it grows long enough that his friends would comment on it.

One who is mourning his parents does not wear new clothes during the twelve months of mourning. However, the mourner may wear new clothes if another person wears them first.

54. A mourner does not participate in a wedding celebration. The mourner may attend the wedding ceremony, but he may not participate in the celebration. A relative whose absence will cause the wedding celebrants sorrow should consult a *rav* regarding how to proceed.

One should not greet a mourner during the entire twelve months of mourning. As is mentioned in Section 48, above, a mourner may greet others, and may respond if he is greeted. There are different customs concerning how the mourner should proceed if he is greeted on Shabbos.

As mentioned in Section 48, above, the mourner does not sit in his usual place in the synagogue. There are various customs concerning sitting in his usual place on Shabbos.

Erecting a monument

55.   The deceased's family is obligated to erect a monument upon the grave.
There are various customs concerning erecting a monument. Some people begin working on the monument after the *shiv'ah*, and complete it at the end of the *sheloshim*. Others erect the monument at the end of the twelve-month period. There are other customs as well.

Some people eulogize the deceased when the monument is dedicated.

The anniversary of the death (*Yahrtzeit*)

56.   A number of customs are observed every year on the anniversary of a relative's death. These are mentioned below.

On the Shabbos before the anniversary, a male relative receives an *aliyah* (if it is possible, the person should receive the *maftir aliyah*). Some people observe the custom of leading the Shabbos services. Others only lead *Musaf*. Many people observe the custom of leading *Ma'ariv* on the *Motza'ei Shabbos* preceding the anniversary. Each community has additional customs that its members should observe.

57.   On the actual anniversary the deceased's son should lead the services and recite *Kaddish*. If the Torah is read on that day, the son receives an *aliyah*.

It is customary to study *Mishnayos* on the anniversary date. Before one begins, he states that he is studying for the merit of his deceased relative. After studying, one should recite the prayer *Ana*, which is printed in volumes of *Mishnayos*. Some people observe the custom to study chapters of *Mishnayos* which begin with the letters of the deceased's name, and the letters that form the word *neshamah* ("soul," this custom is discussed in Section 39, above). Sephardic Jews have a *Hashkavah* for the merit of the deceased.

A memorial candle is lit for the merit of the deceased.

58.   It is customary to visit the graves of deceased relatives on the anniversary of their death. It is also customary to recite the following chapters from *Tehillim*, in the order listed: 33, 16, 17, 77, 91, 104, 130. These are followed by the sections from chapter 119 which begin with the letters of the deceased's name and the letters of the word *neshamah*. (*Tehillim* 119 consists of different sections, each eight verses long. All the verses in each section begin with a different Hebrew letter. For example, all the verses in the first section begin with the letter *alef*, the first Hebrew letter.)

The chapters of *Tehillim*, as well as other prayers which are recited in the cemetery are available in small booklets.

* * *

As mentioned at the beginning of this chapter, only the most common *halachos* are discussed here.

"May death be swallowed up, and may Hashem wipe the tears from every face."

We will conclude this section with the final article from the Thirteen Articles of Faith:

> I believe with total faith that the dead will come to life when the Creator, may His Name be blessed, wills it, and may His remembrance be glorified forever until eternity.

Hebrew
Source Notes

מקורות הלכתיים

מובאים כאן מקורות ההלכה משולחן־ערוך חלק אורח־חיים ומהמשנה־ברורה.

פענוח ראשי־התיבות הוא כדלהלן:

סי' = סימן, סע' = סעיף, משנ"ב = משנה ברורה, ס"ק = סעיף קטן. לדוגמא: סי' ל"א סע' ב' במשנ"ב ס"ק י"א, פירושו: סימן ל"א סעיף ב' במשנה־ברורה סעיף קטן י"א.

"ביאור הלכה" ו"שער הציון" הם שני חיבורים נוספים, שחוברו ע"י מחבר ה"משנה ברורה". שלושת החיבורים מהווים יחידה אחת והם נדפסו יחד עם שולחן ערוך חלק אורח־חיים. מספר פעמים צויינו בספר כמקורות, גם ספרים אלו.

מן הראוי לברר את ההלכה במקורה, בהתאם למקורות המצויינים כאן.

פרק א

1. סי' א' סעיף א'. 2. סי' א' במשנ"ב ס"ק י'. 3. סי' א' במשנ"ב ס"ק ח'. 3. סי' ד' במשנ"ב ס"ק י'. 4. סי' א' משנ"ב ס"ק ב'. 5. פרטים נוספים בסי' ד' סעיף י"ג ובמשנ"ב ס"ק י"ד. 6. סי' ד' במשנ"ב ס"ק א'. 7. סי' ד' סעיף ב'. 8. סי' ד' סעיף י'. 9. סי' ד' סעיף ב' ובמשנ"ב ס"ק י'. 10. סי' ד' סעיף ז' ובמשנ"ב ס"ק ט"ו. 11. סי' ד' סעיף ט'. 12. סי' ד' במשנ"ב ס"ק ט'. 13. סי' א' במשנ"ב ס"ק ב' וסי' ד' סעיף כ"ב. 14. ראה פרטים נוספים בסי' ד' סעיף ט"ו ובמשנ"ב ס"ק ל"ד. 15. סי' ד' במשנ"ב ס"ק ט'. 16. סי' ד' סעיף י"ח. 17. סי' ב' סעיף ו' ובמשנ"ב ס"ק י"א. 18. סי' ב' סעיף ב'. 19. סי' ב' במשנ"ב ס"ק ד'. 20. סי' ב' סעיף ד'. 21. סי' ב' סעיף ה'. 22. סי' ב' במשנ"ב ס"ק ז'.

פרק ג

1. סי' מ"ו במשנ"ב ס"ק א'. 2. סי' ו'. 3. סי' מ"ו במשנ"ב ס"ק ג'. 4. סי' מ"ו סעיף א'. 5. סי' ד' סעיף כ"א. 6. סי' מ"ז סעיף א' ובמשנ"ב ס"ק ב'. 7. סי' מ"ז סעיפים ב', י"ג. 8. סי' מ"ז במשנ"ב ס"ק י'. 9. סי' מ"ז סעיף ט'. 10. סי' ד' במשנ"ב ס"ק כ"ז. 11. סי' ד' במשנ"ב ס"ק ל'. 12. סי' מ"ו במשנ"ב ס"ק כ"ד. 13. ראה בסי' מ"ז במשנ"ב ס"ק כ"ח. 14. סי' ח' במשנ"ב ס"ק מ"ב. 15. סי' צ' במשנ"ב ס"ק א'. 16. סי' נ"ב במשנ"ב ס"ק ט' וסי' מ"ז ס"ק י"ד, י"ז ו־כ"ח. 17. סי' ז' סעיף א'. 18. ראה בסי' ג' סעיפים ב', ד'. 19. חזון־איש חלק אורח־חיים סי' כ"ד ס"ק כ"ו. 20. סי' ד' במשנ"ב ס"ק מ'.

פרק ד

1. סי' צ"א במשנ"ב ס"ק י"ב. 2. סי' נ"א במשנ"ב ס"ק י"ט. 3. סי' פ"ט סעיף ב' ובמשנ"ב שם. 4. ראה בסי' פ"ט סעיף ג' ובמשנ"ב שם. 5. סי' פ"ט סעיף ו' ובמשנ"ב ס"ק ל"ד. 6. סי' פ"ט סעיף ג' ובמשנ"ב ס"ק כ"ב. 7. בשולחן־ערוך החל מסי' ע"ג ועד לסי' פ"ז מובאות הלכות רבות בעניינים אלו. 8. סי' ג' סעי' י' במשנ"ב שם וסי' ע"ו סעיף ה'.

נ״ה. 38. סי׳ ל״ח סעיפים א׳, ב׳. 39. סי׳ מ״ב סעיף ג׳ ובמשנ״ב ס״ק ט״ו. 40. סי׳ כ״ח
סעיף ג׳. 41. סי׳ כ״ה סעיף י״ג ובמשנ״ב ס״ק נ״ה, נ״ו. 42. סי׳ כ״ה במשנ״ב ס״ק
נ״ו. 43. סי׳ כ״ח במשנ״ב ס״ק ו׳. 44. ראה בסי׳ כ״ח סעיף ב׳ ובמשנ״ב ס״ק ז׳. 45. סי׳
כ״ח סעיף ב׳ ובמשנ״ב ס״ק ו׳. 46. סי׳ ל״ט סעיף י׳ ובמשנ״ב שם.

פרק ז

1. סי׳ א׳ סעיפים ה׳-ט׳. 2. סי׳ א׳ ס״ק י״ג. 3. סי׳ מ״ח במשנ״ב ס״ק א׳. 4. סי׳ נ״א
במשנ״ב ס״ק א׳. 5. סי׳ נ״א סעיף ד׳. 6. סי׳ נ״א סעיף ח׳ ובמשנ״ב ס״ק כ׳. 7. סי׳ נ״א
סעיף ט׳. 8. סי׳ נ״א סעיף ז׳ ובמשנ״ב שם ס״ק ט״ו, ט״ז. 9. סי׳ נ״א סעיף א׳ ובמשנ״ב ס״ק
י״ח, י״ט. 10. סי׳ נ״ז סעיף א׳. 11. סי׳ נ״ב סעיף א׳ ובמשנ״ב ס״ק א׳. 12. סי׳ נ״ב ס״ק
ו׳. 13. כל הדינים מובאים בסי׳ נ״ב. 14. ראה בסי׳ נ״ב במשנ״ב ס״ק ו׳. 15. סי׳ ס״א
סעיף א׳ ובמשנ״ב ס״ק ג׳. 16. סי׳ ס״א במשנ״ב ס״ק ד׳. 17. ראה בסי׳ ס״א סעיפים
ט״ז-כ״ג. 18. סי׳ ס״ב סעיף ג׳. 19. סי׳ ס׳ סעיף ה׳. *19. סי׳ ה׳ ובמשנ״ב ס״ק ג׳. סי׳
ס״א סעיף ו׳. 20. סי׳ ס״א סעיפים ד׳, ה׳. 21. סי׳ ס״א סעיף י״ג. *21. סי׳ ס״ג במשנ״ב
ס״ק י״א. 22. סי׳ ס״א סעיף ג׳. 23. סי׳ ס״ג סעיף ו׳ ובמשנ״ב ס״ק י״ז, י״ח. 24. סי׳ כ״ד
סעיפים ב׳, ד׳ ובמשנ״ב שם. *24. סי׳ ס״א סעיף כ״ה. 25. סי׳ ס״ג סעיף ב׳. ראה את
הטעם במשנ״ב ס״ק ה׳. 26. פרטים נוספים מובאים בסי׳ ס״ה סעיף ב׳ ובמשנ״ב שם. 27.
סי׳ נ״ח סעיף א׳. 28. סי׳ נ״ח סעיף א׳. 29. ראה פרטים נוספים בסי׳ נ״ח סעיף ג׳
ובמשנ״ב ס״ק ט״ו, י״ז. 30. ראה בסי׳ נ״ח במשנ״ב ס״ק ה׳. 31. סי׳ נ״ח סעיף ו׳ ובמשנ״ב
ס״ק כ״ז. 32. סי׳ צ״ה במשנ״ב ס״ק ג׳. 33. סי׳ קי״א סעיף א׳. 34. סי׳ ס״ח במשנ״ב
ס״ק ד׳. 35. סי׳ קי״ט סעיף א׳ וראה במשנ״ב סי׳ קכ״ב ס״ק ז׳. 36. סי׳ קי״ט סעיף א׳
ובמשנ״ב שם. 37. סי׳ צ״ח סעיף א׳. ראה פרטים נוספים על הכוונה בתפילה בסי׳ צ׳ ובסי׳
ק״א. 38. סי׳ ק״א סעיף א׳ ובמשנ״ב ס״ק ג׳, ד׳. 39. סי׳ צ״ה במשנ״ב ס״ק ה׳. 40. סי׳
צ׳ סעיף כ״ג ובמשנ״ב ס״ק ע׳, ע״א. 41. סי׳ ק״ד במשנ״ב ס״ק א׳. 42. סי׳ צ״ו סעיף
א׳. 43. סי׳ ק״ד סעיף ז׳ ובמשנ״ב ס״ק כ״ו. 44. סי׳ קכ״ב במשנ״ב ס״ק. 45. סי׳ ק״א
סעיף ב׳. 46. סי׳ ק״א סעיף ב׳. 47. סי׳ צ״ד סעיף א׳. 48. ראה בסי׳ צ׳ סעיפים כ״א,
כ״ב ובמשנ״ב שם. 49. סי׳ צ׳ סעיף ה׳ ובמשנ״ב שם. 50. סי׳ צ״ד סעיף ד׳. 51. סי׳
צ״ה סעיף א׳ ובמשנ״ב ס״ק ג׳. 52. סי׳ צ״ד סעיף ח׳ וראה במשנ״ב ס״ק כ״ב. 53. סי׳ צ״ה
סעיף א׳. 54. סי׳ קי״ג. 55. סי׳ קי״ג סעיפים ו׳, ז׳. 56. סי׳ קכ״א סעיף א׳. 57. סי׳
קכ״ג סעיף א׳. 58. סי׳ קכ״ג סעיף ב׳ ובמשנ״ב ס״ק י׳. 59. בסי׳ ק״ב סעיפים א׳, ב׳, ג׳
מובאים פרטים נוספים. 60. סי׳ ק״ב סעיף ד׳, וראה במשנ״ב ס״ק ט״ו. 61. סי׳ ק״ב סעיף
ה׳. 62. סי׳ קי״ד. 63. סי׳ רצ״ד. 64. סי׳ קי״ז. 65. סי׳ קכ״ד סעיף י׳. דיני ״יעלה
ויבוא״ בחגים השונים מובאים בשולחן-ערוך במקומות הבאים: בהלכות ראש חודש בסי׳
תכ״ב סעיף א׳, בהלכות סוכה בסי׳ תרס״ג סעיף ב׳ ובהלכות פסח בסי׳ ת״צ. לגבי חג השבעות
עיין בסי׳ תצ״ד סעיף א׳ וראה עוד בסי׳ קכ״ד סעיף י׳. 66. סי׳ תרפ״ד סעיף א׳ וסי׳ תרצ״ג
סעיף ב׳. 67. סי׳ תקפ״ב. 68. סי׳ ק׳ ובמשנ״ב ס״ק ג׳. 69. סי׳ פ״ט סעיף א׳. 70. סי׳
פ״ט סעיף א׳. 71. ראה בסי׳ פ״ט סעיף ח׳ ובמשנ״ב שם. 72. סי׳ פ״ט סעיף א׳. 73. סי׳
קכ״ד. 74. ראה בסי׳ קי״א סעיף ב׳. 75. סי׳ קכ״ד סעיף ד׳ ובמשנ״ב ס״ק י״ז. 76. סי׳
קכ״ד סעיף ז׳ ובמשנ״ב ס״ק כ״ב, ל״ז. 77. סי׳ קכ״ד סעיף ו׳. ראה במשנ״ב ס״ק כ״ח. 78.
סי׳ קכ״ה. 79. סי׳ קכ״ה במשנ״ב ס״ז. 80. סי׳ ק״כ סעיף ב׳. 81. סי׳ ק״כ סעיף ב׳
ובמשנ״ב ס״ק ז׳. 82. סי׳ קכ״ז סעיף א׳. 83. סי׳ קכ״ז במשנ״ב ס״ק ג׳. 84. סי׳ קכ״ח
סעיף ב׳. 85. סי׳ קכ״ח סעיף א׳. 86. סי׳ קכ״ח סעיף א׳. 87. סי׳ קכ״ח סעיף ד׳
ובמשנ״ב ס״ק י״ב. 88. ראה פרטים נוספים בסי׳ קכ״ח סעיף ו׳. 89. סי׳ קכ״ח סעיף ח׳
ובמשנ״ב ס״ק כ״ה, כ׳. 90. סי׳ קכ״ח סעיף ט׳ ובמשנ״ב שם. 91. סי׳ קכ״ח סעיף כ״ג

ובמשנ"ב שם. 92. סי' קכ"ח סעיף י"ב. 93. סי' קכ"ח סעיף י"א וסעיף י"ט ובמשנ"ב
שם. 94. סי' קכ"ח סעיף י"ג. 95. סי' קכ"ח סעיף י"ח. 96. ראה בסי' קכ"ח סעיף
מ"ה. 97. ראה בסי' קכ"ח סעיף כ"ד ובמשנ"ב ובביאור הלכה שם. 98. סי' קכ"ח סעיף
י"ד. 99. סי' קכ"ח סעיף ט"ו. 100. סי' קכ"ח סעיף ט"ז. 101. סי' קכ"ז סעיף
ב'. 102. סי' קכ"ח סעיף מ"ד ובמשנ"ב ס"ק קס"ד וסי' קכ"ט סעיף א'. 103. סי' קל"א
במשנ"ב ס"ק ג'. 104. סי' קל"א סעיף א'. 105. סי' קל"א סעיף ב' ובמשנ"ב ס"ק
י'. 106. ראה בסי' קל"א במשנ"ב ס"ק ט', י'. 107. סי' קל"א סעיף ב' ובמשנ"ב ס"ק
י"א. 108. סי' קל"א במשנ"ב ס"ק א'. 109. סי' קל"ד סעיף א'. 110. סי' קל"א סעיפים
ו', ז' ובמשנ"ב שם. 111. סי' קל"א סעיף ד' ובמשנ"ב שם. 112. סי' קל"ה סעיף
ב'. 113. סי' קל"ד סעיף ב' ובמשנ"ב ס"ק י"ג. 114. סי' קל"ד סעיף ב'. הטעמים מובאים
במשנ"ב ס"ק י"ד. 115. סי' קמ"א במשנ"ב ס"ק כ"ה. 116. סי' קל"ה סעיף ג' ובמשנ"ב
ס"ק ט', י'. 117. סי' קמ"א סעיף ז'. 118. סי' קל"ט סעיף ד' ובמשנ"ב ס"ק ט"ז. בסי' ק"מ
סעיף ג' מובא כיצד ינהג מי שהראו לו בטעות פרשה אחרת בתורה והוא בירך עליה. 119.
סי' קל"ט סעיף י"א ובמשנ"ב ס"ק ל"ה, ל"ו. 120. סי' קמ"ז סעיף א'. 121. סי' קל"ט
במשנ"ב ס"ק י"ט. 122. סי' קל"ט סעיף ו'. 123. סי' קל"ט סעיפים ז', ח'. 124. סי'
קמ"א סעיפים א', ב' ובמשנ"ב ס"ק ט'. 125. סי' קל"ט במשנ"ב ס"ק ל"ה. 126. סי' קמ"א
במשנ"ב ס"ק ט"ז. 127. ראה פרטים נוספים בסי' קמ"ו סעיף ב' ובמשנ"ב שם. 128. סי'
קמ"ו במשנ"ב ס"ק י"ט. 129. סי' קמ"ו במשנ"ב ס"ק י"ח. 130. סי' קמ"ו סעיף א'
ובמשנ"ב שם ס"ק ב', ג'. 131. סי' קל"ט במשנ"ב ס"ק ל"ה. 132. סי' קל"ט סעיף
י'. 133. סי' קמ"א סעיף ז' ובמשנ"ב ס"ק כ"ו. 134. סי' קל"ד סעיף ב'. 135. סי' קל"ד
במשנ"ב ס"ק י"א. 136. סי' קל"ד סעיף ב'. ובמשנ"ב ס"ק ח'. 137. סי' קמ"ז סעיף
ג'. 138. סי' קמ"ז במשנ"ב ס"ק ב'. 139. סי' קמ"ט סעיף א'. 140. סי' קל"ב סעיף א'
ובמשנ"ב ס"ק ה'. 141. סי' קל"ב במשנ"ב ס"ק ג'. 142. סי' קל"ב סעיף ב' ובמשנ"ב ס"ק
ט"ו. 143. ראה בסי' קל"ב סעיף ב' ובמשנ"ב ס"ק י"ז. 144. סי' קל"ב סעיף ב' ובמשנ"ב
סעיפים ז', ח'. 145. סי' נ"ה סעיף א' ובמשנ"ב ס"ק ב'. 146. סי' נ"ו סעיף א'
ובמשנ"ב ס"ק א'. 147. סי' נ"ו סעיף א' וראה במשנ"ב ס"ק ז', ח'. 148. סי' ק"ח סעיף
ב' וסי' ק"ה. 148*. ראה בסי' ק"ח סעיף ז'. 149. סי' ק"ח סעיף א' ובמשנ"ב ס"ק
ז'. 150. סי' ק"ח במשנ"ב ס"ק י"א. 151. סי' ק"ח סעיף ט' ובמשנ"ב ס"ק כ"ה. 152. סי'
ק"ח סעיף ד' ובמשנ"ב ס"ק ט"ז. 153. סי' ק"ח סעיף ו'. 154. סי' ק"ח במשנ"ב ס"ק
ד'. 155. סי' קנ"ה סעיף א'. 156. סי' קנ"ה במשנ"ב ס"ק ב'. 157. סי' קנ"ה במשנ"ב
ס"ק ד'.

פרק ח

1. סי' רל"ג סעיף ב' ובביאור הלכה שם. 2. סי' רל"ג במשנ"ב ס"ק כ' וראה בסי' צ"ב סעיף
ד'. 3. סי' רל"ד סעיף א' וסי' קל"ב סעיף ב' ובמשנ"ב ס"ק י"ב, י"ג. 4. סי' רל"ד במשנ"ב
ס"ק ו'. 5. ראה בסי' נ"א סעיף ז' ובמשנ"ב ס"ק ט"ו, ט"ז. 6. סי' רל"ד סעיף א'. ראה
במשנ"ב ס"ק ה'. 7. ראה בסי' קל"א סעיף א'. 8. סי' קל"א סעיף ג' ובמשנ"ב ס"ק ט"ז,
י"ז. 9. סי' קל"א סעיפים ו', ז'. 10. סי' קל"א במשנ"ב ס"ק כ"ה. 11. סי' רל"ג סעיף א'
ובמשנ"ב ס"ק א'. 12. ראה פרטים נוספים בסי' רל"ג במשנ"ב ס"ק י"ד. 13. בהלכות אלו
מצויים פרטים הלכתיים רבים, ראה בסי' רל"ב סעיף ב'.

פרק ט

1. סי' רל"ג סעיף ב' ובמשנ"ב ס"ק ט"ו, ט"ז. 2. סי' רל"ו במשנ"ב ס"ק א'. 3. סי' רל"ו

במשנ״ב ס״ק א׳.   4. סי׳ ס״ו במשנ״ב ס״ק כ״ז וראה בביאור הלכה שם.   5. סי׳ ס״ג סעיף
א׳ ובמשנ״ב ס״ק ז׳.   6. סי׳ רל״ו סעיף א׳.   7. סי׳ רל״ו סעיף ג׳ ובמשנ״ב ס״ק י״ב.   8.
סי׳ רל״ה סעיפים א׳, ג׳. ראה שם בסעיף ד׳ לגבי חלה.   9. פרטי ההלכה מובאים בסי׳ רל״ה
סעיף ב׳ ובמשנ״ב שם.   10. סי׳ רל״ח.   11. סי׳ רל״ט סעיף א׳.   12. סי׳ רל״ט במשנ״ב
ס״ק א׳.   13. סי׳ רל״ט סעיף א׳ ובמשנ״ב ס״ק ד׳.   14. סי׳ רל״ט במשנ״ב ס״ק ב׳.   15.
ראה בסי׳ רל״ט במשנ״ב ס״ק ו׳ ובשער הציון אות י׳.   16. סי׳ רל״ט במשנ״ב ס״ק ו׳.   17.
סי׳ רל״ט במשנ״ב ס״ק ט׳.

פרק י

1. סי׳ קצ״א סעיף ג׳ ובמשנ״ב שם.   2. ראה בסי׳ קפ״ה במשנ״ב ס״ק ג׳.   3. סי׳ קע״ב
במשנ״ב ס״ק ז׳.   4. סי׳ קנ״ו סעיף א׳.   5. סי׳ רט״ו סעיף ד׳.   6. סי׳ רט״ו במשנ״ב ס״ק
י״ח.   7. סי׳ ר״ו סעיף ו׳.   8. סי׳ ר״ב סעיף ג׳.   9. ראה בסי׳ קפ״ד סעיף ד׳ ובמשנ״ב שם
ס״ק ט״ו.   10. ראה בסי׳ מ׳ במשנ״ב ס״ק א׳ ובסי׳ ר״ט במשנ״ב ס״ק י׳.   11. ראה בסי׳
קכ״ד סעיף ה׳.   12. סי׳ קכ״ד סעיף ו׳.   13. ראה בסי׳ רט״ו סעיף א׳.   14. ראה בסי׳
קכ״ד סעיף ח׳.   15. סי׳ קכ״ד סעיף ו׳ ובמשנ״ב שם.   16. סי׳ קכ״ד במשנ״ב ס״ק
כ״א.   17. סי׳ קכ״ד במשנ״ב ס״ק כ״א.   18. סי׳ נ״ד במשנ״ב ס״ק ג׳.

פרק יא

1. סי׳ קנ״ח סעיף א׳.   2. סי׳ קנ״ח במשנ״ב ס״ק ט׳, י׳.   3. סי׳ קנ״ט סעיפים א׳-ה׳.   4.
סי׳ קס״א.   5. ראה בסי׳ קס״א סעיף ג׳.   6. סי׳ קס״א סעיף ד׳.   7. סי׳ קנ״ח במשנ״ב
ס״ק ד׳.   8. סי׳ קס״ב סעיפים א׳, ב׳.   9. סי׳ קס״ב במשנ״ב ס״ק כ״א.   10. סי׳ קס״ב
סעיף ד׳.   11. סי׳ קנ״ח סעיף א׳.   12. סי׳ קנ״ח סעיפים י״א, י״ב.   13. ראה בסי׳ קס״ב
סעיף י׳.   14. פרטים נוספים בסי׳ ק״ס.   15. סי׳ קס״ה סעיף א׳.   16. סי׳ קס״ז סעיף
ו׳.   17. סי׳ קס״ו.   18. סי׳ קס״ז סעיפים ב׳-ד׳.   19. סי׳ קס״ז סעיף ה׳.   20. ראה בסי׳
קס״ז סעיף א׳.   21. סי׳ קע״ז.   22. סי׳ ק״ע סעיף א׳.   23. ראה פרטים נוספים בסי׳
קס״ד סעיף ב׳ ובמשנ״ב שם.   24. סי׳ ק״ע סעיף א׳ ובמשנ״ב שם.   25. ראה פרטים נוספים
בסי׳ קע״ח.

פרק יב

1. סי׳ קפ״ב — סי׳ ר״א.   2. סי׳ קפ״ד סעיף ו׳.   3. סי׳ קפ״ג סעיף ט׳.   4. ראה את פרטי
ההלכה בסי׳ קפ״ד סעיפים א׳, ב׳.   5. ראה בסי׳ קפ״ד במשנ״ב ס״ק כ׳.   6. פרטים נוספים
בסי׳ קע״ז סעיפים א׳, ב׳.   7. סי׳ קפ״א.   8. סי׳ קפ״א במשנ״ב ס״ק א׳.   9. סי׳ קפ״א
סעיף ד׳.   10. ראה בסי׳ קפ״א סעיף י׳.   11. סי׳ קצ״ג סעיף א׳.   12. סי׳ קצ״ג סעיף
א׳.   13. סי׳ תרפ״ב סעיף א׳, — ״על הנסים״ בחנוכה, סי׳ תרצ״ה סעיף ג׳ — ״על הנסים״
בפורים.   14. סי׳ קפ״ח סעיפים ה׳-ז׳.   15. סי׳ קפ״ב סעיף א׳ ובמשנ״ב ס״ק ד׳.   16. סי׳
קפ״ב-קפ״ג.

פרק יג

1. סי׳ ר״י סעיף א׳.   י׳. סי׳ ר״ו סעיף ד׳ ובמשנ״ב ס״ק י״ח.   2. סי׳ ר״ו סעיף ג׳ ובמשנ״ב
ס״ק י״ב.   3. ראה בסי׳ קס״ח סעיפים ו׳-ט׳.   4. סי׳ קע״ד סעיף א׳.   5. סי׳ ר״ב.   6.
סי׳ ר״ד וראה גם בסי׳ ר״ב סעיפים ח׳-ט׳.   7. סי׳ רט״ז במשנ״ב ס״ק ט׳.   8. סי׳
רט״ז.   9. סי׳ רט״ז סעיף ב׳.   10. סי׳ רי״א.   11. סי׳ ר״ו סעיף א׳.   12. סי׳ ר״ו סעיף

א'.   13. סי' ר"ד סעיפים ז'-ח'.   14. סי' ר"י סעיף ב' ובמשנ"ב ס"ק י"ט.   15. סי' קנ"ח
סעיף ד'.   16. סי' ר"ד סעיף י"ב וסי' רי"ב.   17. סי' קס"ח סעיף ו' ובמשנ"ב ס"ק
כ"ד.   18. ראה בסי' ר"ב סעיף ז' ובמשנ"ב שם ובסי' ר"ח במשנ"ב ס"ק ל"ח.

פרק יד

1. סי' ר"י סעיף א'.   2. דיני שיעור "כזית" מובאים בסי' תפ"ו. לגבי "רביעית" ראה בסי' רע"א
במשנ"ב ס"ק ס"ח.   3. סי' ר"י סעיף א'.   4. סי' ר"ח סעיפים א', ב'.   5. ראה בסי' קס"ח
סעיף ו'.   6. סי' ר"ח סעיף י"א.   7. סי' ר"ח סעיפים א', י'.   8. סי' ר"ח סעיף י"ב.   9.
סי' ר"ח סעיף י"ב ובמשנ"ב ס"ק נ"ח.   10. ראה בסי' קע"ח סעיף ה' ובמשנ"ב שם.   11. סי'
קפ"ג סעיף י' ובמשנ"ב ס"ק ל"ה.   12. סי' ר"ז.   13. סי' קע"ד סעיף ל"ו.   14. סי'
ר"ח במשנ"ב ס"ק ס"ב.   15. סי' ר"ח סעיף י"ג.   16. סי' קע"ד סעיף ב' וסי' ר"ח סעיף
ט"ז.   17. ראה בסי' קפ"ד במשנ"ב ס"ק כ'.

פרק טו

1. סי' רכ"ה סעיף ג'.   2. ראה בסי' רכ"ה במשנ"ב ס"ק י"א.   3. סי' רכ"ה במשנ"ב ס"ק
י"א.   4. סי' רכ"ג סעיפים ג', ו'.   5. סי' רכ"ג במשנ"ב ס"ק י"ז.   6. סי' רי"ט בביאור
ההלכה.   7. ראה בסי' רי"ט סעיף ט'.   8. סי' רי"ט סעיף ג'.   9. סי' רכ"ז סעיף
א'.   10. סי' רכ"ז במשנ"ב ס"ק ה'.   11. סי' ר"ו במשנ"ב ס"ק י"ב.   12. סי' רכ"ז סעיף
ג'.   13. ראה בסי' רכ"ז במשנ"ב ס"ק ה'.   14. סי' רכ"ז סעיף ב' ובמשנ"ב ס"ק ח'.   15.
סי' רכ"ט סעיף א'.   16. סי' רכ"ו.   17. ראה בסי' רכ"ו במשנ"ב ס"ק א'.   18. סי' ק"י
סעיף ד'.   19. סי' ק"י סעיף ד'.   20. ראה בסי' ק"י סעיף ז' ובביאור הלכה שם.   21. ראה
בסי' ק"י סעיף ז'.   22. סי' ק"י סעיף ה' ובמשנ"ב שם.   23. סי' ק"י במשנ"ב ס"ק כ"ו.

פרק טז

1. סי' ר"נ במשנ"ב ס"ק ג'.   2. סי' ר"נ סעיף א'.   3. סי' ר"נ סעיף א' ובמשנ"ב ס"ק
ב'.   4. סי' ר"נ סעיפים א', ב'.   5. סי' רס"ב סעיף א' ובמשנ"ב שם.   6. ראה בסי' רס"ב
במשנ"ב ס"ק ג'.   7. סי' ר"נ במשנ"ב ס"ק ג'.   8. סי' רס סעיף ג'.   9. סי' ר"ס סעיף א'
ובמשנ"ב שם.   10. סי' רס"ב סעיף ב' ובמשנ"ב ס"ק ה'.   *10. סי' רמ"ב סעיף א'.   11.
סי' רמ"ט סעיף ב' וראה במשנ"ב שם ס"ק י"ז.   12. ראה בסי' רנ"א סעיפים א', ב'. ובמשנ"ב
שם סוף ס"ק ה'.   13. סי' רס"ג סעיף י'.   14. סי' רס"ג סעיף ג'.   15. סי' רס"ג במשנ"ב
ס"ק מ"ג.   16. סי' רס"ג סעיף ה'.   17. ראה סי' רס"ג במשנ"ב ס"ק כ"ו, כ"ז.   18. סי'
רס"ג סעיף א' ובמשנ"ב שם.   19. ראה בסי' רע"א סעיף א' ובמשנ"ב ס"ק א'-ג'.   20. סי'
רע"א סעיף ד' ובמשנ"ב ס"ק י"א.   21. סי' רע"א במשנ"ב ס"ק י"ח.   22. סי' רס"ג סעיפים ו',
ז' ובמשנ"ב שם.   23. סי' רס"ג סעיף ט' ובמשנ"ב ס"ק מ', מ"א.   24. סי' רס"ג סעיף ז'
ובמשנ"ב שם.   25. סי' רס"ג סעיף ח'.   26. ראה בסי' רס"ג סעיף ח' ובמשנ"ב ס"ק
ל'.   27. ראה בסי' רס"ג במשנ"ב ס"ק ב'.

פרק יז

1. סי' רס"א סעיף ד' ובמשנ"ב ס"ק ל"א.   2. סי' רס"ג סעיף י"ב.   3. סי' רס"ז סעיף ג'
ובמשנ"ב ס"ק ט'.   4. סי' ר"ו במשנ"ב ס"ק י"ב.   5. סי' רס"ח סעיף ב'.   6. סי' רס"ח
סעיף ז' ובמשנ"ב ס"ק י"ט.   7. סי' רס"ח סעיפים ז', ח', י"ב.   8. ראה בסי' רס"ח סעיף
י'.   9. סי' רע"א סעיף א'.   10. סי' רע"ה סעיף ב'.   11. סי' רע"א סעיף י' ובמשנ"ב

ס״ק מ״ב-מ״ד.   12. ראה פרטים נוספים בסי׳ קפ״ב סעיף ו׳, ז׳.   13. סי׳ רע״א סעיף י״ג
ובמשנ״ב ס״ק ס״ח.   14. סי׳ רע״א במשנ״ב ס״ק ע״ג.   15. סי׳ ער״א סעיף ט׳ ובמשנ״ב ס״ק
כ״ה ראה גם בסי׳ רע״א במשנ״ב סוף ס״ק מ״א.   16. סי׳ ער״ב סעיף י׳.   17. ראה בסי׳
רע״א סעיף ט׳ ובמשנ״ב ס״ק מ״א.   18. סי׳ רע״ג.   19. סי׳ רע״ד סעיף א׳ וסי׳ רע״א סעיף
י״ב.   20. ראה בסי׳ רע״ד סעיף א׳ ובמשנ״ב שם.   21. סי׳ רע״ד במשנ״ב ס״ק ה׳.   22.
סי׳ רע״ד סעיף ג׳.   23. ראה בסי׳ קס״ז סעיף ט׳.   24. סי׳ ר״נ סעיף ב׳ וסי׳ רמ״ב במשנ״ב
ס״ק ב׳.   25. סי׳ קפ״ח סעיף ה׳.

פרק יח

1. סי׳ רפ״ב.   2. עניני חלוקת הפרשיות מובאים בסי׳ תכ״ח.   3. סי׳ קמ״ג סעיף א׳.   4.
סי׳ רפ״ב סעיף א׳.   5. סי׳ קל״ה סעיף ד׳.   6. סי׳ קל״ט סעיפים ד׳-י׳.   7. סי׳ קל״ט סעיף
ה׳ ובמשנ״ב שם.   8. סי׳ רפ״ב סעיף ד׳.   9. סי׳ קל״ד סעיף ב׳ ובסי׳ קמ״ז.   10. ראה
בסי׳ קמ״ז סעיף ז׳ במשנ״ב ס״ק כ״ג.   11. הטעם לקריאת ההפטרה מובא בסי׳ רפ״ד במשנ״ב
ס״ק ב׳.   12. ראה בסי׳ רפ״ד סעיף ג׳.   13. סי׳ רפ״ה.   14. סי׳ רפ״ה במשנ״ב ס״ק
ב׳.   15. סי׳ רפ״ה סעיף ב׳ ובמשנ״ב ס״ק ה׳.   16. סי׳ רפ״ה סעיף ד׳.   17. סי׳ רפ״ה
סעיף ג׳ ובמשנ״ב ס״ק ז׳.   18. סי׳ רפ״ו.   19. סי׳ רפ״ו סעיף א׳.   20. סי׳ רס״ח סעיף
ב׳.   21. סי׳ רפ״ט סעיף א׳ ובמשנ״ב ס״ק ב׳.   22. סי׳ ער״ב סעיף ט׳ ובמשנ״ב ס״ק ל׳, סי׳
רפ״ט סעיף ב׳.   23. סי׳ רפ״ט סעיף א׳.   24. סי׳ רע״ג במשנ״ב ס״ק כ״ה, כ״ו.   25. ראה
סי׳ מ״ו סעיף ג׳.   26. ראה פרטים נוספים בסי׳ ר״ג ובמשנ״ב שם.   27. סי׳ ר״ג סעיף ב׳
ובמשנ״ב שם.   28. סי׳ רצ״ב סעיף א׳ ובמשנ״ב שם.   29. סי׳ רצ״ב סעיף ב׳.   30. סי׳
רצ״א סעיף ב׳.   31. סי׳ רצ״א סעיף ד׳.   32. סי׳ רצ״א סעיף ד׳.   33. סי׳ רצ״א סעיפים
א׳, ה׳.   34. סי׳ קפ״ח סעיף ח׳.   35. סי׳ קפ״ח סעיף ט׳.   36. סי׳ קפ״ח במשנ״ב ס״ק ל״ג.

פרק יט

1. סי׳ רצ״ג.   2. סי׳ רצ״ד.   3. סי׳ רצ״ה סעיף א׳.   4. סי׳ רצ״ה ובמשנ״ב ס״ק ד׳.   5.
סי׳ תכ״ו סעיפים א׳, ב׳, ד׳ ובמשנ״ב ס״ק כ״א.   6. ראה בסי׳ תכ״ו סעיף ד׳ ובמשנ״ב ס״ק
כ׳.   7. סי׳ תכ״ו סעיף ג׳.   8. ראה בסי׳ תכ״ו סעיף ב׳ ובמשנ״ב ס״ק ג׳ וס״ק
כ׳.   9. סי׳ רצ״ו במשנ״ב ס״ק ה׳.   10. ראה בסי׳ רצ״ו סעיף א׳.   11. סי׳ רצ״ו סעיף
א׳.   12. סי׳ רצ״ח סעיף ב׳ ובמשנ״ב שם ס״ק א׳.   13. יתר פרטי ההלכה מובאים בסי׳
רצ״ח.   14. סי׳ רצ״ח סעיף ב׳ ובמשנ״ב שם.   15. סי׳ רצ״ו במשנ״ב ס״ק ו׳.   16. סי׳
רצ״ו סעיף ב׳.   17. סי׳ רצ״ו סעיף ח׳ ובמשנ״ב שם.   18. ראה בבאור הלכה סוף סי׳
רצ״ו.   19. סי׳ רצ״ט סעיף א׳.   20. סי׳ רצ״ט סעיף י׳ ובמשנ״ב שם.   21. סי׳ ש׳
ובמשנ״ב שם ס״ק ב׳.   22. סי׳ ש׳ במשנ״ב ס״ק א׳.

פרק כ

1. סי׳ שי״ח סעיף י׳.   2. ראה בסי׳ שי״ח במשנ״ב ס״ק קי״ג.   3. יתר פרטי ההלכה מובאים
בסי׳ תי״ג סעיף ה׳ ובמשנ״ב ס״ק פ״ו ובסי׳ שי״ח סעיפים ו׳-ח׳.   4. סי׳ שי״ח סעיף ט׳.   5.
סי׳ שי״ח סעיף י׳.   6. סי׳ שי״ח סעיף ד׳ ובמשנ״ב ס״ק ל״ג.   7. סי׳ שי״ח סעיף ה׳ ובמשנ״ב
ס״ק מ״ב.   8. שם במשנ״ב ס״ק מ״ה.   9. סי׳ שי״ח במשנ״ב ס״ק ס״ה.   10. סי׳ שי״ח
ס״ק ל״ט.   11. ראה בסי׳ שי״ח בשער הציון אות ס״ה.   12. סי׳ שי״ח סעיף י״ח.   13. סי׳
תנ״ד סעיף ד׳.   14. סי׳ רנ״ג סעיף ב׳.   15. סי׳ רנ״ט סעיף ז׳.   16. סי׳ תנ״ג סעיף ב׳
ובמשנ״ב ס״ק נ״ד, ס״ח.   17. סי׳ תנ״ג סעיף ב׳ ובמשנ״ב שם.   18. ראה בסי׳ רנ״ג במשנ״ב

20. ראה בסי' רנ"ז סעיף ח' ובמשנ"ב ס"ק מ"ג ובסי' רנ"ח במשנ"ב ס"ק ב'.   19. ס"ק ס"ז.
23. סי' ש"כ סעיף י"ז.   22. סי' ש"כ סעיף ד' ובמשנ"ב ס"ק י"ז.   21. סי' ש"כ.   סי' רנ"ח במשנ"ב ס"ק ב'.
25. ראה בסי' שכ"א   24. סי' שכ"א סעיפים ז'-י"ב ובמשנ"ב ס"ק מ"ה.   סי' ש"כ סעיף ז'.
28. סי'   27. סי' ש"כ סעיף ט'.   26. סי' ש"כ סעיף ט'.   סעיף י"ב ובמשנ"ב ס"ק מ"ד, מ"ה.
ס"ק   29. סי' שכ"א סעיף ט"ז ובמשנ"ב ס"ק   שכ"א סעיפים י"ד-י"ט וסי' ש"מ סעיף י"ב.
32. סי'   31. סי' שכ"א במשנ"ב ס"ק ט'.   30. סי' שכ"א סעיף ב' ובמשנ"ב ס"ק ט'.   ס"ו.
35. ראה פרטים   34. סי' שי"ט במשנ"ב ס"ק כ"ח.   33. סי' שי"ט במשנ"ב ס"ק כ"ד.   שי"ט.
37. סי' שכ"א סעיף י"ד ראה בשער   36. סי' שי"ט סעיף י'.   נוספים בסי' שי"ט סעיף י'.
ש"מ   39. ראה בסי'   38. ראה בסי' שי"ז סעיף א' ובמשנ"ב ס"ק ה'-ז'.   הציון שם אות צ"ג.
41. סי' ש"כ סעיף י"ב.   40. ראה בסי' ש"א סעיף מ"ו ובסי' ש"ב סעיף י"ב.   סעיף ג' ובמשנ"ב שם ס"ק מ"א.
נ"ט   42. ראה בסי' ש"ב במשנ"ב ס"ק ס', בסי' ש"כ במשנ"ב ס"ק נ"ה, נ"ז,   סי' שכ"ז סעיף י"ז.
44. סי' שי"ד   43. סי' שכ"ג סעיף ו' ובמשנ"ב שם ס"ק קמ"ח.   ובסי' שכ"ח במשנ"ב ס"ק קמ"ח.
46. סי' שי"ד   45. סי' שכ"ז במשנ"ב ס"ק ל'.   ראה בסי' שכ"ו סעיף י' ובמשנ"ב ס"ק ט"ז.
ס"ק   48. ראה בסי' ש"א סעיף ז' ובמשנ"ב שם   47. סי' ש"א סעיף מ"ו וסי' ש"ב.   סעיף י"א.
50. סי' ש"ב סעיף א' ובמשנ"ב ס"ק   49. סי' ש"ב סעיף א' ובמשנ"ב ס"ק ו'.   ל"ב-ל"ד.
53. סי' ש"ב סעיף ג'. ראה   52. סי' ש"ח במשנ"ב ס"ק ס"ג.   51. סי' ש"א סעיף מ"ה.   ג'.
ס"ק   55. ראה בסי' שכ"ז ובמשנ"ב   54. סי' שכ"ב במשנ"ב ס"ק י"ח.   במשנ"ב שם ס"ק י"ט.
57. סי' של"ח סעיף   56. ראה פרטים נוספים בסי' של"ח במשנ"ב ס"ק ט"ו.   ט"ז.
60. סי' ש"מ   59. סי' ש"מ סעיף ד' ובמשנ"ב ס"ק כ"ב.   58. סי' של"ט סעיף ג'.   א'.
ס"ק כ"ד-כ"ה.   62. ראה בסי' ש"מ במשנ"ב   61. סי' ש"כ במשנ"ב ס"ק נ"ט.   במשנ"ב ס"ק כ"ב אות ח'.
סי'   65. סי' ש"מ סעיף ג' וראה   64. סי' ש"מ סעיף ד'.   63. סי' ש"מ ס"ק ט"ו.
סי'   67. סי' ש"מ סעיף י"ד.   66. סי' ש"מ במשנ"ב ס"ק ט'.   במשנ"ב שם ס"ק ט"ו.
ס"ק   68. ראה בסי' ש"מ סעיף ו' ובמשנ"ב   שכ"א במשנ"ב ס"ק נ' וסי' שי"ד סעיף י"א.
סי' ש"מ סעיף י"ד ובמשנ"ב ס"ק   70.   69. סי' ש"מ סעיף י"ג ובמשנ"ב ס"ק מ"א.   כ"ז.
73.   72. ראה בסי' ש"מ סעיף ז' ובמשנ"ב שם.   71. סי' ש"מ במשנ"ב ס"ק מ"ה.   מ"ה.
75. סי' שי"ז   74. סי' שי"ז סעיף א' ובמשנ"ב ס"ק ז'.   סי' שי"ז סעיף א' ובמשנ"ב שם.
78.   77. סי' שכ"ג סעיף א'.   76. סי' שי"ז סעיף ב' ובמשנ"ב שם.   במשנ"ב סוף ס"ק כ"ג.
בדין זה   80.   79. סי' ש"ו סעיף ז' ובמשנ"ב ס"ק ל"ו.   סי' ת"ק סעיף ב' ובמשנ"ב ס"ק ח'.
82. סי'   81. סי' שט"ו סעיף ב' ובמשנ"ב ס"ק ט"ו, ט"ז.   מצויין פרטים רבים — סי' שט"ו.
סי' של"ז סעיף   84.   83. ראה בסי' שט"ו סעיף ח' בביאור-הלכה.   שט"ו במשנ"ב ס"ק א'.
86. ראה בסי' של"ז סעיף   85. סי' של"ז במשנ"ב ס"ק י"ג.   ב' ובביאור הלכה שם.
89. סי' שכ"ח סעיף   88. סי' ש"מ סעיף א' ובמשנ"ב ס"ק א'.   87. סי' ש"מ סעיף א'.   ג'.
91. סי' ש"ג סעיף כ"ז ובמשנ"ב ס"ק   90. סי' ש"ג סעיף כ"ה.   ל"א ובמשנ"ב ס"ק צ"ט.
שכ"ו   94. ראה פרטים נוספים בסי'   93. סי' ש"ג סעיף כ"ו.   92. סי' ש"ג סעיף כ"ו.   פ"ז.
96. סי' של"ט סעיף ב' ובמשנ"ב ס"ק   95. סי' שכ"ו במשנ"ב ס"ק כ"א.   סעיף א'.
סי'   99. סי' שכ"ט-ש"ל.   98. דיני רפואה בשבת מובאים בסי' שכ"ח-ש"ל.   97.   ב'.
102. סי'   101. סי' של"ו במשנ"ב ס"ק י"ב.   100. סי' של"ו סעיף י"ג.   של"ו סעיף א'.
י"א,   104. סי' של"ו סעיפים ד', י"א,   103. סי' של"ו במשנ"ב ס"ק ס"ג.   של"ו סעיף י"ג.
107. סי' של"ו סעיף ג'   106. סי' של"ו סעיף ג'.   105. סי' של"ו סעיפים ז', ח'.   י"ב.
סי' של"ו במשנ"ב   109.   108. סי' שכ"ו סעיף ג' ובמשנ"ב ס"ק ה', ו'.   ובמשנ"ב ס"ק כ"ה.
סי' ש"ו   111.   111. ראה בסי' ש"ו סעיף ג'.   110. סי' ש"א סעיפים א', ב'.   סוף ס"ק נ"ד.
115. סי' שי"ז סעיף   114. סי' ש"ו סעיף ו'.   113. סי' ש"ו במשנ"ב ס"ק ל"ג.   סעיף א'.
ג',   117. סי' ש"ו סעיף א' ובמשנ"ב ס"ק   116. סי' ש"ו סעיף ח' ובמשנ"ב ס"ק ל"ט.   א'.
סי'   120.   119. סי' ש"ז סעיפים ב'-ה'.   118. סי' של"ה סעיף ה'.   ד'.

שמ״ה-תט״ז. 121. סי׳ ש״א סעיף ז׳ וסי׳ ש״ג. 122.סי׳ ש״ח-שי״א. 123. הקדמת
המשנ״ב לסי׳ ש״ח. 124. סי׳ ש״ח במשנ״ב ס״ק קט״ו.

פרק כא

1. ראה בסי׳ שי״ח במשנ״ב ס״ק ל״ט. 2. ראה בסי׳ שי״ט סעיף ח׳ ובמשנ״ב ס״ק
כ״ח-כ״ט. 3. ראה בסי׳ של״ט סעיף ד׳. 4. סי׳ ש״מ סעיף י״ג ובמשנ״ב ס״ק מ״א. 5.
סי׳ רנ״ב סעיף ז׳. 6. סי׳ תקי״ד במשנ״ב ס״ק י״ח, ל״ה. 7. סי׳ ר״ס סעיף ב׳ ובמשנ״ב שם.

פרק כב

1. סי׳ תצ״ו. 2. ראה בסי׳ תצ״ו סעיף ב׳ ובמשנ״ב שם. 3. סי׳ תצ״ו סעיף ג׳ ובמשנ״ב
שם. 4. סי׳ תצ״ה. 5. סי׳ תק״ב סעיף א׳. 6. סי׳ תקי״א סעיף ד׳ בביאור הלכה. 7.
סי׳ תקי״ד סעיף א׳ ובמשנ״ב ס״ק ט״ז. 8. סי׳ תצ״ה סעיף א׳ ובמשנ״ב שם. 9. סי׳ תצ״ה
סעיף ב׳ ובמשנ״ב ס״ק י״ב. 10. סי׳ תק״ו סעיפים א׳-ב׳. 11. סי׳ תק״ד. 12. סי׳ תק״י
סעיף ב׳. 13. סי׳ תקי״ח סעיף א׳. 14. ראה בסי׳ תצ״ה סעיף ד׳. 15. סי׳ תקכ״ז סעיף
א׳. 16. סי׳ תקכ״ז סעיפים ב׳, ד׳ ובמשנ״ב שם. 17. סי׳ תקכ״ז ס״ק ג׳ ובמשנ״ב ס״ק
ח׳. 18. סי׳ תקכ״ז סעיף י״ב. 19. סי׳ תקכ״ז סעיף י״ב ובמשנ״ב ס״ק ל״ט. 20. ראה
בסי׳ תקכ״ז סעיף י׳-י״א ובמשנ״ב שם. 21. סי׳ תקכ״ז סעיף ט״ו ובמשנ״ב ס״ק מ״ו. 22.
סי׳ תקכ״ז סעיף ט״ז ובמשנ״ב ס״ק י״א, מ״ח. 23. סי׳ תקכ״ז סעיף י״ג. 24. סי׳ תקי״ד
סעיף י״א ובמשנ״ב ס״ק מ״ח. 25. ראה בסי׳ רס״ג במשנ״ב ס״ק כ״ו. 26. סי׳ תקי״ד סעיף
י״א. 27. סי׳ תקי״ד במשנ״ב ס״ק מ״ח. 28. סי׳ תקי״ד במשנ״ב ס״ק ח׳. 29. סי׳ ק׳
ובמשנ״ב ס״ק ג׳. 30. סי׳ צ״ו במשנ״ב ס״ק ח׳. 31. סי׳ תקכ״ט סעיף א׳. 32. סי׳
תקכ״ט במשנ״ב ס״ק ג׳. 33. סי׳ תקכ״ט סעיף א׳ ובמשנ״ב ס״ק י״ב. 34. סי׳ תקכ״ט סעיף
ב׳. 35. סי׳ תקכ״ט סעיף א׳. 36. סי׳ תצ״א סעיף א׳. 37. סי׳ תצ״א במשנ״ב ס״ק ב׳,
ג׳.

פרק כג

1. סי׳ תי״ז במשנ״ב ס״ק א׳. 2. סי׳ תכ״ב סעיף א׳. 3. סי׳ קל״א סעיף ו׳. 4. סי׳ תכ״ג
סעיף ג׳. 5. סי׳ תכ״ב סעיף ב׳. 6. סי׳ תכ״ב במשנ״ב ס״ק ט״ז. 7. סי׳ תכ״ב סעיף
ב׳. 8. סי׳ תכ״ב סעיף ז׳. 9. סי׳ תכ״ב סעיף ג׳. 10. סי׳ תי״ז במשנ״ב ס״ק ד׳. 11.
סי׳ תכ״ג סעיף ג׳. 12. סי׳ תי״ט ובמשנ״ב ס״ק ב׳. 13. סי׳ תכ״ד. 14. סי׳ תי״ח סעיף
א׳. 15. סי׳ תי״ז סעיף א׳ ובביאור הלכה שם. 16. ראה בסי׳ תכ״ה. 17. סי׳ תכ״ה
סעיף ג׳.

פרק כד

1. סי׳ תקפ״א סעיף ב׳. 2. סי׳ תקפ״א סעיף א׳. 3. סי׳ תקפ״א סעיף א׳. 4. סי׳ תקפ״א
סעיף ג׳. 5. סי׳ תקפ״א סעיף ד׳. 6. סי׳ תקפ״א במשנ״ב ס״ק כ״ו. 7. סי׳ תקפ״א
במשנ״ב ס״ק כ״ה. 8. סי׳ תקצ״א-תקצ״ב. 9. ראה בסי׳ תרב״א ס״ק י״ד. 10. סי׳
תק״צ סעיפים א׳-ב ובמשנ״ב שם. 11. סי׳ תקפ״ו. 12. סי׳ תקפ״ה סעיף ב׳. 13. סי׳
תקפ״ח סעיף א׳. 14. סי׳ תקפ״ט סעיף ג׳. 15. סי׳ תקפ״ה סעיף א׳ ובמשנ״ב ס״ק
ב׳. 16. סדר תקיעת שופר מופיע בסי׳ תק״צ. 16.סי׳ ת״ר סעיף ג׳ ובמשנ״ב שם. 17. סי׳
תקצ״ב סעיף ג׳ ובמשנ״ב ס״ק י״ב-י״ד. 18. סי׳ תקפ״ח סעיף ה׳. 19. סי׳
תקפ״ג. 20. סי׳ תקפ״ג במשנ״ב ס״ק א׳. 21. סי׳ תקפ״ג במשנ״ב ס״ק ג׳, ד׳. 22. סי׳

תקפ"ג במשנ"ב ס"ק ג'.   23. סי' תקפ"ג סעיף ב' ובמשנ"ב ס"ק ט'.   24. סי' תקפ"ג סעיף ב'
ובמשנ"ב ס"ק ח'.   25. סי' ת"ר סעיף ב' ובמשנ"ב שם.   26. ראה בסי' תר"א.

פרק כה

1. סי' תקמ"ט.   2. סי' תק"נ סעיף ג'.   3. סי' תק"נ סעיף א' וסי' תקס"ז סעיף ב'.   4. סי'
תקמ"ט במשנ"ב ס"ק ג'.   5. סי' תקס"ז סעיף ג'. ראה פרטים נוספים במשנ"ב ס"ק י"א.   6.
ראה פרטים נוספים בסי' תקס"ד.   7. סי' תק"נ סעיף א' ובמשנ"ב ס"ק ב' ו-ה'.   8. סי' תקס"ו
סעיף ד'.   9. סי' תקס"ו סעיף א'.   10. ראה פרטים נוספים בסי' תקס"ז סעיף ו' ובמשנ"ב
שם.   11. סי' תקס"ו סעיף א'.   12. סי' תקס"ה סעיף ג'.   13. סי' קכ"ט סעיף א'.   14.
סי' תקס"ו סעיף א'.   15. סי' תקס"ו סעיף ג'.   16. סי' תקמ"ט סעיף א' וסי' תר"ב סעיף
א'.   17. סי' תקמ"ט במשנ"ב ס"ק ב'.

פרק כו

1. סי' תר"ג סעיף א'.   2. ראה בסי' תר"ג במשנ"ב ס"ק ב'-ד'.   3. ראה בסי' תר"ג סעיף
א'.   4. סי' תר"ב סעיף א'.   5. סי' תר"ב במשנ"ב ס"ק ב'.   6. סי' תקפ"ב.   7. סי'
תקפ"ב סעיף א' ובמשנ"ב ס"ק ב'.   8. סי' תקפ"ב סעיף א'.   9. סי' תקפ"ב במשנ"ב ס"ק
ט"ז.   10. סי' תר"ה ובמשנ"ב ס"ק ב'.   11. סי' תר"ו.   12. סי' תר"ו סעיף א' ובמשנ"ב
ס"ק ח'.

פרק כז

1. סי' תר"ה סעיף א'.   2. סי' תר"ד סעיף ב'.   3. סי' תר"ז סעיפים א'-ה'.   4. סי' תר"ז
סעיף ג' ובמשנ"ב ס"ק י'.   5. סי' תר"ז במשנ"ב ס"ק י"א.   6. סי' תר"ד סעיף א' ובמשנ"ב
ס"ק א'.   7. ראה בסי' תר"ח סעיף ד' ובמשנ"ב שם.   8. סי' תר"ו סעיף ד' ובמשנ"ב
שם.   9. סי' תר"ח סעיף א' ובמשנ"ב שם.   10. ראה בסי' תר"ח סעיף ג' ובמשנ"ב ס"ק
י"ב.   11. ראה בסי' תר"י סעיף ד'.   12. סי' תרי"ט במשנ"ב ס"ק ד'.   13. סי' תר"י סעיף
ד'.   14. סי' תר"י סעיפים א', ב'.   15. סי' תר"י סעיף ד'.

פרק כח

1. סי' תרי"א סעיף א'.   2. סי' תרי"א סעיפים א', ב'.   3. סי' תר"ב סעיף ה'.   4. סי'
תרי"ג סעיף ד'.   5. סי' תרט"ז סעיף ב'.   6. שם ובמשנ"ב ס"ק י'.   7. ראה פרטים נוספים
בסי' תרי"ג סעיפים ב', ג' ובמשנ"ב ס"ק ד'.   8. סי' תרי"ג סעיף ג' ובמשנ"ב ס"ק ז'.   9. סי'
תרי"ד סעיף א'.   10. סי' תרי"ד סעיפים ב'-ד' ובמשנ"ב ס"ק ה'.   11. ראה בסי'
תרט"ו סעיף א' ובמשנ"ב שם.   12. סי' תרי"ז-תרי"ח.   13. סי' תרי"ט סעיפים א',
ד'.   14. סי' תרי"ט סעיף א' ובמשנ"ב ס"ק ג'.   15. סי' תרי"ט סעיף ב'.   16. סי' תרכ"א
סעיף א' ובמשנ"ב ס"ק ב'.   17. סי' תרכ"א סעיף ו'.   18. סי' תרכ"א סעיף ד' ובמשנ"ב ס"ק
י"ד.   19. סי' תרכ"ב.   20. ראה בסי' תרכ"ב במשנ"ב ס"ק ז' ובשער-הציון אות ו'.   21.
סי' תרכ"ג.   22. סי' תרכ"ג סעיף ו'.   23. סי' תרכ"ד סעיפים א', ב'.   24. סי' תר"ב
ובמשנ"ב ס"ק י'.   25. ראה פרטים נוספים בסי' תרכ"ד סעיפים ג'-ד'.   25. סי' תרכ"ד
סעיף ג' ובמשנ"ב שם.   26. סי' תרכ"ד סעיף ה'.

פרק כט

1. סי' תרכ"ה במשנ"ב ס"ק א'.   2. סי' תרכ"ו.   3. סי' תרכ"ה ובמשנ"ב ס"ק ב'.   3. סי'

תרכ״ה ובמשנ״ב ס״ק ב׳. 5. סי׳ תר״ל. 6. סי׳ תר״ל סעיף י׳ ובמשנ״ב ס״ק מ״ז-נ״א. 7. סי׳ תרל״ד סעיף א׳. 8. סי׳ תר״ל סעיף ט׳ ובמשנ״ב ס״ק מ״ב. 9. סי׳ תרכ״ט. 10. סי׳ תרכ״ט סעיפים ט׳-י״ב. 11. סי׳ תרכ״ט סעיף א׳. 12. ראה בסי׳ תרכ״ט סעיף ו׳. 13. ראה בסי׳ תרל״ה ובמשנ״ב ס״ק י״א. 14. סי׳ תרכ״ט סעיף ז׳ ובמשנ״ב סוף ס״ק כ״ב. 15. סי׳ תרל״ג סעיף ח׳ ובמשנ״ב ס״ק כ״ה. 16. סי׳ תרל״א. 17. סי׳ תרל״ב סעיף ב׳. 18. ראה בסי׳ תרל״ח סעיפים א׳, ב׳. 19. סי׳ תרס״ז. 20. סי׳ תרל״ח במשנ״ב ס״ק ד׳. 21. סי׳ תרל״ח סעיף א׳. 22. סי׳ תרל״ח סעיף ב׳ ובמשנ״ב ס״ק י״ד. 23. סי׳ תרל״ח במשנ״ב ס״ק כ״ד. 24. סי׳ תרל״ט סעיף א׳. 25. סי׳ תרל״ט סעיף ב׳. 26. סי׳ תרל״ט סעיף ח׳ ובמשנ״ב ס״ק כ״ט. 27. סי׳ תרל״ט סעיף ב׳. 28. סי׳ תרל״ט סעיף ח׳ ובמשנ״ב ס״ק מ״ו. 29. ראה פרטים נוספים בסי׳ תרל״ט במשנ״ב ס״ק מ״ז. 30. ראה בסי׳ תרל״ט סעיפים ה׳-ז׳. 31. סי׳ תר״מ סעיף א׳. 32. סי׳ תר״מ סעיף א׳ ובמשנ״ב ס״ק ה׳. 33. סי׳ תרל״ט סעיף א׳ ובמשנ״ב שם. 34. סי׳ תרל״ט סעיף ג׳. 35. סי׳ תרל״ט במשנ״ב ס״ק כ״ב. 36. סי׳ תרל״ט סעיף ג׳ ובמשנ״ב ס״ק כ״ז. 37. סי׳ תרל״ט סעיף ג׳. 38. ראה בסי׳ תרל״ט סעיף ה׳ ובמשנ״ב ס״ק ל״ה. 39. דיני לולב מובאים בסי׳ תרמ״ה, דיני הדס בסי׳ תרמ״ו, דיני ערבה בסי׳ תרמ״ז דיני אתרוג בסי׳ תרמ״ח. בסי׳ תרמ״ט מובאים דיני פסול המשתייכים לכל ארבעת המינים ובסי׳ תר״נ שיעור גודלם של ההדס והערבה. 40. סי׳ תרנ״א סעיף א׳. 41. סי׳ תרנ״א סעיף א׳ ובמשנ״ב ס״ק ח׳-י״ד. 42. סי׳ תרנ״א סעיף ה׳. 43. סי׳ תתנ״ב סעיף א׳. 44. ראה פרטים נוספים בסי׳ תרנ״ב סעיף ב׳. 45. סי׳ תרנ״א סעיפים ב׳, ה׳. 46. סי׳ תתנ״א במשנ״ב ס״ק י״ז. 47. ראה בסי׳ תרנ״א במשנ״ב ס״ק כ״ד-כ״ו. 48. סי׳ תרנ״א סעיף ה׳. 49. סי׳ תתנ״א סעיף ב׳. 50. סי׳ תתנ״א סעיפים ח׳-י״א ובמשנ״ב וסי׳ תרס״א סעיף ב׳. שם. 51. סי׳ תרנ״ח סעיף ב׳ וראה שם לגבי טלטול אתרוג בשבת. 52. סי׳ תרנ״ח סעיף ג׳. 53. סי׳ תרנ״א סעיף ג׳. 54. סי׳ תרנ״ח סעיף ד׳. 55. ראה בסי׳ תרנ״ח סעיף ו׳. 56. ראה בסי׳ תרנ״ד ובמשנ״ב ס״ק ג׳. 57. סי׳ תת״ד. 58.סי׳ תרמ״ד סעיף א׳. 59. ראה בסי׳ תרמ״ד סעיף א׳ ובסי׳ תפ״ח סעיף א׳. 60. ראה בסי׳ ת״צ במשנ״ב ס״ק י״ט. 61. סי׳ תר״ס. 62. סי׳ תר״ס סעיף א׳ ובמשנ״ב ס״ק ד׳-ו׳. 63. סי׳ תקכ״ב סעיף ב׳ ובמשנ״ב ס״ק ט״ז. 64. סי׳ תק״ל במשנ״ב ס״ק א׳. 65. סי׳ תרל״ג. 66. ראה בסי׳ תק״ל במשנ״ב ס״ק א׳. 67. סי׳ תרל״ג. 68. סי׳ תקל״ז-תקל״ח. 69. סי׳ תקל״ח סעיף א׳. 70. סי׳ תקל״ח סעיף ו׳. 71. ראה פרטים נוספים בסי׳ תקמ״ב במשנ״ב ס״ק ב׳. 72. סי׳ תקל״א. 73. סי׳ תקל״ב. 74. סי׳ תקל״ד. 75. ראה בסי׳ תקל״ט. 76. ראה פרטים נוספים בסי׳ תקמ״ה. 77. סי׳ תרס״ד סעיף א׳ ובמשנ״ב שם. 78. סי׳ תרס״ד סעיף א׳. 79. ראה בסי׳ תרס״ד סימנים ב׳-ז׳. 80. סי׳ תרס״ז. 81. סי׳ תרס״ח-תרס״ט. 82. סי׳ תרס״ט במשנ״ב ס״ק י״א. 83. סי׳ תרס״ח סעיף ב׳ וסי׳ תרס״ט סעיף א׳. 84. ראה בסי׳ תרס״ח סוף סעיף ב׳ ובסי׳ קי״ד סעיף ב׳. 85. סי׳ תרס״ח סעיף א׳ ובמשנ״ב ס״ק ה׳-ח׳. 86. סי׳ תרס״ט. 87. סי׳ תכ״ט במשנ״ב ס״ק י״ד.

פרק ל

1. סי׳ תרפ״ב סעיף א׳. 2. סי׳ תרצ״ג. 3. סי׳ תרפ״ד. 4. סי׳ תרע״ב במשנ״ב ס״ק י״ט. 5. סי׳ תרס״ב סעיף ב׳. 6. סי׳ תרע״ז סעיף ב׳. 7. ראה בסי׳ תרע״א סעיף ב׳ ובמשנ״ב שם. 8. סי׳ תרע״א סעיף א׳ ובמשנ״ב ס״ק ד׳. 9. ראה בסי׳ תרע״א סעיף ב׳. 10. ראה בסי׳ תרע״ג סעיף א׳ וסי׳ תרע״ה סעיף ה׳. 11. סי׳ תרע״א סעיף ה׳. 12. סי׳ תרע״א סעיף ז׳. 13. ראה בסי׳ תרע״ב סעיף ב׳. 14. סי׳ תרע״ב סעיף א׳. 15. סי׳ תרע״ה סעיף ב׳. 16. סי׳ תר״פ במשנ״ב ס״ק א׳. 17. סי׳ תרע״ו סעיפים א׳, ב׳. 18. סי׳ תרע״ו סעיף ה׳. 19. ראה בסי׳ תרע״ו במשנ״ב ס״ק ט׳. 20. סי׳ תרע״ו סעיף ד׳ ובמשנ״ב

סעיף א'.   12. ראה בסי' תנ"ג סעיף ד' ובסי' תנ"ח, ת"ס ותפ"ב.   13. ראה בסי' תע"ה סעיף
א' ובמשנ"ב שם.   14. סי' תע"ג סעיף ה' וסי' תע"ה סעיפים א'-ג'.   15. סי' תע"ה סעיף
א'.   16. סי' תע"ז.   17. סי' תע"ו סעיף א' ובמשנ"ב ס"ק ו'.   18. סי' תע"ז במשנ"ב ס"ק
א'.   19. סי' תע"ח סעיף א'.   20. ראה בסי' תפ"א סעיף א' ובמשנ"ב שם.   21. סי' תע"ב
סעיפים ב'-ז'.   22. סי' תפ"א סעיף ב' ובמשנ"ב ס"ק ד'.   23. ראה בסי' קי"ד סעיף
ג'.   24. סי' ת"צ.   25. ראה בסי' ת"צ במשנ"ב ס"ק י"ט.   26. סי' תכ"ט ובמשנ"ב ס"ק
י"ד.   27. סי' תמ"ח.

פרק לד

1. סי' תפ"ט.   2. סי' תפ"ט סעיף א'.   3. סי' תפ"ט סעיף א'.   4. סי' תפ"ט סעיף א'
ובמשנ"ב ס"ק ד'.   5. סי' תפ"ט סעיף ח' ובמשנ"ב שם.   6. סי' תפ"ט סעיף ד'.   7. סי'
תצ"ג סעיפים א', ב'.   8. סי' תצ"ג במשנ"ב ס"ק ג'.   9. סי' תצ"ג במשנ"ב ס"ק ב'.   10.
סי' תצ"ג סעיפים ב', ג', ובמשנ"ב ס"ק י"ד-ט"ו.   11. ראה בסי' תצ"ג סעיף ב'.   12. סי'
תצ"ד סעיף ג' ובמשנ"ב ס"ק ט', י'.   13. סי' תצ"ד.   14. ראה בסי' ת"צ במשנ"ב ס"ק
י"ט.   15. סי' תצ"ד סעיף ג' ובמשנ"ב ס"ק י"ב, י"ג.   16. ראה בסי' תצ"ד סעיף ב'.

פרק לה

1. סי' תקמ"ט סעיפים א', ב' ובמשנ"ב ס"ק ב'.   2. סי' תכ"ח סעיף ח'.   3. סי' תקנ"א סעיף
ב'.   4. סי' תקנ"א במשנ"ב ס"ק צ"ח.   5. סי' תקנ"א סעיף י"ז ובמשנ"ב שם.   6. סי'
תקנ"א סעיף י"ב ובמשנ"ב ס"ק פ"ב.   7. סי' תקנ"א במשנ"ב ס"ק כ'.   8. סי' תקנ"א סעיף
א'.   9. סי' תקנ"א סעיף ז'.   10. סי' תקנ"א סעיף ג' ובמשנ"ב ס"ק כ"ט-ל"א.   11. סי'
תקנ"א סעיף י"ד.   12. ראה בסי' תקנ"א סעיף ט"ז.   13. סי' תקנ"א במשנ"ב ס"ק
צ"ד.   14. סי' תקנ"א סעיף ט'.   15. סי' תקנ"א סעיף י' ובמשנ"ב ס"ק ע'.   16. סי' תקנ"א
סעיפים א', ט' ובמשנ"ב ס"ק ו'.   17. סי' תקנ"ב-תקנ"ג.   17. סי' תקנ"ב סעיף ח'.   18.
ראה בסי' תקנ"ג סעיף ב' ובמשנ"ב שם.   19. ראה פרטים נוספים בסי' תקנ"ד סעיף י"ט
ובמשנ"ב שם.   20. ראה בסי' תקנ"ג סעיף ב'.   21. סי' תקנ"ד.   22. סי' תקנ"ד סעיף
ו'.   23. סי' תקנ"ה במשנ"ב ס"ק ח'.   24. ראה בסי' תקנ"ד סעיף ט' ובסי' תרי"ג במשנ"ב
ס"ק ד'.   25. סי' תקנ"ט סעיף ג' ובמשנ"ב ס"ק י"א.   26. סי' תקנ"ה סעיף ב'.   27. סי'
תקנ"ד סעיף כ"ב.   28. ראה בסי' תקנ"ד סעיף כ'.   29. סי' תקנ"ד סעיפים א'-ג'.   30. סי'
תקנ"ט סעיף ב'.   31. ראה בסי' ת"צ במשנ"ב ס"ק י"ט.   32. סי' תקנ"ט סעיף ג' ובמשנ"ב
שם.   33. סי' תקנ"ט סעיף ב'.   34. סי' תקנ"ז.   35. סי' תקנ"ז.   36. סי' תקנ"ו.   37.
סי' תקפ"א סעיף א'.   38. ראה בסי' ו' במשנ"ב ס"ק י"א.   39. סי' תקפ"א סעיף א'.

RABBI ZE'EV GREENWALD
ILLUSTRATED GUIDES TO JEWISH LAW

The Kosher Kitchen

This volume, the third to be translated from
the popular Hebrew series *Itturei Halachah*,
presents the laws and practices of kashrus,
including a special section on inspecting
fruits and vegetables. Every page is graced
with wonderful, detailed drawings that
illustrate a living kosher kitchen.

VOLUME 3 IN THE SERIES

GRAINS AND CEREALS

OATS, MATZAH MEAL, BREAD CRUMBS, AND GRANOLA

◆ Canned oats are considered halachically to be free of infestation and need not be checked. Those packed in bags should be emptied into a strainer to see if any insects fall through. Then the oatmeal flakes should be scattered over a plate and checked thoroughly. If infested, they should be discarded.

◆ Fresh oats in some areas of the world are considered clean. In the U.S.A., oats and other grains supplied by the government to schools are often infested.

◆ Matzah meal is frequently infested. It should be spread over a plate and thoroughly checked. If signs of infestation are found, the matzah meal should be discarded.

◆ Bread crumbs should be spread out and checked. It is difficult to check granola and it is best to make it at home after checking the individual ingredients. Otherwise, it should be spread out and checked thoroughly.

PROHIBITION OF A MIXTURE OF MEAT AND MILK

◆ The Torah prohibition of meat and milk includes cooking meat and milk together, even if one does not intend to eat the mixture afterwards.

◆ It is also forbidden to derive any benefit whatsoever from a mixture of milk and meat that was cooked together. This includes feeding such a mixture to one's pets, selling it to a Jew or to a non-Jew, etc.

It is forbidden to
cook meat with milk.

It is forbidden
to benefit from
meat cooked
with milk.

It is forbidden to
benefit from meat
cooked with milk.

**Perfect for students & educators!
A practical guide for the whole family!**

FELDHEIM PUBLISHERS
TORAH LITERATURE OF QUALITY